What follows is the story of our tra
through Africa, Australia and Sout
mainly on the contents of the website created whilst "on the
road". When on re-reading I have found factual or typing
errors I have corrected them, but when I haven't obviously I
haven't.

It was written as it happened or a few days later, which
explains the rather cavalier use of the past and present tense.

The writing in italics is later additions and is the result of
entirely superficial and perfunctory research on Google (other
search engines are available).

The views and opinions expressed are mine alone as are the
typos and grammatical errors. The jokes have been
unashamedly stolen when I think I can get away with it, and
as you would expect, no account has been taken of other
people's sensibilities and feelings.
The historical facts should not be relied on as accurate, and if
you are thinking of using this book as a reference for a
planned overland trip, you would probably be well advised
not to.

The "book" is copyright of Jeff Watts although why anyone
would wish to copy from it I cannot imagine.

If you have any comments, suggestions, claims for damages
etc you can contact us at travelswithmyloo@hotmail.com

ISBN-13: 978-1508632948
ISBN-10:1508632944

The Customs House in Genoa is old, dusty, dignified and immovable, so like the customs inspectors themselves. It was a hot Saturday afternoon and it was quiet, just the background hum of flies settling, taking off then settling again. What they wanted was to sleep off their pasta and red wine lunch on a warm, heavy Italian Saturday afternoon. What they didn't want was what they got, an old Englishman with time on his hands on the trail of a refund.

Now I'll be the first to admit (and I bow here to the views expressed by most who know me) that I'm a miserable sod! Not just miserable but short tempered as well,(I love the word irascible) and before I left England everyone told me I must smile and, no matter what the provocation, not to lose my temper. When I accepted their advice with a smile, they looked at it, winced, shook their heads and walked away.

With their advice in mind I painted on my "I want something from you but I am really a nice person anyway" smile and presented my documents for the recovery of the VAT that I'd paid on all of the changes I'd made to the vehicle. A lot of money!
A cursory disdainful glance and the papers were thrown back! "No! Absolutely impossible!" (the smile apparently didn't work but I persevered)
I adapted my smile slightly to my "Listen I am trying to be nice here but don't push it" and pushed the papers back to him,
"Yes! All you need to do is sign there that I am leaving Europe for more than a year so that I can reclaim the VAT."

"NO!" he pushed the papers back at me but I was ready for him... I resisted, my fingers on the opposite side and the papers bent slightly in the middle,

"Why not?"

I was getting fed up and needed to grit my teeth so the smile didn't slip and my teeth were beginning to ache with all the gritting. I pointed out the words on the form which showed I was right ... I'm not sure that was a good move! Being right doesn't always make you popular!

I waited.

He waited.

Eventually,

"NO!"

"Yes!" The smile by now was losing its superficial facade of sincerity and deep inside me a small voice said,

"Hit him Jeff!"

I resisted (just) the growing temptation to emphasise my perfectly valid legal position with a slap across his head, and pushed the paper back to him.

He looked round hopefully for assistance from his friends but they were leaning back on ancient chairs, looking at the ancient ceiling, counting the ancient cobwebs, or checking their ancient eyelids for holes.

In desperation he reached under the desk and produced a copy of the European VAT legislation in English and Italian and German (I'm not sure why the German came into it! but they seem to get into everything else these days)

I ploughed through the English version and suddenly knew this was why I love travel... to be reading European Tax legislation on a hot Saturday afternoon in Italy.

We eventually found the relevant section that showed me to be indisputably correct, and very reluctantly he relented. Either it was the power of my reasoned argument, or more likely it was just to stop the God-Awful smile that by now was scaring him as much as it was hurting me.

He reached slowly for his stamp; it hovered over the form, tantalisingly close.

"I will make an exception for you!" And let it fall very softly. The inner voice had murmured seductively in my ear,

"As soon as he stamps it, slap him Jeff, you know you want to!"

With difficulty I ignored it and reached for the form, smiled, thanked him in all the European languages I could think of (English! Other languages aren't available) and left.

Once outside I looked at the form, he'd stamped it, but he hadn't signed it. Was this a mistake or a deliberate ploy to get rid of me...what do you think?? Yes and me! Bastard! Pause, scowl, ignore inner voice (which by now was becoming insistent), paint on my number 4 "No more Mr Nice guy" smile and went back in.

He had, by this time, joined his friends looking at the ancient cobwebs on the ancient ceiling, and if he was pleased to see me he hid it well, so he made me wait before finally reluctantly acknowledging my presence. Wearily he came back to the counter and, still smiling, I pointed out that he hadn't signed it. He looked carefully at the form, as if surprised, then searched slowly for a pen and signed it even more slowly. I continued smiling, cheeks now really hurting, until he handed me the form and I turned away.

My inner voice was by now deafening and I was finding resisting it increasingly difficult, but instead I just scowled, why waste a smile when you can scowl?. Now even if I say it myself I do a good scowl, the ravages of age, alcohol, sun and an inbuilt bad temper (irascibility!, other words are available) makes scowling one of the few things I'm good at! On thinking about it, it's the only thing I'm getting better at as old age approaches.

"Approaches Watts? You've overtaken it!"

As I went out a young child was passing with his mother and I scowled at them, the child screamed and hid behind his mothers' skirts.

I felt inner warmth, all was well with the world!

IN THE BEGINNING

"Far better is it to dare mighty things, to win glorious triumphs, even though chequered with failure, than to rank with those poor spirits who neither enjoy much nor suffer much, because they live in the grey twilight that knows no victory nor defeat" Theodore Roosevelt.

Like most great adventures it started in the pub. Well that's not true, alcohol as usual made me say what I'd been thinking for a while,

"I've been thinking it might be fun to buy a 4x4 and drive to Capetown!"

It went quiet as they looked at each other over the tops of their beer which is unusual for that lot as they usually view the world though the bottom of a beer glass.

"You know I thought you said you were going to buy a vehicle and drive from Europe to Capetown. You must be bloody mad. You can't even find your way to ASDA without getting lost!"

I'm famous for my ability to get lost, albeit confidently lost, inextricably or even to my mind inexplicably, lost, but lost nevertheless. Friends soon learn that following me inevitably means getting nowhere. Well that's not true, obviously you get somewhere, but it never quite coincides with where you wanted, expected or even intended to be.

The others nodded in agreement; I looked hurt, they pretended not to, or more likely just didn't, notice.

"In Greek mythology there was this bloke, Sisyphus, who was condemned to continually roll a stone up a hill only to find it rolling back down again"

"Oh well that makes total sense then, this imaginary bloke Syphilis.."

"Sisyphus"

"OK Sisyphus, pushed a rock up a hill and that made you want to drive to Capetown…yes! I can see that it's obvious now…. err …No sorry I don't follow!"

"Well don't you see we're all like that in life, pushing rocks pointlessly up hills, the best we can hope for is another hill and another rock!"

"Right! I get that now! … I think!"

"Listen, whatever you do for a living you have to keep starting from zero again, each new job, each new project, each new day…"

I looked around, hoping for a nod of agreement but all I got were blank stares through the bottom of their beer glasses,

"Look it's obvious. If you're a chéf each new meal you cook you start from the bottom of the hill, if you're an accountant each new

set of accounts you start from zero, if you're an housewife it's the same … See??"

"Aaaaah now you explain it like that! …"

"It's obvious isn't it?"

"No!"

Time for another pint, I headed for the bar, got lost, and finished up in the ladies loo.

"It's OK! Don't stand up! But could you tell me where the bar is?"
When I eventually found my way back to the table, they shook their heads
"… and he thinks he's going to drive through Africa…………..."

> *"If this myth (of Sisyphus) is tragic, that is because its hero is conscious. Where would his torture be, indeed, if at every step the hope of succeeding upheld him? The workman of today works everyday in his life at the same tasks, and his fate is no less absurd."*
> *Albert Camus*

I'm not sure where or when the idea started; perhaps it's always been there, festering away. We'd started camper-vanning many years ago. At first a trip to France was exciting; then we travelled further, Spain, Portugal, Italy, even overland to Greece, until suddenly we realized it wasn't exciting; it wasn't challenging; it wasn't dangerous, although in truth danger is an ever present when I'm driving, as of course is surprise and disappointment when I am navigating.
Jean was the same and, both having a love of Africa and of travel, it seemed inevitable that the idea of driving to Africa would be conceived, (with my bad back it's about the only thing that will be these days) that, and the fact that she wouldn't trust me to find Africa on my own.

We all need something to kick us into action, with me it was a letter from the Pension Company whose records obviously are in
need of audit as they seem to show that I was nearing my Sixtieth Birthday, an obvious and unforgivable error which should be brought to the attention of someone, the amount

they charge in fees you'd think that they could at least get peoples ages right.

"Look I was born in 1943 that makes me 50 doesn't it?"

"No! 60"

"Nooo! 2004 minus 1943 is..4 minus 3 is 9, carry 1 take 0 from 4 that makes me 32 … No ... Where's the calculator..2003 – 1943 that's 60 ... Blimey you're right! Where the hell did 60 years go?"

"Well you were drunk for many of them!"

"That'll be why I don't remember them!"

So that's what decided me! Enough of this daily work earning more money than I was worth, (and I wasn't paid that much!) sitting at whatever desk I had found myself at, peering earnestly at a computer screen with an expression which, to an untrained observer appeared to be intense concentration, but which was in fact complete bewilderment! Wondering what it is I was meant to be doing, and trying to remember if I'd already done it, or whether I could get away with not doing it and still charging for it!

From now on it was time to fill the rest of my life with action; albeit arthritic, asthmatic, and also aching action (in case you never noticed that is the current world record for an alliteration!), but action nevertheless, and if you think action is an overstatement, let's agree on activity.

When I broached the subject tentatively to Jean she reacted exactly as she has reacted to most (no! all!) of my harebrained schemes, by nodding and waiting; waiting for the idea to go away; waiting for me to forget what I had suggested or waiting for me to make all the arrangements and then correcting them and making the idea work. I make the broad strategic decisions and leave things like "Where are we?"

"Which way do I turn?" "What's for dinner?" and "Where's my socks?" to Jean.

"OF ALL THE SAD WORDS OF TONGUE AND PEN, THE SADDEST OF THESE "IT MIGHT HAVE BEEN""
John Greenleaf Whittier

We hummed and we aaaarred between Africa and the Silk Road, and Africa won (in truth it was never a contest!), and because you have to have some idea where you're going (well I say that, but life has shown me that I'm better at conceptual horizons than knowing which exit to use on the island at the end of my road). The route is going to be France, Tunisia, Libya, Egypt, Sudan, Ethiopia, Kenya, Tanzania, Zambia after that I'm not sure ... but that is Plan A ... and as every one knows you should never worry about plan A as it never happens it's only A plan! (admit it! that's clever)

At the time of writing there are only two ways to drive down through Africa, the West route; Morocco, Mauritania, Nigeria, Cameroon Congo Angola, etc; or the East route through Egypt, Sudan, Kenya, Tanzania etc. The central route through Algeria, Chad and Central African Republic is impassable, well impassable unless you happen to be an American backed by thousands of other Americans all armed to the bloody teeth and with air support.

The decision to travel the east route meant that we would be travelling through English speaking countries, and is, from all the accounts I've read, the easier of the two.

WHAT VEHICLE? WHAT EQUIPMENT?

Right if we're going to drive to Africa we're going to need a vehicle!

"Wow! Watts you're certainly on top of the problem, I for one certainly wouldn't have thought of that!"
Only a fool learns by experience when he can ask! And with many years of living with a basic and proven lack of an ability to make
the correct decision (or even a decision correctly) about almost anything, I decided to ask the experts at the 4x4 Land Rover Show at Billing Aquadrome!

Being British we'd initially thought "Land Rover", with the vague idea of buying an ex-army Land Rover based ambulance and converting it into a camper van type vehicle.

Blimey there are some characters that drive Land Rovers! There's army Land Rovers owned by men who dress up in army uniforms but they are not, and have never been, soldiers; there are Land Rovers equipped to go anywhere, which are so clean they obviously have never been anywhere! In fact there are Land Rovers converted to do anything you can think of,
"Fish and chip vans?"
"Ok then converted to do anything except be fish and chip vans!"
They park in lines or circles and secretly compare their accessories, and the man with the largest air snorkel smirks and stands proud amongst the lesser mortals.
Phallic symbolism pervades!
The owners of Pre-Series Land Rovers scorn the Series 1 owners who in turn scorn the series 2 owners and so on up (or in some opinions down) to the latest Discovery owners who look down on everyone else because they are rich enough to buy a luxury off-road vehicle (complete with traction control) to take the children to school!

We met Paul Blackburn on the "One Life Live It" stand. Paul spends his life travelling to exotic places for a living, and he told us we needed a Toyota Land Cruiser
"You mean it's his job?"
"Yes it's disgusting isn't it, why can't he get a proper job and a mortgage, and electricity bills, and a garden like the rest of us?"
"Someone once said if you find a job you love, you never work again!"
"That's so true who was it?"
"Does it matter?"
"I suppose not!"
"Confucius!"
"Confucius said that the best vehicle is a Land Cruiser?"
"No! He said the bit about loving your work!"
"Oh ok! So he prefers Land Rovers then?"
"Seeing the age of some of them at the show it's quite possible"

At the Footloose 4x4 stand we met Paul Marsh, who had, as they say, been there, done it, bought the T shirt (well it was a safari shirt, but you know what I mean), and he agreed, no insisted, that Land Cruisers were the answer, not just any old Land Cruiser (and definitely not any new Land Cruiser) but a mid 90's, 80 series, and he sold us a dream, and in the months to come he sold me nearly everything else I didn't realise I needed.

Paul at least had the decency to look guiltily over his shoulder when he said,
"I know I shouldn't say this because it's a Land Rover Show but you should only do a trip like this in a Toyota Land Cruiser!"
"Why"

"Look let's put it this way, do you know what to do with a spanner!"
"Of course I do. I immediately hand it to someone who knows how to use it!"
"Well, in that case you definitely need to drive a Land Cruiser, if you drive a Land Rover you'll spend your life under the bonnet!"

When I asked Paul how much it would cost, he told me to remember to park so that in the morning you wake up and see the sun rise; when I asked him for a fully costed and detailed list of work to be done he described the deafening silence of the desert in the morning and the uncountable millions of stars at night.
What can you do when faced with logic like that particularly as Jean agreed with him totally?

I did, incidentally, get lost at the Billing show, causing Jean some consternation and our friends Diane and Neil much amusement,
and confirming everyone's belief that on my own I'd never get out of England, let alone get to Africa.

Reactions to our plans varied from,
"Great!"... The minority.
"Why?"... Unanswerable, if you need to ask you'll never understand the answer!
"It's dangerous!"...Read your local newspaper.. There's danger everywhere
"Isn't it expensive?"... Yes! But you can't take it with you."
"I know that but weren't you planning to keep just a little back until you go?"
"Watts I wouldn't trust you to drive to the local ASDA"...
Now that is a good point and the view held by the majority.

After a while you get bewildered at all the advice you receive about what equipment you should take, there's "must" and "should" and "would be nice" and "If I were you".
Until finally you realise that if you took it all you'd need a removal van (and trailer).

The first item imposed on me! No argument, no negotiation, was a plastic toilet bucket!! I'd done the macho thing, designed the vehicle, kicked the tyres, and decided on spares. When I showed the finished unit to Jean she looked, looked again and then said,
"Where's the toilet?"
"Aah I've thought of that!! I've bought you a trowel, and it's a new one, never been used before" She looked at the proffered trowel and it was readily apparent that what she was considering doing with it wasn't quite what I had in mind when I bought it.

"If you think I am going out into the bush with a trowel in the middle of the night you can think again!, anything could happen, I could get spiders up my... err..."
"With your bladder they wouldn't stay there long!!"

A small trowel takes less room, is cheaper and doesn't need emptying, but who am I to argue?
I gave in on the loo expecting to win other arguments later. I didn't of course and I was dissuaded from arguing further by Jean's folded arms across the chest and one of "those looks" and I quickly realised that logic was not in order, that and the big cardboard box containing a pale blue plastic bucket with a toilet seat on top which sat in the middle of the lounge for a week until I threatened to use it at a dinner party one night.

Having "agreed" on the plastic loo bucket there's tyres,
"Oh yes you'll definitely need tyres!"

"Aah! But how many?"
"One on each corner for a start!"
"Spare?"
"Oh yes I'd think so!"
"How many?"
"One?"
"No two!"
"Blimey!
"And of course there's the wheels"
"Didn't it have any when you bought it, how did you get it home?"
"Yes, but they were alloy wheels"
"And we don't like alloy wheels do we? Umm! Remind me why we don't like alloy wheels"
"Because they crack!"
"Do they?"
"Yes and so you need steel wheels!"
"Because they don't crack!"
"No they bend!"
"And that's good?"
"Yes! Because then you can hammer them back into shape!"
"If you have a big hammer! As a matter of interest do you have a big hammer?"
"No!"
"Best get one then!"

In one of my (many) past jobs I worked for Southam Tyres, and so, following my own advice, (which I may as well as no one else does) I decided to ask the experts Dave and Allan. Having known me for some years Dave looked at me and said,
"You want some good advice? Don't go! What do you think Allan?"
"Definitely Dave that would be my advice too!"
Bloody comedians!

"Ok then Dave, if I still want to go, what tyres do I need?"
"BF Goodrich All Terrain, and you'll need a couple of Michelin inner tubes, and a repair kit, and some spare valves, anything else Allan?"
Allen got his small calculator out and after a couple of seconds said,
"There must be more, we only need a few more quid and we'll hit this month's target!"
Dave thought for a minute, then smiled slapped himself on the thigh, winced because he's a powerful bloke, (and because he was holding a wheel wrench at the time) and said triumphantly,
"Got it! A set of locking wheel nuts!"
"Well done Dave" said Allen and they danced together round the car park punching the air. I got the feeling they'd seen me coming... Oh well!
Before I left they wanted our picture, they said it was for publicity, but I think it was for the "sucker of the month" section of the company magazine.

Next consideration was the roof tent. We were going to be sleeping in this in all weathers so decided that it was going be the best we could afford and were torn between Howling Moon and Eeze-awn. The decision was made for us because there were only two tents of the size we wanted available, both Howling Moons, so I ordered one quickly.

That's my idea of decision-making! Where there isn't an option.

Not only did we buy a roof tent but also a skirt that hangs under the tent for privacy, and an awning, the penthouse of all tents. If it were in the middle of London it would be worth £1.5 million but as it was it cost me £1600.

(The skirt was heavy and only ever used twice! not one of the better buys!)

We all have sayings that keep us going through life, "This too will end", or "If God sends you a problem he sends you the strength to solve it".
Then there's "troubles don't build character they reveal it!"
Then there's...
"Get on with it Watts it's getting boring.."
Mine is "Life can be difficult in the absence of beer, life can be impossible if the beer is not cold"
"Oh yes very profound!"
We bought a 'fridge, an Engel 'fridge, a prince amongst 'fridges. No expedition should be undertaken without a 'fridge.
"What about an expedition to the Arctic?"
"Well Ok, you wouldn't need one then!"
"Or the Antarctic!"
"Or then, any more?"
"Iceland, Siberia, Alaska...?"
"Ok Ok ... You've made your point"

Right that's tyres, tent, 'fridge, what else? Additional fuel, jerry cans on the roof; additional water jerry cans inside the vehicle, Sand ladders in case I need to climb some sand; Satellite 'phone in case I want to 'phone someone in a satellite: etc, etc, in fact 38, no! 39 etceteras!

MEDICAL PRECAUTIONS
If you're planning this trip be prepared to end up like a colander, and I don't mean people keep pouring cooked vegetables over your head. The nurse at our local surgery seemed to know what she was doing but we confirmed what she'd said with Nomad, the travel company.

We already had yellow fever (the injection that is) and Tetanus so it was Hepatitis A, Hepatitis B, Rabies, and Meningitis but the biggest problem is of course malaria.

Having taken Larium before during a contract in Central Africa and suffering from delusions and hallucinations, the most bizarre being that I was attractive to all females ... absolutely ridiculous ... I won't be taking that again! ... The disappointment of reality proving almost too painful, but not as painful as the ensuing slaps!

Apparently Doxycyclin is the anti–malarial we need and this will also stop stomach bugs but is only fine for short-term use because of the adverse skin reaction it causes when in sunlight!

The other contents of the first aid kit will be a balance between what to take, with what we can use and what to take that other people can use. By definition accidents are difficult to forecast but we expect the biggest problem will be in cuts and burns, so we'll take the usual first aid kit plus butterfly stitches and a range of needles.

We searched the house for odd bandages, plasters, old pills, some suppositories; a twenty five year old packet of condoms (still unopened), which I took, but that was more in hope than expectation! And that should do it…

If I need anything else for broken bones, open-heart surgery, hysterectomy, etc., I've always got my vehicle tool kit.

> BOREDOM WARNING!!!! This next section will cause drowsiness and should be avoided if you are planning to drive or use machinery at the same time as reading.

VISAS AND BUGGERATION

The problem with the east coast route is that visas are hard to get, well probably not hard, but slow, and the two worst I have heard of are the Sudanese and Libyan ones …

Sitting here with everything ready, drumming my fingers waiting, which I'm sure will be good practice as I am going to Africa. I've waited and waited and I knew something would stop me going and it turns out to be the Sudanese visa.

Perhaps it's a good thing not to rush and to have time to reflect.

But I don't do reflection!!

(Or should that be "I don't see myself as reflective!") You see what happens when I've time on my hands I waffle on... will the 120 meg that this website offers be enough? what is a meg? Do I like megs? Could I eat a whole one? Perhaps I should pay for more megs!

But I don't do paying more!!

(Or should that be "To sum up I don't do paying more!") This trip is costing more than I thought but then I've always been paid more than I'm worth, even when I was underpaid, perhaps I should have tried to get a proper job.

"So what was your job then?"

"I was an accountant!"

"Oh yes? Where you any good?"

"Absolutely not! All the countries I worked in and the majority of the company's went bankrupt! I was so bad I could hardly count to ten!"

"So when twenty was needed you had problems!"

"There's a twenty? …. Really? So how does that work then???

Drumming your fingers eventually hurts, I wonder whether to 'phone the Sudanese embassy and explain to the man there that when you say,
"A maximum of four weeks", you really shouldn't then go on to say "…. or maybe five weeks, or six weeks!" He probably found it difficult to think as my fingers were around his throat at the time ... perhaps, on reflection, that didn't help!

I should I suppose have been more grateful for the McVitie's Rich Tea biscuit ("It's OK Sir it's low fat!!" was there a hidden message there?) he offered me, perhaps I could go to Weston Beach and pretend I'm in the Sahara … perhaps ... perhaps… perhaps!

Life is full of perhapses (perhaps's?) I think I'll go and practice using the portable loo bucket!!

OH GOD THE PAPERWORK!! Visas, licenses, insurances, it's not difficult but what a pain!

PASSPORT
Although I had nine months before my passport expired, I decided to renew it; apparently you can do this up to nine months before the old one expires.
I made the mistake of having a very very short haircut and my passport photo looks a bit like an escapee (or is it escaper?) from the French Foreign Legion, no it doesn't! It looks exactly like an escaper (or is it escapee??) from the French Foreign Legion after he's been trod on by a camel whilst hiding in the sand. (No hump jokes there you'll notice but don't worry they'll come later!). We went to the post office and for an extra £5 each they fast tracked the processing and we got it back in a week, which was another of my great ideas as it sat in the drawer for weeks whilst I waited for the visa's.

PASSPORT PHOTO'S

I used my Photosuite program to print off a few pages of passport photo's ... Everyone says that you'll need them on the road.

COPIES OF DRIVER'S LICENCE

I photocopied our pink driving licenses and enveloped them in plastic. These can be used as disposable proof of identity at campsites, roadblocks etc. When the nice man at the roadblock asks for your driving licence then refuses to return it without the payment of a "fine", to see his face as you say, "No problem sunshine you can keep it!" will make life so satisfying!

INTERNATIONAL DRIVING LICENCE

We both have full English driving licenses but I felt we needed an International Driving Licence as back up so I downloaded the form from the RAC website and decided I'd get two each. They cost £8 each and were delivered back within a week, and then sat comfortably next to my passport as we waited for the Sudanese to give me a visa.

CARNET DE PASSAGE

The Carnet de Passage is a document that allows you to import a vehicle into a country without paying import duty, so if you get an offer you can't refuse and sell the car whilst you're there the RAC will pay the import duty for you.
The value of the carnet will be the maximum duty payable in the countries to which you're travelling and in Egypt it's 500% of the value of the car!!

Which sounds fine, unfortunately the RAC, before they will issue with a Carnet (being cynical sods), will insist on an insurance policy for the full amount of the potential duty payable, which will cost you 10% of the value of the carnet, but you get 5% back if they don't have to pay out. (Come on try and keep up!! It's not that difficult to understand, I understand it so anyone can, but I admit it took me about three weeks before I had any idea what they were talking about)

Getting a Bank Guarantee is cheaper but you'll need to give the bank a back up surety, either by lodging the amount of the guarantee (it could be £50,000! yeah right!!!); by giving them a charge on your house; or by pleading with a rich relative (or someone else's rich relative) and for this the bank will charge you about £250.

It's at about this time you begin to wonder if overland travel is worth it, but before you decide, let's talk Visas.

<u>DOUBLE WARNING this next bit is REALLY boring..in fact just skip the next five pages..if you don't please don't blame me you were warned</u>

VISAS

LIBYA
This information was valid when we went, since that date things have gone little "frisky!" so what follows is of historical interest only (using the term "interest" very loosely)

You will need a letter of invitation from someone in Libya, (How many people do you know in Libya?) then you need to have a stamp in your passport translated into Arabic and then they'll give you a visa which is valid for forty five days from the date of issue, but of course they won't tell you how long it will take for them to issue the visa, so from the time they issue the visa to the time you leave Libya you have forty five days. Forty-five days to collect the visa, finalise the arrangements, and drive from UK to the far side of Libya! Sometimes you get the impression they don't want you there! The other alternative is to ask an agent to do it for you. United Travel in London will do it but it will cost you £240, and you will still have the forty-five day problem. Kalif Ahmed is another contact but he makes the expression "laid back" seem manic.

We finally decided to trust Kalif (the fact that he quoted £80 each perhaps contributed) and after a number of calls and visits we left the passports with him and he got them back within a week complete with our invitation. The £80 each is only for the visa and you'll need to budget another £80 odd for their services at the Libyan border, and yet another £50 per day for the guide whilst you're there, but diesel is only 1p per litre!

SUDAN
I am reliably informed that you can get a Sudanese visa in Cairo for $60 but the thought of waiting in long queues in Cairo doesn't excite me. The problem isn't getting the visa issued; it's the sending the application back to Sudan for approval that takes the time, four weeks to be precise! For all you English students out there "precise " and "Sudan" are what's called an Oxymoron...Sudan and waiting are what's called a pleonasm!
Where was I?... Oh yes... apparently once you've got the permission it only takes 24 hours to issue the visa in London.

We went along to the Sudanese Embassy in London who were extremely helpful and pleasant (he gave us a Rich Tea biscuit!) and he agreed that it would certainly be possible, as an alternative to waiting in England for the visa, for the application to be made in London and when they receive the permission back they would send it to Cairo... simple!!!! ... err ... We looked at the helpful smiling man, looked at each other and decided not to risk it, but to wait until we got the visa before leaving ...yes I know I'm an old cynic ... but it's my only weakness ... well no it's not, it's just one of them, one of the others is losing my temper when confronted by mindless bureaucracy in forty degrees of heat.

I also contacted George and Mike at the Acropole Hotel Khartoum as I was reliably (there's that word "reliably" again!!) informed that they will get it in five to ten days, but time will tell, for the Sudanese have more time than they have grains of sand. That sounded like an old Arabian proverb but in fact I have just made it up!

Oh yes! Be prepared to pay £53 each for the privilege, but the wait is thrown in for free.

NEW 04/05/04
That's it we've had enough! We're going next Tuesday (11th may 2004)...We'd contacted various people and they all said in spite of what they might promise in the Sudanese Embassy in London you can't get a visa from there ... you need get it yourself or get
someone to get it for you in Sudan ... why the bloody hell don't they tell you and stop messing peoples lives up!!!

I'll try and get it in Cairo or get London or Khartoum to forward it to Cairo when it comes in....dream on Watts ... and as a fall back there's always George at the Acropole.

EGYPT

Easy! We went to London, applied in the morning, and collected them in the afternoon. They didn't smile at my jokes but then that's not a uniquely Egyptian trait, people rarely do ... although they did smile when they asked me for £18 each for the visa and I said, "That's cheap!"

INSURANCE

Campbell Irvine arranged worldwide insurance, which seems reasonable at £375 each as long as we don't go to America. We are heading for Africa but as I've already said my navigation leaves a lot, if not everything, to be desired, but surely even I can't finish up in America after landing in Africa... can I?

"Do you want an answer Watts?"

"Best not!"

That insurance only covers medical emergencies, the car isn't insured, so I will develop the trick of driving with my fingers crossed and have faith in God, which particular God will depend on the country I happen to be in at the time.

SORN

If you don't prepare a Statutory Off Road Notice (SORN) and you have a vehicle that you're leaving behind and the road tax expires before you return it'll automatically cost you an £80 fine for not renewing it.

So get a SORN form from the post office and declare the vehicle "off road" ... at the same time you can rant ineffectually about the hidden taxes they keep introducing such as the automatic £80 fine and various other new ways they have of extracting money from the middle classes especially the middle class motorists ... and no doubt people will ignore you also!

As an aside it's almost impossible to remain legal. There is an agreement between countries that you can drive a car anywhere providing you are "road legal" in the vehicles' home country, but of course if you have "SORNED" the vehicle you're not road legal so shouldn't drive. BUT!

"I said BUT!"

"Whoops sorry I was losing interest there!"

BUT.. If you don't SORN the vehicle and when you're away you need to re-tax it, for which of course you will need an MOT, but you can't get an MOT when you're abroad and you can't get a Road Fund Licence without an MOT, so how do you do it?

"That's a good question so what did you do?"

"I phoned the Motor Vehicle Licensing people and explained the problem and they were very helpful, they said I must have an MOT and should drive back to England and get a one!"

"That was helpful! So what did you do?"

"I broke the law of course and SORNED it!"

We're fed up with paperwork ... it's boring,(I can see you nodding in agreement there but I did warn you!) but we know if we don't get it right we'll have hassle at the borders when it's hot and we're tired, sticky and bad tempered which is not a good idea. But then with me "tired" and "sticky" are variables, "bad tempered" is a constant!.

Welcome back!

THE EXPEDITION STARTS HERE!

Well they said it would be dusty!

SOMEWHERE IN THE MIDDLE OF FRANCE

On the first night we stopped next to a English camper-van in a small free camp site and it turned out that girl went to school with Jean, was brought up in the next street and played on the same fields!! Malcolm, her husband kept saying,
"Well it's a small world" and I'm not sure if it was good manners on my part or the fact that I didn't think of it at the time that stopped me saying,
"You wouldn't say that if you were driving to bloody Africa!"
When we were shopping for equipment for the trip this very nice friendly helpful man at Nomad (the expedition equipment suppliers) helped us pick a sleeping bag. He recommended a thin waterproof sexy one that covers all seasons; very helpful advice and absolutely wrong! That first night I've never been

so cold in all my life so the first thing we did the following morning, well in

truth it was the second thing, the first was to thaw ourselves out, was to find a unfriendly unhelpful Frenchman who knew enough to say absolutely nothing and we bought cheap, warm, non sexy sleeping bags.

The options for crossing from Europe to Africa are to sail to Tunisia from either Marseilles or Genoa. I do not know a joke about Marseilles so we decided to sail from Genoa… and ..

"Oi! What's the joke about Genoa?"

"Don't ask! You really don't want to know!"

"It's OK I'll risk it!"

"Well don't say I didn't warn you! Ready? .. You have to say Genoa"

"Ok! Genoa!"

"Not yet!"

"Sorry!"

"Ready?"

"I've got to say Genoa right?"

"YES! Now are you ready?"

"Ok!"

"My wife went on holiday to Italy!"

"Genoa?"

"Of course I know her she's my wife!!"

"Do I have to say Genoa now?"

"Just forget it!"

"Forget what?"

Italian drivers obviously take part vicariously in every Grand Prix and scorn my funereal pace as I drive slowly down the middle lane. God! It's fun! And I'm learning lots of new words and gestures. I'm not sure I understand what they all mean but I doubt that they are complimentary

.

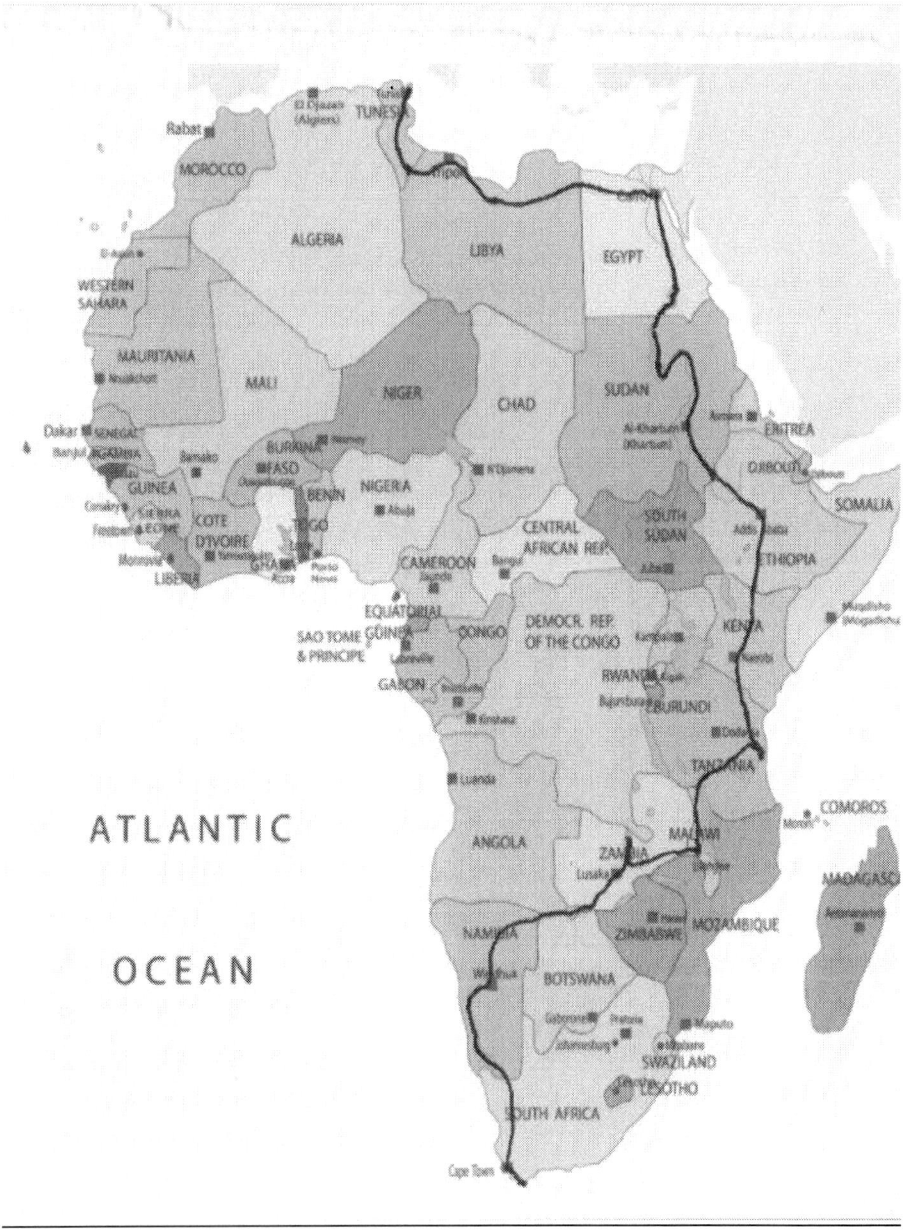
Rabat
MOROCCO
ALGERIA
LIBYA
EGYPT
WESTERN SAHARA
MAURITANIA
MALI
NIGER
CHAD
SUDAN
ERITREA
DJIBOUTI
SOMALIA
Dakar
GUINEA
COTE D'IVOIRE
NIGERIA
BENIN
CENTRAL AFRICAN REP.
SOUTH SUDAN
ETHIOPIA
CAMEROON
SAO TOME & PRINCIPE
CONGO
DEMOCR. REP. OF THE CONGO
RWANDA
BURUNDI
Luanda
ATLANTIC
OCEAN
ANGOLA
COMOROS
MOZAMBIQUE
ZIMBABWE
BOTSWANA
SWAZILAND
Cape Town

TUNISIA

We waited in the queue for the ferry to Tunisia, watching the other travellers. Families going home; overlanders on motorbikes and in trucks; overloaded cars filled with trade goods.

Africa here we come!

The ferry crossing between Italy and Tunisia takes twenty-one hours and all that can be said for it is "it passes", some reading; some sleeping; some drinking and reluctant eating in the restaurant, but it passed. The only "on board" entertainment was queuing for the immigration and customs documents

So having already filled in the immigration, car import and "other imports" forms on board, it was only after much shouting and engine revving that we rolled off the ferry into

Africa and joined the end of the queue, the first of many queues that we would endure in the next few months.

The man in the little box took the immigration and the car import forms and stamped the passports, I smiled, and this I believed helped, as he winced visibly and quickly waived us on...easy or what?

The expedition starts here!
But we joined the end of another queue.
This time the customs man wanted to see the passport and the declaration of goods to be imported; he glances at the list and indicates he wants to look in the back of the car. I smile and he quickly takes one step back and signs my form without even looking into the car.

The expedition starts here!
But we joined the end of another queue.
This man takes my passport and the vehicle registration (they call it the Carte Gris) and stamps the passport with another stamp thus pre-empting my smile.

The expedition starts here!
But we joined the end of another queue.
She was beautiful, dark brown eyes, teeth as white as the head of a well poured pint of Guinness, a wisp of black hair peeking from beneath her cap. When I passed her my passport, the immigration card for the car and the declaration of goods to be imported, did our fingers touch? Was that a spark of electricity joining two people together?
As we looked into each other's eyes, I softened (Oh! for the days when the opposite happened!).
She started to type in the details for the "Permission d'Conduire"
"Meeesterrrr Watts!" it had never sounded so good,

"Yes.."

"Nationality? Allemande?"

"Mmm ... yes! ... EH! NO! Allemande? OI! I'm British ... Not bloody Allemande!"

She was bereft but we both knew it was over and with sadness we waited together for the computer to chatter out the paperwork.

She wrote something in my passport (perhaps it was her 'phone number?), she smiled! I didn't ... I was learning not to when it mattered.

Back to the vehicle, the custom's officer avoiding meeting my eyes muttering something in Arabic to his colleague, which was probably,

"That's the one.. No! don't look! He'll bloody smile again!

The expedition starts here!

"But?"

We joined the end of another queue.

This time the customs officer, at first wearing his sunglasses rakishly pushed up into his hair, but which he quickly dropped down over his eyes when hit (slapped is probably a better word) with my smile, collected the second copy of the permission to drive with the original vehicle documentation form (still with me?) and waved us through.

48 minutes not bad!!

We looked for another queue to join.. No queue, only open gates!

The expedition really starts here! Sorry that should be,

THE EXPEDITION REALLY REALLY STARTS HERE!

Everyone says you should spend the first night in the Hotel
Amilcar in Tunis, if anyone says this to you in future just say,
"You can bloody stay there if you want to! I'd rather sleep on
the beach"
One good thing that can be said for the Hotel Amilcar is that
it's reasonably close to Tunis and has a secure car park, and
the other good thing is ... er... you know there isn't another
good thing.
Built in the seventies it was probably attractive once in a pre-
cast concrete sort of way, and, as with all of these buildings
found everywhere along the Mediterranean and Aegean coast,
it's noisy.
The sound of high heels on concrete resonates through the
walls and floors. Someone breaking wind in any part of the
hotel causes every one to look suspiciously (or innocently) at
his neighbour (I know I could have said "her" neighbour but
I'm from the generation that really doesn't believe that
women do that sort of thing!)
The term is "seen better days" and I'm trying here to think of
the word for what it needs,
"Make over?"
"No!"
"Renovation?"
"No!"
"Demolition?"
"That's the word!"
It needs demolishing!! With most of the staff still in it!!
But here we are at the top of Africa with 10,000 miles or so to
go!

Sometimes you just have to cover the miles to get away from
the crowds, and this is what we did in the few days in Tunisia;
drive and watch the scenery gradually changing from harsh
low rise unfinished, unpainted buildings where the Tunisians

live, to superb startlingly white and manicured hotels where (at least for two weeks) the tourist live.

Driving south through endless miles of olive trees planted in serried lines, and then finally into the first indications of real desert, sand dunes, camels and palms, both date and the perpetually upturned ones attached to the hands of the Arabs.

Through Kairouan, pausing on the side of the road outside the town to put our recently uncovered white knees away in deference to local sensibilities; then through to Tozeur on the very edge of the desert (or if you could see the amount of sand in the vehicle ... almost in the middle of it) ... And finally Douz.

It's difficult to imagine that we're only a week away from England, week in time, a couple of centuries in attitude, and come to think of it, in street cleaning.

Anyone who thinks that small Arab towns are quiet is sadly mistaken!! The noise continues throughout the night with no discernable decrease in decibels; barking dogs, baying donkeys, and finally the calling to prayer of the faithful by someone who must have lungs like a camel, and at three o'clock in the bloody morning!

You'd think with modern technology they'd simply message them on the mobile! I was seriously thinking of getting up and having a word, I'm sure they'd have been grateful for the advice.
The other alternatives that crossed my mind were becoming a Moslem or starting another crusade, the jury is still out on this!
So there was this Imam or Mullah ...

It is in fact it was a Bilal or Azan; Bila being the name of the Prophet Mohammed's companion (and ex-slave), the actual call to prayer is called the Adhan, and the daily prayer is one of the five pillars of Islam. The others being the profession of the Islamic faith; giving alms; fasting and visiting Mecca.

Or whatever he is called, shouting at the top of his bloody voice, and of course this woke up the dog next door, one of those dogs with a deep morose bark, with long but varying pauses between the single bass woofs!
I lay awake in the early hours becoming increasingly homicidal towards this bloody dog, and even seriously contemplated killing it, skinning it and making a casserole with it.
Some salt, pepper, garlic, and a bottle of wine poured over and left to simmer for a few hours … it would have been delicious!!!!
Sucking the bones dry I'd have put them in a bowl and taken them to the dogs' owner and had great pleasure in saying, "I've brought these bones for your dog!!"

Okay Okay I'm sick, but in defence it was by now four o'clock in the bloody morning and I had been eating pasta for a week! So I had a bad nights sleep and this I put forward as my excuse for the unforgivable way I treated Mohammed.

Mohammed wanted to be my guide, well he really wanted to sell me a tour in an air conditioned Land Cruiser… but as we were leaning on my Land Cruiser at the time he felt he should change his argument, so he offered to guide me.
Now in truth I wasn't against this.

What I was against was the price he was asking, and after a full and frank discussion (He eventually understood what "are you totally mad do I look as if I can afford that?" means) we negotiated a price that was probably twice what he really wanted! And for the first, but unfortunately not the last, time in the next few months, an Arab would try and rip me off.

Of course it didn't help that, just because I'd said "bonjour!", he'd got it into his head that I was a linguist and he went off on one in French and Arabic and I have truly no idea what he was talking about!

He took his sandals off, pointed animatedly to his missing right small toenail, pointed at my feet and amongst many other words (many many other words!) I picked out "Poisson! So we arranged to meet him the next morning and to seal the deal he brought us two boxes of dates. At the price I'd agreed he could easily afford them, in fact he could have afforded the whole bloody calendar but it would have been churlish to say it, well in truth I couldn't think of the French for it, churlish has never stopped me, ability often has.

When he left I sat down and tried to think of any scenario that would include a missing toenail, my feet and a fish.
I couldn't then and I still can't.

As we sat in the campsite we realised that thus far we've travelled nowhere that we couldn't have done in our camper-van. Well we could have done it if some the sod whose testacles (if my prayers have been answered) should by now be festering and dropping off, hadn't stolen it.
In my anger at having the van stolen I had forgotten that I was, in fact, going to sell the van for £3500 less than the insurance company, without question, paid me. Instead of being pleased I was annoyed that I could have claimed more and didn't.

And another thing, the bloke in the pub that I arranged to steal the van temporarily (well until the insurance company had paid out) actually did steal it! I suppose he'll be swanning around the continent somewhere!
Bastard!

The good news was that we were beginning to meet up with other overlanders and at Douz we chatted with three Swiss travellers Kurt, Nadja and Mindli. Kurt confided in me that you should treat vehicle engines the same way you treat women, give them a bloody good servicing when you first get them then ignore them after that.

I, of course, vehemently disagree with this chauvinistic and callow attitude.. er ... (in truth Jean tells me that I vehemently disagree with this chauvinistic and callow attitude!!!) However I must confess there are areas that are a complete mystery to me and buttons and things that I'm never sure what will happen if I touch them…come on you know me well enough by now for me not to have to finish this sentence!! Kurt's attitude to vehicles and females probably explained why our first meeting involved me jump-starting his vehicle!!
"And his wife Watts?"
"Behave!"

So for the first time, the first of many times we hope, we met up with fellow travellers and changed our plans, the plan that originally included Mohammed but now didn't. We could wait, face him and tell him that we'd changed our minds or we could be cowardly and creep away. We had an agreement after all and an Englishman keeps his word and Mohammed had brought us two boxes of dates as a gesture of mutual good faith.
We crept away! If you are reading this Mohammed I'm sorry!

I love the desert, vast flat saltpans, mountains and surreal Dalliesque shapes formed over eons by desert winds. Each day the temperature builds but every evening it plummets and the desert wind sandblasts you!

So far we've camped in some good, some bad and some plain bloody awful campsites. One of the best was in Douz in the desert! Wonderfully peaceful and tranquil, well wonderfully peaceful and tranquil if you ignore the dogs, the donkeys and of course the call to prayer

The road between Matmata to Medenine was "under repair!" So under repair that I followed the bulldozer as it opened the road, so any of you who complain about road works on the M6 think on!!!

You get to bed early…you need to …in three hours you'll be called to prayer. Say what you will Islam is a very noisy religion! If there is a heaven and it's full of Muslims you're in for an

eternity of being woken up every three hours to pray and then there's all those wives… I'm going to have to think seriously about this!!!

STUCK IN THE SAND!!

Well, I suppose it had to happen, I got stuck in the sand!!
Now to all of you who, when next driving to work, suddenly find yourself confronted with a bloody great sand dune, some words of advice, DO NOT, as you are speeding up a sixty degree sand dune with engine running in the red, suddenly realise that you don't know what's over the top, and decide to brake gently…this makes you stop quickly. Very quickly!! And you settle into the sand!!

Also it's probably best do not do this in front of a large group of French 4x4'ers who look up from their red wine, turn their chairs around, and settle back for the afternoon's entertainment!! The entertainment of course being watching me digging out a 3.5 tonne vehicle with a shovel in 35 degrees heat!

When this happens to you what you then have to do is reverse back, engage low range second gear, and drive like a French man in the Champs Elysees on a Saturday afternoon, straight up and at the last moment close your eyes and hope!!! The landing loosens your teeth but it works nearly every time, you then open your eyes, smile but in future you resolve to make sure that top is on the red wine more tightly before attempting off road expeditions!!

Oh yes and there's something else. If you see a bump, or a hole in the road approaching ...(well if you're approaching a hole to be strictly accurate) make sure your not braking when you hit it…your front suspension will already be fully compressed and there will be nothing left to cushion the thump, this will not only loosen your fillings even more but will also empty the remaining few drops of wine still left in the bottle after the excursion into the sand dune.

I speak from personal experience here!

Tunisia is a strange mix from the tourist north and the desert south.

Although predominantly Muslim, you have as much chance of being kept awake by a noisy bar as a call to prayer from the mosque, sometimes both!
The desert is everything you have ever imagined it to be, and more. In addition to being very very sandy the stars are so close you can reach up and pick one. It's not silent though, the wind makes the sand talk as it shifts constantly, and continually tries to reclaim the road that we have presumed to build through it.

The sand on the road grips the car and you feel a resistance like a hand holding you back before it releases you and you surge through, but the desert knows that sooner or later it will win,
"You might bully me, but try that on my big brother up the road!"

Driving in sand dunes is a balance between momentum and prudence; get it right and it's great fun, get it wrong and it's out with the shovel!! And you learn the lesson "Digging sand is mans work or "blue job" as Jean insists!"

The campsites are best described as basic, basically crap, but the people are wonderful, always smiling, always friendly, always trying to overcharge you!!
I smile and feign a heart attack at their first price and we get on better after that!

It's an easy introduction to travel in the Sahara…to any of you out there thinking that Tunisia is just high-rise tourist hotels. It's not, but it soon could be. Until then though, if you want to see poverty, dreadful unfinished low-rise buildings, and nights uncontaminated with man made light, broad smiles and piles of rubbish, Southern Tunisia is for you!

I suppose it had to happen to me, after all I get lost between the bedroom and the outside loo, so driving in the Sahara it was inevitable that I'd get lost, but it wasn't my fault, no seriously it wasn't.
The road had already split into three or four parallel tracks when suddenly they diverged. Left or right? (At first I wasn't really worried , I had an almost full tank of diesel, a Jerry can

full of water and a "Desert navigation made simple!" book with me) but I had to admit it, we were lost!

Lost is an emotive word, but if you don't know where you are and you don't know which direction you have to go to get to where you'd really like to be, then, by those rather harsh criteria, we were lost!

I got out of the car, gasped at the heat, got back in and found my compass, located the sun (not that difficult even for me in the desert), lined them up, thought for a moment then suddenly remembered something important that I had forgotten, namely that I have no idea how to use the damn thing.

In the absence of anything better to do we waited, and we waited! Then, in the distance, we saw a hooded and robed figure slowly approaching (remember we'd been driving for a few hours and we hadn't seen anything except scrub desert), a shimmering spectral at first and then we realised that it was a man, an old man, carrying a long stick and a water bottle, his cloak and hood off-white and stained. In the shade of the hood his face was deeply lined but his dark brown eyes sparkled. He stood and waited patiently whilst we explained in English and broken French that we were lost; he exuded stillness!

I got the map out and laid it on the bonnet and he looked at it with interest, perhaps he'd never seen the area that he obviously knew so well reduced to lines and colours on a piece of paper; eventually he realised where we wanted to be…and the interesting thing was that he ignored the map and drew with his stick in the sand.
When we shook hands his was dry, bony and hard, then he smiled again and started to walk away. I offered him some money. He refused.

I felt crass.

He ignored the track we were on and walked straight off into the desert and he never looked back.

I remember him now. I doubt he remembers me!!

I don't know what the moral is!!

At the camp site in Jerba we met two characters Ali and Mohammed who tried to overcharge me two pounds for the nights stay, and we argued for two hours over this, (You will gather that I hadn't got much planned for the day!) and the discussion ranged through the state of English football, the last African Cup of Nations, Cous Cous, the rather attractive bottom of a young (female) jogger, and finally the Internet.

They were very keen to appear on the Internet so I took a photograph of them and promised faithfully, that it would appear on my website, (I lied!). So anyone who stays at the camping at Jerba look out for Ali and Mohammed and bear in mind that they are a pair of thieving rob dogs who I wouldn't trust with next doors ginger tom let alone anything else!!!!

I didn't pay the two pounds and they didn't give me a receipt for the money I did pay!

So perhaps we can call it a draw.

LIBYA

The last night in Tunisia was windy!! Very windy! The wind is called the qibli, which is an unimpressive name for a very very impressive wind. The alternative name is Sirocco, which is a more impressive name, but which is just as windy.

Wind and sand together makes life interesting and your skin sore! All day, as we neared the border, the wind was getting stronger, but insulated as we were in a large heavy Land Cruiser, we didn't really appreciate how strong it was. Sure! It was funny to see the local Tunisians being lifted up by the wind as it got under their robe thingy's (Jalabah's) but it was only when we actually stopped and got out that it hit us. The top layer of skin was scrubbed off in a few seconds and every orifice, both personal and vehicular, was instantly full of sand.

We'd decided to "wild camp" near the Libyan border so that we could get an early start. A mile or so before the border there's a sandy open plain, and sandy open plains are just the thing you don't need when you are looking for somewhere to shelter. The few small trees that had managed to take root were bent over arthritically, almost horizontal to the ground, like us trying to hide from the wind, the stunted trees giving protection to the vehicle but none to the tent sitting as it was on top of the car.

The wind blew and the vehicle rocked, I know I should have been kept awake by the incessant noise and the fear of being blown over. Jean was! So that meant I was too, by Jean not by the wind!

Up early in the morning to face the first of the difficult border crossings, but it would be fine now that Colonel Gaddaffi was back in the world community and doing everything he could to appease the west and make visiting the country easy.. Hmmm yeah right and if you believe that......!

Some people of course would be cynical and say that the only reason he changed was that the alternative would be to risk being invaded by the Americans; I, of course, disagree with that shameful libel of a fundamentally good and decent man! Although some might say getting invaded by the Americans is hard to avoid if you're sitting on oil and are Islamic (some might say it, I of course, wouldn't!)

"The only part of that last bit I believe Watts is the "mental" in "fundamentally""

> *You will recall that this was written in 2004, since then things have changed in Libya. In 2011 the world leaders in the West in their wisdom decided that they would purely as a humanitarian act, change the system and remove the Colonel. Of course since then the whole country has imploded with thousands of deaths and anarchy, but of course that wasn't the West's fault and couldn't possibly have been foreseen!*
> *That's called irony in case you didn't spot it.*

Although we had already been given (Given? Been ripped off for more like!) a Libyan visa in London, we had heard on the road that it was in fact much easier to get it at the border, no-one told that to the Tunisians, in fact the they insisted on you having a Libyan visa before they would let you through their exit barriers!
As we neared the border we couldn't help noticing that there were plastic containers of fuel for sale on the side of the road. Being sensible and not wanting contaminated diesel in my tank I filled
up at the fuel station, where for once, amazingly, there were no cars queuing! In fact it was surprisingly empty. I found out why later when I realised that I had paid five times more at the fuel station than the roadside black-market price.
"Hey! But that's the kind of guy I am!"
"What sort of guy is that Jeff?"
"STUPID!"

At the border we joined a queue of petrol smugglers, all pushing their cars (business must be good!) and presented our passports, no problem (but then this "no problem!" had cost me £150 so far).

Khamiss our guide met us full of effusive greetings, and the car clearance began.

(Before I start this I suggest you go to the loo as it takes a long time.)

First stop at the number plate issuing section where, as the name implies, they issue you with an Arabic number plate, at a price of course. The customs man had a face like a bulldog that had just chewed a wasp.

I think the word is lugubrious!

He looked at the documentation and grunted, then threw the papers disdainfully onto his desk.

My Arabic is rusty but I think this meant,

"Good morning how nice to see you, welcome to our wonderful country, we are here to make your life as easy as possible! What you need to do now is walk out through that barrier over there and get your Carnet stamped at the Libyan equivalent of the RAC, that'll be free; then go next door and get your third party insurance, fourteen days will cost you about £5, Oh! By the way please don't forget to change some dollars into dinars on the way ... You'd better get about $100 worth, that'll give you around 130 dinars!!"

Well I think that's what the monosyllabic grunt meant!

Lugubrious is definitely the word!

I followed his advice and in truth had to do very little, perhaps Khamiss helped! Perhaps he didn't, I'll never know.

Back to the friendly customs man whose demeanour had changed from miserable to downright difficult, obviously the wasp was still there!

I was tempted to turn my smile on, but then thought, "bugger it", and let my face fall into its normal miserable bastard self, he looked at me and recognized a fellow traveller, a beautiful moment as two miserable old bastards enjoyed a miserable old bastard moment together!

He grunted again, my Arabic had improved so much that by this time that I knew what the grunt meant,
"Well done you've managed to get all of these forms which are in Arabic filled out correctly, now I'm going to issue you with local number plates but only after you have given me 110 dinars 25 whatever's and when you return them when you leave Libya we'll give you half back" (they didn't of course!)

I put 110 dinars and a 25 whatever's coin onto his desk just out of his reach so he had to lean forward, he looked at me and waited, I had time, I waited too. Then with grudging respect (a look sometimes I am sure mistaken for hatred!) he reached over and picked it up, he counted it twice and bit on the coin to show he didn't trust me, but as there was only one hundred and one ten dinar note and one coin we both knew he was merely making a point.

The whole business of getting a visa is a rip off and before we had even reached Libya it had cost £150. So when they tried to get more from me in Libya it will come as no surprise to you that I became slightly tetchy, no that's wrong! I became bloody tetchy!
Visa and Translating services in London told me one price for the guide (a guide is apparently compulsory!) the local agent told me another price...
"Now here's a competition for you! Which do you think was the highest?"
"The one in Libya?"

"Well done! How did you guess? And by over £500!"
We settled down for a discussion!!! A long and very frank discussion, and although they spoke English well, they had to leave twice to look up the meaning of some words I was using…only to come back and complain that they couldn't find them in the Arabic/English dictionary.
We eventually "agreed" on a price, which I still wasn't happy with, but being relatively new to this type of travel, in spite of my confident exterior, I felt vulnerable.
The unfortunate outcome is that Libya is an expensive but unavoidable transit country. So we finished up just driving the 1500 miles or so with a guide costing £50 a day, simply driving ahead of us, and it still took seven days!! Seven days of driving on a ribbon of road laid through the desert.
Just a word on guides! Or guards as I prefer to call them! The word I'm thinking of isn't expensive, well it is! The word I'm thinking is ... Compulsory!
Khamiss is a great chap. But why do I get the impression that everywhere we went he reported to "someone"?.. After he had found us good free camping places he then disappeared and when I asked him if he'd "okayed" it with security he just smiled and said it's "for your own good!" and this in a country where they boast of very little crime. Add to this the piece of paper he hands to every roadblock. So call me suspicious!!!
"You're suspicious!"
"You're damned right I'm suspicious!"

I'm disappointed as I really wanted to go down south to see the desert but as I was paying a daily rate the cost was prohibitive.
So Khalifa (our initial contact in London), for your incompetence I'm praying that you get a boil on your bum and that there are only hard seats to sit on!

Forget anything I said about Italian and Tunisian drivers, the Libyans are the worst, by far. It was, shall we say hair raising, no! Let's say bloody frightening. They have a death wish, which wouldn't really worry me at all if the death they are wishing was their own, but when it involves me in any way I get nervous.

A BBQ OF CAMEL

Tonight I'm sitting on a remote beach with my computer in front of me just about to have a BBQ of camel meat, which I bought from a small local shop, it was probably a butcher's but in light of what happened it could have been a cobblers. I didn't know what it would taste like but if it was good enough for the thousands of flies that were happily eating it, it was certainly good enough for us ...

How wrong could I be?

"Right who wants what? Fillet, sirloin, leg or hump?"

"Don't you mean Rump?"

"No I mean hump!"

"I bloody knew that as soon as camels were mentioned you wouldn't be able to resist using a "hump" joke"

"So glad I didn't disappoint you!"

Just as an aside and contrary to what I believed, the hump on the camel doesn't store water it's simply a store of fat, the water is stored in sacs in the stomach

NEXT DAY

"Right! So in case you interested camel tastes just like beef"

"Oh yes Jeff? Fillet?"

"Err Nooo not quite!"

"Sirloin?"

"Nope!"

"Umm topside?"

"Backside?"

"Close!"

"Ok! I give in, which piece?"

"Well you know the part that goes into making shoes??"

"That bad huh??"

"Worse, chewing that was the most exercise I've had in weeks!

Eventually I gave up, and threw it away, it was only by dipping my bread in the marinade did I save the meal. We went to sleep to the sound of waves breaking against the shore, the wind
whistling through the trees and a seagull choking on the remains of the camel!

There's a road between Ahjahivya and Tobruk that's straight, and I mean straight, 250 miles of straight, as if the designer simply put a ruler on the map, ruled a line, and said,
"Oh bugger it, that'll do! Let's go for a pint!"
But at 125 miles, out of the blue (well! out of the yellow in truth, we are in the Sahara remember), there's a service station;
A clean air-conditioned service station;
A clean air-conditioned service station with hygienic toilets;
A clean air-conditioned service station with hygienic toilets and serving the best egg and chilli sandwich you've ever tasted!!
Truly!! Three sandwiches three coffees £2. Wonderful!

Mohammed, one of the assistants, made us very welcome and even gave Jean a rain umbrella, I noticed that he had quite a few; now, considering he was in the middle of the Sahara, rain umbrellas was perhaps not one of his better buys! Then back onto the road, mind wandering, looking wistfully at the vastness of the desert on both sides, wishing I could turn off and just drive.

TOBRUK CEMETERY 28/05/04

In the early years of World War II an area along the Mediterranean coast between Egypt in the west and Tunisia in the east, was alternately controlled by the Allied (British, French and Commonwealth) and Axis (Italian and German) forces as they fought back and forth until finally, after Hitler had sent in Rommel and his Afrika Corps to assist the, let's be honest here, unsuccessful Italian forces, on the 10th April 1941, the Allied forces were besieged at Tobruk.

It was only a spirited a desperate defence of the town, mainly by Australian seventh and ninth divisions' forces that caused Rommel to stall. The Australians held out for 240 days before being gradually withdrawn and replaced by the British 70th Infantry Division and the Czechoslovak 11th Infantry Division who continued to hold out until they linked with the advancing UK Eighth Army at the end of November during operation Crusader.

The siege of Tobruk was only a couple of months old when the Lord Haw Haw, who after the war was hanged as a traitor, broadcasting from Berlin, coined the description "Rats of Tobruk," because of the way they disappeared underground when they were being bombed.

The term "desert rats" was intended as an insult, but the besieged men, being mainly Australian, instead of being offended, revelled in the term and even struck an unofficial medal, made from the skin of a downed aircraft, with a rat motif.

The term "besieged" usually implies the defenders hiding and the attackers attacking, but no–one told the Australians what was expected of them and being Australians they decided to take the battle to the enemy by making raids against the besiegers, perfecting the art of stealth and bush craft, and, unusually for Australians, to see without being seen and heard , creating psychological as well as physical pressure by creeping up on the enemy surrounding them and attacking with bayonets killing silently.

So successful, persistent and deadly were the Australian night patrols that the enemy was reduced to a state of panic and on the slightest provocation, and often with no provocation at all, they would put down indiscriminate artillery and mortar barrages.

Another innovation was their method of fighting tank attacks. Traditionally the tanks led the infantry into battle and the combined firepower of the tanks and the infantry behind usually resulted in immediate capitulation. The Australians changed that by simply letting the tanks through and attacking the following infantry, leaving the tanks isolated and vulnerable.

Tobruk remained in Allied hands until the 21ˢᵗ June 1942 when it was recaptured by the Axis forces and was finally retaken by the Allied Eighth Army in November 1942 as part of the long drawn out final battles, which culminated in the surrender of the Axis forces in May 1943.

In all there were over 3000 killed or wounded and over 900 taken prisoner and there are now 2,282

*Commonwealth buried or commemorated in Tobruk
War Cemetery.*

The graveyard for the Australian and Allied troops killed in
the Second World War is just outside Tobruk, and like all the
Commonwealth War Cemeteries we've seen in many
countries, it is kept immaculately. In a country where there is
rubbish in even the remotest parts, the allied graveyard is
militarily neat!
The Commonwealth War Graveyards in Europe are
predominantly grass but here it is sand and the absence of
grass, along with the heat of the Libyan sun bouncing back
from the bare sand and white gravestones, makes you realise
how hard the conditions were that the defenders of Tobruk
had to endure.
I'm not ashamed to admit that tears flowed, but they always
do when I visit these places.

So many graves, so much waste…

The grave of H Abbot in Tobruk cemetery

So who were you H Abbot? (Harry, Herbert,?) 62 years ago exactly today you woke up under the Libyan sun, full of life and hope with a wife May (or Mary) and two children Aileen and Mary. They would lose you today and perhaps spend the rest of their lives looking at a picture of you on the wall.

I wonder if Aileen and May remember you as a person or just as a picture, whether your grandchildren ask about the black and white photo on the wall and wonder what life would have been like with you as a father?

> *Later research in the Commonwealth War Graves revealed these details*
> *Lance Corporal 241309 RASC   28/05/1942   age*

36

> *"Son of J H & E Bricknell & husband of Gladys Mary Bricknell of Derbyshire"*

Khamiss told us a story about an old lady he took to the cemetery, and they found the grave of her fiancé, she'd never married and she knelt at his grave, took off the engagement ring, buried it, and turned away!

52

Each of the graves has something inscribed, "He gave his life that others may live!" Or "In Gods hands". But the one that struck me, and perhaps came closest to expressing the bitterness that many must surely have felt was,
"To you he was one of many, but he was ours!"
I wrote in the book of Remembrance,
"Perhaps the most fitting memorial is not only that we remember but also that we learn!" if only I believed that it will ever happen.

The Rats of Tobruk medal

ALONG THE LIBYAN COAST
SABRATHA
I've seen many Roman ruins in my life, Tunisia, France, Italy, so it was with something less than excitement I visited Sabratha, but it turned out to be one of the better preserved i.e. least fallen down, Roman ruin still in existence.

What did make it special was that there was no one else around. So we were shown the early toilets, holes cut into stone in the communal loos, the residue (see I am getting better in the past I would have said shit!) being floated away in channels cut into the stone.

What was impressive was the amphitheatre, which was almost totally intact and like all other amphitheatres was built with the prevailing wind at the back of the stage so that the voices are carried out to the audience.

Clever heh!

LEPSIS MAGNA
Right if you're talking Roman ruins Lepsis Magna is the place. It's got everything, the swimming pool (natatio), the cool room (frigidarium), the hot room (tepidarium) (I wondered if they called the loo the crapaderium) they certainly loved their baths. It's got wide roads with the cobbles still there from when it was laid two thousand years ago and the roads have grooves, worn by the chariots, and even speed bumps, nothing changes!

At Lepsis Magna we met and chatted briefly to an American female tour operator (wearing a green eyeshade for Gods sake!) who was planning to start tours to Libya.

I suggested to her that it would be a pleasant change for Americans to visit an Arab country without first bombing it. I could tell from the look on her face that she found this really amusing and would have loved to have stopped and chatted further!!

A final thought about the ruins at Sabratha and Lepsis Magna, which as I've already written puts all the other Roman Ruins I've seen to shame in their completeness and their size, I cannot help but wonder if they were all, as is too easily trotted out, "ruined by earthquakes!"
I'm more of the view that following generations, perhaps intent on destroying the memory of the occupation, deliberately destroyed them. Or perhaps they just wanted the stone to build an outside loo or a bedroom extension for the wife's mother.

One telling point to me being the way the faces were all destroyed on the statues and the friezes. If I understand it correctly, Islam frowns on idolatry of any description, which may explain the particular destruction of the faces. I wonder??

As always happens the truth is probably somewhere in the middle. I learnt later that there was an earthquake but the vandals attacked and finished the work off. Just as an aside the three major cities in the northern region of Libya, which was called Tripolitania, were Lepsis Magna, Sabratha and Oea. The first two diminished in importance over the centuries and the third eventually became modern day Tripoli. So "tri" is three and "polis" is city so Tripoli means three cities!
"Clever hey? Look stop sighing you could learn something here!"

The Libyan people are wonderful. We went shopping in a local market, filling our bag with freshly picked local vegetables, and when we went to pay the stallholder waved us away and said,
"You are welcome, as our guests take it!" I was so annoyed that I'd only filled one bag.

55

Although open and generous individually we were herded along the sterile coast, monitored, discreetly but surely, wherever we went, and frankly treated like the old time camel trains which had to pay transit tax for passing through a territory.

At each road block Khamiss handed over a piece of paper and we were then waived through, with smiles and guns! The only thing that could really be said for Khamiss was that he found us some good free camping sites, including the olive grove and the French Military Cemetery in Tobruk.

The olive grove was his second choice that night! Firstly he took us to a beach, which was fine by me, miles of sand dunes with the Mediterranean waves breaking onto it!
Wild camping at its best! Wonderful!
Well it would have been if Khamiss hadn't returned and said,
"It's too dangerous!"
"What is?"
"This!"
"What?"
"This!"
"Ok! Why is it dangerous?"
"Foreigners!"
"Just in case you hadn't noticed we are foreigners"
"Other foreigners!"
"You mean security don't want me here!"
"It's for your own good!"
He moved us near an olive grove and left. Nearby there were some workers, so we wandered over to introduce ourselves.
Nice people who couldn't speak English and of course our Arabic is limited to err ... err ... well Ok! non-existent!
They said to us,

"You don't want to sleep there, it's much better down the track amongst the trees but be careful we've just sprayed for locusts.. So you're English? That's interesting!"
Well I think that's what they said, we smiled and nodded as if we understood them totally and followed them away from the main road and spent a wonderful evening under the stars in front of a camp fire with the men bringing us firewood. Magnificent people!

Of course the next morning Khamiss couldn't find us! Because, being childish we'd hid! The sound of burning tyres as he roared off looking for us showed how worried he was. By the time he returned we'd emerged from the olive grove and were sitting grinning in the car, he feigned a smile but he was not happy, obviously not being as easily amused as we are.

In Tobruk we stayed in the French Military Cemetery and we got a shower! Now you might not think that's much but it had been a while, a long while! In fact I suspect the occupants of the cemetery smelled better than we did!

I was wandering around the museum looking for the toilet and I FOUND A SHOWER! Quickly I went back to the car and said to Jean,
"Don't ask questions, just get your wash bag"
"Why?"
"I said don't ask questions!"
"Why not?"
There are better ways to use your breath than to ask Jean not to ask questions. I led her to the shower and stood guard outside as she washed off the sands of days, (as all of the occupants had been dead for sixty-odd years I am not sure who or what I was guarding her from!) Ignore what the guidebooks say these are the high spots of any trip!

The abiding memory of Libya isn't Sabratha or Lepsis Magna or even the graveyard at Tobruk, but the litter. Plastic bags and wind do not go well together. Deep in the desert far from habitation there are dehydrated bushes festooned with plastic bags... so depressing!

BARDIA

I never commented on it in the web site but along the coast in the small fishing town of Bardia there's a remarkable mural drawn by a British Soldier John F Brill of the East York's Regiment who tragically, when you see his talent, was killed on 1st July 1942 aged 22.

When we drove into Bardia we were immediately followed by a car, which turned out to be the all-pervading "security". They were obviously used to travellers as, after a half-hearted attempt at interrogating obviously dangerous spies (us!), they lost interest and took us to the small room where John Brill was held prisoner and, whilst there, he drew the mural in charcoal and he was, we were informed, later executed.

The truth it transpired wasn't quite like that, Brill was the artist but not a prisoner, and he wasn't executed, he was killed in action. His mother in answer to various enquiries later wrote a letter,

"Dear Chief Technician Seccombe
A few days ago a friend brought me a cutting from the 'Old Codgers' column of the "Daily Mirror". It concerned a letter written by you, requesting information regarding a mural discovered in a derelict house in Bardia - and which was executed by

a soldier- J.F. Brill- of the R.A.S.C. in 1942.

*I am the mother of John Brill - the said artist - and as
you have shown such interest in the matter, and have
gone to so much trouble, I think it only right to
enlighten you about the facts of the case. (I hope you
will understand that this is not the rhapsody of a fond
mother, but what actually happened.)*

*As a tiny boy, John was always drawing _ After he left
school he entered the Regent St Polytechnic as an art
student. From there he studied at the Royal Academy
School. He had just passed the entrance exam for a
three year Diploma Course at the Royal College of
Art, when war broke out in '39, and of course he had
to join up. By this time, art had become to him the
ruling passion of his
life, murals being his special love. His creed was that
in order to become a great artist, he must suffer.
Consequently, he joined the Infantry, believing that to
be the roughest & hardest of the services. After going
through Dunkirk, his regiment was posted to the
middle east, within a few months, however, he was
transferred to the R.A.S.C.*

*My husband & I, (I have since become widowed,)
often used to wonder, whether the Army life would not
stifle his passion. On the contrary, it seemed to burn
in him in greater and greater intensity. He formed a
close friendship with one of the lads, who was with
him when he was killed, and it is from this chum that I
have obtained all the following information, he and I
having become very great friends.*

It appears, from him, that John was drawing and sketching at every opportunity. (I imagine that life was somewhat slacker in the R.A.S.C. than in the Infantry.) Consequently, he must have come under the notice of his Officers, who invited him to decorate the walls of their mess. The mural, which you saw, was evidently the only one to remain, the subject being "The Pleasures of Avarice". On the wall opposite, was a companion mural, that subject being "The Pleasures of Art" & this, it appears, was truly beautiful, depicting, as it did, all the lovely & lasting things of life. On a third wall, he started one of "The Last Supper", but this was never finished, as his Company was moved up the Line. However, he had painted a set of murals on the four walls of the lad's canteen, which represented "A Soldiers Leave in Cairo". This I understand, afforded them much interest & amusement!!

*I am thankful to say, that he was never under sentence of death, neither was he ever a prisoner. The Arabs certainly gilded the lily! Neither was boot polish used as his medium, but the paints were bought in Cairo, by the lads on leave & sent by convoy up to Bardia. I understand that the ****(illegible) But he spoke in his letters of the wonderful generosity of his officers.*

Contrary to the belief, that artists are often considered to be weak & effeminate beings, his chum told me that John was the bravest man he had ever known, an instance being the fact, that when their convoy was bombed as it frequently was, John would deliberately go out with his sketch book and pencil, and sketch everything within sight, especially the faces of the lads as they ran for cover. I know it was his great desire, that if he were spared to come

*through the war, he intended to paint such a mural,
depicting all the horrors of war and that it would
contribute to the cause of peace so I do hope that this,
that I have told you, will answer your questions.*

*Please do not think that I need any pity, I am deeply
grateful that I possess a faith that sees through death
to a more glorious life beyond, I am convinced that
John is fulfilling his destiny in a higher plane, so I am
well content.*
*If you would like to accept this copy of the mural, you
are very welcome. I have two more. It was through
the kindness of a member of the forces that I obtained
them & I hope this letter reaches you.*
*May all good fortune be yours, & may God's Blessing
be with you!*

Yours sincerely
E. Brill
p.s.
*I hope you can understand my writing, I have a badly
handicapped hand, so writing for me is difficult"*

Fascinating and like all deaths in war tragic but, eventually
and unfortunately time and the indifference of the local people
means that the mural will disintegrate and disappear.

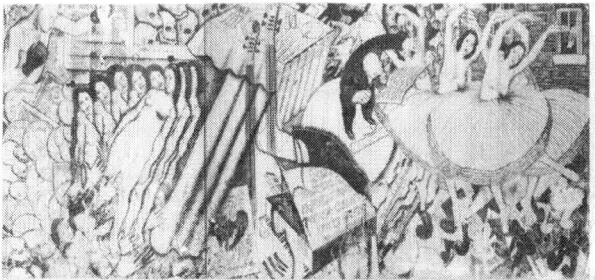

Khamiss handed us over to the Tourist policeman at the Egyptian border who saw us through Customs and we finally left Libya six days after starting off full of hope but in the end just day after day of driving.. such a disappointment!

EGYPT
CUSTOMS AND IMMIGRATION

I hereby claim the world record for passing through customs and immigration into Egypt. Two and a half hours. Impressive huh! ... And this after hearing horror stories on the road of it taking fifteen to twenty hours and involving bribery and corruption.
For those who care I'll run through the procedure as I understand it ... for the rest bear with me, go and put the kettle on and come back when it's over, don't worry you won't miss anything that's even tangentially interesting.

First stop is the entrance gate where a man in a white uniform asked for the passports and after a chat about life in general and a perfunctory glance at our passports he waved us on. Next, another very nice man in another white uniform directed us to the passport hall; he also wanted to talk about life in general but lost interest when we refused his kind offer of black market money!
In the teeming, dusty, hot immigration hall we joined the end of a very long queue, and waited, resigned, but after five minutes yet another very nice man in yet another white uniform gave me some cards to fill in, and took me straight to the front of the queue, amazingly causing no comment or complaint from anyone.

For my part I was really embarrassed at this and tried to explain to him that my strong socialist principles couldn't possibly allow such preferential treatment and that I really should be allowed to wait, like the rest, for two hours until it was my turn…fortunately (and to my intense relief) it turned out he couldn't speak English and so ignored my protestations.

I didn't like to embarrass him by keeping repeating myself so just this once I put my principles, like the other poor sods, behind me. There's a time and place for strong socialist principles and teeming hot dusty immigration halls isn't one of them! However next time I'm faced with a two-hour queue and have the opportunity of being ushered to the front solely on the basis of my colour and age I will certainly refuse, err, or maybe the time after that I'll refuse, or maybe the ……..

The next immigration man took his time examining the passports, before picking them up and taking them away for a discussion, perhaps he wanted to show his boss my hair cut? Who knows? When he returned he passed the passports through to another man who looked at them, looked at us, looked again at the passports, then without any comment, but with a telling shake of his head, passed them back and they were stamped.

Still with me?? … So that's immigration over.

"What do you mean? Are you still only on immigration?"
"Go and sit and drink your tea I'll let you know when we're through"
"Where was I? ... Oh yes!"

Back into the car I was directed to the customs shed. Well, they said it was a customs shed, but to my innocent eyes it looked exactly the same as any other half finished dusty hot shed. We were told to drive over a pit and the customs man told me to open the back and asked what the loo was. I explained and offered to let him examine it; refusing quickly he waived us through, but only after asking us if we had a video camera.

Onto yet another customs shed, another half finished dusty shed, where yet another man checked the vehicle chassis number against the carnet, and also listed the radio make, and wanted to know if we had a video camera..

Noooooooo!

And did we have air-conditioning?.

Nooooooooo!

He wrote something else on the carnet in Arabic and waived us through.

If this is boring for you reading this, I'm bored witless writing it and you can imagine how I felt actually doing it..

Next stop is the traffic police one hundred yards away.

A very nice man with a three day growth of beard and one very spectacular yellow tooth greeted me and said,

"Open!" pointing to the bonnet

As we leant over he said,

"British?"

I nodded and he said,

"Tony Blair!"

I indicated that I thought Tony Blair was perhaps not my world's favourite politician by spitting onto the floor, the sentiments endeared me to him, the fact that I'd spat on his besandaled foot probably didn't!

He laughed out loud, put his arm round me a kissed my ear!!!!

Now you will all be wondering whether receiving a kiss on the ear from a man with one yellow tooth and a three-day growth of beard awoke any latent, hitherto unacknowledged homosexuality within me. I can happily report that it didn't! However still being at the early stages of Customs clearance and not wanting to upset him, I gave him a look that was meant to indicate that should he treat me well, and although innocent and very very shy, who knows what sensual delights awaited him (checking later in a mirror on the look I realised it looked more like I had indigestion!!)

Mr. One Tooth, checked the chassis number again (this time stencilling it onto a piece of what looked alarmingly like toilet paper) and engine number (again stencilling it), and filled out yet another piece of paper.
"GO TO MAHMOOD!" He said, handing me back my Carnet and the piece of paper, which I assumed was details of the car (in Arabic).

Not having a clue who Mahmood was, I acted bewildered, not difficult under the circumstances, and walked around in circles a few times until one of them took me by the shoulders, pointed me back in the direction from where I'd come, and gave me a slight push. The momentum kept me going for a while but I soon slowed to a halt when suddenly I saw a man having his shoes cleaned, a captive audience! So I asked him after the said Mahmood, and he sprung into action, scattering shoes, brushes, polishes and the polisher into the dust.

With shoes that shiny he must have been important, and in very short order were back through the teeming hell which was the customs hall, (or the teeming hall that was the customs hell!) and into Mahmoods' office, where Shiny Shoes and Mahmood proceeded to have a noisy argument until finally Shiny Shoes asked me for $600.This being the recently introduced tax (coincidence or did they know I was coming?)

for vehicles over 2000 cc and staying more than a week. So that'll be me then! Surprise! Surprise!

Mahmood smiled at me, scowled at Shiny Shoes, and Shiny Shoes and I left Mahhood's office, giving him a cheery English wave with a couple of fingers of my right hand. I wondered why he'd smiled at me and scowled at Shiny Shoes and concluded that the $600 must have had something to do with it. Perhaps they couldn't agree on the split between them!
"Cynical? Me? Nooo!"

I had arrived bewildered and was now well into terminally bemused state.

It was at this point I asked an obvious question, "who the hell is Shiny Shoes? " This took some getting through as my Arabic hadn't improved much since the last time I tried to use it which was about two hours ago, but to his credit he understood and he opened an office and showed me papers that indicated that he was the local motoring organization man.

Back to One Tooth, who gave me a toothy smile (obviously) and took a photocopy of my passport, then back again to Mahmood who issued Shiny Shoes and me with a receipt for the E£3000 (that's about 3000 Egyptian pounds or about 450 British pounds) then back to One Tooth who then sent us next door for insurance.
It was at this point that I realised I'd lost my car keys, so we retraced our (and in his case shiny) steps until we found them ... bet you can't guess where?
"I SAID I'LL BET YOU CAN'T GUESS WHERE!"
"Oh sorry I was dozing!"
"I said I'll bet you can't guess where!"

"What? Where?
"The keys!"
"What keys!"
"The ones in Mahmood's office!"
"Oh good … I think!"
Finally back to One Tooth….
"Did I hear the word finally??? At last!!!"
 …. who by now had created a small plastic credit card thing
and given someone some number plates to stick on my
car…still with me???? Good nearly over now!

SHAKEDOWN
So the time to settle up came…
Shiny Shoes gave me a handwritten piece of paper that looked
like this,

E£

```
$600.................................. ..........3672
Indecipherable Arabic    …… … .-3002
Indecipherable Arabic   ………   ..  - 40
Indecipherable Arabic  …………… -  45
Indecipherable Arabic   … ……… -  89
```

He indicated that therefore he owed me 509 less 250 i.e. 259..
Err yes! Err Nooo!
"What's the 250 for?"
"Mahmood!"…. Aaaaah the shakedown!

Seven men in various uniforms, and one tourist, who was
obviously bored and just wanted some entertainment, had
joined One Tooth and Shiny Shoes.

The friendly discussion, which to the layman could easily
have been mistaken for a violent argument, that followed
ranged back and forth and at one stage I thought One Tooth

was going to give me another kiss, and each time they gave me the £259. I gave it back to them acting dim but smiling, in truth I was quite enjoying myself!

So picture the situation! Nine people and me (and one onlooker just passing time) all of whom thought I was stupid for not understanding Egyptian ways. Having spent my life where 90% of the world thinks I'm stupid and 10% couldn't care less but are just looking on, I was comfortable. No! I was more than comfortable, I was having fun!

Eventually they succumbed and gave me all the money I was due. One Tooth probably won't write, and Shiny Shoes went off to find another victim, and have his shoes cleaned.

I'd won my first battle with Egyptian corruption. Well I thought I had ... two days later I went to the bank and realised that the official rate of exchange wasn't six pounds but seven pounds per dollar so they'd ripped me off for £60.

Bastards!

For your information the four charges it later transpired were Road Tax, Insurance, Number plates and something else probably the plastic driving licence!!

SIWA OASIS
We'd heard on the road that the oasis in Siwa was worth a visit, it was, but was it worth a detour of two hundred miles through flat uninteresting country side only to find that the road from there to Cairo was blocked?
"I don't know was it?"
"No!"

Siwa is made of mud, well to be strictly accurate it used to be made of mud until one night in 1926 they had a rain storm, not your average downpour, not even a "raining cats and dogs" rainstorm, but the whole menagerie, the whole cats dogs elephants and perhaps even a ring tailed Lemur rainstorm and it washed the town away.

Now you may be wondering why I've included a picture of a donkey at a filling station, you know what? So am I! All I can tell you is that I found it highly amusing at the time and it kept me happy for the long drive back to the main coast road.

Siwa oasis like so many Egyptian towns, was once a prosperous and influential city being visited by all the pharaohs, by Alexander the Great and of course by me Jeff the boringly average.

The ruins of Shali, a district of Siwa, date back to the 13th century and the houses were originally built of Kershef, a mixture of salt and clay and were only expected to last a couple of decades, and even then had to be rebuilt or repaired even after light rain.

Leaving Siwa and retracing our steps we again joined the Mediterranean coast road and the drive along it is surreal; there are miles and miles of half finished holiday complexes with absolutely no sign of habitation. I don't mean houses I mean vast hotel blocks without roofs, roads without cars and more importantly for us, absolutely nowhere to camp for the night.

Eventually when we were just beginning to wonder if it was a hotel night, we spotted an ambulance station with a large open area behind it. An emergency stop brought the sound of screeching brakes (not ours!), a horn sounded angrily (again not ours!) and what I took (correctly) to be abusive obscene Egyptian (certainly not mine!) directed at me.

By this time I'd been in Egypt long enough to be the subject (or object) of Arabic drivers abuse to be completely unmoved by it (in fact I actively enjoy making them mad!) and waved at him cheerily as he roared by!
"Where was I?"
"Ambulance station!"
"Oh yes! The ambulance station."
The men Mohamed (the older) and Aahmed (the younger) were very welcoming and pointed out a good place to park behind the station, they also suggested that looking for wood for a camp fire anywhere but in the cleared area may not be a good idea as there were still unexploded World War Two bombs there. Being blown up by a British Bomb would have made me really annoyed, so I sent Jean instead!

The two men cooked for us and even, now listen to this..
"OI!! I said listen to this!"
"Sorry!"
"..helped Jean wash her undies and hang them out to dry in front of the ambulance station. Jean had begged for a bowl to wash her undies in (I didn't bother with mine, I'd had them on since England and they were just getting comfortable!), not only did they produce a large bowl but also a packet of industrial strength washing powder all of which Jean poured

into the water and frothed it up, immediately disappearing
behind an avalanche of soap suds.

Aahmed bravely ran to her rescue and dragged her heroically
from the suds, stood her to one side and washed her undies
himself. He paused quizzically over Jeans thong wondering
whether she wore it or used it as a catapult to shoot birds.
Although Jean wears thongs she doesn't think they are all
they're cracked up to be! (I like that joke! Read it again!)

They then proudly...
"OI!! that was a split infinitive!"
"Oh sorry!"
 Then they proudly.."Happy now?"
"Absolutely! So they then what?"
...showed me their ambulance and equipment, which consisted
of three plasters, two bandages, and a plastic tube that he
attempted (unsuccessfully) to explain to me how he used it.

When I still failed to understand he offered to demonstrate on
me but as this appeared to involve me kneeling forward and
him doing something behind me I resisted! (No! I flatly
refused and crossed my legs and clenched my buttocks to
emphasise the point).

I had more equipment in my first aid kit than he did and
probably as much idea what to do with it. If nothing else it
persuaded me that careful driving in Egypt was a good idea.

Being good environmentalists we always collect our rubbish
in plastic bags, which we often dispose of carefully by
dropping it through the sunroof of any car that cuts me up, so
the following morning I handed Aahmed my bag of rubbish
for disposal, and then had to persuade him it wasn't meant as
a token of our gratitude.
"No it's not a present it's rubbish!"

I could see him thinking,
"Yes I think it's a rubbish present as well!"

When I finally got through to him that I was giving it to him
so he could dispose of it, he looked at me as if I was mad and
simply turned and threw it as far as he could towards the long
grass, it didn't quite make it and exploded open when it hit the
ground.

We left with good feelings towards these two men who were
trying to do a difficult job with inadequate equipment and
training, and who had made us welcome and shared their food
with us. I felt bad in not offering them a pair of Jeans thongs
to use as a tourniquet or a towrope but I suspect that the older
one would have worn them so I didn't; I gave him a bra
instead, his need being greater than Jeans!

CAIRO

Cairo has a Ring Road!
Cairo has a Ring Road with directions in Arabic and English!
Cairo has a Ring road with directions in Arabic and English
but the directions bear no relationship with anything that is
shown on the maps!

Which probably explains why we spent three hours driving
round the Cairo Ring Road; doing "U" turns on the Cairo
Ring Road and after filtering off, reversing back onto the
main Cairo Ring Road.

All of these manoeuvres were done under the benevolent (or
disinterested) eyes of the Cairo Traffic Police. I don't want to
bore you with the details (those amongst you who said "why
not? it's never stopped you so far" can leave now, and I pray
that you too one day get stuck on the Cairo Ring Road lost
and needing the loo!)..so I'll move on ..

We eventually found the campsite from which, facing west, you can see the famous pyramids of Giza, the tips reaching into a brilliant blue sky. The pyramids, objects of awe, wonderment and avarice have stood there for 4500 years, which felt to me about the same time that it took us to find the campsite.

Facing east you see a stagnant dark green canal full of rubbish, sewage and mosquitoes, probably of a similar age to the pyramids and a couple of small restaurants with seats stylishly placed so that you can watch Cairo's sewage float by whilst eating.

Whilst we were in Cairo we needed to get our Sudanese visa, which as you know by now, we'd been trying to get since February, and which had become almost a challenge in itself. A challenge to overcome intractable bureaucracy, inefficiency and, dare I say it, common or garden single syllable lies, and should any of you suddenly take leave of whatever is left of your senses and say,
"I know! Why don't I go to Sudan? It should be easy enough to get a visa. I'll apply in good time, say four months, to the Sudanese Embassy in London and they'll give me one"

"Err no, you may get some rich tea biscuits, and a bucket full of platitudes (Duck Billed Platitudes?) what you won't get is a Sudanese visa!"
"Ok you think! What I'll do is get in touch with George or Mike at the Acropole Hotel in Khartoum and they'll apply in Sudan on my behalf and then fax the approval direct to Cairo and I'll just turn up there and collect it, because all the web sites say they can help!"
"Err no, you may make lots of expensive 'phone calls to Sudan from England, and you may wait four days in Cairo,

and receive more Duck Billed Platitudes from George but you won't get a visa because either,

(A) It didn't get faxed; or

(B) The fax was lost in the Sudanese Embassy in Cairo; or

(C) The officer in charge (faxes) at the Sudanese Embassy Cairo decided not to turn up and they didn't like to tell you so they keep you waiting for two bloody hours in a room like the black (sorry! coloured!) hole of Calcutta with your nose stuck in the fetid rotting armpits of various nationalities whose understanding of the term "personal freshness" is akin to mine of Phaeroic hieroglyphics, before finally telling you that he hadn't turned up.

I'm not sure about (A),

I'm not sure about (B),

BUT I'M ABSOLUTELY BLOODY CERTAIN ABOUT (C)!!!!

I admit it I got tetchy at this point and slapped the counter very hard (it hurt like hell as it was made of marble.. but I didn't show it.. well not very much!), and spoke firmly, very firmly, to the immigration man who was either scared of me or didn't like seeing a grown man with tears in his eyes

Eventually I was passed over to Mr. Cream Suit who had been sitting there all the time and who was Head of Immigration, but was wisely keeping a very low profile.(when I discovered this I gave him a black look! And he gave me one in return which was better than mine, but he did have a head start on me!) He finally relented and intervened and asked for four copies of the application. He also tried to ask for the Letter of Recommendation from the British Embassy.

There are many frustrations on the road because of mindless, stupid bureaucracy but none more so than the business of

"Letter of Recommendation" from the British Embassy, which is still required by some countries. A Letter of Recommendation should state that the British Government recommends that you be given entry to the country, and the Sudanese Embassy demands one.

The Brutish (that was a Freudian slip!!) Government's stance on this is that they don't give a Letter of Recommendation, the British Passport is in their opinion sufficient, but they will in fact give you a letter headed "Letter of Recommendation" which states that they do not issue Letters of Recommendation. Which seems to satisfy the requirement, but, BUT! They charge you £36 for that!
"Wow I'll bet you weren't happy with that!"
"You can bet your life I wasn't happy!"

Where was I? Oh yes! when he tried to ask for a Letter of Recommendation he perceived that I wasn't happy (the fact that I'd raised my hand and was about to slap the counter again gave him a clue) and he relented and said,
"Come back in an hour!"
I went back in an hour and they said,
"Come back in three hours"

I raised my hand to slap the counter and I smiled, the combination worked! We were ushered immediately through to the back offices, which were so dirty we started calling them back orifices.

Four orifices later and two hundred dollars poorer and we had our Sudanese visas, two hours from the time Cream Suit got involved! And four months after I applied in London! All I can say to the Sudanese Embassy in London is I hope the next time you dunk your Rich Tea biscuits in your tea they break and fall to the bottom of your cup.

A VISIT TO THE PYRAMIDS
It's hot in Egypt, and the heat gets to you, which may have explained why I upset Ali the Guide (using the term "guide" in its broadest sense), especially when he tried to charge me forty English pounds for a walking tour of the pyramids and when I raised an eyebrow at the amount, he complained that English people were not as generous as Americans and also were more aggressive!!. AGGRESSIVE? ME? (I must confess when I said I
"raised an eyebrow" it may have been just a bit of an understatement!).

I offered him the equivalent of forty pence and he feigned disgust, so I put the money back in my pocket. He assumed an air of injured distain and indicated that he would with reluctance accept the forty pence just to make me feel embarrassed at my lack of generosity. I gave him the satisfaction of making me feel really embarrassed by not giving him anything.

Because of the heat, we took a carriage ride around the pyramids, and were "fortunate" to get Namood who, whilst "guiding" us, also kindly offered us many opportunities to give him money, which we, with reluctance and regret, refused. He took it like a true Egyptian gentleman, first he sulked and then he stopped in the middle of the district rubbish dump and, dropping all pretence of being nice, refused to move unless we gave him more money!

It was an interesting moment, as we looked at each other in the stinking heat of an Egyptian afternoon under the gaze of

76

the ancient Pyramids and rabid dogs. I indicated to Namood (nicely I thought) that if he didn't move the carriage within the next five seconds he would be laying in the towns rubbish tip and I would be driving the carriage back myself.

He believed me and did, I think, learn a valuable lesson that will stand him in good stead for the rest of his unfortunate pox ridden life, namely that grey haired wrinkled Englishmen and their money are very very difficult to separate, but it didn't stop many other Egyptians trying it again and again in the next few weeks

Contrary to belief not all the Pyramids are in Cairo, in fact very few of them are, the whole region down to and including Sudan, abounds with them, some more crowded with tourists than others and some of course which don't look quite as you'd expect.

There are two at Dashur, the Bent and the Red pyramids, which are probably the true ancestors of the pyramids at Giza, being built around 2600 BC a few years earlier than the more famous ones at Giza.

The pyramids of Giza

The Bent pyramid at Dashur

*The Bent Pyramid is named because of the obvious bend in its side, and the Red Pyramid is named because it's, well RED! The Bent pyramid was planned to be larger
than the Great Pyramid built later at Giza, but the foundation was insufficient for the weight.*

Even during the initial construction they were unable to control the shifting and cracking so as a compromise, they reduced the angle of the pyramid, thus reducing the weight of the upper courses. When the pyramid was completed and was named "Sneferu is Shining."

The Red Pyramid was built when the first one went wrong "Plan B" as it were, and it's surprising how much comfort this gave me. It's good to know that the Ancient Egyptians have so much in common with me, starting a project with grandiose plans and then realising that it's impractical.

Eventually we left Cairo after a week, which saw us getting a Sudanese visa, and to our surprise thoroughly enjoying Cairo itself, but the time had come to begin to head south, but not before we had had a (for us) unique experience! We'd eaten at McDonalds! Clean food, clean toilets and air conditioning, Bliss! Pity the food had no taste but then you can't have everything.

GENTLEMEN WE HAVE CONVOY!

First stop after Cairo was EL Menya where, after we booked into a hotel, we became aware that we were not alone. There was a man who followed us everywhere; when we went for a walk along the Nile, our man was there, when we did a sudden left turn, he followed.

It seemed churlish not to be sociable, so I slowed, and with my best smile painted on, I said, pleasantly, well pleasantly for me.

"So who the bloody hell are you?"

"Security!"

"Why do I need security?"

"Security!"

"Right, it's been jolly warm today hasn't it?"

"Security!"

"Supercalliflagelisticexpialidotous" (I had to add that to the spellchecker, but then I also had to add "Wicketkeeper"! that's what you get for using the American version of Microsoft Word!)

"Security!"

We walked ahead and I looked at Jean and whispered, "You carry on, I'm going left!" we separated "That should bewilder him" I thought, it didn't! He simply followed me! Obviously judging me to be a greater security threat than Jean!

We rejoined and I tried another couple of questions but this time I formed them so that "Security" would be the answer but as a game it soon palled and as the conversation wasn't going anywhere, and with him following every movement, neither were we, we went to bed instead!

Next morning he was still there! I sat in the car and started the engine and he guided me out of the very tight parking place but then stood in front of the vehicle, making a very effective human barricade.

He was talking into his radio; I leant out and said,

"You're talking to ...?"

"Security!"

"Thought so!" and I waited,

Suddenly in my rear view mirrors I saw a police vehicle, blue lights flashing, siren wailing, and men with rifles. They slowed, smiled and indicated me to follow them!

With the siren still sounding, the blue light still flashing, and men with rifles still trying to look fierce (difficult when you're in imminent danger of being thrown out the back of the truck!), we left town, cutting a swathe through the morning traffic jam, all the drivers looked at us and wondered who we were. We loved it! Having an armed escort is the only way to travel especially if you are a convicted terrorist or a bank robber or a Prime Minister...erm there's a moral there somewhere!

A suggestion has been made (by our son) that the escort was in fact a normal precaution that all societies make when transporting toxic waste, which is probably what the contents of the loo after

four weeks in temperatures of forty-five degrees could reasonably be classified as.

That suggestion is certainly not to be sniffed at unlike the contents...come on by now you don't need me to finish the sentence...!

I asked Jean to make a noise like a Police Siren but she sounded more like an Ice Cream seller! So I contented myself in looking imperious and joined the chase. I felt very Prime Ministerial and sat there thinking Prime Ministerial thoughts, like, who shall I invade next?

But as there aren't many Arab countries left to invade, I could only think of Dudley or Bradford where there are probably more weapons of mass destruction than there ever were in Iraq! (Think curry houses!).
A rapid slowing down of the escort broke my train of thought. Bugger! over so soon ... But no…as the first peeled off another was there and off we went again!!
I was so into this that I got Jean to get a pair of her white knickers out and to draw a Union Jack on it in red pen (it was in fact a thong so it was only a small Union Jack!) and we hung it on the radio aerial.

Now that really got some attention.
All went well until we had a close shave with a cow and the knickers got caught in its horn and he ran off with a union jack thong stuck in it, causing consternation amongst the populace and at least one old colonial to spring to attention and snap off a very smart salute at the passing Union Jack, knocking over his table and spilling coffee over his crumpled white suit, and dousing the sheesha (a sheesha is the smoking pipe where the smoke is drawn through a bowl of water, sometimes called a hookah, as opposed to a hooker, which is something entirely different!) of the man next to him..
"JEFF!!"
"What?"
"Was all that true?"
"How exactly do you mean true? Truth is such a relative concept!"

"No it's not! It's a simple concept. Try "did all that really happen, is that easier?"
"Well err..."
"The bit about drawing the Union Jack on a white thong...!"
"Um ... well not exactly"
"The cow running off with them stuck to its horn"
"Well it could have happened!"
"Did it?"
"No!"
"The man with the white suit?"
"Err"
"The armed escort?"
"Oh yes now that's absolutely true!"
"Your version of the truth or the one that the rest of the world uses!"
So we were escorted the two hundred miles or so between El Menya and Luxor by armed police "for your safety" and it made what could have been a boring days driving great fun!! I felt quite hurt and abandoned when suddenly without warning they pulled off and left us alone at the mercies of.. well no one really

Since the massacre of tourists in the Valley of the Kings in 1997 when fifty-eight foreign tourists were killed by Islamic extremists, Egypt has been nervous of lone lost wandering travellers (that'll be us then!) and has insisted on the convoy system, although in truth we were more in danger from a traffic accident than from a fanatical El Quaida suicide squad.

NEGOTIATING IN THE BAZAAR
Negotiating soon palls. At first it's fun but it soon becomes boring and annoys me... with this in mind I eventually explained it to the man with a stall who was trying to sell me a casual shirt.

"Right let's change the rules... you tell me how much it is, I decide if I want it, and that's it. One price only! Do you understand?
"Yes!"
"Sure? One price! I say yes or no? ... You understand?"
"Yes!"
"Right go for it. How much?"
"85 pounds!"
"One price? Final price? … Now wasn't that easy?.£85?… Nope! too expensive!"
"So how much you wanna pay?"

In the end we found out about the government store where they don't negotiate, one price! Finish! ... Just what we needed and after running the gauntlet of importuning, or is it imploring, salesmen we found it. Inside we were met by a very nice man and explained to him that what I wanted was a loose sand coloured shirt in medium.
Off he went; back he comes!
"You like?"
"Well yes I do like it's very nice but in case you haven't noticed that isn't in fact a loose sand coloured shirt in medium, it is, if you look closely, a set of aluminium saucepans. Do you in fact have a loose sand coloured etc etc?"
"Wait!"
Off he went; back he comes!
"You like?"
"Well if I needed a pair of black shoes (which if I'm not very much mistaken are both left ones) and which look as if they have been on the shelf since the days of the last Pharaoh, (Cleopatra in case you were wondering) I would certainly be very tempted. However..."
"Wait!"

We backed away and made a run for it as he was laying out a range of brushed nylon ladies full-length nighties with lace around the cuffs in various shades of purple and blue.

I bought the sand coloured etc. from a shop, paying what the first man asked hours ago!

Egypt frankly disappointed. I know it's sacrilege to say it, but too many antiquities get boring. I loved the Pyramids but after a while awe gives way to tedium.
The drive down south took us alongside the Nile, which is even more than you imagine it to be, wide, dominating and in places like a massive moving lake, bringing life to the three mile wide centre band of Egypt, which, unless you travel in other parts of the country, gives the impression that the whole land is rich and fertile.
The Nile retains an air of mystery and you can easily understand why its source has held such a fascination to the nineteenth century explorers such as Stanley, Speke, and Burton.

The other fascinating, but this time man-made, feature is the northern end of the "Cape to Cairo" railway, the unfulfilled dream of that legendry megalomaniac Cecil Rhodes, which now disappears into the sand somewhere in Uganda before reappearing in Sudan. The line we see now is the same one that was built in the 19th century by imported Indian labour, which created a whole new sub-culture within Africa, and ultimately handed over the control of the retail sector to the ethnic Indians, causing resentment that eventually led in some parts, Uganda under Idi Amin for example, to summarily remove them.
The fact is that the work ethic and the accumulation of wealth in hard currency is available to all, the Indians simply put this first in their lives whereas other ethnic groups prefer an

afternoon sleep! I name no names here! But if you're thinking Egyptian you're not far wrong.

Cecil Rhodes had a vision of a rail link connecting British colonies in northern and southern Africa, a vision that came close to fruition, but ground to a halt (literally) between Sudan and Uganda.

A railway already existed in Egypt, started by Lord Kitchener as part of his campaign to relieve General Gordon in Khartoum but it was problems in the southern

countries which, particularly in German East Africa,(later Tanzania), that prevented the completion of the North-South link until after the defeat of Germany in 1918 when most of this territory fell into British hands which made completion politically, but not economically possible.

After World War Two, the independence struggles of Africa and the demise of Colonialism meant that overall control of the continent was lost, the dream faded, and the lines fell into disrepair.

Interestingly the need to open markets between Europe and Southern Africa has made the completion of the project feasible, although the problem of three different rail gauges still remains, as does the vast differences in wealth and the administrative ability between the various countries through which it will have to pass.

You'll have gathered by now that the Nile fascinates me, and the high spot of the trip so far was a gentle sunset boat trip in a felucca, just the three of us, Jean, myself and Mohammed, (he did all the work!).

The triangular sail on the felucca was exactly like old faded drawings you see of these boats in previous eras and obviously hasn't changed in centuries, why would it? It works!

Mohammed, recognising me as someone from a nation with a strong sailing tradition, was comfortable in letting me take over the steering, (that and the fact that when he handed me control there was nothing within hitting distance!) and I lay back relaxing, the tiller nonchalantly under one arm, steering, what has to be admitted wasn't the straightest of courses, and causing a massive Nile cruise ship to perform an emergency stop.

A FELUCCA TRIP ON THE NILE

They all waived and shouted at me from the bridge! People are so friendly!

The setting sun silhouetted the hills in the distance as the sounds of Luxor drifted across the water, was more memorable to me than the visit to the Valley of the Kings and Queens.

ON THE ANAL HABITS OF TRAVELLING

This isn't a pleasant subject so all those of a delicate disposition are probably well advised to move swiftly on. It's not usual in normal conversation when at home to discuss bowel movements, quantity, quality, consistency etc. however this soon becomes perfectly acceptable when on the road.

So far we had been lucky, mainly I suspect because we, well Jean to be honest, have done most of our own cooking. I have had one minor bout caused I almost certainly, by three bowls (or blows even!) of lentil soup.

Jean's was caused by an innocent plate of salad eaten at the Ruzike hotel and was definitely spectacular (not the salad, the results!). A classic case of so much more coming out than ever went in. The good news is we weren't in the tent, having taken a room which was cheaper than camping (why else would we take a room?); the bad news is that the toilet flushing system, inadequate in normal circumstances, simply gave up, and the cistern refused to fill.

This caused an interesting (well interesting to some! Me for instance!) dilemma because the bowl that was on her lap which she was filling orally, was in fact needed to fill with water to flush away the contents of the loo which she was filling (there's no easy way to put this) anally.

There is also a walk, which those who have the dreaded trots develop, which is unmistakable; very short steps, cheeks (bum) locked firmly together, an aura of determination that brooks no interference, as they accelerate penguin like, towards the nearest loo. This form of perambulation I recommend to any athlete as the turn of speed produced is spectacular! But on reflection perhaps it's not to be recommended to hurdlers, or pole-vaulters, and definitely not weight lifters!

We actually changed the hotel name in honour of Jeans' affliction

And never run short of loo paper! Jean did. Fortunately Egyptian currency is mainly paper money so all was not lost. The problem started when the small denomination notes were used up and I was left rushing round the hotel desperately trying to change E£100 notes for smaller ones!!

Unfortunately this being Egypt they soon realised the desperation of my position and started, in the way of all Egyptians, negotiating. At one stage the best bid was 2x20's 3x10's and 2x5's for a hundred pound note, and, of course, refusing coins. I was holding out for more (at a time when Jean couldn't hold out for anything!) when Jean's shout rang through the hotel,

"More paper. NOW!!" Which severely weakened (faecally flawed?) my bargaining position! And I grabbed what I could and ran.

I must also report that Egyptian Bank Notes do not wash easily!!

Moral?

(1) Don't eat salads,

(2) Don't run out of loo paper,

(3) Don't lick your fingers when counting Egyptian money!

The one good thing that came out of Jeans dose of the galloping trots, was that we met this man in Egypt who was so impressed with my writing that he wants to make a film of the trip and particularly Jeans.. er.. illness.

"You're joking Watts!"

"No honestly!"

"He really wants to make a film of Jeans diarrhoea?"

"Yep! Guess what it's going to be called?"

"Aah it's a joke ... go one then what's it gonna be called?"

"You ready for this?"

"If you want the truth I cannot ever imagine being ready for your jokes.. But go on let's get it over with"

"Faecal Attraction!!"

"Good God it gets worse!"

Or what about?

"My wife went on a driving holiday to the desert!"

"So?"

"No! You have to say Sudan!

"Sudan?"

"No! She needed a 4x4"

"Heh?"

"Forget it!"

Talking of Egypt, the Egyptians are without doubt the biggest bunch of thieves and cheats it's ever been my misfortune to meet, and yes this does include that annual conference of Accountants that I now no longer need to attend, and not only because of the unfortunate misunderstanding when they asked me to give a talk on "The joy's of double entry!

From day one when we arrived to the final day when the police wouldn't refund me the deposit on the number plates we were either ripped off or conned.

It came to a head in the market in Aswan when they tried to charge us double what they had just charged an Egyptian for a packet of biscuits (a packet of biscuits for Christ's sake!) so I told them that they were a bunch of cheats and were a disgrace to the human race to which they are only tangentially connected!

He winced and said,

"Don't you trust me?" He looked hurt when I answered truthfully and at great length.

I think he got the gist of what I was saying but he again (like so many before) needed an English/Arabic dictionary…and if you're reading this, the word I used most can be found under "W"

You are expected to pay for even the slightest service, which in any other country on earth would be basic human interaction.

The route down from Luxor to Aswan is a good case in point; it was a difficult journey as Jean was still dosed up with medicine following her dodgy salad so she collapsed in the seat and slept.

I followed a small mini bus carrying two Dutch visitors and the driver, and when we arrived in Aswan he took me to a seedy hotel that tried to charge me double the advertised charge, which I refused and I was highly fed up that Jean had to wait in a hot car whilst feeling so ill.

At this the driver tried to charge me for following him so I offered him the equivalent of five pence for his help and he indicated that he felt this was insufficient and insulting. I took the money back and indicated that (close your eyes children!) that he should go f**k himself! (other swear words are available)

Apart from that we parted on good terms, well that is if you consider one of the good terms to be "go and f**k yourself!!"

We treated ourselves to a good hotel (although even they tried the "rip off" routine) but I was almost too tired to argue too much (but not too tired) and in the ecstasy of a dark air-conditioned room Jean collapsed into bed and immediately slept.

In the corner was a television, and I settled down and tuned into the only English-speaking channel; it was the funeral of Ronald Reagan, four hours of it. Bloody marvellous! Looking over at Jean I imagined that at that precise moment Ron looked better than she did!
No! That was a dreadful thing to say and I really shouldn't have said it.(Ha! Ha! Ha!)

The only way you can travel overland between Egypt and Sudan is by boat (did that make sense?) so we arrived bright and early at the port of Aswan ready to get the ferry to Wadi Halfa, only to be informed that we should have surrendered our Arabic number plates to the traffic police in town.
A frantic race back and a search for the relevant officer eventually left us with the necessary receipt so that we could leave Egypt.

They didn't actually give us out deposit back for our number plates but I'm sure that this was simply an oversight, or it was another example of how the Egyptians can rip you off. I'll leave you to draw your own conclusion; I've already drawn mine!Unfortunately Egypt stands between Europe and the rest of East Africa so you have to go there; off hand I can't think of any other good reason to visits the cesspit of a country and the inhabitants who make it that way.
"So you weren't keen on Egypt then?"

ASWAN TO WADI HALFA FERRY

We bought First Class Tickets on the ferry and were lucky to get them; it cost me an extra $20 to the manager of the Nile Ferry Company Mahmood, who then graciously agreed to give me the last ticket. Well when I say "give" I mean of course "sell". This is only country I've been to where they negotiate before giving the kiss of life!

"Basic, but clean with an evening meal as well!" he promised

When we finally got to the cabin we agreed with the "basic" part of his description, the clean was I suppose a question of definition, the stains that covered the walls and floors being the cleanest parts of the room.

It was air-conditioned though, the air conditioning unit distributing the dust evenly around, but at least the dust was cool. Jean attacked the cabin surfaces with wet wipes and soon it had been improved to "totally disgusting" and the cockroaches felt that it was safe to return, but even then walked on tip toes

They told us that we were next to board after this one and remember that everything has to be off loaded by hand!

We'd arrived early and waited to be told to board, and we waited, and we waited, the sun beat down on us for six bloody hours as we watched an impossible volume of cargo loaded into the seemingly bottomless ship (err no! bottomless is an unfortunate choice of expression when describing an ancient overloaded rust bucket on which we were about to sail) until I was eventually called forward and expected to squeeze into a tiny gap on the pontoon that carried the excess luggage, and which sailed independently to the ferry. They confidently called for me to drive onto the pontoon but I felt the need to point out that there was a large gap between the land and the pontoon.
"No problem all you have to do is drive fast and you'll clear that gap easily!"

Now you know by now that I'm not one to cause difficulties but I felt constrained to point out that whilst their idea was acceptable in normal circumstances, in this particular instance there was a minor flaw, namely that the pontoon was only as wide as my vehicle is long and whilst leaping a gap certainly would get me on, I would then continue straight off the other side, braking in mid air being confined to aircraft and not working too well with Land Cruisers.

One man, obviously trying to help, or more probably just wanting to get home, grabbed a handful of grass and stuffed it between the pontoon and the land. Again not wanting to appear negative I thanked him but pointed out that I didn't feel that a handful of grass would support a three and a half ton vehicle.

They finally found some planks and under the interested gaze of five hundred passengers I edged into the tiniest gap possible. They gave me a sarcastic round of applause and left and so thankfully missed me vainly trying to solve the problem of getting out of the car.

When I shouted for help they tried at first to ignore me but then resignedly, and with little interest, kicked a few bags away and I climbed out of the window thankful for the enforced months of dieting that dry (climatically and alcoholically) Arab countries, and a vegetarian diet impose.

Sailing time was scheduled for five o'clock Egyptian time and we sailed bang on Egyptian time at nine o'clock. We'd watched the pontoon sail two hours earlier than the ferry that by now was filled with over five hundred people crow barred into every corner.
Our own loo as you can imagine was taken on board, even though the toilets were right opposite our door!(I only used them once and can now report that I can tap dance!).

We waited expectantly in our "cabin" for the call to dinner and, after a couple of visits to the "dining room!" to remind them of our presence, the food arrived. Now many of you might think that cold brown beans swimming in olive oil, a half a table spoon of indeterminate salad, a hard boiled egg, a piece of rubbery cheese, and a plastic tub of strawberry jam (or a tub of plastic strawberry jam) all covered with a three day old piece of bread doesn't sound appetizing, nor did we! So we emptied it straight out of the porthole (look the food was going to be going out of the port hole one way or another so we thought we'd avoid the middleman!).

I took a sleeping pill for the first time in my life and slept beatifically all night.

The following morning we passed Abu Simbal. These temples were built by Ramases11 one hell of a long time ago, and when they decided to dam the Nile and create Lake Aswan in 1960, they suddenly realised that it would submerge it, so they moved it. It cost US$40 million paid for by UNESCO.

SUDAN
We finally landed at Wadi Halfa and it was only when the boat stopped moving that heat really hit us, in an already hot country we'd landed in the middle of a heat wave! Still, all we had to do now was get the car from the pontoon and we could hit the road. Talking of which! Where's the pontoon? Following the crowd, (it's something, which if in doubt, we do), we jumped onto a bus, (just as an aside on the bus two men were having an altercation at full volume in Arabic and during a lull one of them looked at the other and said "You stupid boy!" so Dad's Army has arrived in Sudan!).

The first class accommodation of the Wadi Halfa Hotel in the early morning

We were deposited in the customs hall, a brief disinterested search of our bags, a few ticks and we were free to go! .. well we would have been if only we had a car.

As we wandered around wondering what to do next along came Kamal, broad toothless smile, excellent English, he'd been 'phoned by Mahmood and told to look after us. He knew everyone and was a pleasure to be with. He seemed a good person to ask,
"So where's the pontoon Kamal?"

A worryingly vague wave northwards elicited another, to my mind, reasonable question.
"So when exactly will this pontoon arrive?"
"Tomorrow ... Maybe, Insh Allah"
The "maybe" being said very quietly but at least he still smiled.

Shall I argue? No point and any way it was soooo hot; so Jean, me, the loo and a small amount of luggage were deposited in the Nile Hotel Wadi Halfa, a private room no less, everyone else were on beds in the court yards, and so were we after precisely fourteen seconds in the earth covered, cockroach infested, corrugated roofed, baking hot room, the loo remained inside we slept outside, one of the few cases where you go inside to the loo.

The stars in the desert are so close and there are so many of them it's impossible to describe, constellations you don't recognise, and without man made lighting to detract from their beauty. I went to sleep oblivious to the sound of distant music from a cafe enjoying its one busy night a week and awoke with the sun.

The pontoon didn't arrive the next day either, so we spent the day trying to find exciting and interesting things to do, but after seven minutes we gave up and simply looked for shade to hide from a burning sun which contrary to all the laws of nature seemed to spend all day immediately above our heads. Wadi Halfa emptied quickly leaving a few other travellers like us to make desultory conversation and swap tales.

When the pontoon finally arrived the following day we were rushed quickly down to the ferry and then just as quickly waited for eight hours until they had off loaded everything, again by hand. The time waiting had given me a chance to look carefully at the pontoon and the dock.

Now I realise that they knew more about off-loading pontoons than I do, but surely the pontoon being five foot higher than the
dock couldn't be right, and after thinking for a while (needless to say I had to sit down to think, standing and thinking being

impossible in that heat) I approached the Captain and said politely,

"OI! How will I get my car off that bloody pontoon?"

"Easy! As we unload the cargo the pontoon lowers itself to the level of the dock!" he looked at me as if I was stupid,

"Oh sorry! Of course!"

I walked back slowly to Jean, who had squeezed herself into a small space in the shade of the pontoon,

"Where have you been?"

"I was asking the Captain how we would get the car off the pontoon when there's a five foot drop!"

"I was wondering that! And what did he say?"

"Well obviously as they take the cargo off, the pontoon will lower itself to the level …erm…of the … dock…hang on that can't be right! Can it??"

She couldn't be bothered to answer being too busy sweating, but just looked at me, shook her head once, and looked away. Did I have the nerve, or the energy, to ask again? No! So I waited until eventually the car was the only thing left on the pontoon, the same pontoon that was by now six foot higher than the dock!

The Captain and his men looked at me expectantly, although what the Hell they were expecting I have no idea. Kamal arrived, all smiles and goodwill.

"Good! we're ready to clear customs! Come!" he turned and strode off! We watched him go until, realising nothing was happening, he turned back,

"What?"

"Kamal how the hell do I get the car off the pontoon?"

He looked at the Captain and spoke in Arabic; whatever he said in Arabic the answer was a shrug of the shoulders in Arabic! I'll say this for Kamal he's dynamic, tiringly so, but then he hadn't been standing in the heat all day or offloading the pontoon. Kamal high jacked a passing Toyota Hilux,

jumped in and drove off returning a few minutes later towing ,
and I mean towing, a very ancient ramp which left a scar, and
pieces of itself in the sand.

The dockers, who thought their day's work had finished,
sighed (again in Arabic) and carelessly balanced the ramp
between the pontoon and the dock. It looked alarmingly
fragile and, seeing my doubts, the Captain jumped on it to
show me how strong it was, but jumped off quickly as it
sagged under his eight stone or so weight, but still he gave
me a,
"See it's fine!" look, and I gave him a, "Yeah right" look, but
as I didn't appear to have an option and as Jean had refused
my perfectly reasonable suggestion that she do it whilst I
watched from a safe distance, it was left to me.
I was gripping the steering wheel very tightly as I drove the
car nervously off the pontoon, to the alarming creak of the
ancient ramp, the windscreen being filled firstly with the dock
as the nose dipped alarmingly, before I turned the wheel
quickly and the wheels thankfully at last touched Sudanese
land.

The captain appeared suddenly, for the first time in two days
full of smiles and friendship, and I was reminded (by him!)
that it was traditional to give him "baksheesh"
"So you're an Egyptian?" I asked,
"Yes! how did you know?"
"Oh just a wild guess!"
We were getting used to Sudan by now so we were not really
surprised (disappointed but not surprised) that it took a day
and a half to clear us and the car through Customs and this
involved Kamal going to the Chief of Customs home at seven
o'clock at night (long after they'd all stopped work for the
day) and dragging him almost literally by the ears back to the
customs house to clear the vehicle.

Now my golden rule is not to upset customs officers, but Kamal seemed immune to this and we finally drove our car out from the customs compound at 9.30 at night. In truth the Customs Officer was only really interested in whether I had any alcohol!

My reply of,

"If only!" was lost on him!

Kamal was pleased with his days work and it seemed churlish not to offer him a lift home, which he accepted gratefully, in fact he was so grateful he even got us to stop so that he could do his shopping on the way! When he eventually jumped back in he pointed us off into the desert, following what was for him an obvious route, but which to us was just desert blackness, amazingly we arrived at his house and he jumped down, still full of energy, and waived us goodbye.

"Kamal which is the way back?" he looked at us as if we were mad and pointed vaguely over the horizon. Not wanting to appear stupid (or even more stupid) we headed back in the direction he had indicated and almost immediately lost the road.

Jean shouted at me

"Drive on the right!"

"Drive on the right of what? There's bugger all out there"

Suddenly in the distance I spotted a light and in the absence of any better suggestion we drove towards it and, miracle of miracles, we found the road (well we found some tyre tracks) which brought us back into town from completely the opposite direction from which we had so recently left.

By now it was too late to do anything except collapse into (onto) our beds for another night under the stars, which I started to count but was asleep by the time I got to 17.

The next day it only took four hours, and $100, to clear immigration. After the what must have been the fifteenth office I said to Kamal,

"My God Kamal you Sudanese have a dreadful system"

"It's all your fault",

"Why mine?"

"It's the system the British left us"

"Bloody Hell we left in 1956!"

The old Wadi Halfa was buried in 1963 under the water of Lake Nasser (or more correctly Lake Nuba as it's Sudan) along with the only five star hotel north of Khartoum. I like the current one better, it's hot, dirty, has earth floors, cockroaches, lizards, and toilets best left undescribed but it can accurately be called a ten thousand star hotel!

Kamal reckoned that he personally conducted the Duke of Edinburgh around the old Wadi Halfa when the dam was being built,

"You know him?"

"Know who?"

"Prince Phillip!"

"Know him?? Me and Phil great buddies ...Often have a pint!"

"Say Hallo from Kamal next time you see him!!"

"No problem. I'll be seeing him when we get back. He owes me a pint!"

Between 1885-98 Wadi Halfa was the headquarters of the Anglo-Egyptian army as it prepared to re-conquer Sudanese territory from the Mahdi, well in truth they simply wanted revenge for the murder of General Gordon in January 1885 by the followers of The Mahdi which ended the the siege of Khartoum.

Gordon had organised the defence of Khartoum which was under siege led by the Mahdi, the spiritual

leader of the local Muslim tribes. The siege started in March 1884 after the British Government had decided to abandon Sudan, but Gordon (being Gordon)had other plans, and instead of evacuating Khartoum, as he had been instructed, had remained to resist the siege and as time passed the British public increasingly called for his relief, him being one of the military heroes of the day.

It was not until August 1884 that the government finally decided to take steps to relieve Khartoum but it was not until November that the British relief force was ready. The force consisted of two groups; an overland "flying column" of camel-borne troops from Wadi Halfa, and a flotilla of dismantalable boats with more soldiers to sail up the Nile.

The flying column of troops reached Korti towards the end of December, and arrived at Metemma on January 20, 1885. There they found the four gunboats which had been sent south four months earlier from Khartoum, and prepared them for the trip back up the Nile. On the 24th, two of the steamers started for Khartoum, but on arriving there on the 28th, they found that the city had been captured and Gordon dead, having been killed two days previously (two days before Gordons' 52nd birthday).

Gordon facing down the "natives"

The stylised death illustrated above, and as was sold to the British Public, above appears to have been just that, there's no evidence that he stood in front of the invaders and by the strength of his will that he slowed their attack. This appears to be based on a similar incident, that probably was true, when in China (hence his nickname of "Chinese" Gordon). The Mahdi had ordered that Gordon was to be taken alive, hopefully to spare his life, but no one would ever know as the Mahdi himself died a short while later in 1885 from disease, probably typhus.

HEADING SOUTH

There are two routes down from Wadi Halfa to Khartoum. The Railway route which is easier but boring and the Nile route, which is hard! Corrugated and in places rumoured to be impassable, impossible, or even implausible?

Guess which one we chose?

The Nile road is quite a road. No! That's not true, it's not quite a road, it's not even close to being a road. It starts off as a scar covered with stones, and then deteriorates into a tortuous climb through black larval rocked hills before opening out into desert.

In the Sahara there are four types of road surface; hard packed sand which is corrugated and shakes you, the vehicle and all its contents apart; soft flattish sand which SHOULD be taken in low gear and high revs otherwise you get stuck; sand roads with ruts caused by lorries which leave a ridge in the middle of the track, which MUST be avoided because believe me you will get stuck with the centre of the vehicle resting on the ridge, the wheels spinning ineffectually, and finally larval rock which ruins your tyres.
"That's only three!"
"What is?"
"You said "There are four types" you've only told us about three"
"Have I?..hang on!...Oh yes so I have!"
"So?"
"So?
"So what's the fourth?"
"Ok there's the three I've told you about and another that I can't remember! Satisfied?"

The corrugations get so bad that there are sidetracks created by other drivers trying to avoid them, skirting the main route looking for smoother driving and at times they meander far from the main route; and then of course as these side tracks become corrugated so there are side routes off side routes!

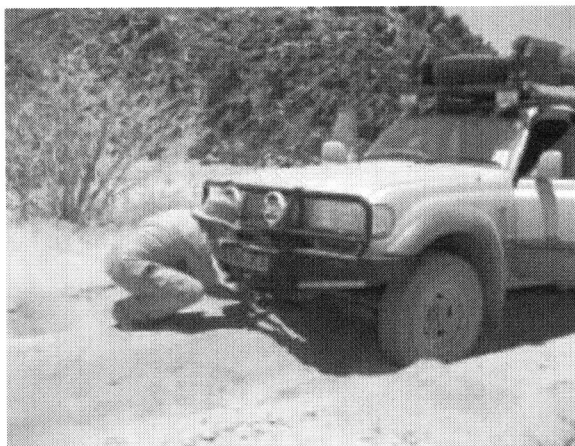

Once you're stuck there's no alternative but to dig, and dig!

The problem lies in deciding what you're driving on and what you're driving into. Get it right and it's the most wonderful feeling in the world (sorry! the second most wonderful feeling in the world!!) as you slide over humps and bounce from track to track.

Get it wrong and you stop! All is silent except for the sound of the hot engine ticking!
No matter how powerful your engine or how good your tyres believe me you ain't going nowhere when the axles and diffs are sitting comfortably in soft and very hot sand.

I just love the corrugations!

There will be those who tell you that the easiest way to drive over corrugations is to drive FAST!! Well yes that does make it smoother but what is happening is that you are simply flying from rut to rut which is not a problem until you need to change direction or to brake when nothing happens as the wheels are not touching the ground

DIGGING

The desert sand is like talcum powder and has the flowing properties of water, as fast as you dig it flows back into the hole. Oh! Did I mention that whilst you're doing this, the air temperature is forty-five degrees, and the sand is so hot you could fry an egg on it,

"Wouldn't it be a bit gritty?"

"Shut up and listen, you might learn something!"

"I have news for you there are some things in life I don't need to learn about and how to dig a big car out of hot sand in 45 degrees of heat is one of them. Do you really think I'm so stupid as to drive in that heat .. No-one in their right mind…."
"Oi watch it!"
You don't sweat! It's so hot it dries instantly and no matter how much water you drink it's not enough, and even worse there's no shade.
The first attempt failed (I tried to drive out straight forward, which even by my standards was stupid as it was driving forward that got me stuck in the first place) so next time after I'd cleared it all again, I was going to go into low first and drive out diagonally over the humps, when help in the form of a Toyota Hilux taxi van arrived with five blokes hanging precariously on (or off) the back.

They stopped, ignored me sweating and digging in the hot sand away from the under body of the car, and asked Jean if she'd like some water and, still ignoring me, one of them grabbed the shovel, and began digging out sand from under the wheels (thus reducing grip even further!). Whilst I was explaining the basic fault in his thinking, the driver jumped in, started up and shot forward at incredible speed, burying the car even deeper.
"Bloody thanks a lot!" I said,
"No problem" he answered.

The English language is wonderful isn't it? The difference between "Thanks!", "Thanks a lot!" and "Bloody thanks a lot!" is so difficult to explain to foreigners!

As I scratched my head wondering how to explain in Arabic that whilst I was grateful for his moral, if not his physical, support, perhaps in future we could think about the problem a bit more, as digging powdery sand for an hour in the blinding sun only for him to bury the car again deeper in five seconds flat was "NOT MY BLOODY IDEA OF FUN!"

Suddenly along came a bloody great big lorry, again filled with people hanging precariously on (or off). Everyone jumped off (one in fact fell off!) and gave us a look that tried unsuccessfully to say
"I meant to do that!") and, again ignoring me, they asked Jean if she wanted some water. Eventually they looked pityingly at my predicament. They looked, and sympathised but of course not one offered to dig! But then of course they knew much more than I did about living in the desert, sympathy doesn't knacker you, digging does!

The driver of the pick up was all for having another full throttle dig into the sand but I quickly jumped into the driving seat! Some advised pushing, some wanted to sleep, some wanted to chat, some wanted to give Jean another drink of water.
At last one of them actually acknowledged my presence!
"Where you going?"
"Well at the moment no f....ng where!"
It was at this point that the driver of the lorry decided to take control, after all he probably had a tight schedule to meet. He came to me, and I got out, thought, and then quickly took the keys away as the pick up drivers eyes lit up.
"Rope" the lorry driver was a man a few words, he reversed behind me and I connected my virgin towrope to the two vehicles as the lorry driver revved his engine impatiently.
The forthcoming action excited the pick up driver so much that he was already in the driving seat of my vehicle and it took a lot of persuasion to let me in. Finally I dragged him out physically and I'd just got myself settled, put the gear lever into reverse and was waiting for the,
"Ready? After 3..2..1.."

But no! With no warning I suddenly shot backwards at fifty miles an hour and was deposited again in the hard road, no longer stuck in sand but with severe whiplash!

I got out rubbing my neck and retrieved my towrope with difficulty from the lorry driver who had already unhooked it and was packing it away in his lorry.

A small Sudanese man in his mid twenties, stood in front of me and looked up at me (physically but not, I hasten to add, metaphorically)
"Now stay on the road!" His whole demeanour showed that he was used to being obeyed and I felt an overwhelming urge to salute, but with all of my fingers for a change! Now this is strange because normally my response would have been along the lines of,
"Blimey so that's the trick! You mean you should try and avoid getting stuck in the sand then having to dig yourself out in the blinding heat ... Wow! Thanks for explaining I'd have never thought of that ... Tosser!" Instead I just said,
"Good idea".
Desert driving is amazing! You're following a vaguely discernable track, then, when even that disappears, you're left with a vast expanse of sand with old tracks heading off in all directions and you are literally guessing which one to take, trying decide whether it's another road or just a detour, or a detour off a detour or a detour of a detour off ....
"Ok Ok! You've made your point!"

Great shimmering lakes appear on the horizon promising cool water... Wow! We could stop and sink our feet into it just to see if they sizzle, then you realise you've seen your first mirage! and they look so real!!

Looking for the route, not forgetting to check the depth of the sand you're driving on; best gear High second? Low first? Watching the rev counter nearing the red, No! Over there! Bugger! Corrugations! The whole vehicle shaking.

Jeans would advise any female doing this trip to tighten her bra up three notches, if you don't your boobs will be going in more directions at the same time than you ever imagined possible,(well not in more directions than I can imagine, but more directions than the average person can imagine) and which, if it could be
replicated would get you a job in any lap dancing club in the world, either as a dancer or to clear the glasses off the first four rows of tables!

Then with a sudden blinding sandstorm you're stuck again and it's off digging sandcastles!!

What I didn't mention was that sometimes there are two foot deep lorry tracks, invisible until the last moment, that cut across at right angles to the route and when you hit one of these at full speed and pitch forward, it hurts! And it was one of these that moved the whole roof rack forward six inches

Finally it's over, the car is filled with sand, you wonder if the computer will ever work again. Jean is pulling her left breast in from where it's stuck out of the sunroof and you know what?
IT'S BLOODY FUN!!!!!!!!!

It took two days to drive down, hard days driving through hundreds of square miles of nothing, only the occasional car, or an Arab child miles from anywhere looking after a few goats; moulting camels in molten heat, looking disinterestedly at you; nights in the desert, total quiet with the stars pressing

110

down. You're asleep by eight o'clock knowing that you have to be awake by six to watch that the sun comes up properly. If I don't do it there's no one else out there to check it.

Do you remember I told you about the small Sudanese man who told me off when I got stuck in the sand? Well he found us again!!

Waiting for the ferry to cross the Nile at Old Dongola he came to the window. "Tacile" turned out to be a General in the Sudanese army (which explains why he was so bossy!) and we finished up having a great time with him!

He took us to his brothers' house who gave us breakfast and lessons in the local Sudanese dialect and in Arabic.

Tacile said

"You need a shower?" a question!

"No! I'm fine!"

"You need a shower!" a statement!

I hadn't washed for three days ... if I'd been in his army he'd probably have had me shot me for less!!

His hospitality characterises the Sudanese, the most generous open friendly and genuine people I've ever met, their only drawback being that they live so close to the Egyptians!!

After Old Dongola the road didn't just get worse, in places it disappeared altogether, and when you ask directions a vague wave of the hand in an approximate direction as opposed to the English pointing, shows the conceptual state of the road and means,

"It's over in that general direction!" In some cases the general direction was flat sand a mile wide.

Apart from playing sandcastles once more we finally crossed the confluence of the White and Blue Nile and drove through Omdurman and into Khartoum.

GORDON AND ALL THAT
The current Presidential Palace in Khartoum is on the site of the old Colonial residence where General Gordon lost his life (and head) at the hands (or I suppose more accurately the spears) of the local populace. The followers of the Mahdi demolished the original one!

A road now runs between the building and the Blue Nile, a road along which you can drive but cannot walk.

This law is (I am assured, but remember I am very very gullible) another legacy from the days of Gordon when he was awoken one night by the sound of a drunken Sudanese chasing a chicken round the garden, that had escaped from the basket when the he fell off his bike,

I imagine the conversation went along the lines of,

"Charles! (that was Gordon's name?)..Charles! What is that bloody awful noise"

"Don't know Memsahib (they did do a lot of time in India). It looks like some native chappy chasing a chicken!"

"Tell him to bugger off"

"OI YOU NATIVE CHAPPY BUGGER OFF! ... It's no use Memsahib he's not going"

"Well shoot him or something!"

"Not sure I'm allowed to do that! I know I'll pass a law forbidding chasing chickens in the garden ... will that do my dear?"

"Charles you're an arse!!"

"Thank you my love!"

The bit about the law is true; I made the conversation up!

"Noooooooo?? Surely not!"

LAND CRUISERS ABOUND
There are more Aid workers in Khartoum than there are people who need help (I half expected to see an agency set up to help unemployed aid workers), and they all seem to drive

new top of the range white Land Cruisers, which can usually be found parked outside expensive restaurants.

They spend their days eating and drinking and discussing no doubt, the humanitarian efforts required to alleviate hunger, disease, tight shoes or whatever is their particular hobbyhorse, and of course shooing away any beggar who interrupts their important work asking for food.

Who's a cynic? Meeeeee? ... Nooo!!!!

When we were in Sudan the starvation in the Darfur region was world news and Khartoum was full of Aid workers there to relieve the suffering,
"Oh so Khartoum is close to Darfur then?"
"Nope it's hundreds of miles away!"
"So why are all the aid workers in Khartoum?"
"My point exactly!"

IT AINT HALF HOT MUM!
The heat in Khartoum is crushing! By eight o'clock you're sweating; by ten o'clock you've slowed to a crawl; and by two
o'clock you'd kill for a piece of shade if only you had the energy!
You need a break from travelling to recharge your batteries (but making sure that the vehicle batteries don't do the opposite). Time for housekeeping and repairs and in our case to move the roof rack back the six inches one of my sudden stops in the sand had moved it forward. This was achieved by tying the roof rack to a tree and driving the Land Cruiser forward ... it worked! Though we resolved in future to find a thicker tree first time, but at least we had some firewood!

The Nile has two major tributaries, the White Nile, this being the source of most of the Nile's water and fertile soil, and the Blue Nile which isn't but is longer.

The White Nile rises in the Great Lakes region of Central Africa, with the most distant source being in Southern Rwanda and it flows north through Tanzania, Lake Victoria, Uganda and southern Sudan, whilst the Blue Nile starts at Lake Tana in Ethiopia, flowing into Sudan from the southeast where they meet near Khartoum

The confluence of the White and Blue Niles

Arrogantly we tend to think only of European Explorers of the nineteenth century as being the "discoverers" of Africa and in particular of the source of the Nile. The truth of course is different, as far back as 1770 James Bruce, a Scot, claimed to have discovered the source of the Blue Nile in his travels around Ethiopia although Pedro Paez, a Jesuit missionary is considered by many to be the first

European to have discovered it in 1618. Bruce disputed this, but it should be remembered that Bruce had a "colourful and fanciful" career and he embraced the "local culture" enthusiastically, especially when the "local culture" was in female form!

Lake Victoria was first claimed to have been "discovered" as the source of the White Nile in 1858 when the British explorer John Hanning Speke reached its southern shore whilst on his journey with Richard Burton exploring Central Africa and the Great Lakes. Believing he had found the source of the Nile on seeing this "vast expanse of open water" for the first time, Speke named the lake after Queen Victoria.

Burton, who had been recovering from illness at the time and resting on the shores of Lake Tanganyika, was outraged that Speke claimed the true source of the Nile to be Lake Victoria when Burton regarded this as still unsettled. A very public quarrel ensued, which not only sparked a great deal of intense debate within the scientific community of the day, but much interest by other explorers keen to either confirm or refute Speke's discovery.

*David Livingstone tried and failed in his attempt to verify Speke's discovery, and it was ultimately the explorer Henry Morton Stanley (of "Dr Livingstone I presume" fame) who confirmed the truth of Speke's discovery,
circumnavigating Lake Victoria and reporting the great outflow at Ripon Falls on the Lake's northern*

*shore at Jinja, four thousand miles from the
Mediterranean sea.*

*Before you ask it was the six main, and many minor,
cataracts on the Nile that prevented boats simply
sailing up the Nile from Egypt to find its source.
Winston Churchill in his 1899 book 'The River War'
described the problems faced by the British between
1896 and 1898 when they returned to reconquer
Sudan and attempted to sail their gunboats up the
Nile.*

*Churchill describes the Second Cataract (now
submerged beneath Lake Nasser) as being "about
nine miles long and having a total descent of sixty
feet. The river flowed over successive ledges of black
granite. During the summer floods, the Nile flowed
swiftly but with an unbroken surface, and the granite
ledges were exposed only when the annual flood
abated".*

*There are several other small cataracts between the
Second and the Third but none of these posed any
problems to the British moving upstream. According
to Churchill, the Third Cataract is "a formidable
barrier."*

*The Fourth Cataract lies in the Monassir Desert, of
which Churchill wrote, "Throughout the whole length
of the course of the Nile there is no more miserable
wilderness than the Monassir Desert. The stream of
the river is broken and its channel obstructed by a
great confusion of boulders, between and among
which the water rushes in dangerous cataracts. The
sandy waste approaches the very brim, and only a few*

*palm-trees, or here and there, a squalid mud hamlet,
reveal the existence of life."*

*To highlight the difficulties The British gunboats El
Teb and Tamai in 1897 attempted to go up the river at
the
Fourth Cataract, but in spite of being helped by 200
Egyptians and 300 tribesmen, the Tamai was swept
downstream and almost capsized. Four hundred more
tribesmen were assembled to help the El Teb, but even
so this too capsized and was carried off
downstream."*
*So it was left to overland explorers to wander
sometimes aimlessly sometimes mistakenly but always
hopefully, through Central Africa looking for the
source and the fame that would come their way*

Kamal (another one not the Wadi Halfa one) made us
incredibly welcome in Khartoum and, unlike so many others
we met, didn't seem to want anything from us. He is famous
amongst the overlanders for his hospitality and even took us
out on his boat to see the confluence of the White and Blue
Niles, something I've always wanted to see. It turned out to be
a bit of an anti climax as a spectacle being just a nondescript
point of land where the two great rivers join.

The Blue Nile was in truth orangey coloured because the rains
had started in Ethiopia, but at the point where they joined they
run alongside each other before embracing and rushing off to
Egypt, a trip I do not envy them!

The week passed in Khartoum, a week in a car park of the
Blue Nile Sailing club, a week getting lost in Khartoum, until
someone finally explained to me that Khartoum's' road
system is based on the Union Jack! Seriously! This of course

didn't stop me getting lost but it made getting lost so much more patriotic.

Jean suffered badly from the heat for three days before I discovered an air-conditioned fruit juice stall, just thirty yards from where we were parked, I'd like to report that when I told her what I'd found she was grateful... but all she said was, "Three bloody days we've been here and now you tell me!" Eventually the time came to move on but only after Kamal arranged for us to join a tour around the sites (or is it sights? Both I suppose!). We were mainly interested in the Whirling Dervishes, who give it a whirl (as it were) every Friday night.

I'm always a little doubtful about watching others go about their normal daily business, (it's weekly but you know what I mean and come to think of it can spinning round and round until you go into a trance truly be described as normal?). But they studiously ignored us and whirled away.

All religion should be like this. Fun!! And the rhythmic hypnotic drumming made it in impossible not to tap your feet, which is about as close as I'll ever get to being a dervish!! They are a sect of Islam I believe, and I would have found out more but they wouldn't stand still long enough for me to ask.

KITCHINER AND ALL THAT
In the latter part of the nineteenth century there was an uprising of the Islamic Sudanese led by the Muhammad Ahmed Al Mahdi or "The Mahdi"
"Gordon old chap.. I think the natives are revolting"
"So do I. So do I!"
The uprising led to the siege of Khartoum, the eventual death of Gordon, and the banishment of the British from Sudan. Revenge was required and Kitchener led an army to overthrow The Mahdi and his Islamic followers and, being

good colonialists, we (The British) despatched gunboats up the Nile to sort him out. The gunboats were stripped down packed in boxes and man-handled up the Nile from Cairo through the cataracts and then rebuilt and went on to shoot seven kinds of shit out of the Mahdist men (Pity the French weren't involved we could have said shot the "merde out of the Mahdi!!").

The state of the British post office now makes me wonder what would have happened if the delivery of the boats had been left to them, three chimneys, no hull, with the engine in America! One boat still remains, the Malik, the personal gunboat of Kitchener

himself. It is now the clubhouse of the Blue Nile Sailing Club and I imagine "if walls could talk" it could tell a tale or two of life (and wives!) in colonial Sudan. It is now badly in need of renovation, and if renovation is too complex, perhaps a start could be made by sweeping it!!

Kitcheners Gun Boat "The Malik"

ROADSIDE REPAIRS

The state of the road, not surprisingly, meant that the pivot seals on the vehicle sprung a leak and one of the members of the Blue Nile Sailing club had a Toyota Spares agency. So, working on the principal that not taking chances is the best policy (and the fact that he was very cheap!) I pulled up outside his small, but incredibly well stocked Toyota Spares shop, at the agreed time, and, this being Africa he strolled in an hour later, full of effusive, but totally insincere, apologies. He had the spares I needed so what to do now? Do I get out my "Mechanicing made easy" book out or ask for help? Having previously had personal experience of my mechanicing, I asked!

A quick shout down the street and we had Toyota mechanics by the score. (What's the collective noun for mechanics? A "fix it"? a "bodge it"?). They stripped the hubs at the side of the road, appearing to know exactly what they were doing (which is more than I did) and they politely listened to my questions and advice and after due consideration, quite sensibly, ignored me.

Sudan is a "dry" country; they banned alcohol in 1986 or so, and in a fit of religious fervour emptied all the beer in the country into the Nile. I believe that fourteen Englishmen died that day, drowned in the Nile ... one after being rescued eight times!

And you know what even when the temperature is forty-five degrees you don't miss a cold beer on the veranda in the early evening! Err ... Hmmmm ... err ...

Mike, one of the members of the Blue Nile Sailing club made the mistake of admitting that he had beer in his 'fridge and he eventually invited us to dinner. I think my hanging onto his ankles when he tried to leave after mentioning the beer perhaps forced the invitation out of him, I'm not sure but then again I'm not proud.

There are two roads out of Khartoum the easy right one, or the sandy difficult wrong one, guess which one we took? An interesting excursion into the sand eventually looped us back onto the right one trying to look as if we intended that route all the time! (I hope you followed that I didn't and I wrote it!)
MAD GERMAN

There are those, dear reader, who think we are mad to do this trip and I count myself amongst that august body! ("August? Is it that time already?") but think of this, as you read this, there's a German man cycling from Frankfurt to Durban, on a budget of USD 3 a day. (This was written at the time of travel...obviously he'll have finished the trip by now)

We were driving along an empty road when ahead we saw a slim hipped cyclist with long blonde hair! You're surprised I stopped and offered him (yes it was a HIM!!!!) a drink of water? (Having been in Egypt I first tried to sell it to him, but Jean intervened),
and we stood in the shade of the car in a temperature of about forty-two degrees, whilst he told us of his trip.
Ronald had cycled overland from Germany through Greece Turkey Syria and Egypt and for a millisecond I was envious, an emotion which was easily, and quickly, replaced with admiration and incredulity!
Talking to him for some reason reminded me I had some crackers in the car, so I prepared some tuna and crackers, which he appeared to enjoy, perhaps the fact that he hadn't eaten for two days helped his gratitude, and I kicked myself for not making a charge.

Having come this far on his own I was surprised when he accepted my offer of a lift for the long leg to our next stop Gedaraif.

During this trip we have wild camped (free camped), in many places with no problems. I love wild camping because you meet different people, see different places..

"And most of all because it's free!"

"Well yes there is that!"

We found a great spot behind a petrol station (the "WE" now being us and Ronald) and settled down for the night, but only after checking with the people at the station that it was permitted. Whoever they were happily gave us permission, then paid for their fuel and drove off!!

Oh well!

A very nice man came over and started a conversation and expressed concern over our safety from scorpions, snakes and thieves and suggested that we move closer to the front of the petrol station.

We really didn't want to, preferring the solitude, but he was insistent, and as he had an air of authority, we moved, set up camp and cooked our dinner; carefully waiting for the arrival of the biggest thunderstorm I've ever seen, before serving it and eating it! Outside in the rain!

We ate quickly; we had to as the bowls of pasta were filling with water faster than we ate.

"We had to eat our pasta faster!"

"Oh yes! very good!"

"You mean that?"

"No!"

Our very nice man appeared later followed by a guard with a gun! "I am concerned for your safety so this man will guard you!"

"Bloody hell", I thought, "he's even older than I am!"

What I said was,

"He's going to shoot the snakes and scorpions then?"

We slept well that night rocked to sleep by hurricane force wind and rain, but I was rudely, (I've used that expression "rudely" but I'm not sure what it means! He certainly wasn't rude when he woke me ... for example by saying,
"OI! You ugly fat old sod ... Come here!!" Although of course he would have been fully justified in doing so!)

Where was I?? Oh yes. Awakened at about five o'clock when the garage reopened and the manager indicated in his best Arabic that he had stopped the Guard stealing my stepladder! The guard was vehemently denying this (I think) and was making his point with his gun.
He eventually stormed off in high dudgeon and the manager smiled at me triumphantly. I said to him,
"When you said you were taking steps to prevent crime I didn't think they would be my buggers!"
I have to report that the joke was wasted on him, but I enjoyed it so much that I reserve the right to use it again in the unlikely event that the opportunity arises!

TO THE BORDER
Sudan was wonderful, the people, the scenery, and the desert, the whole experience, but the time had come to head south again for Ethiopia. Along the road there was the continual cry of "howaya"
which for a while I was convinced was "how are you" as taught by an Australian teacher!

It is in fact Arabic for either "foreigner" or "white man" depending on whom you ask.

The final night was spent on the border on the Sudanese side with Ronald still with us. He didn't have a lot of choice as he had trusted me to put his belongings safely on and in the vehicle which I did, with the exception of his tent which was lost somewhere on the days journey. In my own inimitable style I'd managed in a land of homelessness to make him homeless (or a least tentless!) but he took it better than I expected, he burst into tears then tried to strangle me, which in the circumstances I felt was a perfectly reasonable response and , in his position, is exactly what I would have done! .

That last night in Sudan we slept beside yet another petrol station overlooking Ethiopia, where Abdullah joined us, who although unable to speak a word of English, managed with actions (that I will spare your feelings by not describing) to indicate that he was severely constipated, and had been (or hadn't been!) for five days and wanted some medicine!

Now anyone who has followed this will know that Jean has had recent personal experiences of… err ... bowel irregularities (or in her case bowel too bloody regularities!) ... So I suggested that she deal with him.

She gave him a dose of rehydrant and told him to drink eight litres of water a day. I suggested she also tell him that after drinking all that water not to piss in the Nile without first contacting Aswan Dam to open a couple more floodgates. The next morning he told Jean he'd slept very well, but unfortunately she didn't ask the obvious question.
Because we would be approaching the border at the same time we made a particular point of asking Ronaldo if he had any "funny tobacco" which he denied, and even said that he was going to ask us the same thing. I realised then he thought I wanted to smoke it when in fact I wanted to be sure that we didn't turn up at the border with someone carrying drugs and be damned by association. In the end we went through separately.

I liked and admired Ronald! He'd challenged a continent, its roads, its climate, its inhabitants, but most of all himself!

Post script: We learnt later that he'd made it as far as Tanzania before being robbed of everything, well everything except his tent, he'd already lost that! He's safe now and back in Germany and planning his next trip. Don't feel sorry for him though, unlike many of us he had the strength to ask himself hard questions and found he had the answer, perhaps we all should do the same!

INTO ETHIOPIA

A day of changes from hot to cool; from sand coloured to green; from plains to mountains; from thatch to corrugated iron roofs; from broad open smiles to sullen indifference!

In a continent of "have littles" we'd arrive to a nation of "have nothings!".
The sides of the road are rarely without stick thin people in tattered dirty rags trudging along miles from anywhere who either ignore you completely or scowl sullenly, ignoring your wave, indifferent!

The continual begging is also so depressing (I think I'll have to give it up even though money is running short!) the children are taught from birth to beg from white people and have perfected the sorrowful look with the universal hand to mouth and then to stomach, along with a monotonic gabbled and garbled.
"I have no father mother I am hungry!"
I need more time to think about the whole concept of massive charity aid operations like Band Aid. All I can say is that Ethiopia is a nation of beggars, and a begging nation, even in areas where the land is flat, irrigated and fertile!
Undernourished naked children playing in the filth, donkeys

being beaten for no apparent reason, but eventually you learn to ignore it and thank whatever God you believe in that you were born in the First World.

But the scenery is magnificent, awe inspiring, unending!

LAKE TANA.
As you all know by now when they eventually found the source of the Nile (not that it was lost) it turned out to have two, sources that is, the Blue Nile which leaves Lake Tana in Ethiopia, (although there are sixty small rivers that flowing into it), and the White Nile leaves Lake Victoria in Uganda

Sitting overlooking Lake Tana I was again ashamed of my lack of knowledge of the bird species that filled the overgrown garden of the Hotel Ghion with perpetual noise and movement, small busy with brilliant yellow red, and black plumage and totally unafraid of man.
I asked the waiter what one particular cheeky yellow and black one was called and he looked knowledgably at it, and, after a few seconds said, in all seriousness,
"That Sir is what we call a bird!"
"Err. Thanks. And that red breasted one with a black and white striped head?"
He peered closely, thought for a few moments and then said,
"That Sir is also a bird, but a different one!"
It's good to know that traditional knowledge isn't being lost!
It was the same waiter who brought us the menu and who, when asked if everything was available, replied,
"Of course Sir. You can have anything you want ... providing you want steak or chicken".
It was here also that I first discovered Injera, a fermented pancake which is made by grinding up millet, leaving it to ferment for three days then finally pouring onto a large hot plate to make a something with the colour of a three week old

dish cloth; with the texture of a three week old dish cloth; and with the taste of, you've guessed it, a three week old dish cloth.

As we sit on the concrete veranda of the Hotel Ghion, beer in hand, looking out over the well-established garden of the hotel (for the uninitiated "well-established" is tourist brochure speak for overgrown and uncared for), the soft daily rains drift in over the lake and the horizon disappears.

Later on, just before bedtime I remembered that I needed some hot water for the morning flask of coffee. Wandering back to the bar I was propositioned by one of the local working girls that always frequent African Hotels. Just in case you don't understand what I mean by working girls I don't mean waitresses or cleaners, I mean prostitutes; in many parts of Africa the only way females can earn a decent living or an indecent one come to think of it.

Business must have been very slow that night!! I think she realised that she was on a loser when I asked if there was an Age Concession! When I was younger I'd have asked if they were offering, "buy one get one free".
AIDS of course is rife in the region! which concentrates the mind incredibly ... that and the fact that the hot water in the flask would go cold! (That's me boasting!)

SOME PEOPLE HAVE ALL THE LUCK
Waking up alongside Lake Tana we dawdled around trying to shift a hangover, which I blame Sue-en and Ron for, those final four bottles of wine weren't my idea! and then started chatting to (even) more aid workers!
One in particular was involved in trying to codify the local natural remedies, and seeing how these compare with her knowledge of holistic therapies in the west. I was particularly

interested in this approach and subtly brought the
conversation around to natural cures for headaches and dry
throats. It was hurtful when she suggested that not drinking
alcohol might be worthy of consideration! I quickly
considered it and just as quickly rejected it as a way of life, or
even a way of day!
This conversation of course took longer than we expected but
it was OK as we only had 330 miles to do and about eight
hours of sunlight on (we were informed) a very good road.

Big mistake! The "very good road" was indifferent to say the
least and bloody awful to say the most, and involved dropping
down into a massive escarpment (the Rift Valley!) and then
climbing back up it again. It also involved taking part in the
annual "see who can find the biggest pothole" competition,
which I won!

The sunlight hung about until the massive clouds rolled in and
dumped water by the waterfall full on the road, the
surrounding countryside and us. It was dark earlier than we
anticipated, but the road had, by that time, improved but it
was smooth as marble and covered with a rather attractive
layer of water over it and it was dark, oh yes and I was tired.
An accident waiting to happen and it so nearly did!

Missing seeing a corner until the very last moment and,
knowing I was going too fast to make it, I braked hard and
turned the wheel sharply! Now those of you reading this who
are drivers will immediately say,
"Hmm that's not wise, that can cause a skid"

It did!! We spun across the road, back to our own side, across
onto the gravel then back onto the road again, heart beating
very fast. I do not know what saved us from turning over; it

could have been my feline fast reactions and superb driving skills; it could have
been my shouting "shit!" or it could have been a combination of good luck and good tyres.
I'll leave it to you to decide which.
Oh yes and to the Ethiopian man who was on the gravel when I started and fifty foot up the electric pylon five milliseconds later, sorry! But I must say I'm impressed, not only with your athleticism, but the fact that you took your donkey with you!

We'd broken the number one golden rule of African driving: don't drive in the dark! And we'd nearly suffered for it! We finally arrived in Addis Ababa in the dark, in the rain and with no idea where to sleep.
Addis Ababa is a sprawling town of teeming dark side streets, no driving rules, no street or car lights, and suicidal pedestrians and drivers!
"Bugger the expense let's head for the Hilton" (you probably realise that wasn't me speaking! it was Jean!) and an hour later we found the Hilton and were amazed at the security that surrounded the place.

Once inside we parked under the suspicious gaze of armed security guards, and we eventually found our way over marbled floors to the reception desk, but only after passing through two more security checks, one of which involved being body searched, a task immediately delegated to the youngest member of the team who ostentatiously donned two pairs of rubber gloves (The gloves I could accept, the face mask wasn't really necessary!) before delicately touching various suspicious bulges on my body all of which turned out to be me, smelly but me! The expression on his face made me realise that it had been a while, well quite a while, since I had showered.

At the desk I asked the receptionist, who's name tag read,
"Hi my name is Bethlehem" for a room (in view of what was
about to happen Bethlehem was a suitable name!)
She looked at me askance,
"You want a room?" Incredulous!
"Yes this is an hotel isn't it?"
"We have no room!"
"Why not? We have money!" Having been on the road for a
while I admit we did look dirty, disreputable and destitute.
She explained, and Golden Rule number Two was born (in
case you've forgotten Number One is not driving in the dark)
"Don't arrive in a town which is hosting the current
Organisation of African Unity Conference", and expect a
room."
Bethlehem was a very nice lady and 'phoned around and
eventually found us a small very expensive room in the
nearest place she could…but that was in Stockholm!!
Now those of you who know me will be amazed that, in a rare
attack of foresight and efficiency, only that morning before
leaving Lake Tana I'd 'phoned Henry's office and got his
'phone number in Addis.

Henry had contacted us through the web site and we'd
swapped e- mails on the merits of various portable toilets, and
fool that he is had concluded one by saying,
"If you're ever in Addis ... Etc. etc." ... Foolish man!!
So I 'phoned Henry and explained the problem and he told us
to stay exactly where we were and he'd come and fetch us! By
this time we were tired, lost and hopeless so,
"Stay exactly where you are!" was one of the few instructions
we were capable of obeying! Which we did under the
increasingly suspicious gaze of very well armed security
guards.

Whilst we were waiting for Henry we had the chance to look around at the delegates resplendent in the wonderful colours of their national dress, all sipping champagne and nibbling peanuts. It had been a while since I'd eaten so I reached over and grabbed a handful. The Nigerian delegate looked very nervous at that, so to put his mind at rest I said,
"It's ok! I pay my taxes!"
"Not to us you don't!"
Henry arrived in a pristine white Land Rover with CD plates and the security guards who had been doubtfully watching us actually saluted him!
So who was Henry? Henry turned out to be the second in charge at the South African embassy and he saved our lives, and more importantly my wallet, by inviting us to stay at his fabulous house. Henry's extremely attractive and talented wife Arina nearly managed to avoid wincing as two weary smelly dirty strangers invaded her house, laundry, kitchen, television, bookshelf and map collection!!
Travel is about the people you meet, and this was one of the high spots. In addition to travel, Henry's and my interests coincided in many areas Zimbabwe, Rhodesia, Military History, Rugby, Expeditions, and useless facts. Did you know that the average wind speed in South Africa is 7.5 m.p.h, well thanks to Henry you do now.
The only problem was his house was so comfortable it was easy to relax into it, and leaving two days later was a wrench! Henry, Arina Stefan thank you!! Oh yes and not forgetting Megan the dog, whose reaction to us was at least honest. She looked up, sniffed, covered her nose with her paw and went back to sleep!

THE GREAT SOUTH ROAD
Ethiopia has been a disappointment to me.
The scenery of course is mind blowing. From the mountainous north; great crags and valleys stark and bare; the

middle band with its vast flat fertile plains, the mountains in the distance; and onto the almost tropical south, with banana trees and pineapples growing on the side of the road; lush green vegetation crowding in on you. The rains are impressive, heavy, warm and with a wonderful ability to wait until we are just cooking or putting the tent up!

The people change too! Well in appearance they change. I wrote earlier about the stick thin people in rags in the north. The centre is richer and although thin they look lithe, ploughing the fields
behind two oxen with large wooden ploughs unchanged for centuries. In the south frankly they look well fed.

Unfortunately though the culture of begging is all pervading, both geographically and through all of the strata's of society, and it is so ingrained into the psyche now that it's difficult to see how it can be removed.
Little babies have been taught to stretch out their hands to you, palm up and then touch their tummies. And plead pitifully,
"You, you, you give me money!"
You cannot trust anyone who speaks to you as sooner or later they will inevitably ask you for money and when you refuse they ask again, and again!

They do not like strangers and although I've never felt physically threatened, they make it clear that they dislike and disrespect you just because you are foreign, and being foreign are expected to give them money and they despise you for not giving, not themselves for asking!

When not asking for money they are sullen and unsmiling; arrogant and aloof and asking for money is a reflex action for any real (or imagined) service.

As an example we stayed at a hot spring and the owner was doing some building work and after the owner and me had watched the labourers work for a few minutes one of the them asked me for money,

"Why should I give you money?"

"Because you watched me working!"

Suffice to say he was unlucky!

We stopped at a petrol station and were surrounded by a group of youths and one of them said,

"I want a lift!"

"No!"

"I am a student you must give me a lift!"

"No!"

"I will show you my student card!"

"No!"

"Why not?"

"I don't need to give you a reason!"

"But I am a student!"

"Ok! what are you a student of?"

"English!"

"So how come you don't understand NO then!"

They left! I felt happy that I'd beaten them, well I did until I realised that one of them had pinched my mobile phone!

"Bastard!"

I cannot see how the culture will change when it's inbred from such an early age and while the First World countries keep pumping in Aid (Why? Perhaps to assuage their guilt for being white) as they do, and any American reading this who has warm inner feelings with the knowledge that your taxes are paying for free food for the starving Ethiopians, the bad news is that "vitamin enriched cooking oil. A gift from the USA" is on sale in all the supermarkets!

I had so wanted to meet the people who had never been conquered; where an ancient civilisation existed when we in England were still living in mud huts. Instead I found a society that seems unwilling to help itself, and that obviously feels that the rest of the world that it looks down on as inferior has a duty to continually feed it.

For Ethiopia's sake let's hope that one-day we see sense Henry used the phrase "a society ruined by AIDS; not Acquired Immune Deficiency Syndrome but Aid Income Dependent Society"

The west gave them food and they got on with the war!!

So we finally left Ethiopia, the long run down had brought us gently into the East African Savannah. A final stop in Ethiopia at Moyale where we were just in time to see the customs officers disappearing off for their two-hour lunch. A bit of a paradox really as today was one of their fasting days!! So why do they need a two hour break for lunch on a fast day? Don't ask! I didn't but only because they were all at lunch. After clearing immigration we wandered around but with the customs offices closed we re-entered Ethiopia (which simply involved walking back up the dusty main street), to spend our last few burr.

It goes without saying that beggars and moneychangers approached us, that there was lots of shouting of YOU! YOU! YOU! And "FIRENGE"! The insulting description of white men or foreigners, but by this time we were inured to it and ignored everything. Well I did! Jean was shouting back "lime leaves!"
The subtlety of this was lost on me and certainly on them. Jean explained that she meant "Kaffir Lime leaves" but didn't want to say "kaffir", which is a highly insulting word to use in Africa.
I decided that it was definitely time to move on.

The Ethiopian customs officer wanted to see in the vehicle and when he asked what the "loo" was I told him and I suggested that he really didn't want to see in it! He readily agreed and waved me off ... well he waved me off with one hand, the other was covering his nose!

Michael Burks in his report on the BBC in1984 described the famine in Ethiopia as "a biblical famine in the 20th Century" and "the closest thing to Hell on Earth" and the horrific images shown motivated Bob Geldof and Midge Ure to get a group of their pop friends together, call themselves Band Aid, and make record, "Don't they know it's Christmas", which until overtaken by "Candle in the wind" Elton Johns tribute to Diana, was the biggest single seller of all time.

The success of the record led to the "Live Aid" concert the following year which (reputedly) had four hundred million viewers world wide. The actual

amount raised is almost impossible to calculate but a
conservative estimate is £120 million. Once again the
west tried to salve its conscience the only way it knew
how..with money! And it was a spectacular failure!

All the money raised couldn't overcome the basic
logistical problems within the country, and deliver the
food to where it was needed quickly, so it failed in the
short term; and it failed in the long term by making
local farming unviable, why buy food, why grow food,
when it is being given away for nothing?

So a society that was dependent upon aid was
created, and not only were they dependent but they
expected it, resulting in automatic begging on both an
individual and a governmental level. At the lowest
level the expectation
has led to aggressive begging, almost
indistingushable from mugging.
The pride of a nation was lost, because the pride of
the people was lost!

KENYA
Moyale
Everyone warned us about the dangers on the road between
Moyale and Marsabit. Mike in Khartoum shook his head
sagely and his farewell had finality about it,
"The area is full of thieves and murderers!" was the common
theme, and so it transpired.
With no camping place apparent in Moyale we went to the
police station and chatted with the Officer in Charge who
happily agreed that we could stay in a large open area
between the police station and the local cells, and sure enough
as we feared we are surrounded by thieves, rapists, robbers,
computer consultants and other low life! Fortunately they had

all been caught and convicted and were now gainfully employed cutting the grass. But they seemed a friendly enough group and waved cheerily at us. They would of course, they were going back to safe warm cells, we were sleeping in a tent!

BANDIT COUNTRY
Apparently roving bands of Shifta's (bandits from Somalia) shot at and robbed travellers in this area. Even Paul Theroux in his book Dark Star Safari reported he was shot at, whilst I didn't think that the book was particularly well written shooting at him was a bit over the top and I dread to think what they'd do to me!

Natja, the German girl in Wadi Halfa, reported that two Swedish female travellers had been held up and robbed of everything, being left in only their undies. It was at this point that I took an interest! and asked what I felt were pertinent questions like,
"What colour were the undies? Were they see through? Um were they.. err BIG girls?",
"Stop it Jeff!"

From Wadi Halfa all the way down through Sudan and Ethiopia, our minds have been occupied with thoughts of the Moyale to Marsabit road. Jean's about with Shifta's with guns, mine with the thoughts of two Swedish girls jogging down the road in their tiny undies, blonde hair flowing in the wind, buttocks round tight in their...
"STOP JEFF!"
"Sorry! Where was I?"

Perhaps this, in truth, was what caused the near crash outside Addis.

The received information on the road was that you waited in Moyale and joined a convoy to Marsabit, the theory being presumably that there is safety in numbers, I wondered at the logic of this believing firmly that, if one vehicle was held up the others, like me, would say,

"Bugger this for a game of soldiers!" and hightail it out of there.

As I have already said we stayed the night in the police station compound and had asked Inspector David if there were any problems in the area and he seemed very relaxed, but then he would be wouldn't he. He travelled everywhere in an armed truck with four armed policemen round him, and wearing a bulletproof jacket.

We turned up at the appointed early morning hour and found that the convoy would be a convoy of one.. Us! But Inspector David still kindly gave us an armed guard, who, in addition to an automatic rifle gun also had half a sack of onions!

I was trying to work out the defensive or offensive qualities of onions in a hold up situation (tear gas perhaps?) and it was only when he also produced his clothes bag that I realised that all he wanted was a lift!

Jean took one look at the gun, an automatic, and decided to sit in the back.

Our guard/passenger sat in the front and when we eventually set off, he pushed the magazine firmly into the gun, and started nervously flicking the safety catch on and off whilst peering intently out of the window hoping to see a shifta to shoot at, whilst

I peered equally intently out of the other window hoping to see the "lesser dressed Scandinavian" that species found so

often in Europe but so rarely in Africa unless you are very
very lucky!
The guard and I were both unlucky!!

He insisted on my driving fast, ignoring pot holes, logs and
doing anything that could in any way be construed as safe
driving, leading me to believe that there was in fact an
imminent danger of being robbed, either that or he just wanted
to get home.
So the dire warnings were ill founded ..er.. except that we
later discovered that man had been shot through the head the
previous week on the same stretch of road!

Arriving in Marsabit you can't help wondering who put it
there and why? As far as I could tell on first acquaintance
there was no real reason why you would be pleased to be
there, except perhaps that you have arrived there with the
same number of holes in your body as you had when you left
Moyale!

On the left as you arrive is the Jay Jay hotel, where for $5 a
night you could have a room or for $4 you could sleep in your
vehicle in front of the hotel. The room, of course, wasn't "en
suite" but then as regular readers will know, we do have our
own Loo!

The town of Marsabit is sandy. The streets are sand, the
pavements are sand and the wind blows the sand about. The
only good thing to be said for the sand was that it gives you a
thirst. No! that's not true! It gives you an excuse for a drink!
So like all great explorers before us we explored, and
explored and explored until we found what we were looking
for, no! Not the source of the Nile!.. a bar!

We sat alone in the front room and it took a while before they eventually discovered us. The bar girl was pre-occupied when she came in and jumped in fright at the sight of two ancient white people clutching their throats and gasping "beer, beer". Service was surprisingly slow but the drinks and glasses finally arrived and it soon became apparent why the service was so slow, they had been out to buy glasses, we knew this as they still had the prices on!

On the wall was an empty free condom machine and ancient posters and we were surprised just how quiet it was. Then we discovered why, everyone else was in a back room having a great time, and drinking from bottles! Picking up our glasses we joined them, for a moment everything went quiet then the noise resumed; we joined an Indian looking man at a table, he smiled, looked at me and said (obviously trying to get in my good books)
"How old are you?"
I told him the truth but knocked five years off!
He looked at me again, thought for a moment,
"My God your face could do with some bodywork!"
My inner voice said, " Oi! Bloody cheek! Don't stand for that! Slap him!" Excellent advice that I resisted, but only because it might have spilt my beer.

We chatted on and, suddenly in the middle of talking about something else, he said
"What does Red wine taste like?"
"Umm nice err it depends, why?"
"I've never tasted it, they say it's good for your heart!"
"Mmm I've read that too"
"But smoking is bad for your heart!" (Lighting up another cigarette!"
"Oh yes definitely!"

"Right! So I thought that if I drank red wine and smoked they would cancel each other out"
I knew his argument was flawed but I was buggered if I could think where, so I simply said,
"Well that sounds a good plan to me!"

He also explained that although he was a devout Muslim, he drank alcohol and to his family's annoyance had married a "local". "Local" as in black! Perhaps all religions should give you options to select which of their doctrines you want to follow! I've always thought that the adultery ban should be negotiable. I haven't actually brought it up with Jean yet, I thought I'd get the easy bit over with first and start with God!

When we got back to the hotel there was a South African registered Blue Land Rover outside, with the tent up and the gentle sound of snoring coming from inside. So it was only in the morning we met Rob and Lisa and it turned out that they had been behind us all the way down from Moyale and that at each checkpoint they had been told,
"Your friends are ten minutes ahead of you!"

Rob couldn't catch me up which gave me tremendous pleasure! Not because I'm anti-social but it's so rare for me to be able to stay ahead of anyone!

We travelled with them and spent a couple of nights under Mount Kenya where we managed between us to eat our way through two massive fillet steaks that we were assured were beef but all secretly suspected, from the size, were elephant!

It's not always hot in Africa, try getting up at 5.30 to see the
sun rise over Mount Kenya, only for the clouds to hide it. Jean
thoroughly enjoyed being woken so much that after looking
and shrugging she went back to bed.

Rob was one of those intensely annoying people who seem to
be good at everything they do! In addition to being a medical
doctor, he was also a mechanic and could point out various
constellations in the thousands of stars we could see on the
clear nights in northern Kenya!

I can, thanks to Rob, now find the Southern Cross. Now that
might not mean much to you but to me it's quite an
achievement, not only being able to follow Rob's explanation
but to remember it the next day, and Rob isn't one of those
annoying Doctors who feel that excessive alcohol
consumption is bad for you, in fact he leads by example!

He was permanently tinkering with his Land Rover (all Land
Rover owners seem to do this) and even looked under my
Land Cruiser and announced in his best medical voice.
"Well everything seems to be fine there now, but if there's a
problem, just keep dropping a couple of Aspirins into the tank

and let's see what happens! Pay the receptionist on the way out!"

I suggested that he looked so at home lying under the vehicle that perhaps gynaecology was his future! After all a good gynaecologist should be able to do a complete engine rebuild through the end of the exhaust pipe!

We drove in convoy with Rob and Lisa down to Nairobi where we met Christine and Glenton and together with another itinerant South African couple Natalie and Jeremy spent the evening eating out at an Indian restaurant celebrating Lisa's 27th Birthday. It was nice to be back in civilization again eating at a table with tablecloths and waiters serving us. I rather ruined it by throwing the bones over my shoulder but my excuse was that we had been on the road a long time; but at least we didn't take the loo in with us.

When I recounted the story of the man in Marsabit and his comment about my face needing some bodywork, Christine said that she thought laughter lines were attractive (I don't believe her but she'll do for me!), Glenton reckoned that having this many lines on my face is really useful as if I fall on my back in the pub, wherever they pour beer onto my face it'll run into my mouth...good point!!

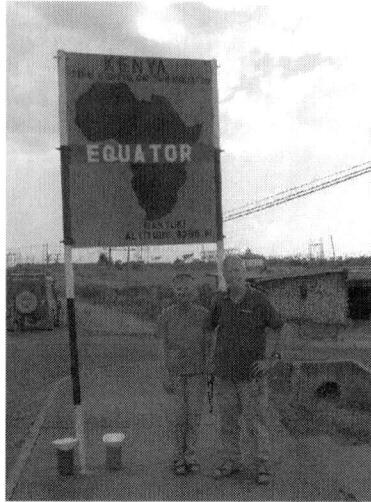

Does water really disappear down the plughole in different rotational directions between the northern and southern hemispheres I wonder?

> *The Coriolis effect is a hard to explain phenomenon that is caused by the rotation of the earth and affects large air masses, and this has led to the urban myth that water will act in the same way when flowing out of a plughole.. it doesn't! The rotational direction depends on whatever forces (which way the bowl was filled or the way hands were washed) are applied to the water immediately before the plughole is opened.*

> *There's a man who spends his days standing on (or near the equator) who purports to be able to demonstrate this effect by first filling and letting the water run out, standing to the north of the "equator" then moving to the south, and "it's a miracle!" it runs out in the opposite direction.*

It's not!

He achieves it simply by turning round whilst holding the bowl thus injecting a "force" into the water in the bowl, which will cause the difference in the direction of the rotation!!

Christine told the story of the Chinese tourist who got out of a game viewing bus and went up to a lion and poked it so he could get a picture of him with the lion roaring, the lion of course killed and ate him. I suggested that the only trouble with the lion eating a Chinese was that after a short while he'd want another one. Christine said I was sick, I agreed quickly for reasons that will become clear later.

Nairobi is a an extremely cosmopolitan city and we had coffee in the coffee bar of the famous New Stanley Hotel and got chatting
to a fascinating Samburu Kenyan who was looking at a book with pictures of the Rift Valley that he'd had just completed. With typical African hospitality he invited me to join him at a circumcision ceremony, which I quickly declined as having been to these sort of things before I know from bitter experience that they always get someone from the audience to come up and join in!! And it's usually me! He also offered to arrange for me to taste the traditional drink of blood and milk, unfortunately he didn't have any with him at the time and even offered to go and get some from somewhere else but we were in such a hurry we couldn't wait.. Damn it I would have loved to try some of that!

As eventually always happens on the road the time had come to part and Rob and Lisa headed off and we followed Glenton and Christine down from Nairobi to Arusha in Tanzania.

Having struggled through Libya, Egypt, Sudan and Ethiopia, Kenya and Tanzania seemed rather, what's the word, easy!, the other word is expensive! So we really just drove heading for Zambia which if not our main geographic destination was certainly our emotional one.

CUSTOMS LAW AGAIN
We had a major argument with the head of customs at Namanga who tried to charge us $40 road tax, based on the entirely spurious argument that it was the law, the fact that he was right and I was wrong, was I feel the only reason he won the argument and although we'd argued vehemently for one and a half hours I'm happy to report that we parted the best of enemies and I hope that if he's ever in England and is passing near us, that he keeps on passing!

Christine was also involved in the argument, now Christine is slightly built, has a lovely smile and is very very scary. After seeing her in action with the same customs man I immediately realised that the safest thing to do is to agree quickly with anything and everything she says!

TANZANIA
MASAI CAMP SITE ARUSHA
Overland trucks are my idea of living hell. For those who don't know overland trucks are groups of people thrown together covering long long distances to visit briefly sites of interest, whether they are or not! And then drive on.
Imagine if you will, being stuck next to me for three months in an enclosed lorry!!
"I'd rather not Watts!"

NGORONGORO CRATER

One of the "must see" places for the trip was the Ngorongoro crater and it lived up to all expectations. Wanting an early start in the morning we camped the night before in the Simba campsite, crowded and dirty, but right on the craters edge and me, being a consummate outdoor man, went off looking for wood to light a campfire. So there I was happily tromping through the thick bush when I came across a mound of…. err well it was brown and steaming, so you can decide on the word to use! And the thought suddenly struck me that there are not many animals that have a back passage large enough to produce that amount of err (what was the word you used?) and also as it was still steaming it had only recently left its owner… so I quickly returned back to the campsite!
It turned out the next morning that he (or she or it) had in fact visited the campsite the previous night and came upon a group of campers who I've no doubt added to the amount of (whatever the word you decided to use is) around the site. Up at five o'clock to ensure we were in the crater before the crowds and I saw the back end of the largest wild pig ever, she (he or it) went one way I the other, just the way I like encounters like that!

There were other reports of elephant, hyena and water buffalo around the camp, which I'd love to have reported that I saw, I didn't. I sleep through anything!

At the gate they tried to insist that we had a guide, at a cost of course, "for your own safety". I demurred (I love that word, it is a "nice" word for describing me having a raging temper and refusing). Remembering the "guide" from Libya, a guide was the last thing I needed or wanted. I pointed out that we didn't have a seat for a guide and that being experienced in the African Bush we didn't need one. When reasoned arguments failed I simply refused! And they relented.

As you drive down into the crater you feel how God must felt when he created the world (and if you believe that etc!), from afar it all looks so magical, the pale blue turquoise and orange sky waking up the earth, mirrored lakes, reflecting the purple of distant mountains, pale brown grass dotted with trees against dark blue hills in the background.

The first animals we saw were delicate (and I'm sure delicious) little Impala, fawn, with black and white stripes, even the males were no bigger than a retriever in height but much more delicately formed. Occasionally one would look at us, and then turn to another as if to say, "Hmm that's a British Registered Land Cruiser, and look the drivers got more white hair than I have"
"Shush don't be so personal he'll hear you!"

Impala's in Early Morning in Ngorongoro

After managing to blag my way in without a guide we were left in peace and could drive slowly selecting our own route, and at that early hour there was only a couple of other vehicles in the whole area, so we could stop and look at individual animals on our own; a lone bull elephant with large tusks reaching lazily up and selecting the choicest leaves like

a dowager picking a pastry; a hyena emerges out of the long grass, his colouring hiding him until the last minute, looking strangely morose for something usually called "laughing". As he walked by I told him my world's favourite joke about the man who got a job in a game park circumcising elephants, the salary was poor but the tips were enormous!!
He looked at me sadly and muttered,
"Heard that one hundreds of times!" and disappeared.

The wildebeest, or gnu, (oh look a gnother gnu!) that amazing deer designed by a committee, the males desperately rushing around trying to keep their harem in check, the harem waiting until he was somewhere else and wandering off. Two big males charging each other meeting head on with a hollow "BOING!" staggering back looking slightly cross eyed and cross legged before rushing back to their ever-decreasing harem!

The aptly named secretary bird, looking over his specs in distaste at everything; a pod of fat hippo's too lazy to live up to their reputation as a very very dangerous animal: Cape Buffalo looking at you through hooded eyes that remind you very quickly that they certainly are not to be messed with!

Two male lions; they really are only great big pussy cats, licking their flanks rolling onto their backs, shall I get out and scratch their big white tummies...? err perhaps not!

Two ostriches silhouetted against the sky line with legs that really should be encased in black fish net stockings and appearing in a comic transsexual act: a hartebeest watching us watching him, before we both get bored and leave!

A large male Kudu, resplendent horns, almost lost against a tree, and us, not being food or a female Kudu, also indifferent

By now the park was busier and the dust plumes of the other vehicles (almost all being Land Cruisers on organised trips) criss-cross the skyline. Then one of the wildebeest changes shape and wow! It's a rhinoceros! tripping along parallel with the path, obviously out for a morning constitutional, occasionally glancing over at the convoy of vehicles keeping station with him.

Suddenly a vehicle comes the other way and for some reason, perhaps he was startled, perhaps annoyed, perhaps he was a Land Rover lover or perhaps he just had a perverse sense of humour, which ever it was, he charged it!

I am sure he enjoyed as much as I did seeing a Land Cruiser full of screaming Japanese tourists, reversing at high speed, cameras flying in all directions as they fell backwards! He stopped just in time then walked across the path in front of the Land Cruiser and, with only one glance back, tripped off again!

I applauded him, I know he didn't hear me but I like to think that he looked at me and winked!

Rhinos are either white or black rhino's and both are grey unless they take on the colour of the earth they roll in! The term "white" is a corruption of the Afrikaans "wyd" or "wide" which describes the shape of its mouth, long and wide, shaped this way as it eats by grazing; the "black" rhino has a pointed mouth which is used for "browsing" or picking leaves from bushes and trees! But just to be difficult it can also fold the pointy bit back and graze!
"Now wasn't that interesting?"
"Fascinating!"
"So go on what's the difference between White and Black Rhinos then?"

"The Black rhino's are black and the White rhinos are … erm … white?"

"You've not been listening have you?"

"No of course not!"

A couple of million years ago a 19 000 feet volcanic mountain, about the size of Kilimanjaro erupted and imploded forming the 8300 square metre Ngorongoro crater. In fact, if I am going to be pedantic, it's not really a crater it's a caldera, or collapsed volcano. The crater (we'll still call it a crater) has a diameter of 19km and is about 600 metres deep. The bottom is flat, almost treeless and filled with small creeks and lakes, and forms a natural sanctuary for thousands of animals, insects and birds. Countless numbers of gazelles, zebra's, elephants, hyena's, buffalo's, hippos, lions and birds including ostriches, co-exist there in a mini environment, but there are surprisingly at first sight no giraffes until you remember the steepness of the pathway down into the crater.

Only the indigenous tribes such as the Masai are allowed to live and keep cattle within the crater, the domesticated and wild animals happily co-existing. Well the lions are happy, perhaps the cows have other views.

The crater is part of a larger conservation area which also includes the Olduvai Gorge, considered to be the seat of humanity after the discovery of the earliest known specimens of human beings were found by the Leakeys who discovered the 1.8 million year old skeleton called Australopithecus boisei, one of the distinct links of the human evolutionary chain. They

*also came upon a complete series of hominoid
footprints estimated to be over 3.7 million years old.*

AID PROJECTS!

"Hey! Just remembered something I meant to tell you about
Aid projects"

"God Watts you're not gonna witter on about that again are
you?"

"You remember the bar in Marsabit there was a condom-
dispensing machine,"

"That's nothing new, they have them in all the toilets in
Europe, remember you thought they were chewing gum
machines at first and loved the flavour of the banana ones!"

"Shush!"

"Anyway this condom machine was affixed to the wall and
had written on it "FREE CONDOMS. ALWAYS USE A
CONDOM. PREVENT AIDS" The idea conceived…

"Unfortunate choice of word when we're talking about
condoms"

"…. in some office in the west. It was empty and had
obviously been so for years, another great plan, no doubt
millions spent and it worked for a couple of years, and is now
ignored, just like thousands of other projects!"

"Finished?"

"Yes!"

BREAKDOWN

Well, I suppose it had to happen we had car problems!
Coasting happily along the road after a night at the Indian
Ocean, the car hiccupped! Hmmm! It's ok it was just wind!!
A few miles further, there it is again! .
Having put diesel in that morning I thought,
"Bugger! Dirty diesel. Either that or the clutch is going!"
Then it cleared and it's ok, working on the premise that if you
ignore it, it will go away, I ignored it and guess what?

"It didn't!"

"Exactly,"

So I pulled into a petrol station and negotiated with the man to drain the tank! God that was painful! I pick the country with the second most expensive diesel on the continent, and I drain an almost full tank into bloody plastic containers

"I think you have water in the diesel sah!" he said,

"Of course I have you silly sod! It's where I was crying into it!"

More expensive diesel in, start up and it's worse! Pushing the car out of the way I decide to change the fuel filter!

Now! Changing a fuel filter surely must rank low in the list of interesting things to watch, so why within fifteen seconds of opening the bonnet was I surrounded by all shapes and sizes of Tanzanians all of whom claimed to be expert mechanics? Just a philosophical question for you! If there are so many good mechanics why are there so many broken down cars? Everyone touched things and tried to get hold of the spanner. One in particular was very keen on undoing things that even I knew had nothing to do with the fuel system so I tapped him on the fingers to dissuade him, the fact that I was holding a four pound hammer at the time served to emphasise the point and added a physical exclamation mark to my verbal, "Don't touch that!"

In the end I accepted help from a man who appeared to be an expert, well enough of an expert that he knew that you used a spanner to turn things and not to hit them! (I didn't know that.. clever isn't it!)

Eventually we got the new diesel filter on, and in spite of many many hands it took a long time, a case of "many hands making more work". When we got everything back together and started it up, it ran wonderfully.

As always happens I was then confronted with a queue of "mechanics", all with upturned palms and all of whom claimed to have been integral in the successful repair and as such worthy of payment, but I will say this they took my refusal in the manner that it was given; with aggression and malice!

The man who had in fact helped me refused my offer of money, perhaps that I offered him my remaining Egyptian Pounds was the reason, but money is money!

I drove off with a smile and they all waved after me! Some of them were even using more than one finger, and the man who's fingers I'd tapped (well "tapped" might have been the merest understatement) with my hammer was still dancing round the car park, one hand under his armpit, doing a more than passable impression of a whirling Dervish!
I roared off relaxed in the sure and certain knowledge that I'd repaired it ... err... I hadn't!
By the time we reached the Mikumi National Park it was hiccupping again, but this time even worse and I was slowly stuttering to a halt, I wasn't worried, much!, and the notice on the side of the road gave me sooo much comfort!
"PLEASE DO NOT LEAVE YOUR VEHICLE WITHIN THE PARK WILD ANIMALS ARE DANGEROUS"
See what I mean?..Comforting!

A final thought! I changed the CD from John Denver to Rod Stewart... it worked for a few minutes then hiccupped again! Limping into the hotel on the outskirts of Mikumi a mechanic was called, and when he arrived he looked dirty enough to be a real one, so I trusted him, his name was Peter!
"We go for drive!"
Wouldn't you believe it? It ran like a dream!

"Faster!" he muttered,
I accelerated into the dusk,
"Faster!"
I floored the accelerator before suddenly remembering that I was in the middle of a game park in the dark, driving at nearly 100 m.p.h. and I knew for certain that if I didn't slow down it wouldn't be dirt in the diesel tank, it would be at best the front bumper or at worst an elephant!
When we got back to the hotel I opened the bonnet and we leant over, now joined by Godfrey, the hotel manager.
Peter said,
"Drain the tank?"
"Done it!"
"New filter?"
"Done it!"
"Check filter on the Injector?"
"Ok do it ... but don't touch anything else!"
As I always do in times of stress I retired to the bar: five minutes passed Godfrey re-appeared.
"Come"
The three of us peered over the bonnet; Peter spoke in Swahili to Godfrey, Godfrey listened (presumably also in Swahili) and interpreted,
Listen listen listen
"Peter say's it's not the diesel!"
Listen listen listen,
"Peter says it's not the oil filter"
Listen listen listen,
"Peter says it's not the Injector Filter"
Silence! I wait,
"And?" I ask
"And?" Godfrey answers,
"I mean we now know what it's not, ask Peter what it is!"
Swahili Swahili Swahili,
"He says he doesn't know!"

I say!

"Well if the diesel is clean, and all the filters are clean, that leaves the pipe between the tank and the filter, someone will have to suck the diesel through!"

Godfrey translates and we look at each other. Godfrey is the manager so he's not going to do it; I'm paying so I'm certainly not going to do it; Peter looks defensive and then sighs!

I retire to the bar. After a five minutes Godfrey appears clutching a small piece of metal gauze.

"Come!"

Back to the car! Godfrey and I lean over the bonnet, trying to ignore Peter who is vomiting copious amounts of my expensive diesel against one of my wheels, I make a mental note to deduct a nominal sum from his final bill to cover the cost of the diesel (but not too nominal!)

Obviously the piece of filter must have come from somewhere and the only place left is from inside the tank. Decision time! Do I accept things as they are or do I get the tank removed?   I hate decisions; I always get them 100% wrong!

Getting out my decision making coin I toss! Heads! Remove the tank!

The next morning Peter and his brother, Omara (where the Hell do they get the names from?) arrived and started to remove the diesel tank with me watching closely, partly out of paternal interest in my car but mainly because there's nothing else to do.

After much sweating and swearing in Swahili, and advice from me (do try and stop bumping your head on the vehicle you'll make yourself bleed ... Oh! you have already!) Eventually Peter says,

"We must take the prop shaft off!"

"NO! You take my prop shaft off over my dead body!"

I have to say he looked tempted!

I wriggled under and spotted what the problem was, apart from the fact that he was a shit mechanic!

I told him, and he and Omara slid back under, followed my advice and undid a couple of bolts. The tank dropped suddenly and heavily onto their heads, closely followed by half a ton of Sudanese sand, which I had unknowingly smuggled down through Africa.

I was going to give them more advice but, seeing the looks on their faces, which by now were covered with blood, sand and sweat, I changed my mind! Opening the fuel tank we spotted the problem, a small filter at the outlet pipe had disintegrated and been sucked into the pipe.

End of story ... the car works, there was only a small square of rubber left over, probably not important, but it's working, thanks Peter, thanks Omara! And I hope the cuts on your heads heal quickly.

It was at this stage I realised that I didn't have enough diesel to get me to the next fuel station ... Peter shook his head and sucked in through his teeth, in the way of mechanics the world over,

"No diesel in town!"

"So what'll I do?"

"Come!"

We went to his workshop where there was a queue of customers awaiting his return, but he ignored them and said,

"I can give you 20 litres"

"Give?"

"Sell!"

"Thought so!"

"You sure this isn't the same diesel that you've just drained form my tank?"

He looked hurt at the slander, left and a few minutes later came back with a bucket of diesel, probably mine or siphoned

from a nearby lorry. I was doubtful about the quality but what could I do?
Oh well! More work for some mechanic further down the road.

At the start of the trip we had an ambition to touch four oceans on the trip so the next stop was the Indian Ocean. The roads by now had improved and it was in truth quite easy to make a detour eastwards to Tanga. The campsite was humid and the breakers white against a white sand..everything you imagine the Indian Ocean to be.

Bliss (and the loo) near the Indian Ocean

Coming out of the showers I bumped into Lisa last seen in Kenya, I looked over and saw Rob under his Land Rover!

Nothing changes! Although Africa is a massive place you inevitably bump into the same people, it's comforting somehow that others can get just as lost as you

It's a small world as they say

TANZANIA ZAMBIA BORDER

The first thing I noticed was that he was wearing an Arsenal Shirt and when he tapped the window I'd opened it a little and very suspiciously.

"What have you got in your vehicle!"

"What's it got to do with you?"

"Customs!"

"Ahh!"

I got out, looked at his shirt and said,

"Are you an Arsenal supporter?"

"Yes! They are my team!" chest pushed out proudly,

"I don't talk to Arsenal supporters!"

He remained unfazed,

"What is your team?"

"Coventry City!"

He looked at me for a moment, frowned, then placing his hand on my shoulder, said,

"You may go Sir, you already have too many problems!"

Bastard!

ZAMBIA

It was eerie arriving back in Zambia after so many years, and as I crossed the Tanzania Zambia border I achieved a feat that anyone who has crossed a land border in Black Africa will appreciate! I hurt the feelings of a money changer, who made the mistake of thinking that old and grey hair equals nice…those of you with the extraordinary doubtful pleasure of knowing me will appreciate immediately that this isn't the case.

He offered me a rate of exchange that relied on my being,
(1) Generous
(2) Too shy to argue
(3) Unaware of the rate of exchange
(4) Last, but not least, trusting

I believe my final assault on his delicate sensibilities was when I asked him, after questioning his parentage and his tangential connection to the human race, if he thought I would really do business with anyone wearing such a damn silly tie as he had on, was the final straw, and he left with what I'm sure was a tear in his eye, vowing never again to steal cheat and rob but to change his life marginally for the better and become an accountant, when he could do all of those things legally.

The first night was spent at a religious campsite, now by that I don't mean that by the end of the evening everyone was on their knees, we've stayed at many of those (many many of those!) but a real religious one where all of the staff and managers walked around with a great big beaming smiles being really nice to us.
It really got on my nerves!

The camp was clean, well-built, safe, quiet and (or but) of course alcohol free. Now will someone tell me where in the Bible it says you can't drink!! Anyway in truth they are smashing people and listen I've learnt something. Zelley was telling me that God made us all in his own image. So when you get to Heaven remember that if you see a pretty black girl of about twenty-eight with a wonderful smile and large breasts.. That'll be God!!

The Great North Road from Kapiri Mposhi to Tanzania is a new road and a good road, one of the best we've driven down and we covered many miles easily before finally arriving at the Forest Inn campsite.

We've had discussions on the road about the criteria for a good campsite and number one on everyone's list is security! Just in case you're interested noise (silence) comes second with ablutions (sanitation) fourth behind cold beer!
I know dear reader that there will have been times when you perhaps thought I was guilty of exaggeration, no matter how slight! (I've told you a million times Watts! Don't exaggerate!)

Tonight we had the first in abundance, that's security in case you've forgotten already, because believe me or believe me not
"Given the choice Watts I'll stay on the "NOT" route if it's Ok with you!"..

....tonight more firearms, both large and small, than could be found in Baghdad on any Saturday night, surround us, and I mean during the war not now there's peace (err of a sort!)

THE PRESIDENT IS COMING!!!!!!!!
We were sitting quietly having a drink at four o'clock (tea of course! we are English after all!) When in roars a convoy, a cavalcade, a column of Land Cruisers, all colours and all new including an ambulance and another one that looks suspiciously like a hearse, and out fall army, police and other indeterminate (but determined) military bods each one of them looking around very aggressively, and all with alarmingly clean firearms, desperately searching for anything that looked remotely suspicious and which therefore could reasonably be shot.
As we were the only ones around they all looked at us then as one relaxed, obviously I don't look like a hired assassin,

which will be useful to bear in mind should I ever decide on a career change.

The manager of the campsite, a young, white, very Afrikaans South African lady went to greet them and two minutes later twenty or so very big, very hard looking military and para-military were backing away, each trying to stand behind the others.

The reason soon became obvious; they had informed her that the President of Zambia wasn't coming on Sunday as had been arranged. There had been a change of plans and he might be coming tonight instead so, just in case, they wanted all the rooms! Never mind the other guests who are already booked in.

From the volume and virulence her outburst I (and they) gathered she disagreed.

After a while someone else arrived in yet another Land Cruiser,

"It's ok! He's not coming until tomorrow! We only want half your rooms"

"Good"

"But we need a telephone in his room!"

"I've been trying to get a phone up there for five years! They told me it's technically impossible! "

"Wait!"

I estimated thirty minutes; it was twenty-seven before the telecom van arrived to install the phone!

So here we are in a campsite, lone white campers surrounded by police, army and a chef, that's right he even brought his own chef! (And they call me paranoid!) You never know I might hang around and try for an invite to dinner, but now I'm going to go and grab a shower. I don't want to be stuck behind the President and his bodyguard in the shower queue, they are all such big buggers there'll be no hot water left!

As we left in the morning the poor lady had just been asked to provide a flagpole for the Presidential Standard!!...I think that was what caused her final breakdown!!

CENTRE PIVOTS ARE SEXY

I'll bet you didn't know that centre pivots are sexy! Well believe me they are! If you're a sexy blonde, naked except for a layer of sun cream there is at least one farmer as we speak in Mkushi who will look around you and gaze lustfully at a centre pivot in full flow. In the past I'm afraid I wouldn't have looked round you but now I certainly would.

Sitting in the bar (just for a change) at Forest Inn (remember the President's coming!) we got chatting to Alex and Nicky who'd come out for a early evening quiet drink and were suddenly confronted with two itinerant Brits and by the end of the evening we were invited to their farm, well we invited ourselves if I am going to be strictly accurate!

Alex, was another of the farmers from Zimbabwe now resurrecting the Zambian agricultural economy after they've been made unwelcome in Zimbabwe (good move that Mugabe! ... get rid of all the whites...never mind the consequences...) and vast tracts of brown bush in Zambia are being turned into green oasis's (oases? Oasisisis?) by the Zimbabwean farmer's vision, skill and energy.

We arrived bright and early only to find that they'd been up for hours, and, after showing us around for a while Alex asked us if we'd like to see his new Centre Pivot. Now at the time I had no idea what a Centre Pivot was but anything that caused the far away glow in his eyes must be worth seeing!

I didn't like to admit my ignorance but agreed excitedly;
Nicky and Jean decided to come along as chaperones ... damn
it!!
Nicky and I jumped on the back of the pick up and, with the
wind blowing through her long blonde, and my short grey,
hair, we set off over bumpy tracks and onto the main road, a
swift acceleration creating G forces that took thirty years off
my face and suddenly there we were in a large field of young
green wheat.
I sniffed the clean African morning air whilst leaning
nonchalantly on the watering contraption thingy, and felt the
wrinkles fall back into place and old age return to my face!

I looked around for the Centre Pivot ... nothing. I looked
around for the blonde wearing just sun cream; I even looked
for two Swedish blondes in their undies still running from the
Shifta's (a man can but hope!) ...still nothing!! I looked at
Alex who was lovingly stroking the watering machine that in
truth looked like a tangled mass of scaffolding that had fallen
over but had wheels on!
"So what do you think then?"
"Impressive!" desperately looking around,
"I'm just gonna set it going do you want to watch?"
"Do I ever!! Can't wait!!" It then dawned on me, as he leant
over and kissed the scaffolding gently, that the scaffolding on
wheels, the object of Alex's lust, was a Centre Pivot, which
I'm sure you all know is a bloody great watering machine.
It is a spectacular piece of equipment stretching some, what?,
one hundred yards long, which when switched on rotates
slowly around the field and waters whatever is under it! And
it costs $125,000!!

I was truly amazed, so impressed that if Nicky and Jean had in
fact taken their clothes off and sprayed themselves with sun

cream; I too would have looked past them at the Centre
Pivot!!   Well I might have glanced!
We left after lunch in awe of everything we saw, we were
hoping for an invitation to their wedding on August 15th, I
even promised them a toast rack, but even their good manners
and kindness didn't run to that.
Good luck Alex and Nicky you deserve it!!

*Zambia, formerly Northern Rhodesia, achieved
independence from Britain in 1964. In the late 1950's
and 1960's the "Independence" movement in Africa
had developed an unstoppable momentum and it was
obvious to the old Colonial Powers that militarily,
economically and morally fighting to retain their
control of areas of Africa that they stole in the 19th
century, was impossible and the famous "winds of
change" speech given by the British Conservative
Prime Minister Harold Macmillan to the South
African Parliament in February 1960 highlighted an
acceptance of the inevitable and triggered a change
in British policy in Africa.*

**"The wind of change is blowing through this
continent, and whether we like it or not, this growth
of national consciousness is a political fact. We must
all accept it as a fact, and our national policies must
take account of it".**

*After Ghana (formerly Gold Coast) gained
Independence and majority rule in 1957 it was
followed quickly (some might say too quickly) by
Kenya, Uganda, Tanzania (Tanganyika), Malawi
(Nyasaland), Zambia (Northern Rhodesia) and
Botswana (Bechuanaland Protectorate). To avoid
what they considered to be precipitous majority rule*

*the white Government of Southern Rhodesia made a
Universal Declaration of Independence (UDI) in
1965, thus retaining white control of government and
the economy.*

*As early as 1953 Britain had created a Federation of
Rhodesia and Nyasaland, made up of Northern
Rhodesia, Southern Rhodesia and Malawi then called
Nyasaland. Economically this made sense. The
mineral and Agricultural wealth of Northern
Rhodesia and Southern Rhodesia; the broad
industrial base of Southern Rhodesia and the
unutilised potential of Nyasaland, did on the face of
it, make an ideal partnership. Unfortunately it quickly
became apparent that the wealth generated was under
the control of, and channelled to, Southern Rhodesia
and that the demands of the Black residents for voting
rights were not met by the Federation and it was
inevitably doomed to failure and was finally
disbanded in 1963.*

*In Zambia prior to independence 99% of the
agriculture and small industry was white run,
although of course many of the whites were second,
third and fourth generation Rhodesian, and Copper
Mining, the bedrock of the countries wealth, was
owned by foreign companies and run by white
expatriates. Majority rule and Independence wasn't
greeted by the whites with any enthusiasm and the
agricultural sector, so susceptible to confidence,
suffered almost immediately with the exodus of white
farmers mainly to Southern Rhodesia (now
Zimbabwe), and Zambia went from being an exporter
of food to an importer in just a couple of years.*

Over the next twenty-five years the Zambian economy suffered a massive and rapid decline caused by successive droughts; a fall in the world price of copper; poor decision making and corruption, which combined to create poverty and starvation. AIDS arrived in the early 1970's with the result that the life expectancy of the average Zambian is now in the mid 30's.

At the time of Independence Zambia's copper mines were owned by Rhodesian Selection Trust (later Roan Selection Trust) a UK company; and Anglo American Copper Mines a South African company. All of the profits were made outside Zambia and all of the middle and senior management, apart from a few personnel managers, were white expatriates. It represented 95% of the countries exports so the Nationalisation of the Copper Mines in 1970 was inevitable, as was the immediate rapid promotion of inadequately trained Black Zambians as unfortunately was the rapid fall of in efficiency that this brought.

The arrival of Robert Mugabe in Zimbabwe and his subsequent action of expropriating the farms from the white farmers resulted in many of them moving into Zambia and bringing with them their skills and energy and, with the ready availability of finance, agriculture in Zambia is once again feeding the nation.

SHIWA NGANDU
The book "Africa House" by Christina Lamb recounts the true story of Stewart Gore Brown who in the early part of the twentieth century built an English style country house and estate in the heart of Africa. He called it Shiwa Ngandu (The

Lake of the Royal Crocodiles) and the folly was financed from his family fortune in Brooklands, and from the old race track attached to it; and although it was an incredible achievement it was ultimately and inevitably a financial failure, a magnificent failure, but a failure nevertheless.

We had to see it and it was pretty much what I expected, as were the numerous pictures of him on the wall unsmiling, arrogant, aristocratic and haughty, I'd have loved to have spent the evening with him teasing him gently ... I know he'd have enjoyed it.

Members of the family were still involved in running the house and campsite, although one gets the distinct impression that they are not "overkeen" on each other, or the guests come to think of it, being very keen to part you from your money and not so keen to have you on their property.

There's a natural hot spring there that feeds the pool, which was occupied that night with a mix of nationalities, sharing experiences and cold beers before wandering drunkenly back to the dining room for a communal dinner. The company and the conversation more than compensated for what the dinner lacked in culinary excellence, or even competence.

Shiwa Ngandu   Or is it Berkshire?

HARVEST HELP

If I write that we did this trip for charity it would be a lie. We did it for us, but took the opportunity to make some money for the Harvest Help charity on the way and people were extraordinarily generous (especially, but not surprisingly, those that I have incriminating pictures of) so we wanted to call into the Mpika project office of the charity, just to say "Hi!"

Anyone who has read this far (I admire your perseverance, but have to warn you that the best bits are over and it's all downhill from here, like Africa really) will know that I am very cynical about charities and the way they work, or more relevantly, how they don't work!

Harvest Help is unique in my experience in that it asks the potential recipients what they need, now there's a first, and then they let the recipients control, now there's a first (second?) and they don't provide Land Cruisers! Anything else notwithstanding, any charity that doesn't provide Land Cruisers gets my vote (or in this case goat!)

The message that we were coming to visit them hadn't arrived, perhaps the man carrying the message in his stick and jogging up the five hundred miles from Lusaka tripped up or found a decent bar, or more probably an indecent one ... so at least we got an unsanitised impression of the work, which was good.

If you drive northeast from Mpika, which itself is one hell of a way from almost everywhere to start with, for forty-two kilometres over a road that starts awful and then deteriorates, you get to a village called Kaluba.

In the past the villagers of Kaluba were hunters in the area of what was to become the North Luangwa National Park, who fed their families by hunting animals, but then this job description was changed to "poaching" when their traditional hunting grounds were set aside as a National Game Park and the rewards for hunting suddenly became a bullet if you were lucky, or a prison sentence if you were unlucky.
No! I didn't get that the wrong way round!

The problem is that when they were hunting for themselves they killed what they needed to eat and naturally they found it easier to kill the older animals. Then the white man arrived bringing foreign currency and demanded bigger and better trophies, killing only for the tusks, horn, or skin and suddenly the villagers became criminals.

The North Luangwa project, which Harvest Help is funding, trains the villagers in agriculture and in organising themselves into units where people are given credit in the form of seeds and the repayment is in goods. It's impressive the way they are working and best of all it's all done by Zambians for Zambians and with Zambians, and they are growing, in addition to the traditional maize, finger millet, beans, sunflower seeds and are (on the basis of a quick visit) doing well!

They complained that "the men with briefcases" were robbing them with the wholesale price they were being paid and asked me what they should do!! I told them that I didn't know and bounced the question back at them.

Unfortunately I think the attitude still pervades that the white man knows all the answers, but this white man for one can't even remember the questions these days, and they didn't realise that this particular white man knows the answers to nothing but it helped my ego that they should at least ask!!

What was interesting was when I asked them what else they needed and they asked for a diesel engine driven milling machine ... err ... if it's difficult to carry maize how you gonna carry diesel? There must be a manual maize mill available somewhere!!
So there we are Harvest Help is funding a change in life style. I suspect that the real benefit will accrue to some man in a briefcase unless of course Harvest Help arranges to buy the produce at a fair market price, and then to distribute it, an impossible dream.

Like all projects in Africa it has to be the Africans who create and motivate, we can enable we shouldn't disable!!
COPPERBELT REVISITED
Well we made it!! The begging letter from the charity said "Coventry to the Copperbelt!" and that's what we've done. The cheques can be cashed and the negatives of all those

pictures destroyed, except for the one with Bryan, Jackie and the Great Dane (and I don't mean Eric the Red!), which I will publish on the web unless suitable payment is received! Sorry Bryan but as you know that's the kind of guy I am. And if you're lost for words at that, the word you're looking for is blackmail which is apposite as we are talking about Zambia.

We arrived in the Zambian Copperbelt for the first time in 1970, and were fortunate enough to be posted to Luanshya. We were all "twenty somethings" disillusioned with life in Britain, looking for something, well in truth looking for money, but we found so much more.

Luanshya in the 70's was a vibrant place, with clubs for all interests, a Copper mine in full production, sprawling dirty and noisy, the smelter belching out sulphur fumes, in spite of which, Luanshya was named the "Garden City".

The streets had names like Poinsettia Avenue, which was, lined with Poinsettia's, Oleander Avenue that was lined with Oleanders, Hibiscus Avenue, which was lined with ....
Come on have a guess! .
Thaaat's it Hibiscus, you are concentrating after all!!

Small terraced houses were replaced by large detached ones; nights and weekends spent in unavoidable tedious gardening and decorating were replaced by nights and weekends playing sport or partying; poverty was replaced by relative wealth; servants did the housework and laundry; gardeners gardened.

The British climate was replaced with African sunshine.

A small mining town in the centre of Africa was a microcosm of any town anywhere! Extramarital affairs abounded; people succeeded and people failed; there was the "in" group who were in the Masons or Rotarians; there was the "out" group who wanted to be in the Masons or Rotarians but weren't invited; there was the rest that didn't even know or care what the Masons and Rotarians were!

The old "Colonials", those that had been in Luanshya before Zambian Independence in 1964, looked down on the newcomers and called them "VC 10'ers" (British Caledonian flew VC10 aircraft then) and this was a pejorative term. In their day they didn't get drunk; they didn't crash cars; they didn't have affairs; but they did. They had just forgotten, they had grown old! They envied us our youth! And in some cases our wives.

We played rugby and cricket and bowls and tennis and soccer and, when needed, we'd turn our hand to amateur dramatics or softball or anything. We played these sports on pitches that would not disgrace professional teams anywhere else; and we played against visiting teams that we'd pay to watch in England, we usually lost but we competed!

At the end of each thirty-month contract we got six months leave and a lump sum to spend on holidays and after six months of high living we needed to work again to get more money.

Life was good!

The married men took to drink; the single men took to drink and looked around; the bored housewives took to drink and looked around. Once again boredom proved to be the biggest aphrodisiac. All this before AIDS, more than religion, tried unsuccessfully to impose celibacy on the world.

We worked from seven in the morning till four in the afternoon, which left a couple of hours of daylight to play sport or drink, and even more hours of darkness just to drink.

Every night there would be a few beers in one club or another. Friday was the "big" night! Darts night, when clubs vied for customers by cooking food and there was very little work done on Saturday mornings! The brilliant morning African sun and hangovers, not sitting easily together.

But it's desolate now, the mines closed, sold eventually to an Indian company who asset stripped it and moved out leaving behind a shell. The mines are flooded, irretrievably damaged; the clubs empty, deserted, inhabited only by ghosts; the playing fields, once nurtured and pampered, scenes of triumph and failures, so important at the time, meaningless now, overgrown.

The rugby posts at 110 feet 4 inches were the highest in the world (perhaps they still are) now rusty, but still standing! Castle Corner on the rugby field where the older members would lean knowledgeably (and drunkenly) against the fence, conveniently close to the bar and the players, and bemoan that the present generation weren't as good as they were, still believing that all they'd need to do is lose a couple of stones (or maybe five) and
they could perform with all their old grace and power; never shy to advise you on your current performance or, more precisely, lack of it.

Thanks, Boet and others. RIP Dick Roy and Mike!

Just in case you're wondering Castle Corner was named after the local beer called Castle the other beer was Lion, but "Lion Corner" doesn't sound as good.

Alliteration Rules OK?

Before one rugby game I took a warm up session of the "Thirds" and, after putting them through a gentle stretching and jogging session, as I walked off I heard Roy Smith say, in all seriousness.
"I thought we agreed at the Annual General Meeting that the thirds didn't need to warm up because it knackered us for the game."

Visiting overseas teams, well aware that we would ply them with drinks, would be careful not to drink too much, well, not until after the game. What they did do however was to sunbathe, not advisable at that altitude where the sun burns, and we'd watch with satisfaction as pure white skin turned pink then red, knowing that hard rough forwards would be in agony when they played the coarse British rugby shirts chaffing their blistered skin. Helped of course by us rubbing their shoulders roughly at every opportunity.

What do you mean "is that fair?" Since when has "fair" had anything to do with playing sport?

The Cricket Club is now an overgrown field, the sightscreens peeling, and beginning to rust through. The cricket square where I spent rather more hours than I should have, batting, keeping wicket, and occasionally, when allowed, bowling, now impossible to find.

To many work was an annoying distraction from what they were really there to do, drink; have sex or play sport; or on a good day all three; and on a really good day, (we were still young remember), to do all three simultaneously.

Alex Milne drove from Capetown to Luanshya some two thousand miles in forty hours to play cricket only to find he hadn't been picked.

Arthur Milnes and I batting for two hours for two runs to save a match against Orientals, a dour Yorkshire man and a just plain awkward Midlander, in the end it became a matter of pride NOT to score.
RIP Arthur.

Revisiting the cricket club now only two photographs remain on the wall, and there I am sitting at the end of the front row. Slim, lithe, athletic, a coiled spring ready to explode ... err... Hang on that's not me ..That's me the fat bloke sitting next to him.

In a town full of characters one of the largest, physically at least, was Keith Hayes. Keith was born and brought up in Northern Rhodesia and had had a number of businesses, some less unsuccessful than others, and I'm afraid that even the successful ones were unsuccessful by other people standards.

One of the wonders of the modern world is the Kariba dam (one of the others is how Sudan can take so long to issue a visa, but I shouldn't go on about it!!). Where was I? , Oh yes Kariba! It was built across the Zambezi River at Kariba to provide power for the old Federation of Rhodesia and Nyasaland.

The Federation was an idea conceived by some British Civil Servant in London, probably on a wet Wednesday afternoon when they'd finished The Times crossword, and imposed on the local population, who didn't want a dam, all they wanted to do is get on with their lives fishing, fornicating and farming, they didn't give a damn about the damn dam.

Not only would the dam provide hydro electric power but it would also become a holiday centre for gambling fishing, water skiing, drinking, and of course extra marital sex ... in fact all those things the colonial whites were good at.

So Kenny bought an island, and was full of enthusiasm for it, he sketched out the plans for the hotel, the game lodges, the casino, and retained an architect.

Well when I say architect, what I mean is a friend from the pub whose day job was driving an earth mover but he was the only one in the pub at the time who had a sharp pencil ... "Now Jeff you know that wasn't true. You just made it up!!"
"Well yes I did sorry..."
"No you're not!"
"True!"

He offered me " a slice of the action!" ("Can't go wrong Jeff you'll be very very rich!") ... in his enthusiasm he let his other businesses slide and flew down regularly to walk out the area, then come back and change the plans.

"Perhaps the runway doesn't need to take a fully laden Boeing 747..."

One year the rains were very good (remember in Africa "good" rains mean lots of rain, "bad" rains means there isn't much) and when he flew down even he noticed that his island was considerably smaller, so he revised his plans yet again.

Yes Kenny's island was getting smaller!! Eventually even he had to admit it; it was definitely getting smaller! ... And he was very fed
up, so he made a formal complaint to the manager of the hydroelectric scheme

Kenny was a big man, a very big man, and he was used to a reaction when he made a formal complaint, or even a mild one come to think of it.

As I'm sure you've guessed the manager not only didn't "do something about this f****ing water of yours that's drowning my f****ng island!" ... (In case you're wondering that was Kenny's idea of a formal complaint!) But also informed Kenny (ensuring that he was protected by his desk!) that within two years his "Island" would in fact be forty feet under water, and that, for good measure he was the fifth one who had bought it.

Kenny can still be found in some bar refining the plans for his hotel complex, waiting desperately for drought to return to Central Africa so the water will drop and he can start building. Either that or sell it to some other mug, but then I suppose so are the other four who bought the island.

> *They built a dam across the Zambezi River at Kariba between 1955 and 1959 to supply cheap electricity to the burgeoning businesses of the Federation of Rhodesia and Nyasaland. Well, in truth, they built it to ensure that the foreign owned copper mines of Northern Rhodesia and the industries of white controlled southern Rhodesia had regular cheap electricity, even the generating plant was located on the south bank in Southern Rhodesia.*

At the time it was built the dam was the largest in the world with a wall 579 meters long and 128 metres high and when it was completed it created a lake 175 miles long by 20 miles wide and the town of Kariba was created for the workers on the dam and in Kariba town is a
church dedicated to the 86 project workers who were killed during the construction.

Legend has it that the 57,000 Tonga people of the upper Zambezi Valley, who were threatened with by the proposed lake called on the fish headed and serpent-tailed Zambezi river God, Nyaminyami, to intervene in order to preserve his own environment and assist them. The construction of the wall was plagued, coincidentally, by unusually severe floods, which destroyed part of the dam in March 1957.

Operation Noah is famous for the rescue of several thousand large animals threatened by the rising water, but the people that it affected had no such help. When the lake flooded the communities where for centuries, they had farmed, fished, worshiped, raised their children and buried their dead, were resettled to poor lands with no development assistance, and left to fend for themselves, and Kariba remains the worst dam-resettlement disaster in African history.

No one knows how big Nyaminyami is because no one has seen him fully, but he is very big, and he is friendly. Legend has it that he even fed the local people in times of famine. Because of this the people pledged their allegiance to him by performing ceremonial dances, and for many years Nyaminyami and his wife stayed safely at Kariba, the spot that was

*their home and near that spot that they started to
build Kariba dam. One season when Nyaminyami's
wife had gone down Kariba Gorge to the valley to
answer their prayers and bless her people, the white
man came to build a wall.*

*It took five long years to build the dam because
Nyaminyami did not want to be disturbed, he caused
some*
*floods and loss of life, but at last he was kind enough
to let the wall be completed. The Tonga's also
believed that Nyaminyami still causes the occasional
earth tremor felt in the lake surroundings. It took the
intervention of the Tonga elders and their medium
spirits to persuade the Nyaminyami to allow the
Zambezi to be tamed.*

*To this day Nyaminyami and his wife have remained
separated, and they believe they will only be reunited
when the Dam is destryed...*

Driving into Luanshya where we used to know everyone. We
needed evidence from upright trustworthy citizens that we had
in fact completed the trip. In their absence we made do with
Joan and Peter Hughes, a view confirmed when their next-
door neighbour Wendy was late for lunch because she had
been detained at the police station following what can only be
described as an "altercation" with the local constabulary.

What is the old town coming too? Wendy finally arrived for
lunch after bribing her way out of, what Peter and I agreed,
was perfectly justifiable and all too brief incarceration. Peter
was all for returning to the police station to bribe them even
more to take her back in. I even offered to contribute, not a
lot, of course, but the thought was there!

Peter, Jean and me toured the town and memories returned of people long gone. Mike Morgan, in a town of drinkers, the undoubted champion. Leaving work on Saturday lunchtime he would report back on Monday morning, never actually having made it home!

One Monday he said to me,
"Jeff, Jackie's not speaking to me, I don't know why, it can't have been anything I've done I wasn't even at home last weekend!"
Peter reminded me of the time there was a party around Mikes house and after an hour sitting at the bar he asked Jackie where Mike was,
"He's asleep down here!" and sure enough he was sleeping peacefully on the floor behind the bar, Jackie stepping over him as if he weren't there.
Mike was promoted, in spite of his drinking he was excellent at his job, and he moved to Senior Staff housing. Soon after the move he returned from his normal night out he couldn't get his key into the lock,(not unusual!) he banged and shouted and swore until the window opened and a strange man said,
"Mike you don't live here anymore!"

The theatre club RADOS with rumours of wife swapping, never substantiated, but darkly hinted at. Harry Williams moving performance in Alfie; Pam leading the dancers in "Brigadoon" which Arthur would insist on calling "Getemdoon".
One busy Friday night in RADOS, reaching in my pocket and accidentally dropping my keys on the floor, and suddenly keys being thrown in from all parts of the room.

Ruth, a big (and I mean BIG) blonde who's err ... err... "enthusiasm" for all things horizontal, vertical and even diagonal became infamous and whose breasts could often be found out on the town on their own if Ruth couldn't make it, or if she had her hands full elsewhere!!

Sandra Rushton (RIP) whose then husband Richard and I played state cricket together saying in all seriousness, "When he's away all weekend I really miss my Dick!" and wondering why everyone laughed!

Gill Kiddell causing whiplash when she walked into the golf club in THAT dress, the women all "tutting" the men all sighing. Jill that was quite a dress! Well in truth it wasn't quite a dress, it wasn't a dress, it wasn't even an adequate top!! It turned a few heads, in fact I still have whiplash! RIP Gill!

The famous streaking incident at the rugby club when, (bugger I can't remember his name), won a bet and streaked across the field after a late night disco, only for someone (who shall remain nameless!) (me!) to switch the floodlights on.

He stood in the middle of the pitch, both hands covering his err ... err.. embarrassment. Running back to the safety of the clubhouse he fell, revealing all. I think it was Toni Duffy, who was heard to say,

"Well he certainly didn't need both hands to cover that!"

It made the national papers, the District Governor closed the club, it took all our powers of negotiation and persuasion, and a donation to the Governors favourite charity; himself, to get it re-opened.

Vicky Jones jumping onto Dot in the pool at Makoma, and pulling down Dot's bra. Arthur calling out,

"Hey Dot if you're drowning those puppies can I have the one with the pink nose!"

The tallest posts in the world

The singing trio, Dave Ross, Terry Morgan and myself who traded volume for quality. Towards the end of one memorable night at the BUFFS Club, Dave turned to me and said,
"Eddie Cochran?"
I climbed straight into "Summertime Blues" and finished to loud applause.
"Was the applause because you'd stopped Watts?"
I turned to Dave and said
"Hmm they like Summertime Blues!"
He said,
"I was playing "Three Steps to Heaven"
We looked at Terry,
"Don't ask me I lost it just after we started!"
"Strange though.. we finished together!" I whispered,
"No Jeff, you finished, we stopped!"

After one night playing Mal Neally came up to me and said,
"Tha knows I'm from Yorkshire and we Yorkshire men speak our mind ... you were crap"
"I'm a Midlander so do we! Piss off!"

My guitar playing proves one thing, if the audience are as drunk as the "musicians", a great night is had by all! At first they used to pay us in beer, but after a while they insisted on paying in money, it was cheaper!

Peter reminded me about Sue McManus who's err ... Attributes almost matched Ruth's (and she could keep fourteen children and a small goat dry under hers!). She was one hell of a golfer. Peter once asked her if when she addressed the ball her arms were above or below her breasts, "Peter I just squeeze 'em together!"

The mortuary with its single dim light, which was lit when someone was inside, in a small town you always knew whoever it was!

Roy Smith had a tree at the end of his drive and as is the way of trees would shed its leaves. Each morning he would tell his gardener to...
"Get those bloody leaves cleared up!"
"Yes Bwana!"
When he returned after work the wind of course had blown some more leaves off,
"I told you t get those bloody leaves cleared!"
"I did Bwana but the wind..."
"Don't argue just do it!"
"But Bwana.......!"
"DO IT!"
This went on for a few days until finally Roy said one morning
"I'm fed up with telling you get it sorted.."
"But Bwana.."
"SORT IT!"
"Yes Bwana"

Roy noticed something different when he got home, there were no leaves but then there was no tree either, just a pile of logs!

My job description was "internal auditor" and I was expected to fight fraud, inefficiency and waste in an organisation covering 200 square miles with 8000 employees! It became clear very quickly that I wasn't up to it and it says much for the perception of the management that in the thirty months I was there they didn't implement a single one of my recommendations.

As Internal Auditor I likened my job to that of Dr Mason the gynaecologist, we both spent our time poking around in the dark because of someone else's cock up! Talk about Sisyphus!

"Who?"

"Ok that's it! go back to the beginning and start again!"

I had a drink for the past at the cricket club knowing the ghost

was laid to rest

RIP Joe McLean, Mike Kelly, Roy Smith, Dave Lumb, Dave Andrews, Sandra, Trevor, Bill Gourlay, Jill Kiddell, Arthur Milnes Vicky Jones and all the others who lived laughed, cried, drank and enjoyed life to the full in Zambia!

Luanshya is the oldest commercial copper mine in Zambia. The existence of copper was known of course by the local tribes for centuries, but it was the discovery by William Collier in 1902 that led to the commercial development of the copper industry.

William Collier was a product of that period in African history that produced larger than life characters like Livingstone, Speke, Rhodes, Burton and Stanley. Born in England in 1870 he was brought up on the fanciful tales of the "dark continent" and of the excitement and fortunes to be made. Leaving England in 1888 at the age of eighteen within two years he was farming in one of the first farms in the new colony of Rhodesia, but the lure of riches and the tales of itinerant prospectors started him wandering again, and like so many of his contemporaries, he alternated between soldiering and searching for the elusive fortune.

In 1902 after the Boer War he joined the Bechuanaland Exploration Company in Bulawayo in Southern Rhodesia (now Zimbabwe) and was instructed to explore north east towards what was to become Ndola in modern day Zambia. Arriving there he saw malachite, a form of green copper ore, in the villages but the natives being scared of their slave trading chief, wouldn't tell him where the deposit was.

Help came in the form of an old Native who invited him on a hunting trip and they trecked twenty odd miles until they arrived at the River Luanshya and the old man pointed along the river and hinted that what he was looking for was there. The following day as he was about to make camp Collier saw a herd of Roan antelope and stalked and shot a large bull which fell across a rock stained with the tell tale green of copper, and so the Copperbelt was discovered and Luanshya Mine got its name of Roan Antelope

Although Luanshya was his most famous find he also discovered Copper at Bwana Mkubwa, and at Chambishi. Now in his early thirties he returned to England but soon returned to Africa to set up his own mine and promptly lost all his money! Returning to Northern Rhodesia he went back to prospecting and found the River Lode at Nchanga, one of the largest ever found.

BIG CITY REVISITED
In the early seventies Lusaka, the countrys' capital, was the largest city in Zambia, but in truth it was still a small city, consisting of a couple of first class hotels (which weren't) and a main street, Cairo road, perhaps because it pointed north/south, and which had all the appearance of an Egyptian market street.

My God it's changed! Now there are shopping Malls with high class shops, fast food outlets that are actually safe to eat at, in the past the only thing that was fast about the food was the speed that you rushed to the toilet, and a car park that's designed to keep your car safe and not to give the local car thieves a better selection without having to travel too far.

They didn't have a car when they arrived, they didn't need one, they had yours when they left.

So obviously I was glad to get out of it, pausing only to meet Rob and Wendy, two economic refugees from Zimbabwe, who managed to produce twins in addition to the rest of the family and who patiently taught me the vagaries of GPS, which he sold me.

For the uninitiated GPS means Global Positioning System and it tells you where you've been; where you're going; where you'll be in ten minutes if you keep going the way you're going; and err ... what time the sun goes down anywhere in the world; and all sorts of other information that you didn't know you needed, and also tells you exactly where you had the accident which was caused by you fiddling with the GPS instead of looking at the road!!

LOST AND FOUND!

15 deg 48 mins. 115 sec E

28 deg 18 mins. 234 sec S

"What's that then?"

"What?"

"15 mins."

"Degrees!"

"Whatever"

"And we're at an altitude of 1056 metres"

"Aaaaah you're playing with your GPS!"

"And guess what? It will tell you where the sun is at any time"

"Look up Watts what can you see?"

"Sky!"

"Any clouds?"

"No!"

"Anything else?"

"Err?"

"I'll give you a clue; it's big hot and hurts your eyes when you look at it"

"Oh yes got it, you mean the Sun"

"There that wasn't hard to find was it? So why do you need a glorified compass to help you find it?"

"It also tells me the XTE!"

"What's that?"

"You know I haven't got the faintest idea but it's currently 23.112 somethings!, and my ETA is 72.4 m.p.h.. Hang on that can't be right.

VICTORIA FALLS

It's impossible to do the "Falls" justice either by describing or photographing them because it's the roar that the Zambezi makes as it plummets the hundred odd metres into the gorge, or the spray that keeps you permanently wet, that adds texture to the view.

The local name is "Musi Oa Tunya" which roughly translates as "the smoke that thunders!", and as always happens when there is an attraction everything in Livingstone is called Musi this or Musi that. From the local hotel to the local beef burger before long you're all "Musied" out.

The town of Livingstone, named after David Livingstone the missionary and explorer who named the falls, has changed since the early 1970's when they really didn't appreciate the asset on their doorstep, but now that Mugabe in Zimbabwe has made

visitors, especially white visitors, unwelcome, Livingstone has boomed and is now on the verge of becoming the tourist capital of Central Africa.

In my early days when I was a lithe sportsman with a feline grace, slim hips broad shoulders,
"Who's this we're talking about Watts? You sure you haven't got the hips and shoulders the wrong way round?"

I used to play for the Copperbelt at cricket but only when no one else was available, and the trip to play Livingstone was very memorable, well it was up to the tenth beer, after that it became a bit of a haze. The game started at lunchtime on Saturday after flying the five hundred miles or so from the Copperbelt, the temperature already in the 90's. We did in truth usually get the better of them up to the end of the first days play. Coming off the field dehydrated we were each given a case of twenty-four beers. Now everyone knows that you do not cure dehydration by drinking ice-cold clear beers with condensation running down the outside of the bottles! Everyone knows that but it didn't stop us trying.
Then they fed us!

The tables groaned under curries that steamed invitingly but that were hot! Quick! Another beer to douse the fire! Eventually a shower then off to town for a couple of beers then an early night, we've long day in the field tomorrow.
The captain's words were wise and sensible,
"Just a couple lads, then back and an early night, you're all grown men I know I can trust you!"
"Sure Skip! You can trust us! Don't worry
He was a good captain but stupid!

Three o'clock in the morning sees us all drunk propping the bar up in the old Musi O Tunya hotel knowing we should be in bed but safe in the knowledge that the opposition are with us.

But of course they weren't, the opposition was safely sensibly tucked up in bed. They conned us again, the oldest trick in the book, which we (willingly) fell for, "fell" being the operative word.

Morning came too quickly, painkillers take some time to work, and playing cricket in the blinding heat with a hangover isn't fun. It was a long day.

Livingston looks the same but it's changing, it's getting busier I'm reminded of the old saying "if this place wasn't so crowded it would be more popular!"

So I sit in the Musi bar drinking my Musi beer looking at the "Musi Eats" menu and I thank God I've seen it before they sell plastic miniatures of the falls manufactured in Taiwan.

Visitors to the camp

We had a visit from elephants that we suddenly realised were getting nearer and nearer, so near that I was beginning to look for escape routes, it's ok! Down the river bank and across the water, no problem I thought, well no problem until someone pointed out the crocodile sitting waiting (well not sitting laying waiting), perhaps they were working together!

WESTERN PROVINCE

Formerly Barotseland, it is the home of the Lozi people. Now the Lozi people have a distinct disadvantage, namely they are not Bembas. Bembas run the country; Lozis are the opposition; Lozi's have a King; the rest of the country has a "democratically" appointed President; result; no investment, bad roads, no development, in a poor country Western Province is the poorest region.

Before Northern Rhodesia was granted Independence in 1964 Barotseland was promised independence as a unique country by the British. The Royal Family in Barotseland had always

been loyal to the British Royal Family and so trusted the British Government to do the honourable thing
Big mistake!
We let them down and now they are the poor relation in a Bemba dominated country. The villages are decrepit mud affairs and I truly fail to understand why everyone is so friendly. I, for one, would be highly fed up being choked by the dust raised by foreign cars driven by white drivers who wave cheerily as they pass, before desperately grabbing the wheel again and hanging on through another bloody great hole in the road (road?? HAH!)

Ngondwe falls

And they have the Ngondwe falls that no one ever visits
Fortunately we'd met up with two Americans Witt and Jennifer, who had built up a Land Rover from spares in America (they may have done better to have used Land Rover spares!) and had driven down the West Coast of Africa before arriving simultaneously at Livingstone and we followed them the hundred and twelve miles taking a grinding six hours. It's always better to travel in pairs on bad stretches so it was a Land Rover leading the way followed by a Land Cruiser picking up the bits that fell off the Land Rover.

Witt being an American blamed the state of the road on the British who built it in 1960 for being typically slipshod and not building anything to last!

I would like to say that good manners prevented me from replying that when oil is found in Western Province we can be sure that the Americans will build good roads for the invasion force!! Or that if they do find oil it will almost certainly have dripped out of a Land Rover. I would like say that good manners prevented me ... but as always they didn't!!!

We called into a small health centre and it was amazing to see the dedication of the nun in charge, the place was clean well run and efficient. I looked through the microscope and saw a TB bacillus, so innocuous to look at and so virulent, and we talked about AIDS. She probably sees more cases of HIV in a morning than most Doctors in the west see in a year, but being a Catholic Nun she violently disagreed with the use of condoms, I find this difficult but who am I to argue with her! Although I wouldn't mind a chat with the Pope!!

Only five foot tall she was scary and quite unashamedly bullied me into giving her nearly all of my medical kit! And in particular the mechanics rubber gloves which she needed for the cleaners! Amazing how something so simple can make a contribution!

Sunset over the Kafue

CAMP VISITORS
And I mean camp as in tented!!

Elephants are a law unto themselves, I still cannot make up my mind whether they are naughty or have a warped sense of humour, but whichever it is they are big enough to do what they want, whenever they want.

The evening had started well enough with a full and frank discussion with the management! We were alone on the campsite above the Kafue River, alone except for the monkeys that we watched playing and fighting, and the hippos that we could hear but not see. The camp owners were concerned for our safety on the walk between where we were camping and the dining room and insisted that we have a guard with us in case a wild animal chased us.

Now I don't have a problem with that, the argument came when I saw the guard. He was young; fit, tall, at first sight everything you need in a guard. But think about this. If an animal is chasing you do you really want to be in the company of a young fit athletic guard, or would you rather be accompanied by an ancient arthritic guard (now here's the point) that you can easily outrun? See what I mean Hmmmm! The management took a long time to see this, and even thought for a while I was joking!

We walked slowly from the campsite to the dining room,(we had to! the guard was really old), and we watched the Kafue put itself to bed from the dining room. As always happens in Central Africa there was no dusk, one minute it was light the next it was dark.
Suddenly there was a crack, then another.
The staff rushed out with powerful torches and there, only ten yards away in the dark was an elephant. We were safe because

there was a big ditch between him and us, but we were still close, very very close. The torches lit his eyes and he watched us, carelessly tearing of limbs the thickness of my arm from trees and after delicately tasting, discarding them!

We were so close we were looking up into his mouth, a surprisingly small pink triangle. Eventually he decided that he'd had enough and with surprising ease he turned in what was a very small space and left. He hadn't finished though, as a parting shot he broke all the fences!
Just because he could!!

Oh yes and he left us a great pile of elephant .. err
...droppings that steamed attractively alongside the dining room. Just because he could!

BEDLESS IN MONGU
After a long drive we arrived but couldn't find anywhere to sleep in Mongu!
Well that's not exactly true, we could have stayed in the grounds of a local bar on a Saturday night.. I don't think so!
Eventually extreme measures were called for and after driving around Mongu for an hour I spotted what I was looking for, a white female, and better still a white female driving a Land Cruiser, she had to be a missionary or a charity worker!!

She was both.

I tried very hard to look refugee'ish and hungry when I drove in front of her and forced her to stop. Jerry had her Methodist missionary zeal put severely to the test when confronted by a grey haired Englishman and a tall American. It caused her a quandary, should she really be helping white people?
Eventually after much persuasion and tears, (mine not hers) she relented and escorted us to the opposition, The Sisters of

the Holy Ghost, a Catholic order, who had built a training centre on the edge of town and, after looking at us nervously, decided that we were safe, beyond redemption maybe, but safe, and let us in.

Sister Ann and Sister Christine Irish Americans, scarily efficient and feisty with it! If you ever meet Sister Ann keep off the subject of President Bush and ants, both of which seem to bring out the most un-nun like feelings in her, and one feels that given the opportunity she would stamp on both of them! She also makes the most wonderful banana bread and pumpkin bread, I seriously considered asking her to forget God and marry me, but it would have been unfair to have made her make a choice!!
We spent two days at the mission; taking the opportunity to repair the vehicles, investigate strange clunks in the suspension, washing, getting haircuts, eating home cooking, and then it was back on the road again.

OLD MAN EMU! HUH!
They said they were indestructible, they even give two-year guarantees, but a combination of African roads and perhaps too much load broke my Emus. For the uninitiated they are shock absorbers, heavy-duty shock absorbers, specifically designed by Australians to withstand the weight of the beers they take when going off road.

Mine broke and with hindsight I think they had been broken for a while, probably on the Moyale to Marsabit road, and it was a very bouncy trip back to Lusaka and into Action Auto's at the top of Cairo Road.

With alarming efficiency they bounced on the bumper and said,

"You're right. The shocks are intercoursed!" (I paraphrase that in the interests of the young children reading this) They wouldn't replace them under guarantee but they did replace them quickly, efficiently, trustingly (I returned the next morning to pay!), and somethingelsly, which writing this later I can't remember.

The loop around was now complete and it's time to cross on the Kazangula ferry into Namibia. Zambia had lived up to what I knew, the people are friendly, annoyingly laid back and destined to wander through life sitting in the shade with a smile on their faces, whilst they are robbed and taken advantage of by foreign businessmen and, even worse, by their own politicians.

NAMIBIA
RUNDU
Yet another campsite that we stayed at was robbed, is it me? People who live in Africa and should know better make the mistake of relaxing just because they are on holiday. You cannot, you're in a part of the world where the "have-nots" vastly exceed the "haves".

I'm not sure what I feel about Namibia yet. It's not a country I know much about, all I know is that the Etosha Game reserve is reputedly one of the best in Africa; that the Skeleton coast and the Namib desert are "must see's"; and that the Fish River canyon make the grand canyon seem like a crack in a newly plastered wall!

WILDERNESS COUNTRY
The north west of the country called Kaokoland is bleak, high, has no rainfall, is searingly hot and is inhabited by people who don't wear bra's or anything else come to think of it.

A bit like Greece or Spain really but they are more kariokiland than Kaokoland! (I like that!!)

The local Himba women smear their bodies with a mixture of red dust and cow fat which, with their natural very black skin, gives them a unique colour, "cow fat orange". This apparently makes them unbelievably attractive to Himba men. I personally think that cow fat looks best on the edge of a large rump steak surrounded by chips and fried onions, rather than a large rumped female, but then I'm not a Himba man!
The women wear a small waist band and ... err ... well that's it, well no that's not it, they all seem to wear a baby on their back! In this heat with all that lard smeared onto them I'm amazed the men can keep hold of them long enough to er..er...I imagine the first time you squeeze her she'd slip out of er.. hmmm.. well you know what I mean!
"Yes we know what you mean!! I suggest you move on quickly!"

Whenever you stop, even if at first you think that there's no one around they appear, and offer to let you take a picture of them. Somehow it doesn't seem right, after all who wants pictures of large breasted naked young women covered in orange coloured animal fat?
Well I know some of you might after all you've read this so far so you must be just sick!

You will not find a picture of a naked Himba lady here. Although they were very happy for me to take their picture, in fact it's how they make money, it makes me uncomfortable and demeaned. I can almost imagine them laughing at western men who take their pictures. If that doesn't make sense it must be just me.

All of the main roads here are gravel and stone but then come to think of it, so are the back roads; the only difference is the size of the gravel. I'm amazed that as yet I haven't had one puncture. A tribute to my BF GOODRIDGE tyres or plain luck?, perhaps a bit of both.

One good thing about the rough roads is that it gets the washing clean!. We put the dirty washing in the loo bucket then put water and detergent in, and drive over rough roads for a day. Result? Clean (ish) washing!. So we now describe roads not as good bad or terrible, but as dirty knickers, dirty knickers and T-shirts, or finally dirty knickers, T-shirts, and socks!! (They have to be really bad to get the socks clean!)
ETOSHA
Everyone told us that Etosha National Park is the best. It's the reason we avoided the others in Kenya and Tanzania, well cost did come into it! And after a day or so in the park I'm not disappointed. Well I'm not disappointed with the quantity of animals although the setting is contrived, sympathetic, but contrived.

Within the camp there are artificial water holes so all the animals come to the camp and you can sit around in comfort watching them. They are there in abundance, Zebra, Kudu, Oryx, Wildebeest, Giraffe, Elephants, Jackals, Impalas, Rhinoceroses (es?), Lions, you name it! It's there!
"Penguins!"
"Well no not penguins!"
"Polar bears!"
"You're just being silly now!"

Last night an elephant watched us! The water hole is separated from the people by a small wall and an alarmingly rickety wire fence. Animals are habituated (now there's a word) to humans, well in truth it is more likely they are simply bored with us and are amazed that we can get so excited about watching them having a drink.

I can imagine the conversation,

"They're still here Gladys!"

"Try to ignore them George! But what pleasure can they get in watching us having a drink I really don't know!"

"I'm fed up with it, watch this I'll give them something to photograph!"

"GEORGE! That's disgusting others have to drink out of this water!"

Last night an elephant came for a closer look at us. We were all sitting quietly watching a pair of young males, well quietly except for the Italians, who cannot do anything quietly and as always were chattering like a troop of monkeys! Suddenly one of the elephants turned, looked, thought for a moment then walked slowly towards us.

Everyone took a picture.

The ones with the massive phallic lenses on their cameras got a wonderful close up of his face

Still he walked slowly towards us!

The ones with normal phallic lenses got a wonderful close up of his face.

Still he walked slowly towards us!

The ones without any phallic lenses got a wonderful close up of his face.

Still he walked slowly towards us!

The ones without a camera got a wonderful close up of his face.

Elephants are big, even small elephants are big!

And still he walked slowly towards us!

A nervous shifting as people suddenly realised that a very large, very wild animal was disobeying the rules.

Finally he stopped and looked at us, idly tearing up clumps of grass, before turning his attention to another group to our left. Time was frozen, we were nervous not wanting to break the spell, fascinated by the patina on his skin, at one stage I was looking directly into his eye as he stood sideways to me, ears flapping, large eye lashes, skin twitching.

He was listening, I am sure, to the various whispered languages, English, German, Afrikaans, Spanish, and Italian, as if making a decision.

Suddenly he turned away, and right in front of the group of Italians he paused, looked, thought, decided, then turned his back towards them, and loudly and quite deliberately, farted!

Elephants are vegetarians! Elephants eat a lot of greens!
Elephants farts set the standard by which all other farts should be measured!.
I was about twenty feet away and it blew my hat off.
But it shut the Italians up! Quite a feat in itself but then it shut everyone up!

I do not, in the interests of those amongst you with delicate sensibilities, intend to describe the smell. But as I said it was that bad it shut the Italians up

For that alone I would have taken my hat off to him, but if you remember he'd already blown it off.

He sniffed the air with his massive trunk as if testing, he was obviously satisfied with his efforts, so he walked away, with just one nonchalant backward glance, to join his friend who

had all this time been watching what was happening and I swear they chuckled together and I'm convinced his friend said,
"You know I've always wanted to do that!"

Whilst all this had been going on no one had noticed two rhinoceroses (es?) arrive and who had been watching all this. One looked at the other and shook her head
"Elephants!!!!"
(I say a she; I didn't get that close as to check! And you know how keen I am to ensure that I only tell you the absolute unvarnished truth, so it could have been a he!)

I'll have to stop writing now I'm still holding my nose and must go and look for my hat!!

I love the pecking order at the water hole, the kudu's bully the Oryx, the Oryx bully the zebras, the zebras bully the impala, the elephants bully everything and the rhinoceroses (es?) just do their own thing.

The giraffes look down on everyone literally and figuratively.

The Oryx gave rise to the myth of the Unicorn as from the side the two large horns look like one, just thought I'd let you know that in case you're sitting there wondering if I'd seen a unicorn.
"Oi Jeff, with all those animals you saw did you see a unicorn?"
"I just told you that!"
"Oh sorry I must have skipped that bit!"

Oh yes I was chatting to one of the game guards and asked him about elephants and he said,
"If you are faced with one and they charge they probably don't mean it!"
"Probably?"
"Yes and the next time they charge there's a good possibility that it's just a dummy charge!"
"Possibility? And if he does mean it?"
"Well the only way to stop him then is to throw human shit at him!"
"And if there isn't any human shit around?"
"Believe me ...."
OVERLAND GROUPS
Last night "overlanders" invaded us! For those of you who don't know Overlanders are groups of people who travel around the sites and sights of Africa usually in converted lorries and who, in doing so themselves, become one of the sights of Africa.

Arriving en-mass they disembark from the lorry and immediately put up their tents. If it's a young group the females wash their clothes and use all the hot water in the showers, the males sniff their clothes and their armpits, decide that both will be ok for another day and go to the bar.

If it's an older group they disembark, stretch their weary muscles and the females wash their clothes and use all the hot water in the showers, the males sniff their clothes and their armpits, decide that both will be ok for another day and go to the bar.

The tour leaders seem to be of an age, usually young, male, usually bored (after all this is the fifth time in six weeks they've done this trip), and very bossy.
I'm not sure I'd like it, they have long long days on the road, early starts, and in truth only see something interesting once every two or three days.

SKELETON COAST NAMIBIA
"You've always wanted to visit the skeleton coast haven't you Watts, read about it, imagined its bleakness so now you're there, are you excited?"
"Mmm it's good!"
"So come on tell all, what's it like?"
"Well there's lots of sand!"
"And?"
"And what?"
"And what else is there apart from sand?"
"Well there's rocks of course and er..er..did I mention the sand?"
"Yes! You did! So there's rocks and sand and what else?"
"Oh yes there's a road going through it"
"So that's rocks and sand and tarmac!"
"Well not exactly the roads made of.."

"Don't tell me rocks and sand…!"

"Yep!"

"Much traffic?"

"Do you really think I'd be the only one stupid enough to travel ninety miles on a bleak sand and rock covered road?"

"So there were how many cars? 100?"

"Less!"

"50?"

"Less!"

"10?, 5?"

"Er"

"2?"

"Nearly!"

"So there was one other car!"

"Mmm!"

"Sounds great fun, any animals?"

"Well now you're talking, as I came a round the bend there was this thing that looked like an elephant!"

"Oh yes and was it?"

"Was what?"

"An elephant?"

"No"

"Don't tell me it was a rock!"

"Yes but it looked like an elephant!"

"Not much wildlife then"

"I saw some birds!"

"What were they?"

"No idea they flew off behind some rocks before I could get my book out"

"Sounds an exciting day!"

"Hey I didn't tell you about the shipwreck!"

"Now you're talking you saw a ship being wrecked?"

"Well not exactly it happened before I got there!"

"So all the excitement was over then, funny I didn't read about it on the news, when did it happen?"

"1976"

"Hey this is interesting, when people drive over the dunes, which they specifically ask you not to, the damage takes decades to repair itself. In fact you can still see the tracks of the convoy that went in to rescue the survivors of the Dunedin Star that went aground"

"When?"

"Don't know"

"And you saw the tracks?"

"No"

"But at least you had the weather! I'll bet it was lovely and warm!"

"It was cold, overcast and windy ... and I was still in my shorts and T shirt from Etosha!"

"So all in all a nothing day, at least it was cheap with nothing to spend your money on!"

"Err well they charged me £6 for travelling on the road and the only hotel charged me £150 for a night!"

"Bloody hell!"

"Exactly I think I'll call it the skeleton cost from now on!" (Pause there and re-read it I said Skeleton COST it's a joke! .. Well! No it's not! £150 is definitely no joke)

"So that's it then?"

"Did I mention the seal colony?"

"No!"

"Ok there's a seal colony!"

"Interesting?"

"Yes, if you like seals!"

"Do you?"

"Do I what?"

"Bloody hell Watts concentrate ... Do you like seals?"

"Not particularly when you've seen one you've seen the whole 80,000, but they are very very smelly!"

"Even worse than elephants wind!"

"Mmm it'll be all that fish!, and they eat 8% of their body weight in fish every day and 37% of their diet is made up of cephalopods!"

"What's a cephalopod?"

"You know I haven't got the faintest idea!"

"So they gave you a brochure then?

"How did you know that!"

"Just a guess!...hang on if you saw shipwrecks and seals that means you must be close to water!"

"Bloody hell I never thought of that. Of course we were near bloody water, it was the Atlantic Ocean, and so that's the Mediterranean, the Indian and the Atlantic Ocean we've seen!"

"Have a swim?"

"With all that seal sh..er.excrement in it? you have to be joking and it was bloody cold"

"So all in all a good day.."

With eyes like that
she's in demand

GATES OF HELL

A writer whom I can't remember but who has obviously more ability than me wrote that the gates to the skeleton coast road are how the gates to Hell will be. True!! (But Hell is cheaper than the lodge.. my idea of Hell is £150 per night!!)

SWAKOPMOND

It rained yesterday in Swakopmond, and it was cold last night too. The guide books apparently all say that Swakopmond is famous for its' mist and rain, but I'd never heard it, because if I had I wouldn't have arrived in shorts and a T shirt and have to get dressed in the middle of the main street. It rained this morning as well, and of course that was when the window mechanism decided to break. Being a trained and skilled mechanic I knew something was wrong because when I pressed the button, motors turned, but the window stayed down. So I stripped the door panel off to get at the mechanism, I'm great at stripping things down; it's putting the buggers back together that gives me a problem.

Before long Nico, a Swiss man with whom we'd been chatting the previous night, joined me and we discussed the problem, as men do, whilst Doris his wife waited patiently for her holiday to continue.

We soon spotted the problem, the arm thingy that fits into the slidey thingy wasn't, err.. fitting that is; (not too technical so far I hope?). Being English I suggested we hit it with a hammer, being Swiss Nico suggested we use a small hammer, and being a wife Doris shook her head and went back to her book.

I was holding the arm thingy whilst Nico held the window and I pressed the button and trapped my finger in the slidey thingy. This didn't help in anyway to mend the window but broadened considerably Nico's command of the English language! Eventually our combined intellect (and a big English hammer) solved the problem and apart from the usual four or five nuts and bolts left over it was solved.

Nico and Doris left on what little was remaining of their holiday. The window works perfectly now, the only trouble is it will only wind up when the headlights are on, obviously a design flaw from the factory, which I will try and get sorted under warranty.

The Namib Desert is what a desert should be like, sandy, but the road is a bit scary. It's just too easy to slide off because the grader drivers who scrape the road are obviously free thinkers and seem to enjoy leaving a mound of sand running along the middle of the road and which, for no apparent reason occasionally, drifts inexorably off to the side of the road. You can't drive over it so you just have to follow it off the road!
Not good news as the edge varies between dangerous, murderous and "Bloody Hell we're going to crash!" It's just too easy to drift off and if you try and do the obvious thing of turning back onto the road you tip over, what you should do is simply drive on into the desert until you stop
"Err but what happens if there is a big drop where you drift off Watts?"
"Well obviously you die. What a stupid question!"

Anyway at the lodge the other night, the one that cost one hundred and fifty bloody pounds for one night .. Did I mention that?"
"At boring length!"
"Any way at that lodge (£150 bloody hell!) was a Trust lawyer from England (HAH! Trust and lawyer in the same sentence, that's an oxymoron!) And he'd slid (or should that be slidden?) off the road and turned onto his side, and had to be pulled out! I suppose he'll have to pay for the damage to the car, but he'll be able to afford it, some poor bloody client will be charged no doubt, lost in the bill for conveyancing some little semi detached house in Wigan will be "site visit",

and I'll bet he wont have to pay the £150 quid accommodation out of his own pocket, and another thing there was no way that was his secretary, it was definitely his wife.."
"Err Jeff I'd be careful isn't there such a thing as slander? and he is a solicitor!"
"LET HIM SUE!! SUE AND BE DAMNED SIR, I SAY, SUE AND BE DAMNED, the truth must out and I am an Englishman and an Englishman's home is his castle, (well it is if your name's Prince Charles), where was I? Oh yes! charlatans to man, the lot of 'em"
"Are you sure you want to say all that?"
"Think I went a bit far?"
"A bit"
"Ok hang on I'll put a disclaimer in "any views expressed in this website are not necessarily the views of the writer who anyway is under considerable stress having just been ripped off to the tune of £150 for one bloody nights accommodation" that should do it!"

Namibia used to be called German South West Africa; it then came under the control of South Africa in 1920 as part of the reparations after the First World War after forty years as a German Protectorate and finally became independent in 1990.

Swakopmond still retains a very strong German influence and its neat clean streets and spotless shopping arcades wouldn't be out of place anywhere in Germany, and the portions in the restaurants are Germanic as were the waistlines of the drinkers at the bar.
But as I wrote earlier the weather was dreadful and we suddenly realised that we hadn't seen rain since Ethiopia and a place that gets dark at 5.30 is cold and wet and deserves one night, which is exactly what it got!

NAMIB DESERT

Now this is more like a desert should be. Wonderful colours of red and yellow green and brown, the occasional glimpse of and ostrich or an Oryx, (which is also called a Gemsbok) and we have the stars back. No one should die before sitting under the Southern Cross in the desert with only the light from a Mopani wood fire to relieve the blackness.

Everyone says you should watch the sun rise at Dune 45; it's one of the wonders of the world. I missed it!! No-one told me that the clocks went forward so it happened without me and I overslept ... Bugger

BOTSWANA

Kasane

It's the game viewing part of the trip; so first stop Kasane and Chobi game reserve. There are sixty thousand elephants in Chobi, and each one is a feeding, knocking down trees and crapping machine, my God they make a place a desert very quickly.

And another thing, they have no road manners at all; they don't slow down at intersections and let you through when you've got right of way! Oh no! They just charge across and have the bloody nerve to wave their trunks at you and make trumpeting sounds and mock charges. This has the effect of inhibiting some people who immediately give in and back off at high speed thus confirming to the elephants that such behaviour is acceptable! Well do I strike

Dune 45 Namib Desert
you as the sort of wimp that would do this?? Err ... Hmmm,
anyway we also saw some sable, kudu, hippos, stranded
Israeli tourists, cattle egret, elephants, and lots of birds none
of which I
can identify

Traffic queue Botswana

Taking advantage of civilization we took a big bag of very
dirty washing to the Chobi game lodge, and, fools that they
are, they promised that their industrial strength washing
machines and detergents would make them pristine in no time.

The first time we went back they said,
"Aah Mr. Watts it's a bigger job than we thought!" they'd
come off second to my underwear. Eventually admitting
defeat and bringing in reinforcements, the Botswana
biological warfare unit who quickly retreated with the loss of
a number of men, and they finally returned our clothes to us
five hours late and about fourteen kilograms lighter. I
immediately suspected theft and emptied the clothes out on
the floor of the reception but the missing fourteen kilograms
turned out to be just the dirt.

MAKGADIKGADI PAN
It's ok! I'll help you MAK GAD I KARDI, it took me a
couple of days to get it right, in fact it almost took longer to
say it than to drive through it.
The pans are vast
"I know I've used vast often but you try and think of a word
for vast open spaces other than vast"
"Gigantic, immeasurable,"
"Yeah ok"

BAOBAB TREES

As I was saying the pans are gigantic, immeasurable and flat
and dusty and you travel all day without seeing another
person, and although there are tracks of a sort you get lost and
need a GPS and four-wheel drive and you know what?
IT'S BLOODY MARVELOUS!!!!!
We saw four ostrich and a small ratty squirrel thing and that
was it, the vehicle is caked with dust, there are scratches along
the side from two inch long spikes that everything appears to
be covered with that really hurt when they scrape down your
arm and you know what?
I WANT TO DO IT AGAIN!!

I thought I'd seen some big baobabs but my God the ones
here are enormous,
"Not vast" Watts?
"Well yes that too and I've a picture of one that's 4704 years
old!
"How do you know?"
"The woman at the campsite told me. When I asked her how
she could be so accurate she said, well they told me it was

215

4700 years old when I came here and I've been here four years!"
"That's not true is it Watts! You made it up!"
"The 4700 years old bit is"
They are sometimes called "upside down trees" by the Africans, based on the legend that God pulled it up and replanted it upside down, and I am assured that the fruit makes Tartar sauce, but come to think of it in all my time I've never seen one with fruit or leaves on.

MAUN BOTSWANA

TAKE ME TO CROCODILE FARM AND THE MAKE IT SNAPPY
It was when I went to shake hands that I noticed that the man who came to show us around the crocodile farm had the bottom half of his right arm missing!!.

I'd stuck my right hand out, and so had he, and there was a gap between us where our hands should have met, and I was left shaking a non-existent hand.

I resisted, with difficulty, commenting, and tried hard to listen attentively to what he was saying as we walked along the sandy track to the crocodile pens, but I couldn't help noticing that he still used his..er..er..well what was left of his arm to point. Perhaps he'd forgotten that he didn't have a hand..
I found it difficult to concentrate my attention being constantly drawn back to his missing arm.

After about eight hundred metres we came to the, thankfully, very well fenced area where thirty or so very large crocodiles lay basking in the sun.

I say very large but he scoffed at this and said that at between three and five metres they were just juniors, OK! But they looked very large to me.

He pointed at the big male (well he didn't exactly point, he aimed his stump at it!) and was telling us how fast they strike, and how they can gallop on land at thirty m.p.h. Now I couldn't help speculating who measured the speed and how? All I know is that if a crocodile were chasing me, the last thing I'd be doing would be taking measurements to check my speed!

I wondered whether now would be opportune to ask if that was the one…No!
The crocodile has apparently remained unchanged for two hundred million years and there's no real reason why it should change, after the first couple of years of life it has no natural enemies, it only needs to eat once every two years and can live for one hundred and forty years.
"… and during the mating season the male can mate up to twenty times a day, and he'll mate with any female who is receptive (I resisted the temptation to say "who wouldn't")..And the females then lay between nine and twenty eggs and then we go into the pen and collect the eggs and put them in the incubator"
"You go into that pen and dig up the eggs? Don't the crocodiles object?"
"Of course they do. But we beat them off with long rubber tipped sticks and then quickly dig up the eggs"
I was going to ask if anyone gave him a hand.. But instead I asked
"Isn't it dangerous?"
"It's a four metre long angry female crocodile weighing well on the way to a thousand pounds, what do you think?"

I hazarded "yes" as an answer and he nodded (would he now mention his arm??..No!)

"We feed them when they need it on donkeys, we shoot them and cut them up and throw them in"
"Oh you don't feed them by hand then?"
"No. Why would we?"
"Just a thought. Tell me do they have names?"
He looked at me as if I was an idiot,
"Why would they have names?"
"So you know which one is which!"
"Why would we want to know which one is which?"
I was going to say "So you know which one ate your bloody arm!" but I again resisted, all I said was,
"I don't know but there's no arm in asking is there?" Even as I said it I knew it was a sick and callous joke, just the sort I love!

I looked again at the one closest to me, (who was certainly a Cyril), and he opened one eye and looked back at me, I quickly put both arms behind my back in case he fancied making a pair, but he continued smiling, perhaps thinking of the day soon when he'd have twenty of the females.

"How to you know which is female and which is male?" I forget the answer but again I don't suppose it's important as long as the crocodiles know.

Gaining confidence now I was trying desperately to bring "armless" into the conversation, but by the time I'd given up he was talking about the problems of getting to work
"At least you don't take work home with you!" he ignored me and said that he had to hitch lifts as the public transport was so bad,
"I'll bet you're late for work quite often!"

"Yes I am. How did you know?"
"Just a guess!"

All in all I think I'd behaved quite well and when we got back to the car I even managed to remember to offer my left hand to him, he again offered his right ... er ... arm so I was shaking thin air again.
Before I left I called into the office and said to the girl behind the counter.
"Er.. You know the guide?"
"What about him?"
"His arm.."
"Car accident!"
"Not..?"
"No..!"
"Ok..Just thought I'd ask.."
"No problem. So you didn't notice him limping, he's got a wooden leg as well!"

THE GUARD IS FLOATING

The campsite at Maun seemed quiet enough and we were invited to kill their last bottle of wine by Helmut and Elizabeth, an invitation difficult to refuse, especially as he'd lit a fire.

So there we were discussing the EEC (seriously we were, and both agreed that we still don't understand how it got to the size it is and who exactly is running it), suddenly we were aware that we had a visitor.

On the very edge of the firelight stood a person,
 "Who are you?" I asked which in the circumstances didn't seem an unreasonable question.
"I am Mishuk; I am your guard and will protect you from thieves and thugs!"

"Good man Mishuk thank you!...I think"
Back to discussing the Euro with Helmut (I also mentioned the first and second world war and of course 1966 world cup when England beat Germany 4-2 ..he still claimed that the ball never crossed the line..),when we became aware that Mishuk was still there.

We looked at each other; I felt I was expected to say something.
"So tell me Mishuk what will you do if thieves and thugs do come here?"
"I will blow my whistle!"
"Why will you blow your whistle?"
"To call Eric!"
"Who the F…. err who is Eric?"
"I am Eric!"
From behind Mishuk, who wasn't particularly large, stepped Eric. He was so small we hadn't seen him there. I felt somewhat less than protected,
"Hallo Eric..er..and.. What will you do if we are attacked?" (I immediately regretted asking)
"I have a torch Sir!". He shone it. Not very bright! But considerably brighter, I suspect, than both Mishuk and Eric.

There was something about them that wasn't right, apart from the fact that they kept giggling and leaning on each other.
We all looked at each other and then I said,
"Mishuk and Eric I think you are either drunk or drugged or both!"
"......and we have an electric fence!. But we've lost the key to the gate and can't lock it, so thieves just walk through it!" he was either ignoring me or didn't understand the statement.
"Well wouldn't you Mishuk?" "Oh yes!"
"I tell you what Mishuk and Eric why don't you and I go to the manager and have a chat?"

"Oh yes Sir! Let's do that!"

They led the way (me walking, them floating!)
until eventually we arrived at the bar, which by that time of
the evening was full of drunken white people who confirmed
that Mishuk and Eric were in fact drunk or drugged or both.
Well I think they did, because they too were giggling and
having such difficulty standing that they needed to lean on the
bar.
We called the manager. Mishuk by this time was also
leaning happily on the bar, and Eric was leaning happily on
Mishuk, both blissfully unaware of what was happening.
Michael the manager arrived and I told him what I thought of
him, his campsite, his guards, and for good measure the state
of the UK economy for all of which he readily admitted total
responsibility.
I then noticed he too was leaning on the bar!

It was at this point I began to suspect the he was simply
humouring me, or that he too was drunk or drugged and I
found myself in a position totally unique in my experience, I
was the most sober person in the room. It was scary and not a
feeling I wish to repeat too often!!
Michael promised he'd,
"Get it shorted! …err …shorted … err shee to it!"
Feeling very pleased with myself I left full of self importance
and dignity only to return five minutes later to ask the way out
as I'd got completely lost and nearly fallen into the swimming
pool.
Outcome? A sleepless night awaiting thieves and thugs, all of
whom were safely tucked up in bed enjoying a good nights
sleep, as I suspect was Mishuk and Eric, all the people in the
bar and of course Michael the manager!

ROBBERY

Since we've been in Botswana we've noticed that there has been an increase in security on the campsites (that is if you class Mishuk and Eric as security) and also notices disclaiming liability for any losses.

The campsite last night was no exception but it seemed well protected so we were surprised when we came to pay in the morning, to find a police van and a group of campers confronting us with quite a story to tell.

Apparently the campers had gone to the bar without locking their vehicles (Oh yes! Very sensible!) and during the evening they'd lost all their money, passports, camera's and common sense (nope they'd lost that already!!).

When they told the camp manager (campsite manager I mean not a camp manager wearing pink hunting gear and mincing round the camp saying "Darling his trunk was enoooormous!!") he had, with the aid of his tracker, followed their spoor (see I am learning things in Africa.)

The spoor led to the bus stop on the main road and with admirable deductive powers they thought.

"I'll bet they caught the bus!", a phone call to the police down the road (remember there is only one road between Maun and Shakawe, and come to think of it only one bus!); the bus was stopped and the criminals were apprehended, and, knowing African police methods, they were probably apprehended by the testacles!

The only point to this story is that they were making their getaway by bus and perhaps I should have been able to make more of it, but I couldn't.

The manager turned to me and said as if in justification,

"Of course they are Zimbabweans"

"Right!".

I suspect that the robbers will be dealt with in a pretty violent way and I also suspect it will not in anyway dissuade them

222

from future crime, what else is there? Tourists are occasionally robbed, and the authorities here don't like it, but then neither do the tourists of course. There is always local crime but robbing tourists gives richer pickings.

I am reminded of the story of the bank robber in America who, when asked,

"Why do you rob banks?" replied

"Obviously because that's where the money is!"

TSODILO HILLS

The Kalahari desert in Northern Botswana is flat, covered with sand and scrub bush, and is hot, just the sort of place the old Bushmen loved. Exploding out of the otherwise flat plain are four hills and these became a sacred place of pilgrimage for the San Bushmen.

The Bushmen drew images of animals on the walls and it surprises me that so much is made of it. The drawings are easily recognisable as animals, Eland, Giraffe, hippopotamus, penguins etc. but why wouldn't they be? Why are we so arrogant as to think that only modern man is capable of reproducing recognisable images?

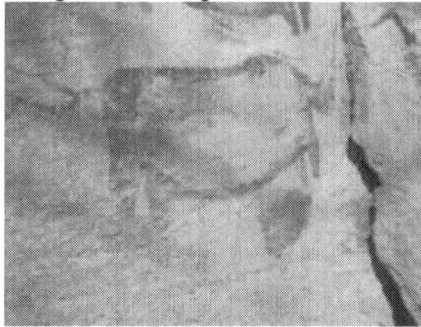

They say the images are over 20,000 years old, but some of them look suspiciously modern, if not in style, then certainly in depth of colour, perhaps a bit of "help" to keep them going, but then perhaps I'm just a cynic!!

The San people believe that human life started in these hills, (I know that's stupid! What really happened was that some omnipotent being created it in six days and put his feet up on the seventh. Sheesh everyone knows that!!), and in the silence of an
African night with the Milky Way draped across the sky, it's easy to imagine families of San Bushmen camping on the same spot, spinning tales and legends and drawing images on the walls with their tins of "Dulux ancient stone" red.

ANOTHER WANDERER
One endangered species that we did see a lot of, particularly in Zambia and countries south (although I suspect there are just as many in Kenya and Tanzania) is the white African who is "getting by" in what are now Black controlled states.

These are white males, who seem to be able to turn their hands to a wide range of jobs and who, when drunk or trying to impress, hint at an "interesting" past involving incursions (or excursions) with obscure army units into neighbouring countries; but who now live from day to day, and who would be lost in a more competitive world.

I have to be careful here not to give the impression that I think the way we have allowed ourselves to become slaves to possessions is the right and only way. But it is so easy in many ways to envy them their feckless way of life.

Such a person was Bart at the Shakawe fishing camp on the Okavango where we spent two days watching birds, wishing that they would stay still long enough so we could look them up in the "Birds of Africa" book.
Bart's first words were "I don't usually speak to Englishmen!".

This was delivered in a broad Afrikaans accent, through a big ginger beard and without a smile to soften the sentiments. "Nice!" I thought, but for once in my life, wisely, kept quiet! As we got to know Bart better it turned out that he was ex South African Special forces soldier who knew Angola well, "but not the towns!" giving the very strong impression that when he went there he didn't actually go through border formalities.

Although he wore the damn silly tiny shorts that all South African men still insist on wearing, he looked very very solid and it wasn't just his ginger beard that was big, everything about him was big, chest, biceps, thighs, waist, the whole package (except the shorts) was BIG!

Bart would be a very useful man to be on your side in an argument. When I say "on your side" I mean of course that I would be behind him, very much like Eric was behind Mishuk.

He'd just recovered from vehicle accident when the car he was driving was in collision with an elephant. He hurt his shoulder but the elephant broke its legs and of course had to be put down. Bart shot it, he gave the impression that he'd do that to a human as well (especially if they were English!). I suspect that if he hadn't had a gun he'd have strangled it! I wish I could have seen the insurance claim.

At 32 he has never had a bank account and now lived in a store room at the lodge earning very little taking out fishing trips into the Okavango, but it's when he talks about fishing and game that he gets the far away look in his eyes.

"What more does a man need than a Backie (a pick up truck), a bed roll and a fishing rod?"

You know what Bart I'm not sure! It sounds idyllic and sitting here writing this I don't know if you have found the secret of a happy life or whether you're naive beyond words.

Hey I've discovered Birds! we borrowed a book and tried vainly to match the birds that we could see in the book with

the ones that were around us. Unfortunately birds being what they are keep flying off and I found great difficulty in finding them in the book. I seriously considered shooting them so I could identify them, but this is apparently considered unacceptable and anyway I don't have a gun. We finally spotted and identified a malachite kingfisher, and when I excitedly told the camp manager he said,
"Oh yes we've all seen hundreds of them!"
"Well I bloody haven't.. er what do they taste like?"

FISH RIVER CANYON
There's a crack in the earth on the borders between Namibia and South Africa and at the bottom of this crack there's a river. The main stone roads take you to look out points but more interestingly there are smaller roads passable only by four-wheel drive vehicles that are irresistible, especially if you are as stupid as I am.
In what is an already quiet area, you can find solitude and there you find the Cairns, built over many years unchanged and undisturbed by other people or by climate. We built one overlooking the canyon in a place of peace and solitude in remembrance of those who are dear and special.

Our Cairn

THERE'S A THIEF IN THE SHOWER

Well we're finally into South Africa on what is the final stage of the journey but I am, as I write this morning dear reader, highly fed up and annoyed.

Last night we pulled into a municipal campsite in Garies and, in truth, it's very good, i.e. cheap. Well, when I say good, it's in need of a clean, the electricity is intermittent the showers only passable but "cheap" makes all this acceptable
One we tried earlier was £15 a night "but you get you own private bathroom and toilet!" yeah right! We moved on!
Anyway it being Tuesday and having lost count of the number of days since I had a shower (I think it was Cairo) I went for a shower.
OH JOY OF JOYS!, someone had left a very expensive, almost unused, shower gel in the shower, and after plain water, a baby wipe, or on a good day, old fashioned Lifebuoy, I was left with a problem, should I use it, or would that be shallow, small minded and penny-pinching? What do you think I did?
EXACTLY!

I've never been so clean and I glowed with the tingling sensation of expensive shower gel. Every orifice was pristine, "Too much information as usual Watts!"
DILEMMA! Do I steal the whole bottle of shower Gel (well what remained of it!) and risk someone returning to the shower and accusing me of stealing it, or do I leave it and return later!.

I decided to return later, then had a drink and forgot. I went over this morning and it was gone! Some other bugger had pinched it! The site is full of South Africans so that'll explain that; you can't trust them to leave other peoples property alone; Bloody Hell fancy pinching a man's shower Gel, I'll be glad to get out of here I am so fed up. I just had to share it with you.

I knew you'd be sympathetic

I think one of the most joyful things in life is discover a forgotten shampoo or gel in the shower.

SOUTH AFRICA

As always happens towards the end of a long trip, without really meaning to you drive faster, and this is what happened again. The western province of South Africa is famous for its springtime flowers and although, to be brutally honest flowers do very little
for me, the scenery in this region is very Alpine, green lush meadows with a backdrop of mountains.

Just a point though, Table Mountain is a famous flat topped mountain seen from the Southern Tip of Africa but there are hundreds of them all the way down, I suppose some volcanic activity took place that formed the whole region.

The flowers, such as they are, were out, but as is ever the case, they were "better last week, next week, last year..etc." the small towns are neat, clean and sun burnt and if you don't look down at the beggars sitting around your feet, you could be fooled into thinking that all is well.

We had been warned of the lawlessness in South Africa so we were on our guard and perhaps this made us neurotic, but when you stopped looking at the buildings and the scenery you suddenly notice the amount of black people meandering, sitting, staring and you become aware that this is still a country, ten years on from independence, of have and have nots.

AND INTO CAPETOWN

The sense of have and have-nots is nowhere more highlighted than in Capetown. The Waterfront teems with beautiful people carrying bags with expensive labels. Ocean side restaurants serve food that cost more than some people earn in a week.

In the centre of Capetown, impressive old colonial buildings fight for shoulder room holding back the younger grey pre-cast concrete monstrosities, the streets feel intimidating, and inevitably you highlight that fact that you are a stranger by looking nervously over your shoulder.

By this time however you know the basic inviolable rule of travel in Africa, if you're approached they want to con you, rob you or beg from you, sometimes all three!
Ah! And whilst we're on the subject of stereotypes here's a couple more.
Italians: noisy and inconsiderate, a good nights sleep is impossible when the Italians arrive.
Japanese: they decant from the bus stand in front of whatever it is they've come to see then swarm all over it, each has to take a picture of everyone else in every possible permutation then they climb into the bus again without actually looking at anything.
Overland Tour groups; no! surprisingly, they are not noisy, the early mornings and long days on the road ensure that; but the females use up all the hot water and hog the mirrors.

Back to South Africa

I can't remember if I told you but in Zambia we met Salome and Mike at Shiwa Ngandu and had a few beers (as you do!) went through all the usual goodbyes and then, roaring down the great north road to Kapiri Mposhi I spotted a broken down hire car. Mike and Salome were "parked" on the side of the road with an oil slick under the car.

"Can't understand it!" bemoaned Mike, "It was OK when I went down the road to Shiwa" (You may recall that road was number four in my list of crap roads in Africa and a road where I thought twice about taking the Land Cruiser) it was there that Mike had taken an overloaded Ford Mondeo!! Result? Hole in the sump!

You may at this point be asking why I mention it now? Stay with me all will be revealed!

So I towed Mike and Salome back to civilisation or close enough for Mike to indicate that he could manage. I was somewhat surprised that he was even going to start the car having deposited most of the oil from his sump on the road, but Hell it's not my car, (but then it wasn't his either!) He unhooked and roared off, as I say I was surprised, but what do I know?

He finally turned into the entrance of Nsobe Lodge on the north road to the Copperbelt in Zambia, where he again demonstrated

the Mike method for driving over poor roads in a saloon car (preferably someone else's) that is to go so fast that you only land on every third boulder and hope that the sump's strong! Had he learnt nothing?

Anyway back to the story.

"At last we're nodding off here!"

The camp site where we stayed in Capetown is at Belleville (Belleville translated literally means "good town!" AAH!!!! It's a rubbish name for a rubbish campsite) it was damp, the weather cold and we were getting fed up. Jean had an inspiration

"You remember Salome said "anytime you're in Capetown etc."" "Why don't we text her?"

"I was going to suggest that!"

"Yeah right!"

So we ..Er..Jean, texted (textd?) Salome...I've never got the hang of texting and now that some thieving bastard has pinched my 'phone with all my numbers in there's no point in even bothering to learn!

Salome, it turned out, was in England visiting some bloke (so who was Mike then? Hmmmm is there some scandal we should know about here?. I'll find out and let you all know!")..but, ..now listen to this.. She said we could use her house and she asked her brother Billy to fetch us from the camp site to lead us there.. Woweeee a warm bed and a bath er.. hang on

"Text her back and ask her if she's got sky sports there's a rugby game on tonight"

"Don't push it Watts!"

Then, Mike texted (?) us to say HI! ..Salome had contacted him from England!.. hang on what IS going on here? ..

To summarise we finished up in Salome's house in Capetown, it's warm there's good books to read, and the 'fridge was full of wine (I use the past tense advisedly!) but no sports channel on the TV. Oh well

PS. In the interests of accuracy Mike has assured me that the car with the hole in the sump was broken when he got it and that He and Salome are just friends!

How many of you would let almost complete strangers use your empty house whilst you were away??..As I said travel is about the people you meet. Anytime you're in England

Salome you can stay with us..only £10 per night..I know! I know! I could ask more but what are friends for?
Salome you're wonderful!

CAPE OF GOOD HOPE
I wasn't going to bother to drive any further but when the shipping company told me that they would drain off all the diesel in the car when they put it on the ship, I thought "bugger that I'm gonna use it myself" they might be the second biggest shipping company in the world but that doesn't stop them stealing my diesel, so we went to the Cape of Good Hope, which isn't I'm sure you know the most southerly point of the African Continent but the most South Easterly point.

We looked out at the Atlantic Ocean! It looked cold and there were no whales, I waited there a long time to get a picture of our Land Cruiser in front of the "Most south easterly point in Africa sign" but bloody hoards of Japanese kept arriving and getting in the way and taking pictures.

In the end I got so tired of waiting that I told the next group that I thought they were selfish, unthinking, short sighted, straight haired Orientals who should stick to waiting on tables in doubtful slop houses, they smiled and gave me their camera to me to take a picture of them .. which I did but kept my finger over the lens..

That'll teach them!.

Cape of Good Hope
Without the Japanese

"So here's a question! What's the most southerly point in the African Continent?"
"Err sorry .err Cape of Good Hope?"

"Aah I knew it! you've not been concentrating!..No! It's Cape Aghuilas..And we went there yesterday to be able to say that we'd done the lot..top to bottom!

"Oh was it interesting?"

"Well it was a pile of rocks and a holiday home resort!"

"So it wasn't interesting?

"And, and, now listen to this, it's the point where the Indian and the Atlantic Oceans meet!"

"And can you see any difference??"

"In truth no!"

"So it's not like the Blue and White Nile?"

"Well even the Blue and White Nile wasn't that noticeable!, but we did see some penguins on the way back ..They were a small and very cute, looking at them I suddenly wondered if they were birds or mammals. They lay eggs so they must be birds! "

"Crocodiles lay eggs!"

"Hmm they can't fly so they must be mammals!"

"Ostriches can't fly and they are birds, you'll be saying next that they swim so they must be fish"

"Ok they swim so they must be fish!"

"No they are birds! And over the years they have lost the ability to fly "

"That's what I said earlier!"

MEDICAL TOURISM

Jean had a shoulder problem that got worse during the trip, you remember Dr Rob and Lisa in Kenya? Well the conversation went,

"Hmm a rotator cup problem I think you should see a specialist! Yes I'd love another beer!"

So he contacted the top shoulder man in South Africa, or even the world, Dr Joe De Beer and when we got to Capetown we'd got an appointment within three days to see him, and, listen to this, even in spite of an unavoidable two-day delay he operated on Jean three days later.

Now that's how it should be! But don't be too impressed! All he did was make some holes in her shoulder and then file the bone down or something. With all the equipment I brought with me I could have done it, but she wouldn't let me, and let me tell you something else, there isn't even a decent scar to justify the expense! Just five little holes!

All this modern development of key hole surgery can't be right, if it was me I'd demand at least a nine inch scar so that I could milk the situation, and it would take a month before I stopped limping!
But no one listens to me, so I'll say no more about it!

And another thing whilst I think about it, in his surgery there are all these pictures of South African Rugby players whose game have been improved because of his surgery, let me tell you this Jean has played a game since and she is still crap, so I ask myself if I believe what anyone says!
I've just thought of something else! Karin van Royan his assistant. No doctor I've ever had examine me looks like that. The ones I get are old male and grumpy, she's young very attractive and pleasant.
It makes me wonder is she's a doctor at all!.

To test out my theory whenever she was around I limped and winced, no reaction!.
I collapsed on the floor feigning a heart attack; did she straddle my chest and give me the kiss of life like any compassionate qualified doctor would?
No she bloody didn't!
And even if she knew I was faking it she could have still done it! I was a private patient after all (well I wasn't but I'd

happily have paid! There's a first! happily and paid in the same sentence when I'm talking!) but it wouldn't have done her any harm and it would have made me very happy, make that very very happy, make that very very very etc. etc.

Simply stepping over me as if I wasn't there as she walked out was hurtful; I think I might write a letter of complaint to someone!.

And another thing whilst we're on the subject, neither Karin nor Joe de Beer wore stethoscopes round their necks like real Doctors, not did they wear crumpled white coats with bloodstains on them.

The whole episode brought home to me something that I'd long since concluded throughout the trip; it's an unfair world. There are people in Africa, the vast majority in fact, who have to walk many miles to get even the basic medical life saving treatment from overworked doctors, whilst others can get world class treatment immediately!
The only difference is money!, not intelligence, not hard work, not fundamental worth as a human being just a simple accident of birth.

It stinks but there it is!

CONCLUSION

So we've done the top to the bottom, from Tunis to Cape Aghuilas, 17000 miles, we've seen the sights we've driven down a lot of roads and up and down some hills. We've touched the four oceans and the conclusion?
It's what we always suspected, travel is about people it's as simple as that.
The good people and the bad people.

The helpful people and the obstructive people.
The generous people and the mean people.
Just like home in fact, just like home!.

Right where's that Atlas of the World.... hmm I wonder what it's like in...

MOROCCO 2005
ANOTHER BLOODY HOLIDAY..ER EXPEDITION

"Guess what!"
"What?"
"We're on holiday!"
"Oh? As opposed to what?"
"We'll as opposed to…erm. Not sure I understand what you mean"
"We'll some people say "I'm on holiday as opposed to working!. Just for the record, when did you last work?"
"March!"
"Which march"
"That's the one that comes after February and before April"
"Year?"
"Which year we on now?"
"2005"
"So that'll be 2004 then!"
"14 months!"
"Yes"
"So forgive me if I'm a bit slow here, you've not worked for fourteen months and only now you say you're on holiday, I repeat on holiday from what?"
"From not being on holiday"

A CRIMINAL RECORD
"No problems so far?"
"Well Saturday morning was a bit of a problem"
"Oh ok!"
"You should now ask what the problem was!"
"Look after all this time I know what I should do, but I also know that even if I don't you'll still tell me, wont you!"
"Not if you don't want me to.. Or will I? Yes I think I will!"
"Now there's a surprise"

238

"I spent all day Friday packing the vehicle making sure ever thing was ok, checked the oil, I knew it was ok it was dripping out from under the engine so there must have been some in, I kicked the tyres, it really hurt!"

"Why?"

"I didn't have any shoes or socks on!"

"Why? on second thoughts it doesn't matter!"

"Because.."

"I SAID IT DOESN'T MATTER!"

"Right where was I? … that's it! Packed the vehicle so we were ready to go, then my clothes, Jean took them all out of course and repacked them properly, then Saturday morning comes and the post arrives A BLOODY SPEEDING FINE FROM CLEVELAND POLICE!, 35 MILE A F*****G HOUR IN A 30 MPH ZONE SIXTY BLOODY QUID! and three points!"

"Perhaps you shouldn't have been speeding, 35mph is quite quick for you, you must have been in third gear for the first time, amazing!"

"It's slow for Jean!"

"How come she's involved?"

"She was bloody driving! And as I had to answer the summons in 28 days I couldn't tell them that because the next summons would come back for Jean and we'd be away and the fine would go up"

"So admit it was you!"

"It wasn't!"

"Admit it was you and pay the fine!"

"They demanded my license to put the three points on it!"

"Hang on! You'll need your license when you're driving in Europe! And weren't you leaving in a couple of hours!"

"EXACTLY!"

"Why didn't you 'phone the court and explain?"

"I did!"

"And"

"Saturday morning, no-one was working!"

"Aahhh difficult! Why didn't you 'phone the police themselves?"

"That's what I did next. Got a very nice lady and I told them very firmly that although they needed £60, an admission of guilt and my license, all that I was willing to send them was an admission of guilt (reluctantly) and that was it....."

"Wow! I'm impressed, so you negotiated and resolved the issue?"

"Oh yes they soon realised that I'm not a man to be messed with, once I've made up my mind I cannot under any circumstances be swayed. So after a lot of negotiating, in the end I agreed to send them the admission of guilt"

"That all?"

"And my license!"

"Anything else?"

"£60"

"I'm sorry I didn't hear that I thought you said £60!"

"Mmm!"

"So after all that negotiating you agreed to send them what they asked for in the first place!"

"Well if you put it like that I suppose I did, but I'd phoned lots of people for advice and not one of them said what I really wanted to hear"

"Which was"

"That's ok Jeff tell them I was driving so I get the 3 points and I'll pay the £60 fine for you!"

"Bastards"

PETROL AND DIESEL DON'T MIX

"Putting unleaded into diesel engine is a mistake any one can make, and when you realise you've done it, under no circumstances do you start the engine, what you do is shout "F….k !" and ask the petrol station for help!"

"And what did they do?"

"They demanded payment for the petrol I'd put in then they suggested I 'phone the RAC!"

"Good idea!"

"I thought so, so I did, but then hit a snag!"

"What was that?"

"When I 'phoned them they reminded me that I wasn't a member!"

"Bloody people nit picking like that! So what did you do?"

"Right it's not a problem draining a tank, you just open a nut and it runs out"

"But you can't just let it run onto the floor!"

"That what I thought, the only thing I could see on the forecourt was the containers that the flowers they were selling were kept in, problem was they were full of flowers!"

"Aah so what did you do?"

"Bought the flowers!..£40"

"Obvious really!"

"Now you had the containers to catch the fuel, but what did you do with the stuff that you took out!"

"Well obviously you offer to sell it back to the petrol station!"

"And did they buy it?"

"What do you think?"

"No?"

"Exactly, so I now had three large flower pots of fuel that I couldn't carry!"

"What you needed was some jerry cans!"

"Which I just happened to have but which I intended to use to carry water in the desert!"

"So you?"

"So I filled the water containers with petrol/diesel"

"But won't that ruin them?"

"Don't ask!"

"So what did you do with the two plastic jerry cans containing thirty litres of petrol/diesel?"

"Took them to the tip!"

"And they took it no problem!"

"No It's illegal to carry petrol/diesel in plastic containers, so they couldn't possibly under any circumstances take them off my hands "More than my jobs worth Guv!", he said!"

"So you?"

"Gave him £10!"

"And?"

"Put them over there behind the shed Guv!"

"Bloody hell so it cost you £10 to get rid of 30 litres of diesel/petrol which is worth, what? £25 bloody hell, then there's the flowers which were £40 so the day had cost you let's see 60 +10 + 25 +40 bloody hell £135 and you haven't even left England yet!. Still nothing else could go wrong!"

"Erm.."

"Nooo!"

I didn't tell the ferry company that my vehicle was over-height so they wanted to charge me an extra £100 on the ferry!"

"What did you do?"

"Screamed burst into tears and threatened to kill myself!"

"Did it work?"

"The nice lady didn't seem to mind too much about me killing myself but it was the tears that got to her, so in the end she only charged me £38"

DATELINE FEZ 19-4-05

Well! After weeks driving through France (everywhere closed) and Spain (the biggest building site (and sight!) in Europe we arrived in Morocco. The border post at Cuerta is easy. It could be easier of course if they put the offices in the order that you have to do things, but the walk does you good and they only seem interested in whether you have a CB radio or a pistol!, presumably they expect you to contact them before you shoot them.

The all-pervading sounds (and smells) are unmistakably Arabic. For a race that prides themselves on personal cleanliness; their country is the pits when it comes to that same attribute. Everywhere there is litter and dirt; the smells are, for want of a
better word Anal, and not just animal Anal, a sewage connoisseur would be in his element.

When we finally entered Fez we resisted with considerable difficulty all temptations to mutter "Juslikethat" (any non English people will have no idea what that means nor will anyone who has never heard of Tommy Cooper!) and despite two motorcyclists and one car driver driving alongside and directing us to one campsite, we chose another (well THE other!), mainly because I'd punched in the wrong co-ordinates into the GPS which not only resulted in us booking in at the cheapest site but also pissed off three touts, all in all, a good result by anyone's standards.

A VISIT TO THE MEDINA
Today didn't quite turn out as we expected. Oh yes! We expected to go to the Medina but not quite by the route we finished up taking. Wandering out of the campsite we were greeted (accosted? waylaid?) by Aziz who kindly invited us to give him money so that we could accompany him around the Medina! He wanted 120 dirham's (around £9) for half a day. I wanted to know what half a day meant; in my book it's twelve hours! In his book it it's four. Oh! We did have fun discussing this! And in the end he agreed that I was of course correct twelve hours is in fact half a day, but in that case the charge would be 120 dirham's for four hours.

I'm not sure that I won that argument.

He told us to get on the bus (number 17 if anyone is interested) and get off at the terminus where he would meet us. He was going to follow us in his own car. No! Don't ask why we couldn't go in his car? I asked and still don't understand. Now that's not a problem is it? Just get off at the terminus..

"Didn't you ask how you would know when the bus was at the terminus?" "Noooooooo it's obvious! Everyone knows that at a terminus there's lots of buses stopped and everyone get's off, the

driver switches the engine off and leans against the bus smoking a cigarette!"

"So was it obvious and did everyone get off?"

You'll have guessed by now that the answer is "no" on both these counts and so we found ourselves still on the bus, happily watching the shops and cafes pass by until the shops and cafes were left behind to be replaced by countryside, nice countryside I'll grant you, but certainly not what we expected to see in the middle of a town.

Bear in mind that we had never been to Fez before, so when a traffic island came into sight with policemen on it, who looked familiar, I knew it was either a case of Déjà vu or that we had done a complete circle on the bus and were back where we started from.

Seeing our vehicle in the campsite confirmed it was the latter. We jumped up and off at the campsite entrance, trying to look as though the circular trip was exactly what we had intended all along, and I think we would have gotten away with it, had the next bus that we caught to return to Fez not been driven by the same driver and conducted by the same conductor.

We ignored their quizzical looks and looked at the fascinating sights that you see when you drive into Fez, wondering if they'd changed since the last time we'd seen them, but they hadn't (it had after all only been 90 minutes!)

This time we got off at the terminus. We knew it was the terminus because this time we asked the conductor! We waited for Aziz but he didn't arrive but then it was ninety minutes later, so we went to the Medina ourselves. You know what we soon realised? You don't need a guide, or a guidebook! It's not as complicated as people think, we wandered around for two hours, again giving the impression that we knew exactly what we were doing and where we were going, a view somewhat diluted by the fact that we saw the same stall five times and the very nice man running it treated us like old friends, which of course by then we were. The meat stalls were very … meaty, having for sale unidentifiable parts of unidentifiable animals. I suggested we get some but Jean demurred (translation! screamed NO! and threw up in a corner)

I think she was worried it wasn't fresh; it must be! ten thousand flies can't be wrong. I suggested that we buy a chicken, at least we knew it was fresh, it was still walking around.

Oh well vegetarian again tonight!

My unerring sense of direction meant we visited parts of the Medina not seen by a white man since the last crusade and just as Jean was about to lose confidence in my navigational powers, (something in truth she first lost about thirty years ago,) we found the way back.

I knew that Jean by this time would be feeling hungry (she often mistakes blind panic at being lost in a strange dangerous environment for hunger) so to placate her I bought her French stick, (cheaper than a meal!) and was very pleased that I had, because had I done with it what she suggested I do with the French stick, the alternative large flat Moroccan bread, especially the ones with nuts, could (in fact certainly would) have proved painful.

So that's it we're back sat the campsite, and Aziz is nowhere to be found (the guide is in fact lost!).

So to summarise, I lost at negotiating, I didn't get off a bus in the right place, I got lost in the Medina, Jean thinks I'm a useless idiot who is too tight to buy her a decent lunch.

All in all it's been a pretty normal day
Off tomorrow into the desert where my unerring sense of direction will get us through five thousand square miles of featureless countryside, that is if I can find my car keys which I've lost somewhere!

CAN LAND CRUISERS FLY
Route De Jaffer.. Midelt to Imichil

Well that was an experience! Only time will tell if it was a good one as the immediacy of ten hours of difficult and at times extremely scary driving fades and the sphincter muscles relax.

And it started off so easily. The book said that the Tour de Jaffer was a pleasant mountain drive through the Middle Atlas which you should take your time over and enjoy the view. What it didn't say was that at times the view as you looked out of the window was downwards and the only thing between you getting a much closer look at that view than you would really want (and which would have certainly been your last) was the friction of the tyres on rocks or sand as one side of the vehicle got higher and higher whilst the side I was sitting on got closer and closer to the ground!, or more exactly to the open air between the vehicle and the ground hundreds of feet below.

The width of the path obviously always exceeded the width of the car (that obviously sometimes being as much as an inch). The edge of the road, or ledge as I prefer to call it, was made of small stones that periodically and for no apparent reason jumped into the gorge.

Jean decided that she could contribute more by being outside the car so she opened the door and climbed out, well in truth up and out, and ran off down the path screaming. Eventually she stopped and turned back, carefully approaching the car, leant back in, retrieved the insurance documents from the glove compartment and from a very safe distance guided me through the tiny gaps by means of a semaphore system invented by and known only to her, and which she was amazed that I didn't immediately understand. Her demented screams which echoed through the valley and dislodged even more stones, eventually got the message home even to me.

Now if there are any tyre technologists reading this who are doing research into the co-efficient of friction between tyres of an overloaded Land Cruiser at an angle approaching forty-five degrees, and smooth rocks, please do not in your research ignore the contribution that knuckles gripping the steering wheel until they bleed whilst the owner of the knuckles mutters,
" Holy Shit!" Over and over again. Just a thought for you!

If you've forgotten let me remind you of what's happening, there's me in a car over a thousand foot gorge, the car leaning over at forty five degrees, and Jean out in front shouting advice at me. (Some of the advice being really helpful like "It was your bloody stupid idea to come this way!!")

It was at this stage that I remembered two things, the first was that all the books say that you shouldn't have too much weight high up on a vehicle as it makes it unstable, and ours had a bloody great roof tent on it, and the second thing was that if you lift the suspension on a vehicle to make the ground clearance better you make it even more unstable. The Land Cruiser had been lifted by two and a half inches!

As you can imagine at that moment neither of these two thoughts gave me much comfort!
Suddenly I had a thought.
"So that's three thoughts then, something of a record for you in a day Watts!"
"Are you going to let me finish?"
"Do I have an option?"

I remembered seeing those yachting people leaning far out to stop the yachty thingies falling over and wondered if Jean could be persuaded to do the same, but I immediately dismissed the idea for two reasons. Firstly we were so close to the rock wall she couldn't lean out and secondly I didn't want the last words I heard as I plummeted over the edge to be Jeans' foul and abusive language.

I considered reversing back along the cliff face but you're talking to a man who can't reverse into parking bay in an empty supermarket car park, so that idea was quickly discarded

Opening my eyes I saw that Jean had waved me on, low first, don't do anything suddenly, the car lumped forward inched even higher then levelled, I closed my eyes, it didn't help, so I opened them! All Ok! Forward again the back wheels slipping in the loose gravel, accelerating gently to lift me over a rock, leaning away from the drop towards the passenger seat (as if that will make any difference!) the car cants over even more, nothing I can do now except ease it forward and hope.

Suddenly a knocking, quiet at first then louder, what the Hell is it? I tear my eyes from the path in front and out of the corner of my eye a little brown hand is tapping the window. I look out and down. Oh my God! The drop is closer than I thought and squeezed between the drop and me is a little girl. "Donnez moi du bon-bon, Donnez moi une stylo, Donnez moi quelle qui chose!"
Bloody Hell I am not kidding, there she was right at the edge of the cliff between a three tonne land cruiser driven by a white haired (the three remaining dark hairs had turned white, in fact even the bald spot had turned white) Englishman, and a bloody great drop, she stood hand extended and she wants a sweet, or a pen or something, I admit I was rude and ignored her but I secretly wondered if I did slide whether hitting her would stop me slipping off the edge
I know I am! but I was under stress!

After eventually crawling through this part of the "Tour", which turned out to be the worst we faced, for the rest of the day we picked our way through a hundred miles teetering on the edge of drops; running out of road, fording oudis (streams), and easing our way round blind bends hoping nothing was coming the other way, or, remembering our earlier predicament, dropping on our roof! About half way along we stopped at an Auberge for mint tea and I asked if he 8had many people through that day.

"Non!"
"This week?"
"Non!"
"This month?"
"Non!"
"Why do you have no visitors do you think?"
"Parce-qui le route c'est trop difficile"
Bloody Hell now they tell me.

When we finally arrived at Imichil it was grey cold and very
windy. I was informed by Jean that we would be staying in a
hotel. A Hotel!!!!!!! I attempted to open negotiations but soon
found I was talking to myself as Jean was already in the
reception. In an attempt to save face in front of the interested
(but in truth not interesting) locals I ended the day by saying
to the Land Cruiser.
"You are joking!" and followed her in.
Inside were other travellers who also had come from Midelt.
"It's strange that we didn't see you on the road" they said
"Yes it's very very difficult isn't it! I was scared of the drops
in places!"
They looked at each other,
"Drops?"
"Drops!"
"What drops?"
"The drops where the road was giving way!"
"There were no drops the road was new and flat!"
It turned out that I'd turned right too soon for, a short way
after we'd turned off, was a brand new road, Jean gave me a
look that was colder than weather, but I am sure she will
speak to me again, possibly, probably, perhaps, eventually.

WE HAVE A STOWAWAY
Oh yes nearly forgot! as a "P.S." to the scary trip, what you
don't do is ask anyone under the age of twenty for directions,

they'll certainly send you the wrong way, I'm not sure why, but it happens too often for it to be a coincidence but that's what they do.
I'd learnt this lesson to my cost when I'd slowed down near a group of Moroccans to ask for directions. I asked the old man who nodded wisely and pointed knowledgeably but obviously had no idea what I was talking about.

One particular youth looked trustworthy, well less untrustworthy than the others, so we asked him and his answer at least appeared to be correct so off we went again, only to come to another cross-roads a couple of hundred yards further on. I stopped and the same youth appeared at the door, and again told me the way, now how the hell did he do that?

After a couple of hundred yards suddenly Jean said, "He's on the back!" and he was! Hanging happily onto the back of the vehicle, feet on bumper holding onto the roof rack. I swerved and braked, trying to dislodge him, but he swallowed a mouthful of sand and when I looked in the mirror he laughed and waved back at me.

At the next crossroads he simply waved me on and I accepted the inevitable, the inevitable being that we were going where he wanted to go and all we could hope was that where he wanted to go was the same as where we wanted to go (I think that's what I meant to write!!!)

At one stage he hammered on the car side and shouted something in Arabic, which turned out later to be roughly translated as,
"You can see my house from up here!"

Finally we arrived at village and he came to the window wanting "une cadeau!" for helping us but seemed to accept my "Bugger off!" quite philosophically, and he then pointed us vaguely in the general direction we needed and ran off.

Finally (and how I will never know) we got out without falling off the mountain, without scratching the vehicle and I'm sorry I am about to swear! Without shitting ourselves, but all three were damned close, and in truth I could be wrong about the third

Ten hours of hard driving to cover one hundred miles to finish up at Imichil, as I've already said, a mountain village that was cold unattractive and so high you have an altitude headache.

So why did you do it you may ask, and the answer from me would be,
"'Cos I am stupid and it was there and it was fun!"
And the answer from Jean would be!"
"You must by now know that Jeff is stupid?"
"I just said that!"

ERG CHEBBI
Erg Chebbi is the remains of an inland sea and throughout the region there are fossils for sale (and in my case as visitors!.. think about it!!) which are thrust at you every time you do anything.

"Yes it's a beautiful stone and yes I know it's cheap but for Gods sake can't a man have a wee in peace!"

From a distance the orange yellow dunes look like waves shimmering in the scorching Saharan heat and which I have to confess, looked irresistible to a man with a 4X4 and who is stupid.

Remembering the Jaffer gorge I hired a local guide to keep us out of trouble. Now at first appearance Hassan is a typical Moroccan, handsome in his dark blue jerbolla, fluent in many languages and with a broad grin he switched on easily when he spoke to Jean, but as we got to know him, to my pleasure and to Jeans disgust, it transpired that in addition to his other attributes he was just as stupid as I am, and when he got bored with the easy road he got us stuck in the dunes, twice!

Now if we had been on our own Jean would have found it impossible not to comment, however it was Hassan, dark swarthy Hassan with white teeth dark hair and handsome face, who got us stuck so no comment was made Huh! And she thinks I didn't notice, and another thing, where was he when I was digging hot sand out from under the car? Chatting Jean up that's where he was!

I dug, they watched, after I'd sweated for a while he wandered over and let some air out of the tyres, and I drove out. Bloody hell how much effort did that take? but that was the answer! Let some air out the tyres and you drive out. I knew that but in the heat I'd forgotten.
EASY!!
Another great day.

IT'S MY TREE

It's a good rule of thumb when on the road that if someone approaches you they want to sell you something, which you wouldn't mind if what they wanted to sell you was an incredible bargain, it never is! The ones who approach you invariably try and rip you off.

I mentioned earlier that when we were approaching Fez two motorcyclists and a car drove alongside us all trying to direct us to a campsite, well it happened again in Erg Chebbi when we were ambushed by a "man on a moped".

We ignored him, and for a while he drove slowly in front of us, until he realised that behind him was an old Englishman just itching to have a(nother) trophy on his bull bars!. We looked for a campsite that we liked but they were all totally devoid of shade or full of French camper vans, so it was with reluctance we agreed to follow the "man on a moped" to his campsite (he'd learnt his lesson by now and was driving alongside us!). His "campsite" turned out to be a small rickety square building and a small tree in the middle of a large area of sand.

"Where's you're campsite then?"

"This is my camp site"

"Aaaaah ... Ok no thanks!"

"You don't like my camp site?" all hurt and injured,

"It's not a camp site it's a hut that's about to fall down and a tree!"

"Yes but it's my tree and you can have it a special rate!"

We left!!

We finally found a campsite that served beer, cold beer, small expensive beer but cold beer! The first beer disappeared very quickly, the second almost as quickly. I asked (nay demanded) a third.

"Not possible Sir!"

Thinking there was a customer limit I smiled my best, "Don't piss with me " smile but he said,

"No Sir! The 'fridge is locked and the bar manager has gone off with the key."

He was surprised when I asked why; well the look of surprise may have been shock as I was gripping him by the throat by this time,
"Well" he explained "if the bar manager leaves the 'fridge unlocked people drink all the beer!"

For once in my life I was speechless, and drowned my sorrows with some water.

It had been one of those days.

MARRAKECH
Driving north -north east from the desert to Marrakech over the High Atlas, the road tarred now, but without the, albeit illusory, comfort of a barrier between the road and the valleys far below, and the temptation to tear your eyes away from the road and look at the view is easily resisted especially with Jean screaming in your ear,
"Look at the road not the scenery!"

When you do stop at the lay-bys the contrasts in the countryside are unique. Orange and green valleys fall away before eventually rising to meet the snow capped mountains in the far distance.

Everywhere men were selling brightly coloured stones, vivid orange and black, but the hassle when you stop and the ever present negotiating makes stopping hardly worth the trouble.

Since the advent of European travel; no that's not true! Since the advent of travel, people have brought back "souvenirs" which were so irresistible at the time and which were bargained for with such intensity, but which stand on shelves forlornly until eventually they are thrown out usually after the traveller had died by people who have no notion of their importance,.

So that's Morocco, a land of contrasts an easy introduction to the delights and frustrations of travel in Africa.

TWO LAST FERRIES

"So you're back in Europe what did you think of Morocco?"

"It was nothing like I expected! I thought there would be lots of sand!"

"Well it is the Sahara!"

"Yes but it also has amazing mountain ranges, the middle and the High Atlas, and the Rif and also rolling countryside not unlike Wiltshire!

"Knowing you're navigation Watts it probably was!"

"And Marrakech itself was fascinating, especially at night when the central square was filled with food stalls and people, I saw a man dancing and playing the guitar with a chicken on his head!"

"Or alternatively you saw a chicken standing on a man who was playing the guitar!"

"That's just silly!"

"And a man playing the guitar with a chicken on his head isn't?"

"It didn't seem so at the time and the chicken was squawking and it sounded to me like it was saying "I can see my coop from up here!"

And there was this other man who had a pile of boxing gloves who asked me if I wanted to fight him, I'm not sure why, but I didn't stop to find out...

"Look this is getting even more boring than usual, tell me nothing else happened so we can get on with our lives?"

"Apart from the problem with the return ferry! No!"

"Good!"

"You're supposed to say, "What was the problem with the return ferry?""
"I know what I'm supposed to say but after all this time I am sincerely desperate not to know!"
"Ok I won't tell you!"
"Yes you will!"
"Ok I will then!"
"How did I know that!"

"You know that Cuerta is a Spanish enclave (well in truth it's an exclave!")
"Well of course it is!"
" Well it's squeezed in between the North of Morocco and the Mediterranean, so when you actually leave mainland Africa you are in fact already in Spain!"
"Ok that makes sense!"
"And when they gave us the timetable it said that the last ferry from Cuerta, the Moroccans call it Sebta, I'll bet you didn't know that,!"
"Why do they call Cuerta Sebta!"
"Now..there's a good reason for that!"
"What is it?"
"I didn't say I knew what the good reason was I only said that there's a good reason for it! Where was I?, Oh yes the timetable said that the last ferry from Cuerta left at 8.30, and as it was only 6.30 we had lots of time, we even thought about going shopping, but what they didn't tell us was that the 8.30 was 8.30 Spanish time not 8.30 Moroccan time, which was in fact 6.30 Moroccan time, and that as we had by now we had crossed into Spain, the 8.30 was in fact 6.30, which was the time of the last ferry, still with me?"
"No!"
"Ok I'll go through it again.. the timetable said.."
"NO! For God's sake no!! just tell me what happened!"

"Well obviously we missed the ferry, and there wasn't another one till the morning, and we had bought a return ticket, and they wouldn't let us use it on the next ferry that was leaving in twenty minutes!"

"You said the last ferry had gone!"

"Yes, well no, the last ferry of the company we had a ticket for had gone but there was one more last ferry of another company"

"Two last ferries then!"

"Yes! So anyway we decided to buy a one way ticket for he second last ferry even though we had the return portion of the two way ticket for the company with the first last ferry!"

"First last ferry?"

"Yes, so you see the problem!"

"No but it doesn't matter, you lost me at the 8.30 6.30 part!"

"The result was that we bought a ticket one way from Cuerta (or Sebta if you're a Moroccan) and the return portion of the ticket for the first company's ferry whose last ferry left before the second company's last ferry I still have!, but it could have been worse. Ask me why?"

"Sorry? I was dozing there. Why?"

"Well by buying a return ticket from the first company operating the first last ferry we got a discount of €20 for the return part, so we in fact saved that on the amount we would have paid if we had have not missed the first company's last ferry and had to spend €100 on the one way ticket for the second company's second last ferry.

No look I'll start again.. Cuerta is in Spain The Moroccans call it Sebta you know!) and is...no don't go come back..It's very rude to walk away in the middle of a conversation..."

AUSTRALIA OR BUST

So I'm not cured!!! But then I don't believe dromomania (From the Greek: dromos (running) and mania (insanity)) is ever truly cured!! I thought I'd got over it, but like the alcoholic or the smoker, I wasn't.

It had started so innocently, in town shopping on a Saturday morning, sulking. I don't like shopping! I particularly don't like shopping for clothes, I have some clothes why would I want any more? So I was sulking, pouting, and generally being even more than usually objectionable, childish and unbearable.

"Look if you're going to behave like a child, just go into the book shop, I'll see you later!"

Now I didn't have to go to the travel section, I could have just as easily gone to browse the fiction or the erotica, these days both the same to me, but I didn't! I was drawn inexorably and irresistibly to travel.

A map of Africa and the southern hemisphere beckoned, I resisted but it proved too much. Without realising it my finger traced a line down through West Africa around the Bight of Benin, through Congo and into Angola, Namibia, Botswana, and I knew the addiction was back.

All it took now was to chat to Jean, and though she went through the motions of complaining in the end all she really said was,

"This time you're not going to put us in the position where we could slide off a mountain track!"

"Of course not!"

"And just because a track goes off the main road we don't HAVE to drive down it!"

"Absolutely"

"And this time we ARE going to book into a good hotel so i can shower and relax!"

"As long as it's not too expensive!"

"DON'T!"

"Sorry!"

"And this time you will change your socks more than once a week!"

"Bloody Hell you're being unreasonable now!"

We had worked with Les and Marian many years ago in Zambia, and we have a lot in common, Les and I love travel, cricket, and beer.

Marian and Jean have a lot in common too, they both think that their (each others, and I suspect everyone else's) husbands are at best incompetent and at worst idiots, so at a dinner party when he mentioned he wanted to see the cricket in Australia, three bottles of wine suggested we drive there and three bottles answered,

"Ok!"

So that's it, we're driving through the Atlantic route of Africa to South Africa then we'll put the vehicles on a boat to Australia and go and watch some cricket!

"Do you think that we are driving to Australia just to watch bloody cricket?"

"Yes dear!"

"WHAT?"

"No dear!"

OFF WE GO!
ENGLAND
Well we got away on time…on the day we intended and with almost everything we need. Unfortunately the most important thing we absolutely shouldn't leave home without was left at home, but only time will tell what it is.

Oh yes! One last thing I made a will! if anything terminal happens on the trip and I haven't got a will the family will get everything!!

The first night saw us in a Bed and Breakfast in Battle, brought about by the most horrendous rainstorm that we have seen, now I know that intrepid expedititioners scoff scornfully (or is it scorn scoff fully) at even the heaviest of rain but as I was only in the south of England at that stage we weren't strictly speaking on an expedition, more like a days holiday, it didn't count.

In case any of you are interested Battle is of course where the Battle of Hastings took place, but I suppose they called it the Battle of Hastings because the Battle of Battle would just sound silly, and the Hastings of Hastings even sillier.
"I was sorry that my name wasn't Harold,"
"Why is that Jeff?"
"Because then I could have phoned Les and Marion and said "Hi it's Harold here, meet me in Battle, I'll keep an eye out for you!""
"Bloody hell how long you planning to be away for?"
"Nine months.. Why?"
"Because if that's the standard of writing it's going to be a long long nine months!"

We met up with Les and Marion at the Dover Docks, which surprised us both and gave us confidence that if we could find Dover Docks then why would we be worried about Africa?, a confidence I am sure that will prove to be misplaced over the coming months.

SPAIN
We took the west coast route down through France entering Spain through the top North East corner and then turned south through surprisingly green countryside and on superb new roads. Things change so much in a year.

We wanted to keep moving south eager to get to the start of the expedition.. Africa! But we couldn't resist a night in Salamanca, wandering around its magnificent central square, which is probably in the top five of my favourite cities, but then I'm a square person.
"As opposed to a round person?"

Our two vehicles attract people who appear fascinated by the concept of roof top tents inhabited by geriatrics; seemingly amazed that we can even climb the ladders let alone drive the damn things. It's a conversation starter, whilst my, "Bugger off and stop asking damn silly questions" is just the opposite.

It's interesting the people you meet. Old hands at travelling and real newbies like Ruth and Jim from the northeast. I love the accent and, believe it or not, they really do say "wayaa aye". They were a month into a six-month tour in a new camper and still had the sparkly eyes that you get when something planned is as good as you imagined! (Unlike my wedding night! but that's another story!)

I told them the trick of putting your dirty washing in a bucket in the morning and then driving all day, preferably on rough roads, so that by the evening the washing is clean (well clean enough! .. we are on an "EXPEDITION" after all!)

WARNING! THIS NEXT BIT ISN'T VERY NICE SO IF YOU OFFEND EASILY PLEASE SKIP IT

Using the bucket in this way is what we do, and of course Les and Marion now do the same. Unfortunately space being at a premium the loo bucket and the wash bucket has to double up. So each morning you have to empty it of its .. erm .. night time emissions, usually over the tents of the noisy neighbours.
"It's pissing down!"
"That's truer than you think!" And, after trying to remember to swill the bucket out thoroughly, the dirty clothes are dropped into the water and detergent added and they mix happily all day until the evening when they are taken out,

rinsed, rung out and hung out to dry, whilst the bucket then reverts to its other function of being a portable loo....

Still with me? No problems? No? Well yes! Now imagine if you will if for some reason, after you have rung out the washing, but then (say) because you are too drunk to be bothered to hang the washing out (yes Marion, drunk was the word I used) what you don't do is simply drop then clothes back into the loo bucket and say,

"Bugger this I'll do it tomorrow!" because if you do, someone (who for the purpose of illustration only we will call Les) will take the loo bucket to the tent and at about two a.m. as the beer works its inexorable way through the system, will use the loo bucket and fail to notice that noise is somewhat different to usual, and not notice the second and third time either...

Marion's morning greeting of,

"Les!!! You've pissed on the washing!" Was as unique as it was loud and caused the other campers to glance nervously at each other. I only hope non-English speakers there do not mistake it for a traditional British greeting.

So we are here at Tarifa, windy Tarifa the Mecca for kiters and wind surfers and after two days resting (and of Marion desperately trying to get the faint odour of Ammonia from her clothes) we are ready for the first real part of the "Expedition" ... Morocco

> *There are over seven hundred wind turbines running along the tops of the hills outside Tarifa and they dominate the skyline, the received wisdom is that they kill thousands of birds each year but apparently they don't! It's a rumour put out by the anti wind turbine brigade. I asked the man at the campsite an obvious question, well obvious to me! "How do you know how many birds it kills? Do they have someone who stands under them and count the dead birds, well count the*

*ones that haven't been eaten by the local foxes?" Of
course they don't! They almost certainly get someone
to pop up every year or so watch the birds for half an
hour and say,*
*"Bugger this let's call it 200,000! Anyone fancy a
paella?"*

*So I suspect that this is another "ahh shame!"
argument put forward by those not wanting wind
power. Risks to birds from wind turbines have to be
weighed against the technology's environmental
contribution as a clean energy source. For example,
the Exxon Valdez oil spill alone is estimated to have
killed between 375,000 and 500,000 birds (but then
again who counted?).*
*Climate change also poses a massive threat to birds,
and wind power's ability to hopefully slow the change
is accepted by the Royal Society for the Protection of
Birds, which actively encourages new wind farm
developments.*

On a more serous note than the effect of global warming on
the future of mankind, I have to top the water in the radiator
up more frequently than I expect to, what I'm really trying to
say is that I shouldn't expect to top the damn thing up at all!
Which could mean anything from a small leak somewhere in
the water cooling system to a cracked cylinder head, not good
news at this stage, but I'll monitor it and keep my fingers
crossed, expecting the worse..

This from the man who, a couple of days ago whilst driving
developed a pain in the hip bone which I self diagnosed as
firstly a muscle pull; then degeneration of the hip joint which
would require immediate replacement in hospital with all the
consequent danger of MRSA; then bone cancer which even as

I sat there was spreading to all four corners of my body and I was going die a horrible and lingering death with my family around me giving me the support I deserve such as,
"For God's sake go if you're going, were missing valuable drinking time and we've already defrosted the vol-au-vents!"

I even drafted out my funeral service but couldn't think of any hymns except "Away in a Manger" and "Leaving on a Jet Plane",
it turned out that I'd twisted my belt when putting it on in the morning and it was digging into my rib!!!

Spain then continues to be an enjoyable place to pass through and a couple of days in Tarifa enabled us to gird out loins (whatever that means!.. has any one ever used the word GIRD in any other context but with ones Loins!!!) before tackling Africa.

MOROCCO
Well we made it into Morocco, where in truth the "EXPEDITION" starts.
Although we were staying in Tarifa the decision was made to sail from Algeceiras, mainly I think because of the rumours of hassle that you get from touts in Tangiers, where the Tarifa ferry sails to. Now hassle never bothers me, in fact I'd go so far as to say I enjoy it… which comes, I am informed by people who know me well, from a deep seated disinterest in the feelings of others, and if the "others" are trying to part me from the love of my life (the contents of my wallet!) so much the better.

An early start to catch the ferry, a couple of right turns brought us neatly into the container terminal, which is exactly the same mistake that we made last year, so, retracing our steps and passing the rotting remains of other travellers who have made the same mistake and never quite made it out. We bought our tickets from one of the row of agents all of whom charge exactly the same amount, but it didn't stop me asking, and joined the queue for the thirty five minute crossing to Cuerta, which the Moroccans call Sebta, before braving the crowded and dusty ride along the Avenue d'Africa. This is a good road and the best feature of it is that it leads you nicely out of town!

(In case you are interested, I'm sitting in the campsite at Chefchauhan typing this with the engine running and the computer plugged into the inverter (what's the difference between converter and an inverter?)…The seat was getting hotter and hotter which obviously meant that the exhaust pipe had got a hole and was due to break off and fill the cab with carbon monoxide and I would sink slowly into a coma. Then I realised I was sitting on the warm connection box thingy that converts (inverts?) the 240 volts that has been inverted (converted?) from the 12 volt battery in the car.. down to …oh bugger, it's not important!.. where was I?)

I had no fears about the border crossing into Morocco as I'd done it last year!

They changed it!!!
And it's better…so the system is as follows.
Ignore the first man who offers you a white immigration card. You'll already have one of those from the people who sold you the ticket…follow the pointed instructions that takes you straight through to the offices and park. A wizened old man comes and tells you where to go.
Obey him he's official! Wizened! But official.
Take your passport with your white card to the man in the first kiosk, he ticks, checks and does whatever and does and stamps your passport.

Go to the next window the man there gives you a three-part form which you complete, in my case totally incorrectly, and hand that and your vehicle registration document to another bored looking man who resignedly changes everything you've entered, and stamps the form.

You then go to a group of uniformed customs men and wait patiently for them to finish their conversation, when they don't you say not quite so patiently.

"OI let's have some bloody service round here!"

Which seems to work. One of them takes your papers and with another man who appears from nowhere comes with you to examine your vehicle. So picture the scene! There's you, a customs man and the third man who turns out to be police, all standing looking into the back of your vehicle and asking disinterestedly, if you have a firearm.

I answered in the negative, and didn't joke; sometimes even I know when it's not appropriate. The policeman who was about 6'3" high and just as wide looked at the map on the side of the vehicle, then told me that the southern part of morocco was not another country as shown on the map on the side of the car but was in fact owned by Morocco.. The intellectual quality of his arguments I found persuasive but not as persuasive as his sheer size so I agreed to agree.

You then take your paper to another man who stamps it! You smile and bid your farewells using the policeman as shade, and that's it. Well apart from having to show the passports to another man and the vehicle paperwork to yet another!

I'm still not sure about insurance and I haven't got a green card so am I insured?, should I have said something?. You know what I have no idea!!!

POSTSCRIPT

Big mistake on the insurance! It turns out I should have bought insurance at the border, but I didn't and luckily got away with it, not being asked for a copy of the insurance and more importantly not having a crash. I don't recommend you follow my actions or advice.

But then I don't recommend you do that anyway!!!

CHEFCHAUHAN

Chefchauhan is an old city famous for its medina and square surrounded with nice cafes, with a good campsite, except for dogs barking (memo to me! prepare poison sausages!) and some sod tried to rip me off!!!!

In case I haven't already told you, and I suspect I might have, I'm often asked what I would never travel without, and people think I am joking when I say "poison sausages" I'm not!! They are soooo useful to quieten the barking dog! And the campers who talk all night depriving me of much needed sleep are invited to a BBQ the following day by "That nice old man in the Land Cruiser" and guess what they are fed on!!! You got it!! Sausages!!!

Bastards!

I had a mint tea and orange juice and needed a wee (the old prostate problem raised its ugly head, unlike anything else in that region these days unfortunately!!)…And across the square was the public loo and here a wizened (I have decided I like that word!) old man was sweeping the steps and, seeing me mounting the steps on tip toes two at a time, rightly surmised that I was a man in need so he rushed to open the locked door… As I passed a small table..

"Was it wizened Jeff?"

AS I PASSED A SMALL TABLE……………!!!!

"Sorry!"

I noticed there was a bowl with a hand written "1 DHM" on it (for those of you not on an "EXPEDITION" 1 dirham (DHM) is about 6p) 6p a pee seemed extortionate (and is also surprisingly difficult to say) but needs must etc. On the way out our wizened friend pointed to the bowl where the paper now read "2DHM" a 100% increase in the time it takes to have a piss. Now I have to admit 1DHM is not a lot but it's not the principle it's the money!.

I demurred! vehemently, violently and vociferously! Reaching forward I turned the paper over. Sure enough on the back was "1DHM". Ahh differential pricing!!!! And he obviously had me down as a "2DHM" man whereas I, who had recently had the evidence to hand as it were, knew I was most definitely only a 1DHM man.

Oh! We did enjoy the ensuing chat and left the best of friends…well we left with me calling him a "cheating old bastard" and him answering me in Arabic…and I doubt he was saying, "thanks for your custom"
It's moments like this that makes travel worthwhile.

I mentioned earlier that I had to top up the radiator with water more often than I should have and sure enough the new radiator, fitted before the start of the trip, had a leak. Being Sunday morning I thought I'd have problems getting it replaced, but of course being a Muslim country and a country where business is hard. The first little workshop we came to simply sent the lad off and a man arrived armed with just one spanner and a screwdriver. I looked unimpressed but he quickly disconnected the radiator, called up a man with a small motorbike, jumped on the back and roared off with the radiator under his arm.

We settled down to wait, and wait, and wait! A couple of hours went by and I was convinced that by now the radiator was half way to Casablanca fitted to another land cruiser!! But all we could do is what travellers do best! Sit at the side of the road, wait and accept that you are the centre of attention.

People spoke and smiled and even got Jean and Marion chairs and cokes! When he eventually came back I looked doubtfully at the repair, it didn't look as nice as when it was first fitted, but it seemed water tight, which is more than the fancy looking one was!

And it was! I changed it 15000 miles later after abusing it dreadfully and the repair held.

MAURITANIAN VISA

Before leaving on the trip we read the web sites; we read "Lonely Planet"; we read "Africa on a Shoestring"; so we set off happy in the knowledge that we could get the Mauritanian Visa from Rabat, and that we would get the Mali visa in Casablanca.

WRONG!!

The Mauritanian Embassy looked strangely deserted as we alighted from the "petit bleu taxi", (it's a taxi, it's small and it's blue!) we stood and waited, a habit that you develop quickly in Africa.

"That's a good point Jeff can you really wait quickly?"

Anyway a man eventually wandered over and said,

"You want a Visa?"

"Yes!"

"Casablanca!"

"Erm! Nooo! The books say that you can get it here by being here at 8.30 and here we are at 8.35 so we'd like a visa please!"

"Casablanca!"

"Sorry you're not listening! Now you're obviously under a delusion here, now go away and find me someone who appreciates the impotence …

"Do you mean importance Jeff!"

"...of my contribution to the Mauritanian economy and who will not only want to give me a visa forthwith but who will probably also want to make me honorary Prime Minister "Casablanca!!"

So that's it! the visa is now apparently issued in Casablanca.

HOWEVER!!!!!!!!!!!!!!!!

Just a hundred yards further on there is the Malian Embassy. Now according to Rough Guide, Lonely Planet etc. the Malian Visa is issued in Casablanca…so to confirm it we wandered down and said to the man,

"Good morning!"

"Visa?" he said, "come!"

We were ushered into a cavernous ornately tiled room, furnished with an outsize empty desk and a few chairs, at which sat a very large immaculately dressed man reading a French newspaper.

"Bonjour", J'ai dis" (that's actual French in case you didn't recognise the accent)

"Nous voudrons une visa s'il vous plait!"

He looked up slowly from his newspaper,

"I will require two passport photographs and two hundred and fifty dirhams, or sixty US dollars!"

"Ahh you speak English!"

He gave me a look that said, "Better than you do Boyo!"

Reaching into a drawer he pulled out four blank documents and dropped them on his desk, and returned to his newspaper.

Underneath his newspaper was the post, four unopened letters which I presume he was not rushing to open as there was obviously not much going on and if he did it now, there would be nothing else to do all day.

We completed the forms and waited whilst he finished another part of the newspaper at his own pace, my little voice inside me said,

"He's taking the mickey Jeff... give him a kicking!"

I coughed, he read more slowly, and the only thing that prevented me from following the perfectly reasonable advice from my inner voice was that,

(a) I hadn't got my visa yet,

(b) He was about 6' 5",

Eventually he looked up and feigned surprise that we were still there.

"Sixty Dollars!"

He took his time counting three twenty-dollar notes before saying,

"When do you leave Rabat!"

"Tomorrow. Early!"

"Come back this afternoon after three o'clock" and returned to his newspaper. Apparently we were dismissed!!

There is little else to tell you. To get to the Embassy from the camping in Sale you get a "grand taxi" from Sale to Rabat (30 dhms) then a "petite bleu" from the centre of Rabat to the embassy (it's on a meter but it's about 20 dhms).

The only other thing to report is that we decided to get the local bus back to town from the embassy (4.60 dhms) and a charming lady offered me the last seat,

"Ah non merci madame" j'ai dis (French again) "après vous"

"Non monsieur pour vous"

"Non madame pour vous"

"NON!"

"OUI!"

I was determined that she would learn that she was in the presence of an English gentleman even if I had to slap her. Eventually she said,

"Monsieur je suis la conductress.. Maintenant ASSEYEZ VOUS!!!!!

I sat!

The collection of the visa "come back after three o'clock" was uneventful. We sat in the same cavernously ornate room with the same immaculately dressed man, the newspaper finished, and two of the letters still unopened.

He looked at us without smiling, he opened his lunch box hopefully but was disappointed to see it was empty, then sipped equally hopefully from an equally empty water bottle, and it was only with great difficulty I prevented myself from approaching him (by the throat!), but experience has shown, as satisfying as this is, this doesn't help, so I tried the diplomatic, oblique approach.

"So how long do you think I should ask the taxi driver to wait?"

Admit it you're impressed, subtle but requiring an answer!

The answer was equally oblique consisting as it did of a shrug and a "vingt ou vingt-cinq minutes!"

I sat down ignoring my inner voice who, as always, was recommending more direct action, until suddenly and for no apparent reason, he left the room returning almost immediately with the passports, and not only with the passports but also with a great big smile.

"They have arrived!"

We were given a book to sign and he continued to smile ingratiatingly,

"I should finish at 3.30 it's now 3.55 perhaps you should pay me $1 per minute overtime"

The little voice roared in my ear!

"That's it! He's taking the piss now hit him, tell him where to stick his visa!"

I smiled feigning ignorance of his meaning and he reluctantly handed over the passports...not too bad though! ... Same day service, and with a smile of sorts. Unusual in Africa. Unusual anywhere!

MAURITANIA

An early start saw us speeding down the autoroute to Casablanca to get to the erstwhile Mauritanian embassy.

It's easy enough to find, the trick being of course firstly to get the right city, and secondly to follow the GPS points you found on the internet, and miraculously you're there, park, go to the window and ask for the form. You'll need two passport pictures and a copy of the information page from the passport, complete the form, show it to the man who looks smiles and says "Attendez". "Attendez" is the same as waiting but so much more "foreign!"

Get to a seat and "attendez" having remembered to take your book in with you, and you settle down until they think you've waited long enough to establish their importance and then for no apparent reason they say,

"Entrez!"

Into the office of the man who sits behind a large desk and
slowly completes his reading of a circular advertising garden
sheds or something before opening your passport and looking
through it,
"Why you want to go to Mauritania!"
My immediate thought was to tell him "So I can get out the
other side as quickly as possible ... Tosser!"
"Because I have read that it is beautiful and I want to see it for
myself!"

Little voice in brain says "Jesus! Watts!" and vomits,
He finishes looking and says,
"Quatre-vingt Euros!" We gave him quatre-vingt euros,
departed and sent Les and Marion in.
Outside I said to Jean,
"How much was that?"
"Eighty euros!"
"But the man there said four hundred Dhms which is forty
euros ... cheeky sod ... time for a chat I think!"
Back into the office where Les and Marion are sitting,
"Excuse me!" I say, "I would prefer to pay in dirhams"
"No! Only Moroccans can pay in dirhams"
"Ok, if it's only four hundred dirhams for two which is forty
euros, why did you charge me eighty euros!"
"He charged us 90 euros!" said Marion
He suddenly reached for his 'phone and made a number of
calls, but I could tell he was stalling for time whilst
desperately trying to think of a good reason for overcharging
us, but, failing to come up with an explanation, he eventually
and reluctantly gave us the forty and fifty euros back, and
mentally cancelled the order for a garden shed.

He told us to return tomorrow for the visa. Time will tell if we get it.

CAMPING OASIS CASABLANCA

Right! So after getting your visa for Mauritania you'll need to camp whilst waiting for the visa, here's what you do.

Leave the Embassy drive up the road, take the wrong turn, drive down a dual carriage way looking for an island, nothing, spot a gap, slow down suddenly, apologise to the man you cut up, shout,

"And you sunshine!" back at him, pull into the out slip of a garage just missing a motorbike. Well I think I just missed him ... (Memo to self.. check front bull bars for unwanted Moroccan body parts, well unwanted by me, I'm sure he's very keen to get them back!), turn right, then right again, then left round and island twice before stopping at a café, ask for croissants, watch man run off to patisserie to buy them, watch him come back, enjoy them so much you ask him for some more, watch him run off again muttering in Arabic,

"Why didn't you ask for eight in the first place?"

Talk to man in cafe who draws you a map of the camping, follow map, realise that whilst man in cafe is a very nice man, map drawing isn't his strong point, spot camping, pull across three lanes of traffic, sound horn in reply to all of the drivers who test their horns (they all work) ... pull into camping ...

We drove seventeen miles and it took one hour twenty minutes. When we asked the man in camping the following morning, the quickest way to get to Mauritanian embassy, he says,

"You can walk it in five minutes it is immediately behind the camping!"

And the moral to that is?

How the hell should I know what the moral is!

MARRAKECH

Well! The bloody Marakeshian taxi driver bringing us back from a night in Marrakech nearly wrote us off. He didn't quite know where the entrance to the campsite was, so he did the obvious thing, he turned onto the opposite side of the road and stopped side on to the oncoming traffic, which was approaching at alarming speed. Looking out at the car lights and I thought "Oh dear!" What in fact I said was "JESUS FUCKING CHRIST" and tried to get out of the car over the drivers lap.

My Christian fist in his Moslem groin galvanized him into action and he accelerated, as the car with its brakes squealing louder than
I was, missed the back of us by inches. Even I was speechless.. so
shocked and speechless that I didn't even argue when he charged us for the journey…as I sit here now I can think of a number of things to say all of which escaped me at the time, and I have to report that words weren't all that escaped me! Looking back now I wish I had got his name and address. I could at least have returned his Islamic testacles, which are now hanging from my rear view mirror as a memento of an extremely scary moment.

FEZ

Just a few words about Fez, which I thoroughly enjoyed, and we spent a long time around the souk, which is what they call the local market, with a guide. Now for some reason I always object to paying for guides, which shouldn't surprise those who know me as I always object to paying for anything. (You'll have noticed by now I am sure how often "object" and "paying" appear in the same sentence).

The guide showed us all the usual things and explained the reasons why Shi'ite and Sunni Moslems kill each other. Which was as unfathomable to me as the reasons why Catholics and Protestants kill each other; why Moslems and Christians kill each other; or why Jews and Arabs kill each other. He spent a lot of time explaining and I am truly none the wiser! I often thank God I'm an atheist!!

I really wanted to see the dying vats, where the skins that have been stripped from the carcasses are dried and dipped in vats of dye, a system unchanged in thousands of years. And from the smell, some of the skins were at least that old. The souk is, in the main, like a massive car boot sale with tat from Taiwan filling the stalls but I loved the metal and wood working areas where the methods and tools that they use are unchanged since biblical times (or should that be from Koranic times) … to watch a man turn a flat sheet of metal into a bowl using just a hammer was fascinating, awesome, and extremely noisy! In spite of our instructions to the guide that we didn't want to buy anything we were taken to a ceramics factory…. Which evoked a Yeah! Yeah! Whatever! reaction from all of us.

Dying pots Fez

After the ceramics factory, came the carpet-making factory, and again we got the hard sell,
"There are 120, 000 knots per inch all tied by hand!"

"Really? That's truly.. erm … erm a lot! So who counts them?"
"We can pack it and send it for you, no problem!"
"I'll bet you can sunshine!"
"And just think you will be helping one thousand three hundred and fifty poor Moroccan women who make them in their homes just for people like you!"
Little voice says,
"He's got his hand on your thigh Jeff!"
"Yes I can feel it!"
"If he moves it any higher you're on your own!!"
I say to the man,
"Right thanks for the information but I don't want one!"
"Wait I haven't shown you all the carpets yet!"
"I don't want to see all the carpets I don't even want to see one!"
"What about the one thousand three hundred and fifty old Moroccan women?"
Little voice says,
"Tell him to..!"

I make to leave and he stands in my way, a stand off, until he says dismissively,
"You asked so many questions I thought you were serious!"
"Aah! You mistook my questions for interest!! Big mistake!"
Outside I said to the guide, from very close up,
"NO MORE SELLING!!!!!!!!!!!!!!"
He smiled and agreed totally and apologetically then deposited us in the shop of a herbal pharmacist who tried to sell me herbs, spices, sweets and other concoctions all of which were designed to make me a better person,
"You have rheumatism this will cure it!"
" I know I can be a pain but I don't have rheumatism!"
"You are losing your hair this will replace it!"
"Women like bald men!"

"This is natural viagra.."
"It's not getting an erection I have trouble with, it's finding someone to use it on!"

Spice stall Fez

I was fed up with being sold to … and it showed.. When the guide realised he was in for a commissionless day he quickly deposited us back at the camp site. So I'd seen the tanneries and upset a guide, a gay carpet salesman and a charlatan pharmacist.

All in all not a bad day! Life can be so good at times!

ZAGORA

Well a few days passed with us travelling generally south eastish, and it's getting hotter. Over the Atlas mountains and by God they are bleak, lunar, not awe inspiring tree topped mountains but sand coloured peaks devoid of any greenery, nothing moved, not a bird in sight just an occasional small white cloud in an otherwise azure sky.

The lava hardened into the shapes that formed when it first spewed out as a liquid millions of years ago, the hot wind drying your skin, I'm not sure what the wind is called the harmattan? The sirocco? I ought to look it up but it's so hot I can't be bothered.

It's probably the sirrocco or is it sirocco
(What's an R between friends? Well, that depends whether you're impotent or important! Don't worry if you missed that joke, I like it so much I'll use it again later!)

Les and I went into Zagora shopping this morning for dinner tonight and for some self tapping screws; fancy leaving home without self tapping screws…sheesh.. With our combined accountants intellect (about 92!) We managed to get some tomatoes (squashed!) onions (rotten!) green peppers (wizened!) and some pasta which when I asked for he kept trying to give me ice cream wafers. Now there's nothing wrong with ice cream wafers, but as a substitute for pasta it has immediate limitations.
Apparently you should ask for macaroni.

Never mind the food, let's get on with manly things, which is looking for self-tapping screws, my Arabic and French beginning to struggle at this point. We stood in the bakery asking for self-tapping screws (well we had to start somewhere!), and we were joined by Lasser, who obviously had nothing better to do, who led us off, much of the disgust of the baker who thought we were asking for a dozen toasties.The man with the self-tapping screws offered us a range sufficient to satisfy the most eclectic of tastes, and we struggled to make a selection. When we finally decided he said,
"Two dirhams Fifty!"
"Ah Les" I said, "differential pricing"
Lasser said,
"Oh no! That's ok! He overcharges everyone!"

Of all the people to meet at the back end of a small town in Morocco trust me to meet the one who understands the word differential..

And I don't include Les in that.

SOME BUGGERS LOST THE LOO SEAT

I like my loo! We've sat through a lot together, it's seen parts of me only very close friends have seen, and from unusual angles. So when suddenly the seat was missing I was desperate. Thinking back I'd had it this morning, and I can remember putting the lid down whilst I threw water over the toilets in a vain attempt to make it fit for human, as opposed to mosquito, habitation.

I had put it safely in a corner but being stupid I left it there, and when I eventually remembered and went back for it, it was gone! I immediately made lots of toilet noise (perhaps "noises about toilets" would be a better description) and demanded immediate action. (I resisted here saying "raised a stink" but as you can imagine only with great difficulty).

The camp manager (no! not that sort of camp) was sent for and I was determined to get to the bottom of the missing loo seat....

"Oh yes very good!"

"What is?"

"The "get to the bottom" joke!"

"That wasn't a joke, I meant it!"

"Oh pity it was one of your better ones!"

"I've lost my thread now where was I?"

"Bottom?"

"Oh yes! so he said.."

"I am going to church, it is not my problem!"

"Listen sunshine.. If you don't find my loo seat you'll be seeing whichever heaven you believe in a bloody sight sooner than you expect!"

Apparently what happened was that he found my loo seat and he put it in the rubbish, the man who emptied that rubbish was summoned and he remembered my loo seat (how could he forget it), and he pointed to the exact rubbish bin into which he threw it… the same rubbish bin that another man came and took to the Zagora rubbish tip..

So that's it! My loo seat with which I have travelled many miles, lies alone somewhere in a Moroccan rubbish tip. Leaving me to suffer the agonies of a thin rim …now we will know what real discomfort is…but that's what EXPEDITIONS are about!!!
I AM NOT HAPPY!!!!!!!!!!

WHERE ARE WE NOW?
Well I can tell you it's hot!! And when I say hot I don't mean "Turned out nice again" sort of hot, I mean "Jesus that's hot" sort of hot; I suppose it should be expected especially as we are in the Sahara. It was my fault of course, most things tend to be, so.. No hang on! I know what I was going to tell you.. I'VE REPLACED THE LOO SEAT!!!!!!!!!!

As you may remember the man at the campsite in Zagora tidied up for the first time this year and managed to throw my loo seat away. After an evening of abusing everyone in sight, well everyone in hearing is truer, knowing full well that it wouldn't do any good but which is tremendously satisfying, when I woke up in the morning I had calmed down, well calmed down to merely homicidal.

The man on whom I intended to vent my justifiable anger had wisely chosen not to return, so I decided to search the town for a replacement to sit on, a replacement for the loo seat I mean, not a man..

But in truth I wasn't that fussy.

When I got into Zagora, it was the Berber market day, where you can buy anything from a camel to the latest DVD but was at a loss as to where to begin to look for a toilet seat amongst all the hundreds of stalls (and stools!!! They sold camels and sheep too!)…
OK before you start smirking and feeling superior, do you know the French for,
"Excuse me but someone stole my toilet seat and it's a special size!"
Help, in the shape of the camp site managers manager (who had heard all about my loo seat) arrived, and between us we searched high and low (I resisted the temptation to repeat the "top to bottom" joke) and the search was made easier because I took the loo with me…. and then we found a seat! a nice shade of sky blue it was….and obviously the word had got round as everyone smiled at me as I walked up the main street of Zagora, with my loo in one hand and the seat in the other… I now know the Arabic for " Nice loo you have there mate!!"

It's taken me a couple of days to adapt it, but tonight it was completed and it's now stuck together with instant glue and cable ties and even if I say it myself it's an improvement on the original and it works!! Memo to self.. make sure next time you repair a loo seat remember to wipe all the instant glue off…Jean sat on it and the rest is too painful to go into details about!..

Well! That's my story and I'm sticking to it, not unlike Jean and the seat! When she came down the ladder from the tent with the
seat stuck to her naked bum and said, "Look!" I know I was wrong to laugh, and I certainly shouldn't have said "Very nice! I've always liked it, but why have you framed it?"
but I didn't deserve the punch!

A NIGHT IN THE DESERT
Right back to the story! Where are we now?.. Well we're about twenty-five miles from the Algerian border and last night and we slept in the desert. In the camp there were only the four of us, plus our guide Abbas (I thought he said his name was Abyss.. which to my mind isn't a good name for a guide who is taking you into the wilderness!) and two others, we have no idea who they were, probably mates of Abbas who fancied a free meal in the desert.

We arrived here by driving through the Sahara from M'Hamed to Foum Zguid and if you look on the map you find the M'hamed at the end of one road and Foum Zguid at the end of another road but there's nothing connecting them. Well that's the road, in truth route would be better word, because we were travelling through the desert.

After negotiating a fee we picked up our guide, Abyss, Abbas whatever his bloody name is, and were taken into the desert where we were given a meal of cous cous and meat under a warm cloudless sky, along with mint tea, I waited hopefully but in vain for a beer.

The mattresses were laid out after our alfresco dinner and we lay there counting the stars and listening to the guide and his friends playing the outa (a kind of three string guitar) and singing a traditional haunting song of a lost love in a far off land whilst the noble desert nomad strives in vain to make enough money to return and claim his bride, I'm not sure if he succeeded as after five minutes I called out…

"For Christ's sake shut the f**k up I'm trying get some sleep here" Sheesh!

Jean waking up in the desert waiting for her coffee

The guide, Abbas, was telling us that although he has a Moroccan passport, he is in fact a Polissario, who accepts neither the Moroccan, Algerian or Spanish claims to the land, and are fighting for independence…and we should, now listen to this! bear this in mind if stopped by the military whilst travelling through the desert. I said,

"Abbas my son, if a Moroccan or Algerian or Spanish man sticks a bloody great gun up my nose and says 'Have you seen any Polissario today? Please be rest assured that the index fingers of both hands will be immediately and firmly pointed in your direction!"

The Polissario Front, the military arm of the Sahrawi Arab Democratic Republic, was formed in 1973 with the express intention of militarily forcing an end to Spanish colonization of Western Sahara, an area covering some 102,700 square miles, sharing borders with Algeria, Mauritania, and Morocco, and with a coastline along the Atlantic Ocean, and is one of the most sparsely populated territories in the world with the largest city El Laâyoune, being home to over half of the estimated 380,000 population of the territory.

In the late 19th century, when the European powers divided Africa up for themselves, Morocco was split between France and Spain, with Spain receiving the portion that is now Western Sahara. Spain began talks with them to discuss a transition of power but at the same time, independent Morocco was laying claim to lands it stated had historically been its own. A UN mission visited the Sahara and reported that the majority of inhabitants favoured independence, rather than remaining a Spanish holding or being transferred to Morocco and soon after that the International Court of Justice reported to Morocco that the historical holdings of the region did not grant it the right to reclaim western Sahara, stating that instead the Sahrawi people had the right to self-determination.

At the end of 1975 Morocco amassed troops along the border, prompting the Spanish to capitulate and cede

*control of the territory to Morocco and Mauritania.
The next day the Polissario Front declared the
formation of the Sahrawi Arab Democratic Republic,
creating a government in exile based in Algeria. The
Sahrawi Arab Democratic Republic first targeted the
southern third of the region, which had been ceded to
Mauritania,
eventually seizing it, Morocco responded by laying
claim to that region as well.*

*In 1991 a cease-fire was achieved, with Morocco
agreeing to hold a referendum to determine whether
the inhabitants of the Western Sahara wished
independence. To date, no referendum has taken
place and large swathes of the territory of the
Western Sahara are mined, particularly along the
Moroccan border, making overland travel dangerous.*

*Morocco fiercely refuses to move from their position
on Western Sahara, which explains the attitude of the
policeman at the border.*

I love the desert and all its contrasts. The driving is fun but as
we are on an "EXPEDITION" I'll have to curb my temptation
to wander and get back to heading south.

TOO CLOSE FOR COMFORT
I know in the past I've been accused of exaggeration,
fabrication, sometimes even down right lies; and I have to
admit that occasionally there may have been some slight
justification for this, but today there is no need for any
embellishments, what I'm about to tell you really happened.
Unfortunately.

The car and all its contents were bogged down within three
yards and fifteen minutes of being engulfed by the Atlantic.

The day had started so easily after spending the previous night at Fort Beau Gerif, and whilst there we made the passing acquaintance of a group of Belgian men who later were to prove important to us.

As we were leaving the campsite, the owner told us about the "scenic" route to the coast…for scenic read rough rocky and interesting. It was, a normal sort of off road piste made of sand and rocks with steep ascents and descents but all well within the capabilities of the cars and their drivers, and of course in addition he recommended highly the drive down Plage Blanche beach.

When we finally got to beach, we met the Belgians again who, after getting stuck and reducing their tyre pressures, needed our compressor to re-inflate them, not a problem, and whilst we were showing them again the wonders of the Kelly kettle, they said that they too had decided that they too would drive down the beach…. so we tagged along…as you do!

They shot off and we followed, pausing only to dig ourselves out of the sand, inconvenient but no problem, fooling ourselves that we knew what we were doing in getting out of "stuck" situations, little knowing that the warm up would come in useful later.

Of course by this time the Belgians were long gone but no problem!! What's the worst that can happen?

The drive along the beach is supposed to be easy, it is easy if you know that after about twenty five kilometres you MUST get off the beach, after that the hard sand turns softer, but we didn't know that at the time. Of course what you do then is to ignore the waves of the local fishermen who appear to be directing you off the beach and think that their shouts of, "DANGER!" is some cute Moroccan joke.

Suddenly the sand got softer and softer, and even with diff locks on, progress slowed dramatically. Les by this time had turned back but unfortunately had turned towards the sea rather than away from it and was now sinking to his axles so I turned to help him, great idea Watts! Les's car weighs a couple of tonnes so I went in front of him and my car weighs three and a half tonnes so surprise surprise I got stuck and dug in even deeper … It was no longer sand but soft shale, soft because it was waterlogged!

Perhaps now it would be opportune to mention the Atlantic, which was receding but which, as is the way with oceans would eventually return, to a line about thirty yards higher up the beach from where I was truly and deeply stuck… and that turn was due, past due, and the enormity of our problem hit us, and we started digging.

At this point three of the Belgians returned from where they too had been stuck further along and started to help us, lots of digging and pushing, resulted in the car sinking even deeper and the near side wheels were by now sitting in a few inches of Atlantic, I dug faster which only succeeded in making the car sink even more.
More Belgians arrived!

The suggestion was made (not by me as by now I had stopped thinking and was allowing panic to set in), that we use the sand ladders and high lift jack to raise the wheels then slide the ladders under the wheels then drop the car back down.. Easy!!.. (Why didn't I think of that? Because you're an idiot Watts) and also let the tyres down to about 20 psi and, again not my idea, take the heavy items from the car…

I was desperately digging now as the car sank and the shale was now against the underside of it. As I knelt to dig, the water was lapping round my thighs. We had one chance for this to work, the tide was coming in fast and we wouldn't have time to repeat the jacking, in fifteen minutes the car would be flooded.

Papy, one of the Belgian lads had already shown that he knew what he was doing and Françoise said

"Would you like Papy to drive it out!"

Now wasn't the time for false pride and I happily, well "happily"isn't quite the right word for what I as feeling, handed him the keys and stood at the back with the others ready to push. By now the water was covering the sand ladders and was half way up the tyres.

Papy started the engine; the thought struck me that if this didn't work it would perhaps be the last time it would ever be started. At the count of three we pushed!, (Bugger three! I was pushing after one!) and desperation lent me strength; the engine roared and the car moved, slowly at first then surged forward, Papy drove at the sea! He'd made a mistake! But no! He knew what he was doing, the bottom was marginally firmer there; as he picked up speed and the spray covered the vehicle momentarily, he turned gently up the beach, engine still screaming.

The car pulled itself slowly out of danger, I couldn't keep up and stood, hands on knees not believing my good fortune! "Don't stall it Papy!" but he didn't, he kept going, climbing higher away from the sea, until finally he stopped, not above the eventual water line but far enough so that we had time, time to get Les out.

Les's car stood forlornly alone, but not for long as we now knew what to do, some lifted, some dug, others let down the tyres and then we all emptied his car.

Francois took pictures!

Papy again was entrusted with the driving and again he proved himself. Slowly at first but then faster, until Les's vehicle too was far enough away from the incoming tide to give us time to repack… and escape…but not too much time, the sea seemed to want us back!

So even now the danger wasn't over, we were still well below the high water line and now we still had to drive over soft sand and find the turn inland before the sea caught us, and we wanted all the cars out, not just ours

Papy and the others ran off to their cars, all now much nearer the Atlantic than was safe, he shouted at me "GO GO and don't stop for anything!"

I put the car in low range and set off, willing the tyres to grip, building up speed, slowly, scared: changing up to second gear as quickly as I could but even as I changed gear the car slowed and I felt the wheels dig in. I decided then to ignore all

293

my instincts, stay in the same gear and worry about over-revving the engine later!!

The engine rev counter was in the red and I was only going 20 mph when the others overtook me, shouting at me to go faster. I knew if I stopped now they would have to leave me. Each time I reached for the gear lever I lost my nerve and stopped myself and prayed that my forward momentum was enough.

By now the mist was down and I couldn't see anything, and most importantly I couldn't see the sea, I darn't go higher as the sand was too soft, but was I driving through the mist straight into the sea?
Ahead the ghostly silhouette of a rusty wreck, I'd seen it earlier but couldn't remember which side I'd passed it, then I saw a set of tyre tracks passing seawards, but would the sea already be covering them in the mist, risking all I turned and followed them hoping that the sand was hard enough.

A nervous glance at the dash board showed the rev counter at 4300 r.p.m. much too high! Then suddenly out of the mist a lone figure waved me inland, still not daring to change gear, I swung round in a large arc and finally saw them parked in the safety of a dune ... when I switched the engine off I sat and gripped the steering wheel, the engine ticked!
Only then did I trust that we would not lose our car!!!!

We cooked them a meal, and I only charged them cost price! Alex Gwen, Francois, Joco, Seb, Papy, Johnny thank you is too small a word for what we feel

The next day it took us all day to drive out to the main road, a day that started with me repairing broken fan belts, a result of the previous days high revolution's no doubt, a day of digging out, but it's strange isn't it that digging out loses its immediacy when you're not looking between your legs at the Atlantic.

My trouser pockets were full of sand and shale where they had been washed in by the sea!!!

I was scared!!!!!!!!

THOUGHTS ON MOROCCO

Well Morocco has shown us all of its facets, the ancient cities of Marrakech and Fez, Chefchauhan high in the Atlas Mountains, the desert in M'Hamed and finally the beaches, well one particular beach that still gives me nightmares.

But we have a long way to go through Mauritania and Mali, and the route south lays before us, and without any decisions to make, it's one long long straight road, no turns, no gear changes. No ....well, no nothing..... miles of fawn nothingness, especially in the mornings when the damp mist envelopes you, yes I do mean damp mist and I am in the Sahara..

The border formalities between Morocco and Mauritania are easy; first you have to leave Morocco, so you join the back of the queue behind a large lorry, then you wait twenty minutes until you get out to investigate why there's no movement and only then realise that the "queue" is in fact a parked lorry, and when you pull round that the action REALLY starts.. Well no it doesn't!
All you do is go to the first door, where a policeman takes your passports off you and writes the information in book, then to the next door where another man takes your green paper that you were handed when you came into the country, and checks it against the vehicle number, then into the next office where another policeman stamps your passport (and

before you ask, "No I don't know why the first policeman doesn't stamp it!")
Then you drive away to be stopped by a policeman who checks your passport, and another man who checks your car documents.. Easy!!!
All you do now is drive over a very poor road, both in surface and in directions, to the Mauritanian officials. Now look I don't want to nag you, but please do try and stick to the path, even if you can't see it, as you are now in what we in the profession call.. A MINEFIELD!

Yes! That's what I said but there's nothing to worry about, well nothing except for the mines, just make sure that you drive behind someone else, not too closely though, until eventually you will arrive at the entrance to Mauritania where you're met by the very nice Mauritanian Policeman who will take your passport and write in a book, he will then ask you for "cadeau". It's at this point that you feign ignorance of his meaning, difficult as up to this point you have been happily conversing in French,
"Sorry I don't understand!"
"Une cadeau"
"Nope sunshine! No idea what you mean!"
"A present"
"Present?"
"Present!"
"Ahh yes I am present!"
His friend arrives,
"You have a present for him!"
"Sorry?"
They converse in Arabic, and even I know that they are saying,
"Can anyone be this stupid"
I think,

"Just watch mate when it comes to being stupid and saving money I am your man!"
I wear my village idiot grin with ease, until eventually he throws down the passports in disgust and I pick them up,
"Ahh" I couldn't resist " Une cadeau pour moi!"
Oh they did think that was funny!!!!

That's immigration sorted (I think) so now it's customs, they give you two bits of scrappy paper (or two scrappy bits of paper) and again begin to discuss presents, and again are met with my well practiced village idiot smile; one of the bits of paper is apparently the customs declaration for currency and the other the import documentation for the vehicle.
"€10"
"Why?"
"That is the fee!"
"I want a receipt!"
"Of course!"
Was I conned? I don't know.

As easy as that! And no "cadeaux" At the barrier (a bent unpainted pole between two bent unpainted barrels) another customs man stuck his face in the window and said "cadeau?" I looked at him, looked at my completed documentation and we looked at each other, and we both knew that, for him anyway, Christmas wasn't going to come early!

An uneventful drive brought us into Nouadhibou, which is dirty, sand blown, and rubbish strewn. The brown square buildings wincing against the swirling Saharan winds, paper bags pirouetting on sandy thermals, goats wandering the streets, stray cats and dogs scavenging for scraps with an all pervading smell of human and animal excrement, burning rubbish, the people cowed and unsmiling! All in all one of the better places we've been through in the last couple of days!

"Oh it's here that you change your money"
"You didn't!!! Tell me you didn't change it at the border!!!!!!"
"Oh well you'll know better next time.."

Now get the car insurance, and contrary to what you read you don't have to go to the police to buy it. Babba at the camping Abba (not quite an anagram and almost a palindrome!) will arrange all that for you.

So that's it! You're in Mauritania. The minimum time you can get insurance for is ten days and it costs about fifteen Euros, ten days is plenty for what I want to do, namely get out the other end.

Oh yes I forgot to tell you, we were wild camping near the sea (but after our Plage Blanche experience.. not too near!) last night whilst we were still in Morocco, when suddenly two men in uniform appeared, I thought we were in trouble, but they were simply looking for "clandestines!" (I thought at first they said "langoustines") apparently these are illegal immigrants from the Canaries.

Looking round at the desolation, I remembered fondly the air conditioned beach bars selling cold beer in the Canaries, and tried desperately to think of something that could motivate me to become a "clandestine" (or even a langoustine) and smuggle myself into the Western Sahara, but nothing sprang to mind.

We were of course in the Western Sahara, a tract of land whose ownership is hotly (well it would be hot! it is in the Sahara!) disputed. To be brutally honest I am amazed that anyone could care less, no one lives here, its landscape lunar,

it's hot in the day, damp and cold at night with a permanent wind....
Let them have it I say! Let's all go to the Canaries!!

Oh yes something else I'd forgotten, on the drive down through Southern Morocco the police blocks became more frequent, all very friendly, but insistent on knowing what we were doing there, and very keen to know if we were "humanitarians!", apparently they don't want us foreigners going in and helping the people in the refugee camps!!

I told them that no one gets something for nothing from me, I'll quite happily feed the refugees but they'll bloody have to pay like anyone else, did I really look that gullible?.. He smiled at me.. Obviously thinking I was joking.. If only he knew!!!!!!!

KIFFA MAURITANIA AFTER NOUABADABOU
"So what you been doing then"
"Well I've been driving through Mauritania, two long days of road and sand, we left nouabadabadababdbaou., bloody hell it's difficult to stop that word once you've started it. I've always wanted to see the ore train that goes from Zouerat to Nouabadabadabbda and it is sometimes two miles long, but I overslept and thought I'd missed it"
"Shame that! All that way and you missed the train!"
"Ahh but I hadn't! I was stopped at one of the many police road blocks and suddenly I saw it and got some pictures!"
"And was it two miles long?"
"I have no idea but it should be possible to work it out because I know what time the engine passed me by the time on the first picture on my camera and the time on the last, and it was travelling at about forty mph so I should be able to work it out, but I can't because I thought I could rewire the inverter"

" I didn't know you were an electrician"
" I'm not! That's why the inverter didn't work so I couldn't work out the length of the train"
" I'm sure that's obvious to you but I think the rest of us are struggling here!"
"Well it's obvious isn't it, after I'd taken the pictures of the train I didn't switch the camera off, so the battery on the camera went flat and I couldn't charge it up because someone…"
"You!"
"Well yes if you're going to be picky, Me! had messed about with the inverter.. But I fiddled about with it again and it's working now.. and sometime soon I should be able to work out how long the train is….any way we drove from Nouabadababadbabouou to Nouakchott which is tarred all the way and runs through miles and miles and miles."
"And miles?"
"Yes, and miles of sand!"
"Sand and the Sahara. Now there's a surprise!"
"Yes and there's a bloody lot of it and nothing else, just the odd camel and a few goats the occasional donkey…"
"And sand!"
"Oh yes and sand!"

You've heard of a camel train .. Well this is one!

After a night in Nouakchott at camping Nomad, which is ok
for one night, it has to be, there is no other option! You set off
for
Kiffa on a road strewn with dead donkeys, cows, camels and
goats. The road is tarred but even if it weren't you wouldn't
get lost, just follow the crashed vehicles and dead animals and
you'll be fine.

On the business of roads it would be possible so far for Auntie
Mabel and Uncle Bill to drive down here in their 1975 Ford
Transit camper, without any problem, providing they resist the
temptation to go to the desert or the beach (I've always
wondered what the point of resisting temptation is! But then
I've always thought anyone who risks getting stuck on a
beach is stupid)
My God they love their road blocks, I suppose over the two
days it's taken us to get from nouab..etc etc to Kiffa we must
have passed through twenty of the bloody things .. No
problem all low key. It's wise to make sure you have plenty of

photocopies of your passport and hand them over…they will ask for a cadeau.. You will say
"Listen sunshine I don't even give cadeaux at Christmas!" and they will wave you on with a happy smile (well sometimes!)

We arrived at Kiffa for a nights stay in the only camp site in town, it's on your right as you drive in just before the police road block, again we were the only ones there, so of course being quiet they had taken the opportunity of having a spring clean, well they could have but they didn't. With this in mind I cornered the first of many staff and said,
"So tell me are you going to clean the showers and toilets or am I"
He was genuinely amazed that there was anything wrong, he looked at me and said something in Arabic, which I took to mean,
"Oh! The cockroaches in the shower tray, they always shower at this time, we pride ourselves on the cleanliness of our cockroaches!"He picked up half of the brush section of a broom head and made a few desultory passes at the Sahara that was the toilet block floor.
A while later Jean said,
"Blimey those toilets are dreadful!"
Off I went to find the patron, and (not for the first time) to cut a long story short we had a discussion, a very full and very very frank discussion, and the toilets were cleaned!
I truly believe that they did enjoy getting feedback from the paying guests!!!

A violent night time sand storm saw us (well only saw us dimly) putting the tent away at two o'clock in the morning and sleeping the rest of the night in the car, being very careful not to stand on some of the largest, fastest and fiercest spiders I've ever seen, definitely a 'leave in peace' spider, I'm not sure what sort it was but I promised myself to look it up on the web.

"NO Jeff!"

"What?"

"You were going to make a web joke about spiders!"

"I wasn't!"

"Just don't! Right?"

"Spoilsport!"

Leaving Mauritania was simple and involved desultory checking of the paperwork and giving back the "laissez passer" that enabled you to bring your vehicle into the country, it's on the side of the road without anything to show you're at the border, probably because you're not; but then there's nothing to show you're at the border, when, a few miles further on you're stopped at a falling down semi thatched mud hut, and a man, who, after waking up and putting his uniform on, well his jacket anyway, takes your passports and stamps them after keeping you waiting the obligatory fifteen minutes whilst he deals with all the other (non existent) customers.

Mauritania saw us leaving as we entered, with a request for "une cadeau" the last, like the first, being unsuccessful.

Nearing the border with Mali, the roadblocks get more numerous and the requests for cadeaux more insistent. They ask about your car insurance, but are really only interested whether you have medicine for "fatigue" which is a euphemism for erectile problems. (Memo to me next time take some Radian B ointment and tell them to rub it on. It won't help their erections but my God it'll improve their tap dancing!)

So that's it the everlasting impression of Mauritania is that it is sandy, large and with permanently open hands demanding "cadeaux"

MALI

Entering Mali is an anti-climax, you're never quite sure when it happened; a man in a mud hut and a uniform sort of waves at you and you stop, in truth he doesn't seem to mind whether you do or not but, as you've taken the trouble to acknowledge his presence, he seems to think it's polite to do the same
He salutes lazily, or perhaps he just brushes a fly away, difficult to decide I do the same and he wonders if I'm taking the Mickey!
I am!

I offer him my passport but he declines and points me in the direction of Niori..
Oh! By the way of you're thinking of following us, the road to Niori, which is marked as a track on the Michelin map and described in the Lonely Planet as requiring a compass, is so easy Auntie Mabel and Uncle Bill in their camper could make tea at the same time as driving it.

Where was I, Oh yes! Getting into Mali, so first into Niori, ignore the "Commissariat du Police" which is just after the airport on the left hand side, but don't forget it because you'll be returning there later.

Go straight into town and look for the customs. As a clue, look for a traffic island with a chunk of concrete in the middle, they (and I suspect the Turner prize committee) would call it a statue, but believe me it's just a chunk of concrete. Turn right (for God's sake don't try and treat it as an island, no-one else does and you'll wipe out sundry local stalls), then twiddle about a bit and follow the directions of the people sitting near the customs house doing nothing, be careful not to mistake theses people sitting round doing nothing with all the others sitting round doing nothing, as they know nothing! and eventually or fortuitously, you'll finish up at the Customs house; No it's not a scrap yard which will be your first impression. For the first time you'll need your Carnet du Passage.

The custom's officer will stamp the Carnet, the effort causing a few beads of sweat fall artistically onto your virginal carnet and he'll hand it back, then falls back into his chair, exhausted at the effort.

Easy!!!

You remember I told you to make a note of the Commissariat du Police. Well the reason is now you have to go back there to get your passport stamped.
If you're anything like me he'll look through it carefully and say,
"Ahh you have no visa!"
I'll give you a clue what you do next, take your passport off him, turn it the right way round, and show him the visa, he looks at it disappointed but stamps it and demands CFA1000.

It's at this point you realise that you haven't got any local money, and bang on cue, as if my magic, a little face appears at the window and asks if you need money changing on the "marche noire", I look at the policeman who looks at me.. Is it trap? I don't think so but I take the easy way out and say,
"No I don't but Les does!"
That way I get the best of both worlds, if it's a trap Les gets arrested, if it's not Les has to pay the money, it's called a "win

win situation!" admit it you're impressed. Ok just a little impressed??..

NO? Please yourself!

Right next stage is off to town with the little man to get the money changed for the car insurance, it's about twenty-five Euros, so we need to change some more money, into town and change the money, back up the road to the policeman to give him the CFA1000 and then back with the same money changer to the camp site.. Err.. Camp site? A car park with trees, but it has cold beer and a restaurant. Well it sells road kill chicken and soggy chips.. But no matter..

We needed an early start in the morning, and we didn't need to worry about oversleeping!. The night club that you're parked outside opens at ten thirty and blasts out God awful Malian music until two o'clock when the patrons leave and then chat happily beneath the Land Cruiser finally falling asleep but waking up at five a.m. to turn on the radio and continue their conversation.

The road from Niori to Bamako would be a bigger test for Auntie Mabel and Uncle Bill's camper but not much, they are working on the road as we speak and it will soon be finished and become another ruler straight line through changing scenery as the desert gives way to greenery and the first signs of rains appear.

We stayed at Jean Bakars camp site in Bamako and it's an oasis in a mad city and a great place to get information and cold beer (The latter more important, to me at least, than the former) and now's the time to get your visa for Burkina Faso, which I'll bet you didn't know used to be called Upper Volta!

It's easy to get the visa, just go to the top of the road from Jean Bakars, get a taxi for the thirty minute drive to the Burkina Faso embassy, give them three copies of your passport photo, and CFA 28,200 and you get your visa back the same day.

Well that's the theory, in our case you get a taxi driver who speaks an obscure French dialect at triple pace; who is on his first day as a taxi driver; who cannot differentiate between Burkina Faso and Senegal, and who's taxi has holes in the floor.

I suppose we should have left when, an hour into the thirty minute drive, he was stopped and dragged off by the police, but no! Being basically nice people, stupid but nice, we stayed until he returned, muttering in Malian, before driving off again.
He stopped and asked directions, and I picked up the word "Senegal" I said,
"Nooo! Burkina Faso" he looked at me amazed as if I hadn't mentioned it before.

For two bloody hours we toured the back streets of Bamako, in blinding heat, whilst he became more desperate for us to go to Sene-bloody-gal, finally, triumphantly stopping outside an obviously residential house and saying
"Voila"
He looks hurt at my cynical expression; I pushed open the gate and called out,
"Err Halloo! Bonjour!!

Nothing! Now even I know embassies have people around, even the Mauritanian Embassy in Rabat had the decency to leave someone at the embassy to tell us we had to go to Casablanca. This one was deserted, and it had a swimming pool in the front of it!! Resisting with great difficulty the urge to strip off and jump in, instead I wandered around calling out, more hope than expectation.

He joined me in shouting, desperate now. I think he was tiring of our company, we certainly were of his…it was at this point he decided the time was right to renegotiate the fare, it seems he now had to get more money to pay the fine that the police had just given him.

Oh! We did have fun negotiating and we finally agreed that he would have another attempt at finding the Embassy of Burkina Faso and I wouldn't "let your bloody tyres down before finding another taxi driver who knows his way round this bloody town"
It was more by luck than judgement that he deposited us at the Embassy of Burkina Faso only forty-five minutes before they closed and two and a half hours after we'd, mistakenly we now knew, hailed him.

As we left the taxi he re-opened negotiations, to my disappearing back. I ignored him and went inside.
He followed!
We filled in the forms, (why do they want to know my mothers name?) and they wanted the CFA28,200
Problem! We didn't have it. We only have Euros,
"Vous prenez Euros"
"Malaheuresment non!"

Our taxi driver was still shouting to me through the window of the Embassy, it was now mid-day and the embassy closed in thirty minutes.
We need a bank! Quick! We need taxi! Quick! We knew that there was a taxi outside but even I wouldn't get back in that one!

We started to walk, followed by our taxi driver, still negotiating with the back of my head. Suddenly another taxi appeared and we jumped in, and our taxi man immediately stood in front, blocking the way and started telling the new taxi driver in great detail about the breakdown in negotiations, and they entered into a discussion.

"I need the bank quick!" shouting over them,

But they talked on.. I said,

"Right out we get" I had one foot on the ground when the new taxi driver started to drive and, with much horn sounding, found us a bank… we ignored the money changers then found the ATM machine, Great!

It didn't take Visa cards! Not Great!

So we joined a queue and resigned ourselves to missing the deadlines for visas.

This is getting boring now so I'll stop, we got back to the embassy, which wasn't closed, a very nice man took our passports and an hour later gave us back our passports and visa's.

Two girls who arrived after us got their passports and visas at the same time as us.. so we needn't have worried or rushed.. Our taxi driver hasn't been seen since, and suddenly it's raining!

We stayed on for a few days with Jean Bakir in Bamako, recovering and housekeeping before the next part of the holiday.. err sorry expedition!

John Bakir's campsite is not in truth the easiest place to find, but if you look for "Tore d'Africa" (which means the Tower of Africa) and resembles an erect penis with an outline of Africa stuck on top, (there has to be a joke there somewhere but I can't think of it).

Look for that and the camp site is within a couple of kilometres of that, but don't expect anything to indicate that you're there, just a lorry scrap yard and some red gates, behind which there is a haven, an oasis of calm which was for us difficult to leave.

BURKINA FASO
Burkina Faso used to be called Upper Volta,(did I tell you that?) which explained why I'd hardly ever heard of it before this trip, sorry EXPEDITION, but suddenly there it was.

Mali was interesting! Suddenly, after the perpetual demands for "cadeaux" in Mauritania, there were almost none in Mali. Why would it change like that, what is it about a border that changes attitudes? So Mali was surprisingly pleasant for West Africa and we were sorry to leave it.

But knowing that we still have to get to Ghana to try and sort out a "bateau" for south we had to. If we can't get a boat it will mean a cross-country dash through Nigeria, Cameroon, Congo, etc. which I prefer but, after the Atlantic experience of nearly losing the vehicle because of my insistence that we drive down the beach, my views on anything are being looked on with great suspicion, well in truth everything I suggest is being automatically vetoed.

Politically I am not saying a lot at the moment but stick with me on this; time will tell what'll happen... after all what's the worst that can happen? Well! Apart from being held up at gunpoint in Nigeria; being stuck in mud Cameroon; getting involved in an uprising in Congo and running over land mines in Angola; it'll be plain sailing, perhaps like the boat from Ghana to South Africa

Where was I Oh yes! Mali to Burkina Faso (which used to be called Upper Volta in case you'd forgotten). Once again it's an Auntie Mabel and Uncle Bill camper van road, but more typically the Africa we know. Laterite edged tarred roads with just the occasional pothole to stop you dozing off.

I could go into details about the borders and perhaps ask questions as to why there are two police posts when you enter Burkina Faso both appearing to do the same thing, but I wont; I could tell you that the customs post appear to be manned by the army, but I wont; all I'll tell you is that there are, and as long as you have a Carnet du Passage you'll get through without hassle.

For one of the poorest countries in Africa Burkina Faso (or Upper Volta as it used to be called!) looks amazingly fertile, fields of sweet corn, rice fields, etc. (I said etc. then because I couldn't identify the other things growing, come to think of it, they could just have been weeds) with people bent over them, tilling and toiling.

A long drive after we left Bamako in Mali, before we arrived in Bobo (on the map it's called Bobo-Dioulasso but everyone knows it as Bobo, which is a damn sight easier to spell) in Burkina Faso; the first real town of any size and a bustling community with hundreds of moped repair shops, most of which we saw as we searched desperately for a place to change money, something that we were stupid enough to think that the banks were supposed to do.

Wrong!

The reaction of the lady in the bank of "pas aujourdhui" left me trifle bewildered, did she mean that she wouldn't because it was Saturday or that she wouldn't because she simply didn't feel like it…I suspect the latter.. But without time to argue we rushed off until eventually we found the bureau de change, which was air conditioned and empty.

Where are queues when you need them? A couple of hours sitting in air conditioned comfort would have gone down well, but it's a fact of life in Africa that if the office is hot, sticky and smelly you wait for bloody hours, if it's cool and air conditioned you're in and out in two minutes.

Who says I'm paranoid? Come on who's has been saying it? I know someone has!

Right! Now you have money, you can buy insurance, for which you'll need the car documents, which of course you've remembered to bring with you…if you did well done!

I, of course, hadn't and had to walk back the "five minutes" to Casa Africa, well it might by five minutes to an Olympic sprinter with severe diarrhoea looking for a loo; to me it was forty-five minutes in sticky heat back to Casa Africa, the bungalow come doss house where we were sleeping in the garden.
The prospect of forty-five minute return journey with attendant offers of postcards, sweets, and suites! meant that a taxi was called for, and in fact called; this despite previous vows never to get in another African taxi after our experiences in Morocco and Mali.

A further sixty minutes watching an insurance man trying to make sense of the British registration document before finally and triumphantly relieving us of the equivalent of £42 passed as slowly as you'd expect; but left us with Insurance cover for the whole of West Africa, and cover for everything except what is almost certainly going to happen. But then that's the case with insurance all over the world not just in Africa.

If you're beginning to think that this is a pretty tedious, even by the normally high levels of tedium achieved, you are of course correct. It's Saturday afternoon in Bobo, it's building up to rain, distant thunder is rumbling and the air is heavy! And there's noting to do but wait. So why should I be bored on my own when I can take you with me?
Don't thank me that's the kind of guy I am!!

The image that you present to the world isn't always what you think, or even what you'd like it to be. Yesterday was a good case in point. Since I've been on this trip I've consciously tried to create he aura of a hardy explorer, make that Explorer, following on from Burton, Speke, Selous, Stanley and Livingstone. Dressing in sand coloured clothes and only shaving every two or three days I see myself as a latter day Hemingway.

I was sitting on the veranda practicing my steely eyed, but approachable look perfected so well by Robert Redford, when a man selling something approached me quietly. Looking nervously over his shoulder he reached into his bag, what would it be? Perhaps illicit diamonds, some poached ivory or even Rhino horn. What could he have to tempt this worldly wise explorer, err Explorer?

It was a wooden carving of a bloody hippopotamus standing upright playing the Xylophone. So that's the image I present to the world, I'm a man who looks as if he would love to adorn his house with a wooden carving of a hippo standing upright playing a xylophone!!

I fixed him with my steely gaze, that I have been practicing so assiduously, and instead of fading nervously away, he mistook the look as intense interest, and so began negotiations. He started at £20! I ignored him…he took this as a negotiating ploy and reduced his price to £17.50. I continued to ignore him; he continued to reduce his price. Until finally I growled,

"I do not want your bloody hippo!"

He smiled, he could tell how desperate I was to own it, he reduced his price even further

"But Sir it is very life like"

"Hippos. don't stand on their hind legs, and they certainly don't play f***ing xylophones!"

He paused and considered this then knocked another £2.50 off.

I turned my back on him!

He took this as yet another subtle negotiating trick and, I felt with some respect, said

"Ok final last price £10!"

I said

"Really? Final last price? Ok then!"

He smiled, a sale at last but I continued,

"No! Now bugger off! I don't want the bloody thing at any price"

"Ok!" he said "how much!"

Right! Does anyone want to buy a rather tasteful wooden statue of a hippo on its hind legs playing the xylophone?? I'll give it to you at a good price..£25! And I'm not even covering my costs!!

OUAGADOUGOU

Be careful! Ouagadougou like Nouababababdo it's another of those words that you can never seem to stop. It's the capital of

314

Burkina Faso (which you know of course used to be called Upper Volta), but indistinguishable from all the other towns we've passed through.

The book and the Internet said the place to stay is in the Cathedral compound with the nuns; you have to have a room but if the are full (they were!) and she likes you (she didn't!) she'd let you camp in the car park (she wouldn't!)
She was a miserable bugger, but she was a nun so I was nice to her. I make a habit of being nice to Nun's,
"I absolutely knew as soon as you mentioned Nun's you'd come up with a habit joke!"
"I'm glad I didn't disappoint you!"
"You did!! Oh believe me you did!"

Back to the story!
"Do you speak English?"
"Non!"
"Ok! (into French now) Avez-vous une chambre?"
"Non encore" (still no!)
"Right, can we camp in the compound please?"
"Non"
"Pardon madame, peuvent nous camper ici"
"Non encore!"

Little voice inside says,
"Slap her Jeff, she might be a nun but she deserves it, you've no chance of going to Heaven anyway"

"Right, Ok, do you know anywhere we can stay?"
"Non!"
We left, but I couldn't help thinking that if she was a Nun and by definition destined for Heaven that Heaven ain't gonna be a fun place, academic to me but worthy of consideration to you out there!

We'd heard on the road that you could stay in the car park of the OK Inn, which eventually we found after visiting everywhere else in town, cunningly hidden behind a large lorry depot. The OK Inn, seriously that was its name, has good free camping under the trees in a large car park, their only proviso being that you drink in their bar.
I, of course, tried to argue with this..
"Listen! I just might not want to drink ice cold beer with condensation running down the outside of the glass in an air conditioned bar (I did in fact really want to drink an ice cold beer etc etc but I wouldn't let them know that)" but I'm afraid to say they insisted.

Oh well you can't win them all.

We were in town to get our Ghanaian visa which is pretty straight forward, you need four photographs and they give you four identical forms to fill in, but no carbon paper, but I smiled, (it was early in the day well before "niceness" was sweated out of me) and returned the forms to them, and told them about the latest wonderful invention called carbon paper, gave them CFA 15000 and are told to return the next day at two o'clock. Simple really!
"Hey! I'll tell you a secret the hotel "The OK Inn" runs its computer network by wireless"

"So what's secret about that?"
"Well they've not protected it so if you were to sign on to your computer which happens to have wireless facility"
"Which yours has!"
"Well yes, and if, purely by accident you happened to click on the connect icon"
"Which you did!"

"Mmm and then, again by accident, you were to click on Internet explorer, and type in Hotmail",
"And your name and password",
"Yes, well if that were to happen you could get unlimited Internet access for free",
"But you wouldn't do anything as cheap as that would you, especially as they were letting you stay for free?
"What sort of man do you think I am?"
"The sort who would, even though you are being allowed to stay for free, would steal internet access!"
"Exactly, you got it!"

The rains have started and we are heading south again into Ghana where I am typing this, believe it or not in another Catholic mission, the air reeks of purity and goodness, and I have an overwhelming desire to be nice to people, perhaps even to lay my hands on their head and say,
"Bless you my child" and not only when they have sneezed, I've just heard that up the road there's a hotel selling beer so I think I'll go and convert a few sinners!!!!
I have to report that the overwhelming desire to be nice wasn't in truth overwhelming or even long lasting, in fact it was quite under whelming, and in no time I returned to my normal miserable objectionable and difficult self!

GHANA
In parts it's not a bad road between Ouagadougou and Ghana; in parts it's an ok road between Ouagadougou and Ghana; and in parts it's a really fun road (translation of fun? impassable!) between Ouagadougou and Ghana.

A combination of detours, laterite, heavy rain and lorries means that the suspension is used to the full and the car takes on a very "expedition" hue, with manly red stains all over it, only some of which are blood!. (Don't ask!.. he cycled into me your Honour! I didn't hit him! Well not as hard as he claimed!)

The Burkina Faso border is, like the rest of Burkina Faso, laid back and chaotic in a gentle sort of way, and Ghanaian customs and immigration clearance came and went with the sort of bureaucratic slowness you expected in East Africa but which has been missing in the west.

Arriving at the Ghanaian border you hand in your Carnet du Passage and the man looks at it like it's a final electricity demand, then tells you to "SIT" and puts the carnet on his desk and goes back to sleep.
Twenty minutes later, just as the little voice in my head was becoming even more than usually persuasive, another man appears with a temporary import license, the very thing that Carnets are designed to avoid, which you complete and give to another man, who stamps your Carnet and you're done.

Well half done in truth, all you have to do now is fill out another form for the police; he's the man that actually stamps your passport, then get your name entered into another book by another policeman, then finally your name is entered into yet another book by yet another customs officer then that's it!..easy! In the interest of truth and accuracy there were probably a couple more entries in a couple more exercise books but I lost count and just "went with the flow"

The route through Ghana took us through Tamale, Kumasi, and finally into BIG MILLIES just outside Accra, how can you resist a campsite called BIG MILLIES?, well OK you might be able to I certainly can't!

Kumasi is reputedly the biggest and busiest market in West Africa, which isn't a problem to the local drivers with years of practice, which has made them experienced in pushing in and turning across lines of traffic and surprisingly everything keeps moving, well almost, particularly as there is a noticeable lack of police interference or involvement, perhaps that's why.

Well! that's how it is most of the time! All goes well until two Englishmen arrive and take the left filter instead of the right filter then try a "U" turn!!
Everything stopped! Horns were sounded; advice was freely and volubly given! (And, in my case at least, returned with interest (for interest read invective!)).
"F**K off back to England!" being the most apposite, but a few deft moves, and a discreet use of the bull bars got me moving again, roughly in the direction of England and all was well, well it would have been until I did it again, and again received (and returned) the same excellent advice.

A man tapped the window and tried to charge me for parking, he didn't seem impressed when I told him I wasn't parking but I was in fact in a traffic queue and I was lost! Stuck! But lost! The sight of him reaching for his parking tickets (about 30 pence) galvanized me into action as this was I felt only adding insult to injury.

The advantage of a big 4x4 is that central reservations, and parking attendants toes, hold no fear(in fact you need have no reservations about central reservations!). A quick change down and a hard left, an (albeit insincere) apologetic smile at the parking attendant who screamed in agony and fell over as he tried to rub both his feet at the same time and we were back on the right road.

Nudging our way into the main road from where we started an hour ago, through the traffic lights (red!) up a one way street (wrong way!) stop and ask the way, have nice conversation with man selling bibles, cause a new traffic jam before finally turning into the Presbyterian guest house, which is what we were looking for.

A good nights sleep in there, until the famous rooster (as promised in the Lonely Planet) woke us up at 4 o'clock. If you're following us down the route don't worry it's dead now, and the chicken soup lasted three days!

The scenery is definitely tropical rainforest and we passed over a very full White Volta (it was orange!) and later over an equally full Black Volta (still orange!) and countless crashed and broken down lorries.

Did I mention that Burkina Faso used to be called Upper Volta?

DEAD RATS

They eat rats here! They big rats and they call them Grass Cutters. At first I wasn't sure what they were as the men stood on the side of the road and hung them up for you to see, but rats they were, as big as cats, big cats at that. I should have taken a picture but I didn't ... So when you hear that the poor starving Africans are eating rats remember they are delicacies to them, a bit like snails to the French! And I'm really fed up that Blackadder beat me to "rat-au-van" or "rat-a-touille" joke!

BROKEN DOWN LORRIES

I have endless respect for the drivers and mechanics here who seem to think nothing of replacing wheel bearings, stripping differentials and even a full engine rebuild in the middle of the main Kumasi to Accra road, (No! it's alright chaps I really love queuing in ninety degrees of humid heat breathing in diesel fumes, you just take your bloody time!) and this coming from a man who can't replace a battery in a torch on the kitchen table without losing a spring!!

From the outset I liked the sound of Big Milley's! And couldn't wait to find out what was big about Milley, (I had hopes of course). Accra turned out to be yet another chaotic West African city with the traffic making its own rules, and particularly….
Sorry hang on just had a thought!
On the road down we were stuck in a traffic queue caused by one of the many many road works, that have been started but which show little sign of being completed. We'd been following this truck full to overflowing with large bags of charcoal, when suddenly a truck coming in the other direction ipped on a large pot hole and caught the edge, and tore open a bag of charcoal; as he drove on he deposited the contents of the bag of charcoal through the open window of a brand new BMW, right onto the drivers lap.

Now I know I shouldn't laugh, and of course I didn't,(well not much) but I couldn't resist saying to the driver as he got out of his car, spilling charcoal from his lap
"Well you'll be ok for a BBQ tonight!"
Oh he did laugh at that one!

Right! Back to Big Milley's, set on the seashore, white sand brightly coloured boats and coconut palms, it's a great place!!
Very laid back and full of interesting people, travellers, medics, aid workers all coming together to drink beer and in some cases to join the local Rasta male population in both of their favourite pastimes, the second one being smoking strange smelling tea leaves!! Oh yes and listening to reggae full blast.. That makes it three!
Set on the edge of the ocean (remembering Plage Blanche I checked the tide levels!) the palm trees (like the Rasta's) sway

gently in the breeze; the beer is cold, the food good, and the second hand smoke from the tea leaves soooo satisfying, or should that be stupifying!!

A time for a rest from the perpetual driving, and also a chance to do some loin girding before the torment that I suspect will be Accra where boats, and visas and traffic jams and new passports look as though they will fill the week.

We had a great time with Mariska, Karen, Nicole from Belgium (I like Belgians!), Jennifer, Erin, Ellen, Emily and of course Kate from America all of whom made us realise again that travel is about people not about places.. Tonight is apparently Reggae night where the music will be blasting out at full volume until, well, tomorrow!
Oh I am looking forward to that!!!!!!!!

I'll have to stop now I need to find the main fuse board that feeds the sound system, then I'll offer, or threaten, to lend them my John Denver CD ...I know they'll be grateful.
As an alternative to driving down through Nigeria we needed to find a shipping agent in Accra, how difficult can it be to 'phone them, get an idea of the cost and the timetable, then we could go to their office once they'd told us where it is. Well very difficult when the only telephone directory available was six years out of date and falling apart.

ACCRA
Two days of rain, not your average English rain but your average tropical, teeming, torrential "coming down in buckets" rain, left our spirits, and everything else we owned, dampened so it was off to Accra, to get the various visas and of course new passports that all of the over-sized West African visas has made necessary.

"As rule of thumb on the road the size of the visa is inverse proportion to the size of the country."
"So what does that mean then?"
"The smaller the country the larger the visa, in fact some of the visa's are in truth larger than the country!"
"Is that true?"
"Well obviously not! that's what's called irony!"
"Or stupidity!"
We loved Big Milley's, well no, in truth we loved the people we met there, people with character who's company was always challenging and interesting.
It was fascinating talking to some of the volunteers who had paid large amounts of money, perhaps as much as $6000, to enable them to teach for a month in Ghana, and how in many cases they were disillusioned by what they found and what they were allowed to do.

They taught at local schools, usually AIDS related issues, and lived with local families. I had not heard of this system before, and my natural cynicism made me raise an eyebrow, well both in fact (and an ear!) and, whilst I am absolutely certain that Cross Cultural Solutions are totally honest and upright and that the Ghanaian managers are doing a wonderful job that helps and enriches both the volunteers and the Ghanaian beneficiaries; it's easy to see that the system could be abused and take advantage of the vast well of goodwill that exists amongst those who wish to help those who need help, or those who wish to help those they think should need help!

Enough of that I've got some scandal!!! Katie and Emily were dismissed from their volunteer job!!! That's it! You're right to ask.. How can you be sacked from being a volunteer, when you've actually paid money to volunteer? If you ever get to meet Katie and Emily and you'll find out!!
Talk about feisty!!

Sheesh!.. Just because one of their male colleagues, …erm how to put this? Enjoyed extending horizontal relationships (or horizontal relationships with extensions of himself, you choose!) between himself and the (female) nationals of Ghana.. And that this exercise in horizontal cross-cultural relationships was not on a one-to-one basis but on a one-to-very many basis.

Katie had commented to the administration (at length and adversely) about this … and, as they say, the brown stuff hit the revolving thingy and the result was she was sent on extended holiday.

I suggested as politely as I could that perhaps it might have been jealousy that had motivated her actions!
Blimey! For a medium size girly she certainly packs a punch but it's ok the bruising is going down now and I should be able to see out of both eyes quite soon.

The good news is that she has promised to show the world her tattoos when she is a bridesmaid at her sisters wedding, AND she has promised us a picture but I had to promise that in no circumstances would I publish it on the web site.

This I promised and at the time (suffering as I was from her recent violent attack) I meant it…. And of course I wouldn't break a promise….!!!!!

Back to the trip

It's so difficult to get GOOD information about driving in Nigeria, of course everyone purses their lips and shakes their heads, but when you question them on actual knowledge they admit they are simply repeating hearsay.

324

What we've decided to do is drive through Nigeria using only
the main roads, stop early in the day at good hotels with
secure car parks, and keep our fingers crossed!
What else can we do?
We stayed last night at the Methodist mission in Accra
expensive, poor food and reggae replaced with hymns, so we
moved to the car park of Ryan's Irish Pub. I know what
you're thinking! You don't need to drink just because you're
in a pub car park! Some people can and do enjoy themselves
without drinking! Well some of you might be able to stay in a
pub car park without drinking, and be able enjoy yourself
without drinking; I don't think I can, and I'm not about to
start trying now!

IN THE BAR RYAN'S PUB

Yes I know I said you don't need to drink just because you're
staying in a pub car park but it's been raining for five days and
I'm bored, the bed gets wet at night (no! not the old problem!)
Then, after a few brief rays of sun, which dries off the worst
of the damp, it then inevitably clouds over and the humidity
climbs, and the rain comes down, and makes everything is wet
again.

We were still not sure whether or not to drive through West
Africa or catch the boat. The problem is of course Nigeria,
everyone says that it's much too dangerous to drive, but when
you question the source of their knowledge, they admit that
they are simply repeating what "everyone knows".
By definition the Lonely Planet is out of date, so what with
that, and the "what everyone knows" it's difficult to make a
decision.

We went to the Nigerian Embassy and the very nice man there
said, not surprisingly, that it was fine and that he did the
journey regularly between Accra and Lagos taking only eight

hours, without problems from customs or police; I resisted the temptation to suggest that his CD plates may help, well I didn't in fact.

A flat part of the trip with really nothing to do whilst waiting for passports and visas, too wet to sit out and at the end of the day we are in a pub car park after all..

So might as well sit inside and drink!

UPDATE
We've decided to continue our drive through West Africa, basically because very few people we met ACTUALLY have tried, and in spite of not doing it or knowing anyone who did it, they say it's dangerous and more importantly, because the alternatives were just too complex and would take too long so it's visa time again. Crazily, well to me, containers filled in Ghana are shipped back to Algeceiras in Spain before being transhipped to another vessel for shipping to Durban.. Taking 6-8 weeks!
PASSPORTS VISAS AND BOREDOM
Well! We've got a new passport, it's called at macro bionic or some such thing and apparently measures the distance between your eyes and ears divides it by your date of birth and if the answer is more than twelve you cannot get back into the UK.
My passport was issued easily but the system wouldn't accept Jeans, and there was no point in them releasing it, as the first time we tried to use it at an electronic border control it would sound red lights and she would be dragged off screaming!
Well I think that was what Joanne; the Consul, was trying to tell me when she was explaining the delay in issuing Jeans passport. Apparently Jeans eyes are too close together so the machine wouldn't accept it.

But then Joanne recently married a Chelsea supporter who also works at the consulate (how do they pass the entrance exams to the diplomatic core these days? .. in my day diplomats didn't even acknowledge that soccer existed.. "Rugger" at "Twickers" was about as close as they got to dirty knees.. But now they accept Chelsea supporters!.. No wonder we lost the Empire!)

Anyway we finally got our new, (it's not macro bionic, it's isotonic), passport, virginally clean of stamps and visas so at last we can get back to the business of EXPEDITIONING!

First stop the Togolese (Togonese?) Embassy and a couple of hours later the virginal passport (it can't be Isotonic that's a drink…ergonomic??) had its first page used up and after that a quick visit to the Nigerian Embassy saw us chatting up the Nigerian Visa man trying to persuade him to break the rules and accept our application so we could get the visa quickly and get on the road.

He listened sympathetically to our plight and fully understood that living in Ryan's bar car park in torrential rain was difficult and that simply by accepting our application and processing it he could improve our lives immeasurably.. He listened sympathetically, looking interestedly at our new egocentric (?) passport, smiled encouragingly, and refused!!

THE BEGGARS ARE GETTING FUSSY

I know that there was something I was going to tell you. We stopped at a supermarket in Accra and a very nice beggar came up and said,

"Sir I am hungry!" which usually means he wants a cigarette or money and is certainly not in the market for the two stale bread rolls that he got from me!! He was somewhat less than grateful but I always say it's the giver who benefits, and not the givee (??).Yes I know what you are thinking and of course you are totally right I do always say that to justify my meanness.

Two days later he stopped me again, obviously he had a short memory or perhaps felt that I could have changed and in the last two days and suddenly become generous and caring, so he was misguided as well as hungry, and said,

"Sir I am hungry!"

"I gave you some food two days ago don't you remember?"

He gave me a look that seemed to indicate that he certainly did remember.

"Ok im going into the supermarket I'll get you a couple of rolls!"

"Err Sir could you make it a French stick please!!!" FRENCH STICK! No less!! Cheeky sod!

In an attempt to embarrass him I said,

"Would you like some cheese in it?"

"Yes please" bloody hell they will be carrying menus around with them next!!

LAKE AKOSOMBO DAM AND LAKE VOLTA

The thought of another night in the car park of Ryan's bar in the rain lacked a certain (well any) appeal so, on the strength of Gillian from the British Embassy's, recommendation we decided on a weekend at the largest man made lake in the world, Lake Akosombo (that is the largest if you discount the puddle in our bed after a rainstorm)

I thought that camping would still be fun (for fun read cheap!), but the idea didn't go down well!

"I want a hotel and a dry bed!"

"But..!"

"I want a hotel and a dry bed!"

"Well we're on an EXPEDITION and...."

"I want a hotel and a dry bed!"

There are times in life when it arguing is pointless so I presented myself to the receptionist at the Akosombo

Continental hotel,
"Right sunshine how much for a night?"
"$60!"
"And for two nights?"
"$120!"
"Erm nooo! All you've just shown me you can multiply by two let's talk discount!"
We negotiated at length and agreed, both reluctantly, on $100.

I filled out the registration form with the information from my new existentiate (?) passport and all went well until I got to the arrival date; Friday 04.08.06, no problem! Departure date Sunday 06.08.06
"Sorry sir, we're full tomorrow!"
"What do you mean full!"
"It means we have no rooms!"
Little voice whispers "Ahh we have a comedian! Slap him Jeff!
"So tell me, these two nights we've just spent twenty minutes arguing about, which two nights did you think I meant? Last night and tonight, tonight and a week next bloody Wednesday?"

So it's back to camping (Jean still doesn't believe me!) on the banks of the Volta River and looking nervously at the heavy black rain clouds that have been locked above us for a week. The good news is that we met a group of Australians over in Ghana learning drumming and experiencing the joys of living in a brothel (don't ask!) Linda, Elaine, Michelle, Sharon and little Joy are being subjected to West African organization for the first time, and, listen to this, made the fatal mistake of saying,
"If you're ever in Adelaide ..etc"
Why do people do it??
Why do we take advantage?

Because that's the sort of people we are…so that's another place to stay in Australia!

In 1957 Ghana became the first state in sub-Saharan Africa to gain political independence from Britain under its first President Kwame Nkrumah "the Father of African Nationalism" and it triggered, literally and metaphorically, the Independence movement that quickly spread East and South through Africa. Ghana, named after the medieval empire on the Upper Niger river, was previously called Gold Coast by the early European explorers who arrived in search of gold in the 15th and 16th centuries, and has more than 100 different ethnic groups, but fortunately has largely been spared the ethnic conflict that has torn apart many other African countries.

When they achieved independence Ghana had been among the wealthiest and most socially advanced areas in Africa, with schools, railways, hospitals, social security and an advanced economy. Under Nkrumah's leadership, Ghana adopted socialist policies and practices and created a welfare system; started various community programs, and established schools. Driven by Nkrumah's socialist zeal, roads and bridges were built to improve communications and the infrastructure. Public health in villages was improved, as were tap water systems and concrete drains for latrines

He also attempted to change Ghana's economy. His reasoning being that, only if Ghana could escape the inherited system by reducing dependence on foreign technology and material goods, could it become truly independent. Unfortunately many economic projects he initiated were unsuccessful, or with delayed

benefits. The Akosombo Damn for example was
expensive at the time, but today produces most of
Ghana's hydroelectric power.

Nkrumah's policies unfortunately but inevitably did
not free Ghana from dependence on Western imports,
and by the time he was deposed in 1966 Ghana had
fallen from one of the richest countries in Africa to
one of the poorest, because of what was to become the
norm in Africa, corruption and excesses by the ruling
elite. He died of in April 1972 at the age of 62.
The Volta Lake where we stayed resulted from the
construction of the dam at Akosombo in 1960, and is
the largest man-made lake in the world, covering an
area of about 8,515 hectares. When it was formed
78,000 people were relocated to new townships,
along with 200,000 animals belonging to them.

Just been told it's apparently a biometric passport!!! Metric?
Blimey is everything European now? What was wrong with
good old feet and inches? Twelve inches to the foot, three feet
to a yard, one thousand seven hundred and sixty yards to a
mile! What's difficult about that????

CALABAR NIGERIA
If you look on the map you will see that Calabar is nearly at
the border with Cameroon (No don't bother! just take my
word for it!)
and, in spite of dire predictions, we have not been robbed
ravished or raped, in fact, if you discount the eighty odd road
blocks in the two days it took to drive between the Benin
border and Calabar, it's been quite tedious, but I jump ahead.
We were in and out of Togo in an hour or so, and apart from
the roads being chaotic I truly can't think of anything to say
about it.

After our night in Hotel Dono Port Novo in Benin an early
start saw us at the border with Nigeria and for the first time
were met with a surprisingly hostile reception, mainly because
I refused to pay a scruffy looking individual 2700 (about £12)
Naira at a makeshift control barrier, a pole between two forty
five gallon oil drums,
"2700 naira!" he barked
"Who are you?" I growled,
"Police!"
"So why should I pay you 2700 naira? and where's your badge
and do I get a receipt?"

He didn't like any of these questions and looked over his
shoulder towards, what looked a first (and second) sight like a
broken down garden shed, out of which came, in high
dudgeon, an equally disreputable character, who demanded to
know what the problem was, I knew this because he said,
"What's the problem?"

Scruff number one conversed quickly and scruff number two
looked at me as if I was a mass child murderer,
"Papers!" he demanded
"Who are you?" by now I was certainly ready to join forces in
battle, but then I remembered that not all police in Africa look
like police, so with great difficulty I controlled myself and
gave him the mass of paperwork that you seem to accumulate
when travelling. He turned and walked off with it and, as you
can imagine, I followed.

Close up the garden shed looked even worse, but he tried hard
to compensate by looking intimidating, in response to which I
looked at a three year old calendar with (feigned) fascinated
interest.

Already inside was another man who did not have the 500 Naira that was demanded (notice 500 not 2700!! (Call me cynical but the only obvious difference I could spot was the fact that I was older than him, oh yes and whiter, well white!!)) He was pleading, unsuccessfully, with the policeman (?) to let him through!

The policeman looked at me as if to say "that's the way you should behave!" and he waited for a fundamental change in my attitude and demeanour, he waited, like so many others, before and since, in vain.
It's amazing how fascinating three-year-old calendars can be! Eventually he tired and reached into his desk and brought out a child's exercise book and officiously, and perhaps even officially, filled in all the details from the Carnet and my International Driving License before getting bewildered, losing interest and throwing them all down dismissively for me to pick up and leave.
Now I don't recommend you to react the same but it was early in the day and they did piss me off!

I am not going to go through details of clearing police, immigration and customs on the Togo, Benin and Nigerian border, all I can tell you is that it takes time, it's not logical but it can be done and in spite of the requests there is never a question of my giving (or unfortunately being given), a bribe.

DRIVING THROUGH NIGERIA

They said it was dangerous and we were stupid to even think about it and, even though I am extremely sceptical about 95% of the information you get, I was on a high state of alert, or is it state of high alert? Well I was awake, so we got to the border early, and were processed through, as I wrote earlier without any real problem.

After clearing customs we took a deep breath and readied ourselves for the inevitable certain death and even worse, robberies ahead. Into first gear, windows locked, bulletproof vest (well two T shirts and double deodorant) and it was a case of,
"All set? Good luck chaps! Right over the top!"

Five yards hard driving brought us to our first police roadblock, and five yards further by another and another and another. The pattern was set for the day and in the two hundred and fifty miles between the border and the first nights stop in Benin we must have been stopped at forty road blocks, manned by police, army, narcotics, highways police and God knows who else. But never a criminal, there's no room for a criminal in between the multitude of other roadblocks.

At each successive roadblock we painted on smiles and acted dim when it came to understanding their requests,
"Something for me?"
A man in Ryan's said,
"Just slip them Naira 500(about £2) and you'll not have any problems!"
Bloody hell I should think not, no problem apart from being eighty quid out of pocket! I'll stick to acting dim. When I was getting bored I slipped them a ballpoint pen and they were happy! Well that may be an overstatement but accepted it and waved us on.

By the second day (and another forty odd road blocks) we were getting into the swing of it, and, accepting the inevitable, joining the game. The constant theme was that driving a right handed drive was illegal in Nigeria and as I was explaining for the umpteenth time that registering a right hand drive was illegal, driving through wasn't, a fact I had confirmed in writing with the Nigerian Embassy in London! (Well I intended to but you know how you run out of time!!). This usually worked but at one he said,

"No you must pay a fine you have broken our law!"

"Ok If I have broken your law take me to the police station and charge me and I will pay the fine there!"

"Come then we will go! But it is very far!"

"That's ok I have time and a car!"

"Can you give me a lift?"

"No chance sunshine you can walk!"

A pause, then,

"You may go but do not do it again!"

"Ok I won't bye!!" (I lied I did!)

At another when we had reached bit of an impasse and I was reluctantly reaching for a pen the man said,

"Is this a missionary vehicle?"

I was so shocked that I could be mistaken for a missionary that I was rendered speechless and my silence was taken as confirmation and he waved me through with a smile.

Jean and I looked at each other and we knew what to do. At the next roadblock when they brought up the right hand drive problem I said,

"Oh that's strange as the mission (clever huh?) contacted the Nigerian Embassy and they said it was fine!" (Double name dropping) this resulted in a very smart salute and we were waved on.

At the next one I let it be known that I was a medical missionary and by now I was on a roll,

"Yes I'm on my way to Angola to train doctors!"

Double respect now but he wasn't finished,

"Why Angola what is wrong with helping Nigeria?"

"Oh I've already done that when I worked in Kano, I worked through the church there!"

Now anyone who knew me in Kano will know that the nearest I got to the church was passing it on the way to the pub but as I was invariably on my knees when going home that must have counted!

So that's it I'm a medical missionary (I even invented a disease!! trygenic myopic myalgea) and on day two I only parted with three

pens all day; and before you think too badly of me Jean started saying "Bless you" and making the sign of the cross at them, which even I draw a line at.

At another roadblock a very very powerful young man with a bandolier of bullets and a very large gun, sleeves ripped off his combat shirt or more likely split from the pressure of his massive biceps, tapped on Jeans window with the business end of his gun!

She wound her window down, looked at the gun and, looking straight into his eyes, said,

"Please don't point that at me I have children older than you"

He glanced over at me and I gave him my "Don't look at me, you're on your own sunshine, but remember you've only got a fully loaded automatic!" .

"Sorry madam" and he moved away, a wise decision!

Just for anyone following then here are the strategies for getting through roadblocks, not necessarily in the order that I would recommend.

(1) When you stop tell them to "Piss off and stop wasting my time",

(2) Immediately slip them Naira 500,

(3) Give them a ball point pen,

(4) Claim to be a missionary on Gods work and offer to pray for them,

(5) Smile and say Hi and ask after their family,

Finally and seriously remember that they are underpaid with families to support and they are simply trying to get by in life; give each and everyone respect and remember it's better to have police roadblocks rather than criminal ones, and feel comfort in knowing that with there being so many roadblocks there is no room for any criminals.

I repeat what I've been saying for a while when you're on the road. BEFORE BELIEVING WHAT PEOPLE SAY ASK THEM HOW THEY KNOW!"

CALABAR

Unlike Lagos and Benin the traffic in Calabar flowed and the streets were clear of rubbish, but in spite of that (or maybe because of that) we missed the turn to the "good" hotels and finished up in the back streets of the docks! The two hotels mentioned in the Lonely Planet were, um? Damn! I can't think of the word that I'm looking for? But bloody awful will do until I can.

We got stuck behind a "happy clapper!" children's parade and as we crawled along, suddenly we saw a LARGE Land Cruiser driven by whites! Now a trick worth remembering when you're lost is to ask a white face!

They turned out to be Japanese who immediately guided us to the Hotel Mirage, and drove off shaking their heads at two old couples who though planning to drive all the way through Africa couldn't even find hotels in a town as small as Calabar.

CAMEROON VISA

Well we're sitting here in Calabar waiting for a Cameroon Visa, which you get from the Cameroon Embassy. What you do is write a handwritten letter asking for a visa, fill in a form, get three passport photos, pay your money and they (hopefully) give you a visa.

What you don't do is get to the Cameroon Embassy on the same day that the Ambassador is at some diplomatic jolly, up to his bloody elbows in free vol-au-vaunts instead of being at his desk dealing with our visas, and not telling his secretary whether or not he will be coming back to his desk.

Also what you don't do is to arrive the day before some other bloody holiday, when he again wont be doing what he was put on this earth to do, dealing with our visas, and we will be left twiddling our thumbs in a Formica hotel for three days!

But I'm not bitter!"

Much!

BUT

The nice man from the embassy (I, of course, never had any doubts about him at all) came back, took our money and gave us a visa. He apologised for the delay and said he would normally do it in half an hour!!

MEMORIES OF NIGERIA

Our route through Nigeria took us through Lagos, Benin, Aba, Owerri, and Calabar and, Calabar apart, each town appears to be more squalid and crowded than the previous one. Rotting rubbish was an introduction to each city, spilling over onto the road; the pollution from the badly maintained vehicles on overcrowded roads and burning rubbish leaves a permanent fog, swarms of smoking and screaming mopeds filling every gap between the cars.

One man said,

"Ahh you are in the armpit of Africa!" I warmed to the analogy of likening Africa to the human body, but the armpit isn't the first area this part of Africa springs to mind!

Calabar is a haven, clean broad streets, and uncrowded roads if you're going to be stuck anywhere it's as good a place as any.

So we don't know anything about Nigeria apart from the main road through, and the Nigerians we met were helpful and efficient (ish) but we were insulated in our cars from the smell and pollution and of course eighty roadblocks made it a memorable section of the trip, sorry EXPEDITION!!!

CAMEROON

AND I THOUGHT THE ROADS COULDN'T BE AS BAD AS THEY SAID!

Right where did we leave you? Oh yes! In Calabar Nigeria which, from what we saw, is the most attractive town in Nigeria.
We wanted to enter the south of Cameroon through Ikom, reputedly quieter than the others, so we left early driving northward in torrential rain, which although making driving uncomfortable at least kept the criminals, and all but the most desperate police, indoors.
The Nigerian border post was the quietest we have been through, and the most laid back, vague waves of the hands in the general direction of some derelict offices, a brief search for the customs stamp (it was at the back of the drawer) and we were through.
The narcotics officer wanted to be invited to England and the immigration officer was so quick in stamping our passports he gave the impression that he was desperate either to get us out of the country, himself home for lunch, or both!!
We asked about the roads in Cameroon, they laughed and said,
"You will see!"

The tarmac stopped at the border, and we rolled gently over the wooden bridge into Cameroon; along a laterite path, smooth! Not a problem! What bad roads?
The Cameroon officials were friendly and welcoming and I asked again about the roads,
"Not very good!"
"When you say not very good what do you mean?"
"Bad!"
Jean had been worried about the roads but I managed to persuade her that they couldn't possibly be as impassable as they were reported, and that the ones shown in the pictures and on various web sites, were in remote areas. The roads that we would be travelling on would be the main trunk roads and so couldn't possibly be that bad! She looked doubtful and muttered something about beaches and Atlantic. I looked at the heavens and hoped!

The customs officer ruined the initial good impression of Cameroon by trying to get a bribe disguised as "overtime" for working on a bank holiday, and he refused to stamp the Carnet until we paid him extra "overtime" money.
"Right let's get this clear, if it wasn't a bank holiday you would stamp it"
"Oh yes!"
"Ok we'll sleep outside tonight and come through tomorrow!"
"Ahh you don't understand this is the law!"
"Aah believe me matey I do understand only too well!"
He stamped the Carnets and smiled; we took the Carnets and scowled…

Staying that first night in Cameroon outside the local police station in Eyumojock gave me the opportunity to get first hand information about the road from the police chief,
"Very difficult!"
Jean said

"I will kill you!"
I eased myself behind the police chief! He saw the look on Jeans face and retreated into his office, conveniently forgetting his sworn duty to protect citizens from the threat of imminent violence, locked the door and 'phoned for reinforcements.

I have to report that the road started poor, moved quickly through hard (well soft in truth), bypassed very difficult and arrived almost immediately at virtually impassable.

You quickly learn that in mud this deep you have very little control over where the vehicle is going, the sheer sided ruts decide that for you, and all you can do is try and steer a general course and avoid over revving and digging in, but you may as well simply take your hands off the steering wheel and just use your feet. The other very real danger is of breaking your thumbs if the wheels suddenly turn in rut which makes the steering wheel spin, so make sure that your thumbs aren't wrapped around the steering wheel.
I managed to make progress of sort for a few hundred yards and with misplaced confidence I reached for the inter-com and called
to Marion and Les to follow my track as best they could but they had already started and suddenly Marion shouted, "We're stuck" five seconds later so was I!
Clutch in, pause, deep breath and into reverse, strange noise from wheels… bugger hand brake still on! How long has that been on? Hands off the steering wheel so that you're not fighting the wheels and they are at least pointing the same direction as the ruts, reverse slowly back until the wheels grip, steady, STEADY! Easy now, look for another line where the ruts aren't so deep.. Into low second…gently now, GENTLEEEEY!, great we're out of the first rut, ease into another, resist the temptation to accelerate too quickly ..the

back slews round so you going sideways ..Not a problem, you're still going forward, suddenly the wheels grip and you're through! .. Stop and switch off!
Wow! That was fun!

What to do now? Go back to help Les? But that means leaving the car.. Two problems with that! Security and being in the way of vehicles coming the other way.
Think Jeff! No reply from the radio so lock up and go back to see what's happening.

It's further than I thought, or perhaps the thick mud made it seem that way. When I arrived Les is in deep mud but already he's being helped. In the distance I could hear the revving of another car coming the other way so I slithered and slid as quickly as I could back to my car and stood helplessly as a grossly overloaded Toyota pick up crabbed sideways towards it, no point in doing anything I waited for the collision, at the last moment it straightened and squeezed by, merely brushing my mud guard.

Where I had been tense and gripping the wheel tightly, this driver, obviously used to the road and the conditions, was relaxed and smiling.
I sat and waited and enjoyed the sounds of tropical Africa.
It was a very muddy Jean who joined me with an update of Les and Marion, they were still stuck but they had all the assistance they needed. We were simply blocking the road so we might as well get out of everyones way. I started the engine but before moving off I turned to Jean,
She was quiet! She'd fallen into the mud, perhaps that was why?

"See it wasn't that bad!"

342

She looked at me! One of her "special" looks, in the heat of tropical Africa the inside of the car chilled noticeably.
By now I had the hang of the driving, easing forward not worrying too much about sliding or tilting just trying generally to watch the tyre tracks of other vehicles that had gone before, down a hill and suddenly a wall of mud, no tyre tracks through it, decision! The edge looks the least worst but no decision was necessary, the mud had already decided I was going off the edge of the road, I had no choice, I put the clutch in too late and dug in.
Stuck!

And this is what was happening to Les!!

Jean fell on her bum

He was dressed in shorts and a dirty T-shirt, and he was
waving his hands,
"Go back, go back!"
Where the hell did he come from?

Suddenly there were more of them, obviously very
experienced, they worked as a team, telling me where to steer,
when to accelerate and miraculously the tyres gripped and I
eased back.
I hadn't noticed the detour that I had driven by earlier and
after I had stopped, he explained that it was them who had
created the detour, and they would guide me through! .. at a
price!
It was a toll road!!

Bloody hell you have to admire them, although the cynic in
me seriously considered whether they had spent all night
pouring water onto the impassable bit just so we would have
to use the detour.. Noo!!!!! Surely not! Why not? It's exactly
the sort of thing I would do!
"Look sunshine get me through this lot and I'll happily pay
you!" (Again the word "happily" and "pay" being found in the
same sentence! God I'm getting old!)

This from a man who will sit for three hours in a traffic jam on the M6 rather than pay the three quid toll on the Birmingham ring road!.

Entrepreneurs they may be, road builders they aint! The detour consisted of two deep ruts filled with stones, tree trunks and various bits of rubbish that successive cars had churned up into glutinous orange stinking mass. This wasn't too bad, but the ruts were different depths so the car leant over and at times it feels like you're driving at 45 degrees, the reason being, of course, that you are in fact driving at 45 degrees!

But there is no way it will tip over; the mud banks are half way up your door.

They pushed, they rocked, they shouted, they jumped fearlessly in front of the vehicle and told me where to steer until finally we arrived at the last section, an almost vertical drop into a ditch and an equally steep climb out.

I paused!

"Why have you stopped?"

"Because I'm shitting myself here!"

"GO GO!"

I went went! The nose dipped alarmingly forward until all I could see was mud, then sky, and suddenly I was out, a quick burst on the engine and I was through!,

Bugger! No I wasn't, my rear axle grounded and I was stuck again. Very very stuck!

They still have mountain gorillas in Cameroon! They live in family groups and the Alpha male is called the silverback and they are big and have the strength of five grown men, and where are they when you need them to push you out of the mud? Sat up some bloody tree munching on Eucalyptus! That's where they are!

345

"It's Koalas that eat Eucalyptus Jeff, Gorillas eat bamboo shoots, or is that Giant Pandas"
"Whatever they bloody eat, one good push from one of them would have got me out no problem!"

I had not of course paid the toll, and this gave them renewed energy, into low first here we go again
"Three, two, one!"

Hands off the steering wheel for a second to let the wheels centralise, make sure thumbs are out of the way, and we (er! they!) pushed! The engine screamed! Too many revs! Ease off, better! Slowly we creep forward.. Power now!! And we were through.. a few more slides and suddenly I was on firmish ground, it was still deep and sticky but by now I knew it was drivable!

I had the same silly grin on my face that I had after the sponsored nudist parachute jump (but that was the straps!) and now the worst was over and Les still had to come through. I got out of the car and listened to the sounds of the rain forest, the cicadas, the ticking of the engine, the soft hiss of air from a damaged tyre, the distant roar of Les nearing, innocent of what was to come, the…. hang on! Did I say the soft hiss of air escaping from a damaged tyre?
"Well bloody thanks a lot God!"

Some wood had found its way between the tyre bead and the rim and sure enough the tyre was deflating, not quickly, but in the way of punctures, inexorably.

There was no way I could jack a tyre up in that mud so we jumped in and drove as quickly as two feet deep mud and a rapidly deflating tyre will allow, which isn't very. Quickly, that is.

We had good luck and bad luck, the good luck was that the next village was only about half a mile away, the bad luck was that the ruts were even deeper as they ran through the village, they resembled three foot deep muddy tram lines, and there was no way I could cross them to get to the only piece of hard ground I could see.

I stopped! Now you have to remember at this point that pushing people out of the mud is the local cottage industry round here and within seconds they were all behind me pushing like buggery before they realised I'd switched the engine off and had the hand brake on.
One of them came to the window sweating from pushing a three and a half ton Toyota with the hand brake on in the mud and spoke to me in his local dialect. I had of course no idea what he said but I suspect it was something like
"Are you taking the piss or what?"
I told him about the puncture and that I needed to get onto the hard ground I had parked near.
In broken English another one said,
"Oh no! he wouldn't like it if you parked there!"
"Don't you worry your pretty little head about him sunshine, when I'm stuck in the middle of the road with traffic coming and a puncture I can be very very persuasive!"

He went to the back, his friends went to the side and I started the engine. No point in trying to steer, the car was going where they wanted, which wasn't where I wanted. We went past the hard ground I had selected and I knew that they were pushing me gently but firmly to where they wanted me to go. If you can't beat

Them, join them, so I decided to cooperate, something I always do when there is no other option!

There is a trick that sometimes works when you're in a rut (literally as opposed to psychologically) and that is not to turn the steering wheel as you normally would, but to turn it sharply then turn it back. Keep doing that and if you're lucky you'll get out.

We were lucky it worked!!! And we eventually rolled sedately, if muddily, into the garden of an old woman who was sitting in front of her house. She looked up and seemed unfazed at the sight of a bloody great orange Land Cruiser suddenly emerging from the mud and appearing in her front garden.
Jean did what I should have done, went and said hello.

I, of course, ignored the niceties and became dynamic. Well I thought I was being dynamic. Jean said later I was rushing round like a headless chicken! At least all the other chickens in the garden had a head.

The inside of the car was a mess, everything having fallen down. Right! First we need the High lift Jack, that's on the floor behind the seats, which of course was covered by everything not tied down. Throw pillows, sleeping bags, books, empty water bottles, a dirty pair of socks (so that was what the smell was!) to the other side and haul out the Jack! What next? The wheel spanner! Where's that? Bugger! Under all the stuff I've just thrown across the car. Round the other side chuck everything back and get the wheel spanner. Reaching behind me I said,
"Hold that please!"

What now? Spare wheel off the roof! No need to use the ladder I'll just climb on the window frame. I begin to climb up and then see the inch deep layer of mud on my shoes that would drop into the window mechanism. I need something to cover the window..

That'll do. A plastic bag, perfect .. inside is another bag filled with peanuts that I had bought earlier. I grabbed the inner bag, "Hold that please!"
The little sod's face lit up and he rushed off, thinking all his Christmases had come at once! He'd pinched my peanuts! He was intercepted by the old woman who slapped his head took the peanuts off him disappeared then re-appeared empty handed!

No time to get them back! I climbed onto the roof and then climbed off again. Damn! I'd forgotten I need a spanner to release the spare wheel. Opening the boot, I see everything had fallen onto the tool bag…
Bugger! Move everything, sweating now, it's running off my nose and my shirt is soaked.. find spanner, climb back on roof begin to undo nut.
Look down and realise that the man I asked to hold the wheel spanner was already undoing the wheel nuts!
"Oi stop that!"

Too late he was on a roll! And on the wrong wheel! Tempted to drop spare wheel on his head but he looked up saw my expression and jumped back.
Spare wheel handed down, athletic leap down and nearly fall over. Give them my "I meant to do that look!"
Now for the high lift jack.

You will remember that the last time I had used the High Lift Jack was on "THE" beach in Morocco. The sand and shells had had a few weeks to congeal nicely in the mechanism of the Jack so naturally nothing worked!
I heaved, sweated, and swore but it wouldn't move,

"STOP! Jeff you're not thinking! Somethings not working..
Think about it logically!" I thought about it logically and
when nothing came to me I did the next best thing, I hit it with
a hammer! That did the trick and it started to move!

Now those of you who do not know anything about High Lift
Jacks won't know that what you have is a large steel pipe,
which goes through a mechanism that acts as a fulcrum,(the
mechanism which works better if not bunged up with sand
and shells) and the other side fits into a bracket on the car. So
as you press the pipe down it lifts the car.. And the car is
heavy!

I was struggling, sweating and swearing, until one of them
lent me a hand, literally! He had more power in his hand than
I had in my whole body! And finally the car was up. Easing
the wheel off I cleaned the kilos of glutinous mud from the
brake pads and discs and then wrestled the new wheel on.
Right! Wheels on now, time to reverse the process. I pressed
the little lever thingy on the jack, which should reverse the
lifting system into a lowering process.
Nothing! It just kept lifting. . Bugger!

I held the pipe down; looked over to make sure that the lever
thingy was down, yes! I let go of the pipe, turned to reach for
the hammer, the little bolt thingy suddenly released and the
pipe shot up and hit me across the face!

Stars came out in the middle of a Cameroonian day!
Bloody hell it hurt!

Remember it had the weight of the whole vehicle behind it..I
staggered and, as I always do at times like this pretended that
I had meant to do it or looked for someone smaller than me to
blame. But no-one truly believed that even I meant to hit

myself across the head with a pipe propelled by the 3.5 ton of Land Cruiser, and the only person there smaller than me was a two year old boy, and even he didn't look as though he scared easily!

He returned my glare impassively,

I lent against the car and the man who was doing the wheel nuts said,

"Ooh sorry!"

"Not half as bloody sorry as I am, sunshine!"

By the time I was seeing straight again the wheel was back on, I climbed back on to the top of the vehicle and they handed me the punctured wheel, now even heavier because of all the mud. More sweat and it was at that moment that Les slithered slowly by, and shouted,

"You ok?"

What I thought was,

"Oh yes I'm standing on top of the bloody car sweating with a blinding headache bird watching! Silly sod!"

What I said was

"Yes! You go on!"

Spare wheel tightened! Another leap off but more carefully this time,

Right that's it, were ready! Everything back in and on the vehicle forgotten anything…Right let's go…hang on.. I have forgotten something! where's Jean?

It seemed a shame to interrupt her, she was having SUCH a lovely conversation with the old lady in the shade of the hut, probably giving her recipes for cooking my bloody peanuts!
 Jean said,

"Who tightened the wheel nuts?"

"He did! Bugger!"

There's something about Africans, spanners and wheel nuts it becomes a macho thing! If there was an Olympic event in wheel nut tightening the rest of the world wouldn't even get to the finals.
Sure enough when I tried to loosen the nuts I couldn't budge them,
"Oi! Get this sorted!" and gave him back the wheel spanner, and he eased it off without thinking and gave me a pitying look that said,
"Get what sorted?"

Bastard!

I paid them the equivalent of £5, which to them is a lot of money (it's a lot of money to me but, even though I obviously thought about it, there was no way I could get away without giving them something).
They offered to escort us through the remaining few hundred yards and as I started to reverse out following their instructions. Jean said,
"Jeff you haven't said goodbye to the lady!"
I leant out of the window and waved cheerily, shouting,
"I hope the bloody peanuts choke you!"
She gave me an equally cheery wave back and shouted something in local dialect, I'm not sure what it was but everyone looked at her shocked so it probably ended in "off"

That's it! They escorted me, running ahead of me up the muddy tracks, easily outpacing me and when we finally stopped, even though they were sweating they weren't even breathing heavily!

I gave them some pens and my Jaguar racing baseball cap (a waste really as I don't suppose they have ever heard of Jaguars or baseball!) and we parted, great blokes!
And a great day!! And seriously the roads weren't that bad, they were only impassable, but fun!!!!!!

It's interesting the change in scenery now that we're in tropical Africa, the combination of warmth and wet makes everything so vibrant. The "jungle" crowds the road and everywhere there are bananas, date and palm oil trees, sugar cane and mango. In fact the never-ending battle seems to be to keep the vegetation from reclaiming the road, and it's all very low tech, men with machetes simply hacking away, stopping as we drive by to return our waves, then starting again.

I wrote earlier about the muddy roads and whilst these are the most spectacularly bad the others are in truth more difficult to drive on. Massive and deep pot holes, filled with water means that you have to be aware all the time, as anyone of them can ruin your tyre at best or rip a wheel off at worst.
The worst part is when you relax and you let your speed build up, then suddenly you see the hole and you brake hard, but it's important that you try to lift off just before you hit the hole, so that at least your front suspension isn't fully depressed, and it can do its job.

But there's no doubt that suspension units are consumables, especially when the vehicle is overloaded, but fingers crossed, so far so good
The traffic weaves around the holes selfishly; the yellow taxis in particular ignore every rule of the road, but all of the other drivers simply look straight ahead and continue driving. At the time of writing I still haven't had anyone actually hit me but I'm fully convinced that this will change.

Today, it's Monday in Yaounde and it's been a visa day for Gabon and Congo, and yet another day of frustration and waiting. The Gabon visa takes twenty four hours and they want us back to collect our passports at three o'clock tomorrow, which is after the Congo visa closes which takes another twenty four hours so that can't be put in until Wednesday. It's frustrating but then much of travel is boring and frustrating.

The Visa for the Democratic Republic of Congo (that's another Congo) takes forty-eight hours but they don't work Friday then it's the weekend so it's probably another week sitting.

Hopefully though with a bit of wheedling and negotiating and paying and pleading, or if I think it will work, tears, we may just be able to get away before the weekend, which is important as we have to be in Libreville by Sunday as the Angolan Embassy only accepts visa applications for processing on Monday for delivery on Friday. It's a pain, and an expensive one at that. The two Congo's and the Gabon visas have cost £240 just so we can drive through the bloody countries.

But the good news is that the weather has changed to dry and for a change we are not sleeping in a damp tent, and at least we can sit out at night, well we can providing we cover up well to avoid the mosquitoes.

As you know malaria is carried by the female anopheles mosquito, which bites from dusk to late evening, so if in that period you cover your bare skin or spray on at least 30% DEET you shouldn't get malaria. Short-term usage of anti malaria pills is fine but long-term use certainly affects your health and wallet.

As always happens on these trips there are dead times, frustrating times, the distances being so large and the visa problems taking so long that we are running out of the time that we can spend in Central Africa and of course our ultimate destination, Australia.

What is noticeable are the different attitudes of the people in the various countries and even regions within countries. In this part of Cameroon they are much less open and welcoming than in the North. No one matches the Ghanaians for friendliness and fun and one wonders why attitudes vary so much, or perhaps it's just reflective of my attitude to them!

I had another flat tyre yesterday, again as a result of the excursion into the mud a couple of days ago. Not a puncture as such! Just a bit of wood getting between the rim and the tyre bead. It's easy enough to repair, all you do is deflate the tyre by removing the valve core, break the bead by either using the high lift jack or simply driving over it, use your tyre levers to ease the tyre back, clean the rim and the tyre, centralise the deflated tyre on the rim, pump it up, remove pump, replace the inner core (when you eventually remember where you put it) and then check the
pressure again: or you take it to a little man give him £2 and let him do it!
Guess which I did!

On the domestic front the damp is making washing difficult to dry so it's dirty clothes and then eventually wearing the cleanest of the dirty. Although in the tropics I'm still managing a cup of tea as often as I can, ever the Englishman, old habits die-hard, as of course do dirty ones! It's easy to get into the habit of drinking beer every night and that, with the lack of exercise, means that my spare tyre is even bigger than the two on the vehicle, travelling ain't a healthy pastime.

I wrote that I didn't see many dogs or cats in Nigeria, (or did I? just in case I didn't .. "You don't see many dogs or cats in Nigeria") and here in Cameroon there are dogs but again I can't remember seeing a cat and I've no idea why. I suspect that with all the rubbish that's laying around the rat population abounds, or perhaps the rats have eaten the cats!

The internet connections are dreadful, which means that although I've taken hundreds of photos I've been unable to transmit them, however they are now on discs and I'll be posting them from Libreville Gabon for inclusion on the website.

We left Yaounde after eventually getting the three visas, Gabon, Congo Kinshasa and Congo Brazzaville in three days, which is a bonus. The female at the Congo Brazzaville embassy achieved a new high (or is it low?) in sheer rudeness. So rude that it was funny, living down to her nickname of on the road of "Laughing Cow", it was a pity she didn't speak English as I couldn't even take the Mickey, and I wonder if it was everyone she disliked, English people in general, or just me in particular, but that's impossible I smiled at her and that's usually enough for any female to want my children without anaesthetic (and no that's not just the conception!)

Cameroon has three distinct climates and the change in climates are reflected in the road conditions, from deep mud in the north, rutted holes in Limbe to smooth almost too perfect roads in the south.

The mission in Yaounde was a good place to stay but beware the of harmless mad man in the grounds who has loud conversations with himself all night, also a bloody yappy dog that was very lucky not to get one of Jeans sleeping pills. I was, seriously, all for it, but after discussions we couldn't decide how much of one of her pills was enough to make it sleep and how much would kill it. My view was for giving it the lot but in the end I was outvoted again.

Instead I got outside of some "whiskey" that Les bought. £1.80 a litre (and it was worth exactly that) and I drunk 45p's worth, which guaranteed me a nights sleep, and a raging hangover in the morning! And it took me three days to get the feeling back in my tongue!
I have suggested that he pours a bottle into his tank, all I know is that if it has the same effect on his injectors that it had on my bowels his performance will improve 150%

BITAM GABON
The border posts between Cameroon and Gabon are so easy they are an anti-climax; don't worry about the distance of ten kilometres or so between the various authorities, or the size of the woman who appears to be the "chief" of immigration.

A BIG girl with so much hair under her armpits for a moment I thought she had Tina Turner in a headlock. To balance it out the man who does the immigration was also large enough not to argue with, and when he insisted that we get a photocopy of the visa page of the passport, for which we had to pay. I smiled and readily agreed, two actions that those of you who know me will know are alien to everything I stand for and which I only do when I want something and/or the person in front of me is big ugly and armed.

As we stood there in his small office, (I later realised it wasn't small it was just that he was filling most of it), a young girl guilty of something no doubt, was peremptorily ordered to go into a cell, which she meekly did. He shouted "Close the door behind you!" which she also did! But all was well as immediately he disappeared to shout at someone else, a policewoman opened the cell door and shooed her out.

He had disappeared still clutching my passports so I wandered off to find him, which wasn't difficult all I had to do was follow his voice. We finally got the photocopies from a little shop along the street, ran incidentally by a man of about the same size as the policeman, brothers perhaps? Surely not! Back at the station he stamped the passports with such violence they are still indented!

It was only when I was driving away the next day that I realised my bag with all the irreplaceable paperwork was missing, I went back to the office and it was there where I had left it, cowering in the corner.
I tried to persuade everyone I had left it there for safekeeping, they looked doubtful!

We're very close to Equatorial Guinea, where of course Mark Thatcher the son of our beloved and revered Ex leader of the Conservative Party Maggie Thatcher, God rest her soul! Had another of his bright ideas..
"She's not dead yet Jeff!"
"Oh isn't she? "(Ok where are them bloody poisoned sausages?)

Anyway he had this great idea to invade the place, and was about as successful at that as at everything else he's tried (Accountancy-failed, Paris-Dakar Rally lost!, secretly invade Equatorial Guinea, found out!) No No! That's so unfair, I am being too hard on him, he is in truth a very successful, astute and able business man, who made a fortune arranging the sale of arms to the Middle East, and it must have been legitimate as sale needed the specific permission of the Prime Minister, or "his mother" as she is sometimes called!

And it certainly wasn't his fault that those responsible for fitting out the helicopter misread the specification and fitted it out as a gunship instead of an ambulance, which he claimed he asked for, but it's a mistake anyone could make!
"Oi Bert! What's this say I can't make it out! Gunship or Ambulance?"
"Give it here let's have a look! It looks like Gunship!, who's the customer Fred?"
"Mark Thatcher, Bert!"
"Oh yes it'll definitely be gunship! Fred"
"Thanks Bert!"
"That's Ok Fred!"
"Hang on, have we been paid in advance! Fred"
"Definitely Bert!"
"Bloody good job Fred!"

If there are any libel lawyers reading this I hereby affirm that none of the above is in anyway intended to impugn his honesty, his ability or his integrity!! And the £500,000 fine and four year suspended sentence imposed on him for his part in the plot was a dreadful miscarriage of justice!
Wanker!!

GABON
What you have to remember about trips like this is that sometimes there is nothing to do but drive. The villages you pass are nondescript, occasionally you get eye contact with someone and they smile, other times they don't, just look sullen and resentful.

At least the children haven't reached he "Donnez moi une cadeau" stage that so many in the north have, and at the road blocks in Gabon you are waved disinterestedly through, or, when they
happen to be standing near the barrier and they feel that they ought to do something, they go through the motions of asking for documents, before losing interest and waving you on.
And not even a hint at a "present"

The road down from Bitam was superb, smooth and flat obviously brand new, so smooth that the artificial flowers in the vase on the table of Auntie Mabels' camper would have been undisturbed.. Well right up to the bloody great pothole that I didn't see and which shook my teeth loose. The bad roads had started again and this slowed us down and, as you know, I'm paranoid about driving at night, especially on roads like this where there are endless convoys of lorries carrying massive trees to the port, raping the forests of its hardwoods. Well the ones that keep going get to the port, the others are toppled over, sometimes on the side of the road sometimes in the middle, and when they aren't toppled over they are broken down!.

I've rambled off the subject there, what was I going to say? Oh yes! It was getting dark and there was nowhere to stay, the "hotel" mentioned in the Lonely Planet, which we headed for, was unappealing, which is a nice word for dreadful! So we fell back on "getting a place to sleep for the night" trick number three and turned into the nearest church I could see. Sure enough, as always happens, the man who could make the decision wasn't there but his deputy was, he of course, daren't make a decision, but with a bit of gentle bullying (and a reminder of the parable of the good Samaritan,) he will let you park till the "chief" returns.

Of course by the time he does you've got the tent up, you've got your gifts of pencils "for the children" out ready, and BINGO another night sorted! We watched a local game of football, typical of African games, dozens of players and a worn out semi inflated football. One player stood out from the rest both in ability and in physique, the sort that if spotted would earn millions in western football, but he'll probably live and die in a small African backwater.

Libreville is a miniature French town, rich from oil money, and the supermarkets are as well stocked as any in France, in fact they are the best stocked since France! Tonight's accommodation is courtesy (courtesy implies free, No! we paid!) of the Catholic mission and Monday will see us with our nose pressed against the window of the Angolan Embassy.

Angola Cabinda is a small state, an exclave, which is sandwiched nicely between Gabon and the two Congo's, (The Congo and The Democratic Republic of Congo, which used to be Zaire..don't worry I'll explain the difference later and that's a threat!). You need a separate visa for Angola Cabinda and for Angola Luanda and the theory is that you can get both visas in Libreville and then whip down the coast from Gabon through Cabinda Angola then through the two Congo's (stop looking like that I just told you, there's The Congo and The Democratic Republic of Congo which used to be called Zaire but that which some people now call Congo Zaire), and on into Angola Luanda, BUT the current view on the road is that the issue of the visa takes a week.

Alternatively you can by pass Angola Cabinda and drive inland out of Gabon into Congo Brazzaville then into Congo Kinshasa (now then! just when you understand the difference between The Congo and the Democratic Republic of Congo which used to be called Zaire and which some people now call Congo Zaire, some other people, or perhaps even the same people on different days, refer to The Congo as Congo Brazzaville and The Democratic Republic of Congo, which used to be called Zaire and which is sometimes called Congo Zaire , as Congo Kinshasa...see it's not difficult is it?) and get your Angola Luanda visa in Matadi, but that involves a round trip of five hundred miles.

Are you following this? Because if you are you're better than I am, I am here and totally bewildered. Bloody hell it's complicated. Anyway we will go to the Angola Embassy on Monday and ask the questions. The problem is of course that we
will ask the questions is English and they will answer in Portuguese which will leave us none the wiser!!!

It's been a boring couple of weeks (I can see you nodding in agreement at that) all we seem to have been doing is driving waiting for visas, and driving again, and I really don't see it changing until we hit Namibia which will take two or three weeks as least.

CAP ESTERIOS NEAT LIBREVILLE GABON

The good news is that we got the application in first thing last Monday morning and sure enough the visa will be issued on the Friday! Waiting again! The man at the Angolan embassy assured us that the roads too and through Angola are passable, but when I asked him when he last drove it he stared at me as if I was mad and gave me a look as if to say "Do I look the sort of person who is stupid enough to drive from here through Angola when there's is a perfectly good airline connecting the two?"
In truth he did look like a man stupid enough...etc. etc!!

The Catholic mission in Libreville is an "ok" place to stay but not really long term, all that bloody singing, so we took up Patrick's, the owner of the restaurant at Cap Esterios, offer of staying there "provided we ate and drank" no great hardship except that he didn't tell us he was closed during the week.

It's an easy place to wait, but all of us are getting bored with it, and will be glad when the next part of the trip through Angola Cabinda, Congo (which some people call Congo Brazzaville), DRC (which some people call Zaire others call Congo Zaire and yet others call Congo Kinshasa) and Angola (Luanda) is over with, glad though for different reasons.

Les is nervous of the reputation of the Congo's, particularly as DRC (DRC? Aah! that's yet another name for Congo, Congo Zaire and Congo Kinshasa) has been having elections and elections and
violence in Africa traditionally go hand in hand. Unlike England where elections and apathy go hand in hand, a bit like erections and apathy go hand in hand really! (That joke didn't work did it? As I was typing it I misspelt election and instead wrote erection and the combination of "erection" and "hand in hand" in the same sentence proved too much for me to resist...blimey I have been waiting for visa's far too long!")

I, on the other hand, am more scared of the boredom of day after day of driving than anything else, although the consolation is that it's quicker to drive through than repeat all the names of the various countries!
Everyone we speak too suck in through their teeth when we tell them where we are driving, but they've been doing this since before Nigeria, so it's lost its ability to frighten, we are still alive and everyone we have spoken to has got clean teeth, so no-one has lost!

I believed it before I came, and this trip has confirmed it, that most people who give you advice have no personal knowledge of travelling and simply delight in forecasting dire consequences if you even think of leaving your own garden! I'll repeat a word of warning, if you're travelling, only believe what people say if they have done it, and remember that in a perverted way most secretly want their worst prophecies fulfilled to justify their decision not to take chances.

Others of course simply, and rightly, ask who in their right mind would want to travel through expensive, squalid mosquito ridden countries where everyone tries to rip you off, where if you can get a shower it's cold, and where for 95% of the nights you're kept awake by dogs, cockerels, music, and shouting.

I wish I could answer that but I can't!

Update from 25 Sept 06...
Mouila Southern Gabon
I'm fed up! Well I'm more than fed up!, I'm totally pissed off. I am not sure how much the victim of a crime is culpable but I suppose not locking the car door properly outside the main post office in Libreville made me contributory to the crime but not nearly as much as the bastard who opened the door and stole my MP3 player and my small camera.

I know it's my fault, when you have been travelling as long as I have I should have known better but I didn't and it cost me. I am aware that the web site so far is an endless litany of how we are always being begged from or ripped off, but that is I'm afraid West Africa.

There are two types of police in Gabon, the ones who wear the typical French police hats and they are very benign and friendly; the others that wear the blue combat uniform are a different proposition, arrogant and aggressive and demanding.

By this time on the trip you become hardened to their wiles, in Libreville their favourite trick is to pull you over demand every last piece of paperwork then say "Controlle technique!!, now I'm not sure what the correct or expected response to this is but from their reaction to my response of,
"I have no idea what you're talking about!" Obviously isn't either.
So they repeat what they said and I repeat what I said, and they shout it at me and I feign ignorance. When it first happened a couple of days ago the policeman lost interest and waved me on.

This second man however was made of sterner stuff and not only repeated it, but brought in reinforcements to repeat it. So I had "Controlle Technique " in stereo and instead of making it clearer it made it twice as difficult.
Eventually a man who was just out for a walk and who spoke English came along and explained that "Controlle Technique" is the local word for the vehicle indicators, but that these police use
it as a catch all offence to extract money from people, by accusing them of not using their indicators and so committing an offence.
Apparently the correct response is to say, "Oh sorry let me give you money!"
Yeah right!!!!

So now I understood what "controlle technique" meant; they knew I understood; and they waited, and waited and the man who was doing the translating waited.
Eventually they spoke to the interpreter,
"They want to know why we are waiting!"
By this time I was pissed off, but then so were all the drivers parked behind me who couldn't get passed,(pissed because they couldn't get passed!)

God I was having fun!!

I told him to tell them that professionals had tried to rip me
off in Nigeria Mauritania and Mali and that if they think that
jumped up little shits like these two tossers think that they can
bully me they can think again!
He looked shocked and translated, but I believe, no I know,
that he watered it down a little, well quite a lot in fact, as it
was only a few words, all of which I understood, in fact he
said,
"He is very sorry!"
Obviously a diplomat used to dealing with men like these,
they said something back and he said, "I'm afraid you must
pay a fine!" In essence my reply was translated to them that if
they want money from me they must take me to the station
and charge me formally. He winced at this but translated, and
they gave me their meanest look, paused but suddenly said,
"Ok you can go! Bonne voyage!" Bonne bloody voyage
indeed! Cheeky sod!

I was pissed off with them and pissed off with the traffic and
when I finally found the post office I didn't close the car door
properly and so lost £250 worth of equipment when had I just
given them the £5 I'd have been ok!
So who is the idiot round here!
Say it! "Jeff is the idiot round here, and most other places
too!"

ALBERT SCHWEITZER HOSPITAL LAMBARÉNÉ

There's not a lot I can say about Albert Schweitzer except that
his story had a profound effect on me when I first heard about
it it many year's ago and the image of him playing the organ
in the middle of the jungle with one hand whilst curing people
with the other remained with me all through the visit,

although the pet pelican that he had was, to say the least, incongruous. I'll leave it to you to look up his life and make your decision, however suffice it to say that his legacy lives on and his hospital is a haven of peace in the middle of chaos.

My French isn't very good but as I understand it Albert Schweitzer was a famous German organist who was doing something (I never found out what) in Gabon who had a revelation from somewhere (God?) and decided that he could cure the local population of all sorts of ills by playing the piano to them.

This he did from 1915 until 1965 when he eventually died. Somewhere in the middle he won the Nobel peace prize (perhaps because he stopped playing for a while and gave everyone some peace!) and won lots other awards, oh yes! he kept a pelican called Percy or something.

That about it really, perhaps there's more to the story than I could make out and I've promised myself to look it up. In the museum there are pictures of him and he looks a lot like Albert Einstein, they have the same first name perhaps they were brothers!

> *"I don't know what your destiny will be, but one thing I do know: the only ones among you who will be really happy are those who have sought and found how to serve."*

> *Albert Schweitzer's basic philosophy was called the Reverence for Life, "the only thing we are really sure of is that we live and want to go on living. This is something that we share with everything else that lives, from elephants to blades of grass – and, of course, every human being. So we are brothers and*

sisters to all living things, and owe to all of them the same care and respect, that we wish for ourselves."

Albert Schweitzer was born on January 14, 1875 in Alsace the son of a Lutheran pastor. A little-known fact is that Jean Paul Sartre was Schweitzer's cousin. Sartre referred to him always as "Uncle Al."

Before setting up his hospital in Lambarene he had enough achievements to keep the average man satisfied for three lifetimes. He began playing the organ and piano and went on to become the world's leading expert on organ building.

In 1893, Albert Schweitzer began his studies at the University of Strasbourg, receiving a Doctorate in Philosophy in 1899, and in 1900 he obtained an advanced degree in theology, and within the next two years was appointed principal of St. Thomas College in Strasbourg, Curate at St. Nicholai, and to the faculty in both theology and philosophy at University of Strasbourg.

Schweitzer had always however felt a strong yearning towards direct service to humanity. In 1904, he read an article in the Paris Missionary Society's publication about their urgent need for physicians in the French colony of Gabon which had a profound effect on him and despite much resistance in January 1905, at the age of 30, he began studying medicine, receiving his degree with a specialization in tropical medicine and surgery at the age of 38, and immediately applied for a post with the Missionary Society.

What he had not anticipated was that, even though he had rearranged his life to meet needs of the Society, they turned him down on the basis of his theological views, they said "it would only intensify their problems by encouraging intellectuals and freethinkers who could only disrupt the mission enterprise and confuse the natives with their theological improvisations...and they were not about to sponsor Schweitzer and open the floodgates to other liberals and radicals."

In short, Albert Schweitzer was "politically incorrect!"

Undeterred Dr. Schweitzer's and his wife Helene Bresslau a trained nurse, joined her husband in a program of fund-raising to supply a hospital and underwrite the expenses for its first two years and on Good Friday, 1913 Dr. and Mrs. Schweitzer left for Africa. Finally they reached Libreville in French Equatorial Africa, now called Gabon, and set off up the great river Ogowe towards their final destination to build the hospital at Lambaréné. They began their hospital in a chicken coop, and gradually added new buildings, and the hospital now treats thousands of patients each year.

One year after their arrival at Lambaréné, World War I broke out, and because of their German citizenship the Schweitzer's were classed as enemy aliens in what was at the time a French colony. Initially they were confined to the hospital and were refused permission to treat patients but then because of the lack of medical facilities the authorities changed their minds and allowed them to practice but in yet another change of mind they were interred firstly in a prisoner of war camp in Bordeaux, and then in St. Remy and upon their release in 1918, Albert and Helen returned to Alsace, where their daughter Rhena was born on January 14, 1919.

In 1920, he was invited to give a lecture in Sweden and there he described how, while being rowed up the Ogowe River from Lambaréné, his search for an expression of his philosophy ended.

"There flashed upon my mind the phrase Reverence for Life. Man's ethics must not end with man, but should extend to the universe. He must regain the consciousness of the great chain of life from which he cannot be separated. He must understand that all creation has its value. Life should only be negated when it is for a higher value and purpose -- not merely in selfish or thoughtless actions. What then results for man is not only a deepening of relationships, but a widening of relationships."

Because of his wife's ill health after his confinement he returned alone to Africa in 1924, his wife and daughter remaining behind in Europe, however they corresponded frequently. Rhena saw little of her father during her childhood, but when her own children were grown, Rhena acquired technical lab skills and left for Africa to serve with her father where she eventually took over the administration of the hospital.

In 1953, at the age of 78, Dr. Schweitzer was honoured for his humanitarian work with the 1952

*Nobel Peace Prize and true to his lifelong principles
he used the
$33,000 prize money to build a new leper ward at the
hospital*

*Albert Schweitzer died in Lambaréné several months
after his 90th birthday the 4. September 1965. At
Lambaréné, Schweitzer was doctor and surgeon in the
hospital, pastor of a congregation, administrator of a
village, superintendent of buildings and grounds,
writer of scholarly books, commentator on
contemporary history, musician, host to countless
visitors.*

*Since his death many have questioned his methods
and his paternalistic authoritarianism towards the
indigenous people and the hospital, but those who do
this do did not live in the Africa of Albert Schweitzer
nor were they the ones who received the skilled and
loving care from a doctor when non existed before.*

DRIVING THROUGH GABON

As we drive through Gabon the scenery has changed from
Tropical to sub Savannah, and the roads from smooth to dust.
We have mixed feelings about Gabon, the people are certainly
not as open and friendly as some other Africans, but Gabon
doesn't have the economic problems of others, it's oil and
timber wealth ensures that and the prices here make its
nickname of "the Switzerland of Africa" well founded.

In the supermarket I queried the price of a small piece of Brie
cheese,
"£4 for a slice of Brie? Blimey that's expensive!"
"It's been flown from France Sir!"
"At that price it must have flown bloody first class!"

Heading out of Gabon the road becomes progressively worse, and the scenery flatter; another new country is waiting and that's "THE CONGO!" a name conjuring up violence and darkest
Africa, the Congo of Joseph Conrad's "Heart of Darkness", of Leopold's genocide, and of the unknown.

CONGO
You clear the Gabon immigration and customs at Ndende, a quiet and sleepy town at the best of times and even quieter when we arrived at ten o'clock on a Sunday morning to a closed and shuttered Immigration office. Some wandering around eventually located the Police Chief. "The house on the left after the third road hump!" they said and there it was!

He was good, efficient and fast, perhaps keen to get back to the female who looked out of the window at us as we interrupted whatever it was he was doing and took him away to process our papers. She scowled at us, I was going to say "gave us a black look!" and only with great difficulty resisted!
"No you didn't"
"You're right I didn't"
A few, slow miles down the road and you're at the Congo border, where the various Border officials are sitting at the local bar (it's Sunday lunchtime remember!) and are so pleased to see us!!! (NOT).
All goes swimmingly, if slowly, but just when we think we have finished they suddenly decide they want to search the vehicle and we're not talking a glance, were talking everything out. Not aggressive just insistent. So picture the scene, a narrow track, in fact the main Gabon/Congo Road, with all of our boxes unloaded, when along comes an officer who looks at us, looks at the boxes, looks at the soldiers and simply says,
"Go!"

We looked at each other and we goed!

So although we started the process at one o'clock by the time we finished here (another control of some description and more stamps in the passport) it was three thirty and with thirty-eight kilometres to go and sunset at six thirty we decided to take no
chances and stay in the village. They are smashing people, better here than some awful hotel in the next town; we sit watching an African sunset over distant hills, what could be better?
"Watching it with a cold beer that's what!"
So that what we're going to do

A good stop if you're running late after the border check, which is probable, is on the football field near the second immigration post, and as always happens we become the centre of attention for all the children who crowd round watching and wanting.
Contrary to what we thought Congo is smashing, the people are nice, the roadblocks such as they are, are benign.
The roads varying from excellent to bloody awful.
Typical Africa in fact!
NKOLA VILLAGE
All day we saw the lorries taking their loads of massive logs to the port, each lorry carrying 10,000 plus years of growth of hardwood for export to Asia and China, the roads to the port smooth and wide, paid for by the timber contractors to make transport easier; the lorries driven by eastern looking gentlemen. The roads opening up the interior so the animals are hunted for bush meat, the local girls prostituting themselves for money, the country prostituting its ancient wood for money. Another example of Africa being raped of its natural resources, and the world's hardwood, desperately

needed to balance the climate, being turned into furniture in India and China.

It was getting dark so we had to stop, and if you're ever in this situation it's easy, all you do is look for a neat village (it means that someone is in control!), find the chief of the village and ask him if you can stay. It's never failed us yet and in this case the chief,
"I'm the big chief you can call me Tatti!" was great!
The "big chief" was in fact hardly "big" but what he lacked in stature he gained in status and presence, and whenever anyone approached him they had to be below his eyeline, difficult when he was sitting down and only five foot tall when he was standing.

Chief Tatti

We lost count of the number of timber lorries that roared recklessly through the village throughout the night. It was so depressing!

A couple of nights in Pointe Noir where we were found in a petrol station by Francois a Swiss motorcyclist who lives in Madagascar, had bought his BMW in Europe and was riding it back through Africa. He is the first "traveller" that we have met for a while and he is convinced that all English men drink beer, bloody cheek, just to prove him wrong I broke the abstemious habits of a lifetime (well it was a day in truth, it just felt like a lifetime) and sat and drank all night and swapped tales of life on the road. His Swiss passport didn't have enough pages left to get his Angolan visa so he was stuck in Point Noir.

We sat on the balcony of a "night club" and watched the flaring of the gas from the oil rigs along the coast (drinking beer..he insisted! You know beer is quite nice! I might try another one sometime) and our reverie was broken by the women practicing for the "Miss Congo" competition. Bloody hell they were skinny, so skinny in

fact if the restaurant had served me a kebab with only that much meat on I'd have sent it back.

I've mentioned at length the begging. It happened again yesterday when a man approached me and said,
" Please give me money I am hungry!"
I looked at the spare tyre around his considerable waist, poked it and said
"Hungry?? You're fatter than I am!"

Suddenly a mobile rang, I knew it wasn't mine I'd left that on the kitchen table in England. He looked around then suddenly realised it was his, tapped his pockets, found his ''phone smiled apologetically and answered it. He had a long conversation periodically holding his hand up in the universal "sorry about this don't go away I'll only be a couple of minutes!" gesture.

He finally finished paused,
"Where was I? Oh yes! please give me money I am hungry!"

"Listen matey if you're hungry you use phone to call for a f*****g Pizza!"

ANGOLA CABINDA
Immigration office Cabinda

There's not a lot to be said about Angola Cabinda except that we drove through it. Everywhere there were vague reminders of how it used to be, wealthy and well run, but now it's a ruin, dirty, square once white now grey houses, with graffiti and no roofs, tired looking people, dirty dusty roads.

We stayed at the catholic mission, the walled garden full of rubbish, old forty foot containers rusting, the whole area neglected and uncared for, only the remains of a flower beds indicating that once someone cared. So like Africa really! Leaving was easy both from an immigration, personal and customs view!

Angola (again)!!

We thought the roads in Congo Zaire were bad, but all they did was whet the appetite for REALLY bad roads in Angola, corrugations, sand and craters gave way to broken tar, the worst sort of bad road, and even I, whose idea of a good road is a bad road began to tire of fighting the vehicle over holes in the road, ten hours of hard driving and you are lucky to manage one hundred miles in a day.

The whole country is still suffering from the after effects of the war which ended seven years ago, and although the capital Luanda shows all the signs of wealth, behind the façade is the squalor and deprivation the we saw in all the other large cities in Africa. The driving matches the lowest standards BUT in spite of my worst expectations I still have not been hit and I have not hit anyone, either with my car or personally, but it's been bloody close on both counts.

376

This type of travel is the worst, no communications with the local people (everyone in the county speaks Portuguese except me) just driving, driving and more driving.

We decided, on the advice of a very nice man we waylaid on the side of the road in Luanda and take the yellow route down to the town of Namibe and then cut across country to the country of Namibia (yes it is confusing isn't it) but not half as confusing as the criss-cross of tracks that resulted in us getting hopelessly lost in the mountains, which gave us a chance not only to look at the magnificent scenery that we wouldn't have normally seen, but also to test to the utmost our off road driving skills.

Inevitably we got lost in the mountains and when the subject of landmines was brought up I of course said that the landmine problem has been blown up out of all proportions.

"But then you would!"

Suddenly on the side of the road was strangely dressed man, blue apron and a large face mask! and he was holding a long stick!.

Behind him was a notice,

"BEWARE MINE CLEARING"

"So what you doing?" (There are times when I'm not very bright!)

"I'm clearing mines, what are you doing?"

Oh dear! I suggested that Jean walked ahead and I would follow her, that way the car would be safe. She demurred (vehemently), and so I did the next best thing and pretended to break down, and let Les drive ahead!

It was long slog of vertical ups and equally vertical downs, of deep sand, and precipitous drops until we finally found the main road again a very few miles further south than when we left it 30 hours and 120 miles previously.

This had taken two days without seeing another vehicle, but strangely during the middle of the night, when fortunately we had driven off the road and were well hidden, three vehicle passed by.. scary!

We were light on water, which wasn't as much as a problem as it could be in some parts of Africa, but it meant that washing was out of the question and we had to resort to baby wipes. Now that's fine but there's a couple of points to remember. When you use your baby wipe the order is face, hands, armpit, groin and feet, do
try and get it in the right order..the other thing to remember is to try and get first use of it!

The trick in building bridges is to explain the theory, start the job then let them carry on, but never, never be the first one over!!!!

For all you 4x4 drivers I did however learn the benefit of using

low first as a means of controlling the downward momentum that 3.5 tonnes of Toyota, loose rocks and a 70 degrees gradient inevitably produces! Oh yes! Closing your eyes and muttering "Jesus Christ!" also helps.

I also increased the tyre pressure by 10 p.s.i to try and avoid sidewall damage caused by hitting the edges of potholes, this I did, of course, half way through the day after the worst of the

road and immediately before we hit miles of deep sand (for those of you
who don't know you should reduce your tyre pressures in sand ..yeah yeah Ok I'm an anorak!.)

Les unfortunately suffered a sidewall blow out, and I spent a happy hour and a half sitting watching him sweat and suffer whilst offering timely words of advice, which I know in time when he has the chance to consider in depth he will appreciate.. Particularly the bit about being careful not to bump his head on the bumper whilst struggling to release the spare tyre, advice that, as always, came just too late.

The after effects of the war were apparent everywhere in Angola, burnt out tanks, people with missing legs, houses with no roofs and a population that frankly seemed tired, but not half as tired as we were after driving on what were the worst roads in Africa

WARS IN ANGOLA
There has been continual war in Angola since 1961, firstly a war to wrest independence from Portugal and then an extended Civil War between the Communist MPLA, (Popular Movement for the Liberation of Angola),which was supported by Cuba, and the Soviet Union; and the anti-Communist, UNITA, (National Union for the Total Independance of Angola) supported by South Africa and the United States and financed by oil and diamonds backed by the Gulf Oil and de Beers respectively.

I warn you now this gets complicated but the good news is that questions will not be asked!

In the early 1960's, MPLA guerrillas occupied ninety percent of the Cabinda exclave,(that's the little bit of Angola separated from the rest of Angola by a small strip of Congo), and when in 1966, the Gulf Oil Company discovered oil there, the Portuguese sent in the army to
clear out the MPLA. People were driven into "aldeamentos (villages) and hundreds were killed.

UNITA fought <u>with</u> the MPLA in the Angolan War of Independence but then <u>against</u> the MPLA in the ensuing civil war.

UNITA (South Africa,USA and China) was founded in 1966 and was pro west and led by Jonas Savimbi who created it the year after he left the FNLA (National Front for the Liberation of Angola) and he took with him Chinese support.

The MPLA,(Cuba and USSR) led by Agostinho Neto declared independence of the People's Republic of Angola on November 11, 1975.

The FNLA was led by Holden Roberto, after the defection of Jonas Savimbi.The FNLA also declared Angolan independence as the Social Democratic Republic of Angola based in Huambo, in the centre of the country but only controlled about 15% of the country.

How you doing so far??? Oh yes I'd better explain something. Foreign powers looking to influence an

African country select a person and get him into
power, then because of the debt he owes them he can
be manipulated. Ahh! But what about the democratic
process I hear you ask! Don't be ridiculous I reply!!!!

Back to the story!
The FLEC, (that's the Liberation Front for Cabinda.
No! I haven't mentioned it before.) declared the
independence of the Republic of Cabinda from Paris
and called it The Democratic Republic of Angola and
was based in
Ambriz,in the north east coast, and was armed and
backed by the French government.

In spite of Cabinda's relatively small size, foreign
powers and the nationalist movements coveted the
territory for its vast reserves of petroleum the
principal export of Angola.

The FNLA and UNITA forged an alliance on
November 23, 1975 proclaiming their own coalition
government based in Huambo with Holden Roberto
and Jonas Savimbi as co-presidents and José Ndelé
and Johnny Pinnock Eduardo as co-Prime Ministers.

On the night of November 10 1975, the day before
official independence, Savimbi secretly flew to South
Africa and in a reversal of policy Vorster not only
agreed to keep troops through November but
promised to withdraw the SADF troops only after the
OAU meeting on December 9.

The Soviets, well aware of South African activity in
southern Angola, flew Cuban soldiers into Luanda the
week before independence. While Cuban officers led

the mission and provided the bulk of the troop force, sixty Soviet officers in the Congo joined the Cubans on November 12. The Soviet leadership expressly forbade the Cubans from intervening in Angola's civil war, focusing the mission on containing South Africa.

The South Africans invaded Angola in October 1975, with orders to support the American mercenaries in combat. On December 17, 1975, South African reservists (who were also conscripted) were deployed. The apartheid government (and the USA) claimed that it invaded Angola because it had a right to protect Africa from communist domination. It claimed also that it had been requested to intervene by the Zaire and Zambian governments. This claim is somewhat dubious, given that the ANC leadership were at the time holed up in Lusaka, the capital of Zambia.
"ANC?"
"Yes the African National Congress that's the political arm of the freedom fighting organisation for South Africa, Umkhonto we Sizwe (spear of the nation) is the military arm but lets not go there!

When the MPLA gained control of Angola's central government in 1976, UNITA and the FNLA, two separate factions fighting for ascendancy, refused to recognize the new marxist-oriented government. In 1977, the MPLA captured the last major stronghold of the UNITA, whose leaders then fled to neighboring Zaire and Zambia, where they regrouped and revived their guerrilla warfare against the MPLA.

White mercenaries, South Africans, and Portuguese
frequently aided UNITA militarily, and covert
American arms and assistance were reportedly
received as well. In 1977 UNITA initiated a series of
guerrilla raids on urban areas in Angola; and a
rebellion that UNITA supported was crushed.

The following year a government offensive against the
guerrillas failed to dislodge them from the large areas
they controlled in southern Angola. Being
sympathetic to South Africa, UNITA let South African
forces maintain bases in its territory for raids into
Namibia, or South West Africa. In the early 1980s,
UNITA guerrillas had extended their control to
central and southeast Angola. Remember they had the
support of Great Britain, France, the United States,
Saudi Arabia, and a number of African nations, while
the MPLA was backed by the Soviet Union and Cuba.

Continual warfare disrupted Angola's economy and
displaced one-sixth of its people, many of whom were
forced to become refugees in Zaire, Zambia, and the
Congo. The United States refused to recognize
Angola's government as long as Cuban troops were in
the country. In late 1988 US-mediated talks led to a
signed peace accord, after which South Africa
removed its troops, but the fighting continued between
the marxist MPLA government and the UNITA rebels.

Another truce in June 1989, signed by Angola's
President Jose Eduardo dos Santos and UNITA
leader Jonas Savimibi , also failed to end hostilities.
Cuba removed its troops in May 1991. After a year of
negotiations, led by the Soviet Union and the US,
Santos and Savimbi signed a peace treaty in Lisbon,

Portugal, on May 31, 1991, officially ending the 16-year civil war.

The peace lasted long enough for elections in 1992, but when Savimbi won 40% of the popular vote to Santos's 49%. Savimbi refused to accept the result and another peace was brokered in 1994, which only lasted about a year. They put together a National Unity Government in 1997 but Savimbi said MPLA wasn't holding up its end of the bargain and started shooting again at the end of 1998. Savimbi was killed in a battle on February 2002 and since then the country has been peaceful, though not yet fully democratic.

The factions and factions within factions, and the swirling changing allegiances based on tribal, political and financial loyalties were typical of emergent Africa; manoeuvring that cost millions of lives and millions of dollars, and continues to this day.

If you think that was complicated multiply it many times for Zambia, Zimbabwe, Mozambique, etc. and you will understand why even now democracy in Africa isn't working.

ZAMBIA
VICTORIA FALLS LIVINGSTONE

"BUGGER! SOD! BUGGER! BUGGER! BUGGER!"
"As bad as that Jeff?"
"Worse! much much worse!"
"Oh dear! Oh well never mind!"
"Well aren't you going to ask?"

"No I've made that mistake before and anyway you're probably going to tell me anyway"

"Ok then I wont tell you.. Ok Bugger it yes I will!"

"I'm soooo pleased!"

"You know I had problem with the computer in the arsehole ..er armpit.. of Africa Nigeria when the screen suddenly went all liney and then just as suddenly corrected itself.. Well it happened again in Angola but this time it didn't correct itself, in fact it got worse, so all I was left with was a blank screen it was dreadful.. I said it was dreadful! OI! Are you listening to me?"

"I'm wrapped in rapt attention!"

"Good! So anyway in Livingstone I found a very nice man who had a computer shop and together we turned the computer on, to try and get it to work! Something I'd tried many times in the last couple of days and guess what!"

"……….."

" I SAID GUESS WHAT!"

"Oh sorry, I'll bet it worked!"

"No it still didn't work, and his opinion was the same as mine that it wasn't the disc but the screen and that, as such, there was little we could do!, so the choice was simple, get a new computer or simply stop updating the website!"

"Please tell me you decided to stop updating the website a decision that would please an inordinate number of people!"

"No I decided to buy a new computer .. a Fujitsu! ..and it cost 650 pounds!"

"Blimey! I'll bet that hurt, is that why you were swearing?"

"Let me finish .. and no that's not why I was swearing!.. Tony, the computer man, transferred all my data from the old hard drive onto the new computer.. It's a Fujitsu you know.."

"I thought that was a Japanese Martial Art...."

"Tony transferred all the data onto the new computer and brought it to me at the camp site and we had a couple of beers an he told me about some of the things they got up to in the Rhodesian war whilst a member of the Selous Scouts (were very very naughty boy's!)..and we agreed I'd collect the old computer the next day!"

"So that's why you were swearing?"

"Why?"

"Because he forgot to bring the old computer!"

"No the reason that I'm swearing is that when I did go to collect the old computer…."

"I know I'll bet it was working!"

"How did you now that?"

"Just a hunch!"

"You're right it was working perfectly so now I have two computers and I'm £650 worse off and I have to carry two computers around with me!"

"Well let's hope the new one writes more interesting stuff than the old one ever did!"

Victoria falls

Because of the time of the year Victoria Falls didn't have much water going over and was frankly unimpressive, as were the changes that were taking place in the shops around the

Falls. Like so many things that we found on the way down once it was run by Africans, things stopped working. The souvenir shop at the Falls which, two years ago was stocked with a whole range of clothing and memorabilia as well as cold drinks, now had empty shelves and the girl behind the counter simply wanted to sleep.

The curio salesmen were the same with a standard patter designed to create a relationship albeit superficial and commercial.
"Where you from?.. what's your name?.. first visit to Zambia?" the answers to which are studiously ignored because they simply want to get down to the business of selling.
I'll let you into my secret of dealing with them.. never ever offer a price!"
He will start at a figure
"Only 170,000 kwacha" (£25!)
"No too expensive!"
"So how much you wanna pay?"

That's when you smile and say nothing! Just watch the price fall but DON"T WEAKEN!..everytime he asks
"So how much you wanna pay?"
SAY NOTHING!
I got the price down from 170,000 to 85,000 in three minutes without saying a word..and then still didn't buy it,
"Still too expensive?"
"No I didn't want it, I was just bored and wanted to pass the time!"
You're sick Watts!

LUANSHYA
It was inevitable that we would return to Luanshya, and of course that we would visit Peter and Joan Hughes.

Regular readers will remember that when we arrived in Luanshya two years ago Wendy their neighbour was in the middle of a personal crisis (she was in prison as it happens!) and the electric power had gone off.

Two years later we turned up again and Wendy was in the middle of yet another personal crisis and again the power was off, so by definition the lack of power must have been my fault!.

To all you interested (as opposed to interesting) readers the bad news is that I promised Wendy that I wouldn't mention anything about her crisis on here and of course a promise is a promise, the good news is that I was lying when I said it!!

As I said, Wendy was in the middle of a personal crisis, and was inconsolable!

Henry had told her that morning that he was leaving her! They had been together for eight years and she hadn't any idea that there was anything wrong! I'm not good in these situations so I did the manly thing and patted her on the shoulder and joined Peter for a drink in the bar.

We could hear the ladies talking and we could make out the occasional word like,

"Nooo!" or "How could he?" Peter and I looked at each other and

raised our eyebrows (and our glasses!) and as is the way of men, stayed well out of it.

It was too late to cancel the dinner party and Wendy didn't eat much, just stared into her drink. I tried to help, but my comment of,

"Never mind Wendy you can always get another!" resulted in her bursting into tears and rushing out of the room, then rushing back in to refill her glass with wine and rushing out again!

Joan said,

"JEFF!"
Jean said,
"JEFF!"
I said,
"What?"
The women looked at each other, I looked at Peter but he was
looking at the ceiling, with a "you're on your own Watts!"
look on his face.

So that's it! The evening wasn't exactly a disaster but certainly
I've been at happier occasions, and all I can say is that perhaps
she found some consolation in the arms of Simon …
"Hang on Jeff did you say she slept with Simon on the same
day that Henry left her? Blimey she couldn't have been too
upset! What's going on here, her husband leaves her and she
sleeps with Simon..sheesh"
"What are you talking about, Simon is her husband!"
"So who the hell's Henry?"
"Henry? He's the cook and a bloody good one!"
As the evening drew to a close Wendy confided that,
'Husbands you can get any day, a good cook is hard to find!'"

Peter looked at me and I looked at him, we both had the same
thought but we were each waiting for the other to speak,
finally he looked at Wendy and said
"Was that rhyming slang then Wendy?"
Peter reminded me of the story of a mutual friend Van who
used to boast about his killer guard dog. One day he sacked
his houseboy acrimoniously, and later the houseboy came
back with his friend and beat Van up. When asked later if the
dog helped Van replied,
"Of course he licked the blood up!"

Zambia as a country is booming, the streets of the capital
Lusaka, clean and lined with Jacaranda. But Luanshya, the

town we love, is slowly dying, the mine operating with a fraction of the staff it had before and the paternalistic philosophy of the mine long since disappeared, as each subsequent owner asset strips and moves on.

The main interest is in the results of the election. The present incumbent Mwanamasa is only the third president since independence some forty-two years ago. Kenneth Kaunda the first President was voted in at the first election after independence in 1964 and, as is the way in Africa, promptly abolished elections. When asked about his pre election slogan of "one man one vote" he is rumoured to have replied, "The Zambian people have had one vote and they have had it once!"

The next President Chiluba lasted ten years or so until even the placid Zambians decided that he had dipped into the petty cash once too often and finally Mwanamasa came to power. Strong rumours of ballot rigging abound but again it says so much for the tolerance, or is it apathy, that even this is greeted with a shrug. Even the election monitors are rumoured to be corrupt, but it's difficult to get a black election official that's whiter than white!
"That's sick Watts!"
"WHAT?????? What?"

WILDLIFE CAMP SOUTH LUANGWA
Against my better judgment we went on a game drive, now for those who don't know, this is where you get into a fancy open topped Land Rover and are driven around the park by a game ranger who confidently identifies the various species of birds and animals that are too lazy to move out of view.
He cannot lose because when we say,
"What bird is that then?"

And he replies,
"Ahh! it is a lesser spotted hairy arsed wag tail."
We have to believe him because if we had known we wouldn't
have asked in the first place.
We came upon two lions, a male and a female, who were
lying in the grass completely ignoring the five vehicles each
with nine people in who were looking at them, willing them to
do something. Suddenly the male remembering that he was
the king of the jungle thought he had better oblige, so he
twitched his tail lifted his head, and yawned.
When this didn't get the expected screams of fear, or even a
round of applause, he laid down again exhausted at all the
effort.

It was a beautiful night with the dark star filled sky
occasionally illuminated by lightening.
"Billy (he was the guide/driver)" I asked "Is it going to rain?"
"Oh no Sir! it is much too early in the year!"
The lightening flashed and the wind started to blow,
"Billy are you sure it's not going to rain?"
"Oh no Sir! Not for three weeks!"
The lightening continued the wind blew and the heavens
opened,
"Billy are you really sure it's not going to rain because I am
getting very very wet back here!"
"Sir I think maybe perhaps there will be a shower later!"
"Billy I think you're taking the piss out of me aren't you?"
"Oh yes Sir I am!"
Bastard!!

Heard a good story about the group who were going on a
game viewing and before they started one of them asked the
guide what they should do if suddenly confronted by a man-
eating lion. The guide said,
"Well you should first, without taking your eyes off the Lion

take one step to the left, then, still without taking your eyes off the Lion, take one step back, then finally, but still keeping eye contact, you should take one step to the right!"
"And will that stop the lion charging?"
"Of course not! But at least it will stop you stepping in your own shit!"

Oh I forgot to tell you. (Well I think I did). When we were in the Eureka camp in Lusaka behind us was parked a drunken white man who introduced himself and told me he had spent his life wandering about in the bush and was an expert in all things to do with animals, and everything else!

The camp had introduced some "wild" animals, two Eland and some zebras and allowed them to wander around. Our drunken friend suddenly leant over to me and said,
"Shush quiet now look over your shoulder slowly!" I looked over my shoulder slowly and he said,
"See those!"
"Yes!"
"They're zebra's"
"Bloody hell!" I said "I'm glad I met you I'll know now what they are when I see them again!"
What I meant to say was,
"You're a Tosser now bugger off!" I should have said it but I didn't, but I did later!!

We had an interesting conversation with Charlene at the Wildlife camp. She and two colleagues were staying there awaiting the clearance of their scientific research equipment, so they could get started on a study into the reproductive cycle of the Tsetse Fly

Now for those of you that don't know the Tsetse Fly causes sleeping sickness and affects both humans and domestic cattle, but not wild animals, and the study was being financed by The South African Government because, with global warming the band across Central Africa that the tsetse fly occupies is getting wider and South Africa is naturally concerned at the impact that this will have on their domestic cattle. So obviously anything that can be done to eradicate them is beneficial to all, er Nooo!!!!

The presence of the tsetse fly is the only thing that gives the wild game animals breathing space, without them domestic cows would take over and the game would disappear. So how do you keep the tsetse where we want them?, that is well away from South Africa, that was their problem. A question which they would have found easier to answer had all their equipment not been retained by Zambian Customs. She explained that when tsetse flies mate the female retains the male sperm in her body, and not only that, but she produces a plug that keeps the sperm in her and prevents any other tsetse sperm from being introduced into her.
So if you can make the first tsetse fly to mate to be sterile then the female wont be able to produce. This appears to be the route that they are taking, although why they don't learn from humans and kill the sexual desire of the females by simply feeding her wedding cake I don't know!
Perhaps I should have mentioned it!
We were sitting in the camp watching the elephants when Charlene came over to us with a bag and said
"I've got something for you!"

Now I love it when females bring me something in a bag, because it usually edible!! Perhaps cakes made to a recipe passed onto them by their old south African Grandmother; or samoosas made with a recipe from their old Indian grandmother; or even miniature steak and kidney pies passed onto them by their old English grandmother.

I grabbed the bag and opened it, inside was what to the untrained eye, appeared to be dead flies! Now I've eaten cooked insects before and they were good, so no doubt Charlene had a recipe for flies from her old South African Grandmother!

"They look like flies!" I said,

"They're Tsetse flies" she said,

"Right!.. er.. Thanks!

I picked one out and laid it in the palm of my hand, Charlene whispered,

"Look at the length of its proboscis!"

I looked but couldn't see anything,

"So it's a male then?" I asked,

"I have no idea!"

"But you said it had a long proboscis!"

"Ahh no! a proboscis is its nose that it uses to stick in you, not its penis"

These scientist women don't care what they say do they!

I looked closer and sure enough its proboscis was impressive, and you could see why they hurt so much when they stick it in you. I looked at another and there was a small white grub attached to it.

"This ones being eaten!"

"No! they sometimes spontaneously abort when they are under stress!"

Blimey I hope she has a good recipe because at that moment they certainly didn't look like a delicacy,

"Right so how do you cook them?"

"Cook them? I don't!"

"Ok so when others eat them how do they cook them, deep fry perhaps?"

"I don't know of anyone who eats them!"

She looked at me as if I were stupid, I recognised it from many years of experience when I am on a tangential path in a conversation.

"Charlene I'm lost I thought you were bringing me them to eat!"

"No I brought you them to show you"

"There must be 2000 of them, one would have been enough!"

I handed her back her dead tsetse flies and she looked hurt, but the thought of food had made me hungry and I reached for the peanuts on the bar, well I think they were peanuts! Who knows we are in Africa after all?

The Tale of Mulenga and his pillows

"Bwana I have a problem!"

"Mulenga I have many problems and most of them are caused by you!"

Mulenga laughed nervously and was relieved to see that Swannie's pipe was laying on the table. Now Swannie's temper was legendry not just in Luanshya but throughout the Copperbelt, his range of invective innovative, unique and in many cases biologically impossible.

A few years ago his family, in the forlorn hope that it would calm him down had given him a pipe, but it didn't! What it do however was give everyone an indication of the state of his temper, ranging from it laying on his desk when he was merely in his normal bad mood; through slowly reaching for it, which meant he was on slow burn; and finally to throwing it with alarming accuracy at the poor unfortunate who had upset him.

With some people their bite is worse than their bite; Swannie's bite equalled, and in many cases far exceeded, his bark, so you can imagine it was with a certain amount of trepidation that Mulenga tapped on his door

"Yes Bwana"

"So what's your problem this time Mulenga?"

"Bwana, my wife's' younger sister she is coming to stay"

"Mulenga you have my sympathy, my wifes' sister comes to stay and I know that is a problem. So tell me is this the same sister whose funeral you went to last month?"

"Oh no Bwana!.. That was my wife's other sister who lives, er lived in Mufulira"

"Ok so what's the problem Mulenga, and I know I'll regret asking!"

"Bwana when you go to the mine stores to get the corrugated sheeting for the engine shop roof, can I come with you to get some pillows for my wife's younger sister to sleep on?"

(For those of you who don't know the Stores on the Copper mines not only stocked the million and one parts needed to keep the mine operating but also stocked household goods that employees could buy and have deducted from their salary the end of the month)

"Mulenga we don't need any sheeting for the engine shop roof, I got it all last week"

"Ah Bwana but we are short by fifteen sheets"

Swannie reached for his pipe, Mulenga took a step back,

"Mulenga how can we be fifteen sheets short when I counted them!"

"Bwana George at eighteen shaft borrowed some to finish his job!"

"Mulenga get them back off Bwana George and next time ask before giving them away!"

"Bwana George is not there he has gone on leave!"

"Jesus Christ Mulenga OK I'll get some corrugated sheets tomorrow!"

"But Bwana my wife's younger sister she arrives today and she has not got a pillow!"

"Mulenga!" he put his pipe in the corner of his mouth ominously "Mulenga I do not give a monkey's toss about your wife's sisters bedroom comfort, and I am certainly not going

to drive fifteen miles in this heat to get pillows for her, now bugger off!"
"Yes Bwana"
He waited
"But Bwana!"
"Mulenga, be very very careful"
But Mulenga didn't need telling, Swannie was sucking deeply on his pipe, never a good sign. Mulenga took a deep breath and edged back towards the door.
"But Bwana remember the Engineering Superintendent wanted the roof finished today for the Managers visit and without the sheets we will not finish it" and left quickly closing the door behind him as a precaution against the pipe.

Swannie was waiting for Mulenga in his van, gripping the wheel tightly and sucking on his pipe.
When Mulenga got in Swannie said,
"Don't say a word Mulenga, don't even breath!" letting in the clutch fiercely and driving off.
Mulenga wisely said nothing for five minutes until,
"Bwana!"
"What did I say to you about not talking Mulenga?"
Swannies' pipe moved as he chewed on it, knuckles white on the steering wheel,
"Sorry Bwana!"
Five more minutes
"Bwana, did you remember to bring the requisition book for the sheets and the pillows?" it came out in a rush,
"Shit! Why didn't you remind me?"
"But Bwana.." But then Mulenga very wisely shut up!
Swannie slammed on his brakes and the car behind only just stopped in time, the driver was about to jump out but seeing who it was, locked the doors and windows, and backed up.

Two hours later Mulenga was standing in a queue at the mine stores whilst Swannie seethed in the background. When Mulenga finally got to the window he greeted the Storeman enthusiastically and for a few minutes they conversed and reminisced, until finally Swannie could stand it no longer and interrupted,

"Mulenga get on with it"

"Aah but Bwana Joseph he is my brother and I was telling him about my wife's younger sister who is coming and how I need some pillows!"

"When you say brother do you mean same tribe or same parents?"

"Aah Bwana we have the same mother but my father was his fathers brother, you know that in …."

"MULENGA!!! GET THE BLOODY PILLOWS!"

"Yes Bwana!"

Mulenga spoke to Joseph who examined the requisition closely then shook his head,

"Bwana Joseph he says that he cannot give me the pillows because Personnel have not signed the requisition to confirm I work for the mine,"

"Mulenga he is your brother he knows you work for the mine, tell him to give you the f……g pillows, NOW!!!"

Swannie was using his pipe to point, always a dangerous sign. Mulenga spoke to Joseph who shook his head, but not before retreating a few steps,

"Bwana he says he cannot, but it will only take a few minutes to go to personnel and get them to sign, I have another brother there who's name is Benedict, who will sign"

They sat in the car in silence for the ten minute drive to Personnel, well, Mulenga was silent Swannie swore and berated each and every other car and pedestrian who dared came near, and his screeching stop and slammed doors outside personnel ensured that if nothing else they were all woken up in time to go to lunch.

Mulenga greeted the personnel officer like a brother, which of course he was, and was in the middle of telling him about the visit of his wife's younger sister and the need for pillows, when Swannie lent over the desk, tapped the requisition and Mulenga's brothers forehead with his pipe and said, ominously quietly,

"Sign!"

Mulenga's brother Benedict looked at Mulenga and Mulenga looked pleadingly at Benedict,.

Not surprisingly Benedict signed!

Back in the van the temperature both climactic and Swannies, was at boiling point and Mulenga did the very wise thing of sitting, looking out of the window, and saying nothing.

Another twenty-minute wait at the stores window and Mulenga was speaking to Joseph again,

"Aah so how is Benedict!"

Mulenga shook his head quickly and handed the requisition over which Joseph examined in closely and smiled, all was well, then he said something to Mulenga and held out his hand, Mulenga tapped his pocket, shook his head and said something to Joseph who again shook his head.

Swannie watched all this and went and stood alongside Mulenga

"What's wrong Mulenga?"

"Aah Bwana Joseph he says he cannot give me pillows until he sees my Mine Identity card to prove I am an employee!"

Joseph showed surprising agility as a he dodged Swannie hand as it closed towards his throat.

"Bwana please it will not take long to go to my house.

Mulenga's house was easy to spot, in an otherwise drab township Mulenga's house boasted a new corrugated iron roof which Swannie examined with interest as Mulenga disappeared indoors, to reappear a few moments later with his wife,

"Bwana Swannie this is my wife!"

Now Swannie had a temper but in the traditional South African way he was also very chivalrous and he greeted Mulenga's wife politely and, as is the case in Africa, asked after her family and children and discussed the weather, and even smiled and agreed that their new roof looked very nice, at the same time looking at Mulenga who smiled nervously back at him, and looked everywhere but at his new corrugated iron roof!

Mrs. Mulenga continued.

"He is working so hard at his new roofing business..!"

Mulenga coughed very loudly,

Swannie just looked, but that was enough,

Eventually Swannie indicated as nicely as he could that it was time to go and Mulenga's wife agreed and sat in the passenger seat. Swannie looked at Mulenga who said,

"Perhaps we could give my wife a lift to the bus station where she will meet her younger sister"

Swannie bit on his pipe and looked ahead whilst Mulenga jumped on the back but as Swannie drove off he banged on the roof,

"Sorry Bwana I forgot my Mine identity card!" jumped off and ran into the house only to return eight minutes later to ask his wife where it was, she got slowly out of the car and waddled into the house. When she got back in she smiled at Swannie, Mulenga smiled at Swannie, Swannie just scowled.

An hour later they were back in the queue at the stores window having deposited Mulenga's wife at the bus station, Mulenga having wisely decided to stay on the back of the van, rather than sit alongside Swannie.

Mulenga finally reached the front of the queue presented his requisition and the Identity card, Joseph smiled and nodded then shook his head and handed them back to Mulenga who smiled sadly and turned back to Swannie.

"What's wrong now Mulenga?" he asked

"Aah Bwana Joseph says that they have been out of stock of pillows for three weeks!

After Swannie had thrown his pipe and hit Joseph on the head with it, it had taken three other workers to physically hold him down whilst Joseph and Mulenga ran and four weeks later Swannie was up in the local court charged with assault with a deadly weapon.

The Magistrate looked around severely and spoke to the court, "This appears to be a very serious case of assault with a deadly weapon on a fellow employee and the court takes a dim view of such acts…Mr. Prosecutor?

"Thank you your honour, the facts of this case are not in dispute the defendant Mr. Henry Swanniepool.." everyone wondered who he was talking about as he was only ever known as Swannie.."

struck the defendant Mr. Joseph Bwalya on the head with a pipe causing severe concussion .."

The Magistrate leant forward

"What sort of pipe was this Mr. Prosecutor? A steel pipe? A scaffolding pipe? Shouldn't it be introduced into evidence?

"It is there Your Honour on the table!"

The Magistrate looked at the table, the defence solicitor looked at the table, the prosecutor looked at the table, in fact the whole court looked at the table.. and someone laughed!

"Silence in court" snapped the Magistrate "where exactly is the pipe Mr. Prosecutor?"

"There! Your Honour on the table!"

The Magistrate looked again and seemed to see Swannies pipe for the first time,

"Is that the deadly weapon to which you are referring?"

"Yes Your honour!"

"Very well carry on I am to say the least intrigued. Usher please confirm that it is not loaded" he waited for the court to laugh at his joke.. In vain..

When Joseph stood in the witness box he was wearing a very very large bandage on his head, so large that it looked exactly like what it in fact was.. a turban

"Your client is of Indian persuasion perhaps Mr. Prosecutor?"

"Not that I am aware Your honour!"

"Then why is he wearing a turban?"

"It is not a turban it is a bandage to cover the wound Your Honour!"

"Please ask him to remove it!"

It took a long time to unravel the turban.. err .. bandage but finally it lay in an untidy heap on the floor,

"Show me the wound please!"

Joseph pointed dramatically at a spot just above his left eye, the Magistrate leant forward and looked,

"I am sorry Mr. Prosecutor I cannot see anything ask your client to step closer!"

Joseph left the witness box, and walked towards the bench, and as

an afterthought limped a little, and showed the Magistrate his wound, who looked, put his spectacles on, looked again and then shrugged his shoulders,

"Carry on Mr. Prosecutor!"

"Thank you Your Honour.. perhaps Mr Bwalya you could tell the court what happened

"Bwana Swannie hit me with his pipe"

The Magistrate looked down at him and said,

"Yes? So what did you do?"

"I ran you're Your Majesty"

"Just call me Sir!"

"Yes Your Majesty Sir!"

"Not Your Majesty Sir.. Oh just get on with it, you say you

ran?"

"Yes Your Majesty I ran very fast!"

"Why?"

"Because Bwana Swannie was mad, I ran very far, about one mile!"

"Why did you run so far?"

"Someone was chasing me, I thought it was Bwana Swannie so I ran faster!"

"And was Bwana Swannie, err the defendant chasing you?"

"Oh no sir it was Mulenga!"

"Why was Mulenga chasing you?"

"Oh he wasn't chasing me he too was running away from Bwana Swannie Your Majesty Sir"

The Magistrate looked at the Prosecutor and said,

"Are you telling me that your client suffered from sever concussion and was still able, by his own admission, to run a mile?"

"I am Your Honour!"

The Magistrate looked at Joseph and said,

"Please go on, I am fascinated to know what happened next"

"I went to the hospital to see the doctor"

"And what did he say?"

"He laughed Your Magistrate!"

"Did he now, and what treatment did he give you?"

"A white tablet and a plaster for my head… oh and a note for the policeman.. And another note for Personnel saying I was unfit for work"

"So you went to the police?"

"Yes Your Majesty and they said it was not very serious and they wanted to hit me again to make it more serious, but they did not"

"I am glad!" the Magistrate looked at the prosecutor,

"Anything to say Mr. Prosecutor"

"Your Honour it is the company policy to prosecute all cases of assault and this was a particularly vicious…"

"Thank you Mr. Prosecutor!. I think I have heard enough, perhaps the defence and prosecuting solicitors would care to have a chat in my chambers!

When they all returned to court the Magistrate said,

"We have discussed this case and I believe that Mr. Swanniepool may wish to change his plea to guilty.."

"I will not!" shouted Swannie,

"Yes you will" shouted Mrs. Swannie, who was wearing her best brown tweed suit for the occasion, and was hot!

"Yes you will" shouted the defence solicitor.

Swannie shut up and reached for his pipe, then remembered it was Exhibit A

The Magistrate continued,

"… his plea to guilty and in which case he will be fined.." he looked at the clerk who held up his hands twice "Twenty Kwacha and the weapon confiscated"

The prosecutor stood up,

"And compensation for my client?"

"Be careful Mr. Prosecutor"

So that was it the story of Mulenga's pillows and Swannies Pipe.

In case you're interested the twenty kwacha finished up in the till of Theo's bar, put there by the court clerk in payment of a previous bar bill and for that night's beer.

The pipe, after a decent interval, could often be seen in the mouth of the Magistrate as he listened tiredly to a case of marital infidelity or double parking whilst he dreamt of his farm on the banks of the Kafue River.

Mrs. Mulenga younger sister never did arrive as her bus broke down just outside Chapata and after three hours waiting she grew tired and went home.

Joseph was off work for three weeks then received word that the assistant storekeeper was trying to take over his very profitable sideline of selling pillows to the local Indian traders and returned to work.

Mulenga's roofing business was put on hold because his source of raw materials was suddenly curtailed.

The mine fined Swannie for taking smoking materials, a pipe, into the stores, which was strictly forbidden, and his family bought him another pipe.

Mrs. Mulenga decided that she would go and visit her younger sister in Chapata, but taking no chances, she took pillows with her. This left Mulenga without any, so, after two sleepless nights he knocked tentatively on Swannies office door.

"Bwana I have a problem!..............."

This story was told to me by Peter Hughes who assured me that, apart from the facts, it is absolutely true and any comments or doubts should be addressed to him and not to me!

MALAWI

I like Malawi and, since the death of the over zealous Hastings Banda its first post independent President, it seems to have so much going for it, the lake, mountains, fascinating history, tea plantations and finally, proximity to South Africa. It's difficult to find anything to write about it though, as from a "travellers" viewpoint it's soft and easy. The Lodges have campsites most of which are well run and clean, and the roads are well maintained, people friendly.. all in all boring as hell for anyone trying to write something interesting on a website for those of you who are reading this instead of working.

Oh yes I'll bet you didn't know that Malawi has massive tea plantations and that all the best leaves are exported, the cynic in me wonders if it is exported under the "fair-trade to help small producers label" when in fact the tea estates are massive operations, they wouldn't do that would they?, but I must say that I've enjoyed some of my best cups of tea ever in Malawi and am now a convert.

Anything else?? Oh yes we stayed in Blantyre where we met a group of trainee doctors from Europe and got to discussing the female reproductive system (as you do!) and in the course of the conversation they pointed out that the reason for the fall off in fertility of western men was the amount of female oestrogen in the water supply.

Apparently when women take the birth pill and she goes to the loo, the oestrogen stays in the water system and when men drink it their fertility falls; well that and sitting with lap top computers on their laps on trains (I got a bit lost there to be honest but didn't like to ask) so any of you out there who want to father children should not do it whilst drinking water and using a lap top on a train.

I think that's what they were saying.
What else.. Oh yes we went to Livingstonia, on the Zomba plateau, which is a mission founded by a chap called Laws who was a member of the Free Church of Scotland and there is a university (small) a primary school (even smaller) and a museum (closed!) … Now I've forgotten what I was going to say… umm..oh yes I remember. We stayed at a camp site that's "ecologically sound", no I didn't know what that meant until I was told that when you go to the loo, you do what you have to do and then you don't use water you simply sprinkle some ash and sawdust on top of it and in time that turns into compost and they use it in their garden.

They seemed very surprised when they asked me if I wanted homegrown vegetable salad with my dinner and I said, "You have got to be bloody joking!"

SOUTH AFRICA

South Africa is the end of the second phase of the trip, and like Nigeria we had dire warnings about the crime rate particularly in the large cities, so we headed for a small quiet town called Umhalanga rocks (pronounced Mshlanga). Well that's the theory, Umhalanga Rocks wasn't the small camp site we expected but a new holiday town on the outskirts of Durban, and we were fortunate as everything we needed was there, including most fortunately of all Toyota Umhalanga who we needed to replace the front seal, which we last replaced in Khartoum two years ago by a group of mechanics on the side of the road.. and they never gave me a warranty.. Bloody hell.

Oh yes! I heard a South African MP on the radio on the subject of "gay" marriages saying "future generations will suffer from gay marriages!!" HUH??? So how does that work then?

I don't know what will happen to South Africa, the tourism potential is amazing, the Drakensburg and the Kruger park which I prefer to Etosha.. at least you have to drive to find the animals.

By the way did I tell you that you can buy Zebras in the shop in Kruger Park,

"Real ones? So did you?"

" I tried but when I got it to the cash till they couldn't find the bar code"

"Ahh that was a joke then"

"Just a little one"

"So little it was unrecognisable"

"AND!"

"And?"

"I tried to buy some camouflage clothing but I couldn't find any!"

"That'll be another little joke then!"

KRUGER PARK

Whilst I was in the shop some sod backed into me into me in a small car park in Kruger then drove off. When I got back to the car a couple of other tourists told me and, highly pissed off, I set out in pursuit into the dusk of an African night, mentally practicing what I was going to do when I caught up with him.

Ten minutes down the road in rapidly decreasing light sanity prevailed. Here I was hurtling through the murk where animals didn't obey the highway code, and bloody great bull elephants get a bit fed up when you run into them; then of course some of the South African drivers are big buggers as well.These two thoughts made me slow down and return to camp, cowardice again in my life getting the better of justifiable anger. The damage is superficial, so much like me really!

Hippo's telling secrets

We stayed at Villa Calla in Umhalanga where Janelle's poached eggs were magnificent, (every time she leant over me

in her tight top and asked me how I wanted my eggs I couldn't get two poached eggs out of my scrambled brain but that's just me!) and we quickly felt part of the Villa Calla family.
Janelle, Calla and Karl showed us what South African hospitality really means.
What else? We went to a sushi restaurant in Umhalanga which is run by an ex South African rugby winger, I didn't realise this until Calla told me and I made the mistake of saying, "Oh yes he'll be the one that kept dropping the plates!!" Well I thought it was funny, unfortunately he was a friend of Calla (and a big bugger!) and Calla said, "Oh he WILL be amused when I tell him that!" so I couldn't go back to try some more raw fish!

ISANDLWANA AND RORKES DRIFT

We spent a couple of days in Isandlwana and walked the site of the famous battle which took place in January 1879 between the invading British Army and the Zulu's, which has given birth to at least two films which even the most cursory examination of the facts are shown to be more entertainment than documentary (I know for a fact Michael Cain wasn't there).

Having said that the site is eerie and remote and dotted with white Cairns marking the spots where men were killed, well the British men, only recently has there been a memorial created to the Zulu's who, it has to be remembered, were defending their homeland and who were reluctant to fight, preferring negotiation.

The British troops were camped under the hill and were attacked by the Zulu's in their traditional Bulls horn formation and if you read reports of the battle it's not difficult to imagine how the last survivors felt as they fought desperately slowly retreating up the hill until finally.....

The ancillary battle of Rorkes drift took place on the same day and eleven Victoria Crosses were awarded but one can't help wondering whether this was because, after the first major defeat of the British Army by a "native" army, the politicians needed to change it into a victory and this could be achieved by awarding Victoria Crosses, the highest award for gallantry England can award, it happened again at Dunkirk when a massive retreat was hailed as a victory.

The battle of Isandlwana was the first of a number of battles in the Anglo-Zulu war, a war created almost entirely by the British High Commissioner in South Africa, Sir Bartle Frere, to counter the growing power of Cetshwayo's Zulu empire, which had first emerged early in the nineteenth century in an area along the eastern seaboard of Southern Africa, north of modern day Durban.

British adventurers had been attracted to Zululand in search of trade and profit, and by the 1840s a British colony - Natal - had sprung up on the southern borders of Zululand. By the 1870s, the British had begun to adopt a 'forward policy' in the region, hoping to bring the various British colonies, Boer republics and independent African groups under common control, with a view to implementing a policy of economic development, and the Zulu's were seen as a threat.

Sir Bartle Frere deliberately created an incident with the Zulu king, Cetshwayo kaMpande, confident in the belief that the Zulu army - armed primarily with shields and spears - would soon collapse in the face of British Army's firepower.

It has to be remembered that in the absence of fast communications, the British High Commissioners abroad were trusted to react as the local circumstances required (although of course they were supposed to act within agreed outlines from the British Government), and the British Government had made it clear that they did not want a war with the Zulu nation if for no other reason that at the time they were involved in many fronts elsewhere in the world.

So Sir Bartle Frere desperately needed a reason to invade Zululand and thus be able to ignore the Governments views and three relatively minor acts (well minor in the context of the times) between July and September 1978 gave him the excuse he wanted.

Firstly a wife of Sihayo, one of Cetshwayo's senior chiefs fled into Natal from Zululand, and she was subsequently seized and executed by his brother and sons.

A week later the same young men, along with two other brothers and an uncle, captured another refugee wife of Sihayo in the company of the young man with whom she had fled. This woman was carried back, and was probably put to death; the young man with her although guilty in Zulu eyes, was safe from them on English soil and they did not touch him.

The last incident was when a Mr. Deighton a surveyor and trader in the Colonial Engineering Department, went down to the ford across the Tugela on the border between Natal and Zululand, there they were surrounded by fifteen or twenty armed Zulus, made prisoners, and taken off along with their horses. They were roughly treated and threatened for some time;

though, ultimately, and at the instance of a headman who fortunately came along, they were released.

None of these three incidents were in themselves serious enough to warrant an invasion but Sir Bartle Frere quickly took the opportunity of escalating a note of protest into a ten point ultimatum with conditions that he knew Cetshwayo couldn't possibly comply with and with indecent haste he ordered the invasion of Zululand long before the British Government could veto it Lieutenant General Frederick Augustus Thesiger, 2nd Baron Chelmsford invaded Zululand with a force of 5,000 Europeans and 8,200 Africans whilst another force of 1,400 Europeans and 400 Africans were stationed in the Utrecht district. Three columns invaded Zululand, from the Lower Tugela, Rorke's Drift and Utrecht respectively, their objective being Ulundi, the royal capital.

Although Cetshwayo's army consisted of some 40,000 men, Chelmsford's three columns were unopposed. On 22 January the centre column (1,600 Europeans, 2,500 Africans), which had advanced from Rorke's Drift, was camped near Isandlwana and on the morning of that day Chelmsford split his forces and moved out to support a reconnoitring party.

After Lord Chelmsford had left, a Zulu army of nearly 20,000 surprised the camp and Chelmsford's refusal to set up a defensive ring contrary to standing orders, and also arrogantly ignoring information that the Zulus were close at hand, were decisions they all were later to regret.

414

The Battle of Isandlwana was the greatest victory that the Zulu kingdom would enjoy during the war and some 1350 British Soldiers and an unknown number of Zulus perished in the battle.

In its aftermath, a party of between 4,000 and 5000 Zulu reserves mounted a raid on the nearby Rorke's Drift, which was heroically and successfully defended by one hundred and thirty-nine British soldiers and the Zulu's were only driven off after ten hours of ferocious close quarter fighting when British reinforcements were seen coming towards them.

Rorke's Drift itself was a small single building mission hospital and former trading post located near a drift (ford) on the Mzinyathi ("Buffalo") River forming the border between Natal and Zululand and got its name from its first owner James Rorke the son of an Irish ex soldier who bought the farm in 1849.

Eleven Victoria Crosses and five DCM's were awarded to the eight officers and one hundred and thirty one non-commissioned ranks of B company 2nd Battalion 24th foot South Warwickshire Regiment, (although made up primarily of Welshmen), seventeen were killed and ten wounded. Zulu casualties are thought to have been around five hundred.

The theory persists that the Battle of Rorkes drift, coming as it did after the ignominious defeat of the British Army at Isandlwana, received a disproportionate number of VC's to deflect the public's attention from the defeat. But the courage shown in a desperate fight for life is different from the courage shown when you have a choice, indeed Sir

Garnet Wolseley, taking over as Commander-in-Chief from Lord Chelmsford, was unimpressed with the awards made to the defenders of Rorke's Drift, saying "It is monstrous making heroes of those who shut up in buildings at Rorke's Drift, could not bolt, and fought like rats for their lives which they could not otherwise save."

It's interesting to note that the consequences of the battle: Corporal Schiess fell "on hard times" and died in 1884 aged 28 years; Pte John Fielding's hair is said to have turned white shortly after the battle; William Jones in old age suffered from nightmares that the Zulus were about to attack; Robert Jones shot himself in 1896. It seems probable that a number of the defenders of Rorke's Drift subsequently suffered from what is now called as Post Traumatic Stress Disorder.

Isandlwana marked the beginning of the end of the Zulu empire and it suffered it final defeat at the Battle of Ulundi (Cetshwayo's Royal household) in July 1979, and he was captured an exiled to London. He returned to Zululand in 1883 but was deposed by a rival and died a few months later, perhaps of a heart attack but more probably from poisoning.

TIME TO LEAVE AFRICA

We knew that the car had to be clean before it would be allowed into Australia so I presented myself to the local car valeting service in Umhalanga Rocks and negotiated the full executive clean! In my defense I did say that I needed it really clean (and I mean REALLY clean) and the next morning I delivered it to them and they said,
"It'll be ready at lunchtime!"

"Look when I said clean it needs to be "running fingers along the chassis with white gloves on" clean!""
They gave me the well known "yeah yeah whatever!" look.

I returned at lunchtime, well after lunchtime in truth not wanting to be unreasonable, and the car was parked outside, superficially clean, definitely superficially, for a quick glance under showed the Cameroonian mud still firmly attached. I mentioned this, at length!, and drove it back in, but this time I decided to stay and watch, then I stayed and advised, and finally I stayed and did the job myself.
I stayed and did the job myself for three days!. Three days and three blocked drains!
I got the impression they were getting tired of me by the time the car eventually passed the "white gloved fingers along the chassis test!" an impression confirmed when I finally paid the bill and said,

"I'll mention you on the website!"
"Please don't, we can't afford business like yours!"

A final thought as we leave South Africa we have achieved the ambition of crossing all of the major rivers in Africa.
The White and Blue Nile
The Congo
The Volta
The Niger
The Ogowe
The Zambezi
And The Limpopo

We left South Africa with a speedometer reading of 141612 miles, which meant we did (141612 - 124500) 17112 miles through Africa in exactly five calendar months

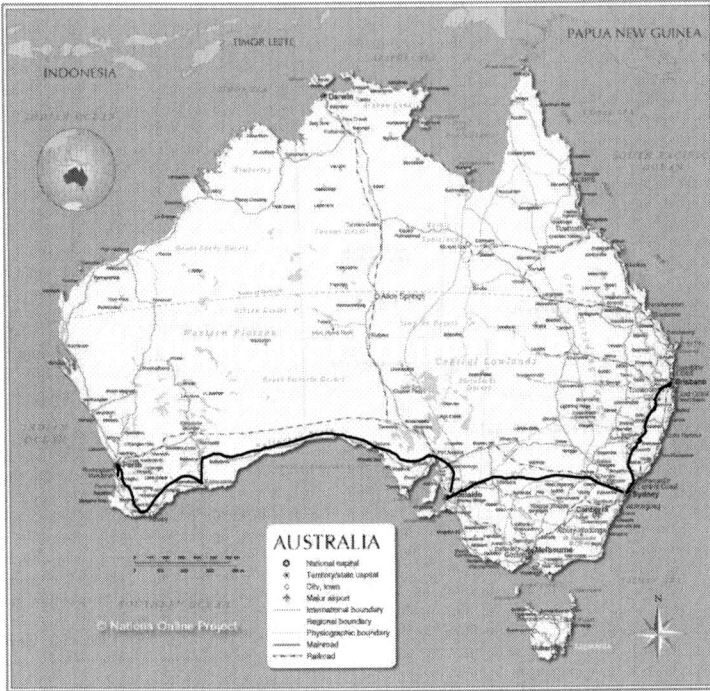

AUSTRALIA

Well it seemed like a good idea at the time to drive the car to and around Australia after all how difficult could it be to temporarily import a vehicle into Australia?.. Answer?.. Not difficult but a pain in the arse!!

CUSTOMS

This part isn't too difficult providing you have a Carnet de Passage that's valid for as long as you want to stay in Australia, and is valued at one and a half times the value of the vehicle plus £5000, a value recommended by the RAC in the UK, which of course the Australian customs, like all the others, completely ignore.

QUARANTINE

The vehicle has to be clean, and I mean clean, I don't mean "bugger it that's close enough". The quarantine inspector was affable enough but he greeted me with the statement,
"I'm looking for just one thing so I can send it for professional steam cleaning!"
And that costs money; I passed but remember it took me three days with a power hose and the complete team at Jeeves in Umhalanga South Africa to get it through.
The quarantine check cost about A$112

FORTY EIGHT HOUR PERMIT TO DRIVE

Now you have cleared the vehicle you have to get a forty eight hour permit to drive, so you can drive the car from the docks to the vehicle testing station, you can do this by ''phone, that is you can do it when you eventually find someone who knows what the hell you're talking about. It'll cost you A$15 and this will give you permission only to drive from the docks to the vehicle testing station.

ROAD WORTHINESS
You go to the local vehicle-testing department who give your vehicle an MOT this will cost A$57. The test is easy enough and it simply confirms that the vehicle is roadworthy. Best not go as we did on the last working day before Christmas because everyone has suddenly remembered that they need to get their car done, whilst the staff have already, metaphorically if not literally, begun their Christmas celebrations.

LICENSE
Armed with the vehicle road worthiness certificate, your driving license and your passport, you present yourself to the vehicle license department who (eventually) issue you with a license which means you are insured against personal injury to third parties. It cost me A$85 for three months, and it means that your car is on the Australian system so they can fine you for being English. As an aside we were classified as a golf buggy, I didn't like to ask why as the girl who issued it was wearing a Father Christmas pixie hat and a silly grin.

THIRD PARTY PROPERTY INSURANCE
The road license means you are insured against claims for personal injury from third parties, you'll need third party insurance against property (car) damage. This cost me A$290 for four months..

Ok that's it; you can now drive in Australia!! Legally and with third party insurance .. Is it worth importing you're own vehicle rather than hiring in Australia?.. Well obviously it depends on how long you intend staying, but for three months it just about breaks even.

But if you think Africa's bureaucratic.. Australia leaves it standing or more correctly sitting in committee!!!!

But I digress; the flight from Durban to Perth was like all long flights! Long (obviously) boring and uncomfortable, reading this you'll be familiar with that feeling! The temptation is to drink but that's a mistake, it feels ok at the time (especially when it's free) but you wake up with a hangover, and that's not nice when you have to queue for customs and immigration, so I was good, I only had a small bottle of wine and a couple of beers, oh yes and a double gin and tonic, the last being as a final treatment for possible insipient malaria!

After being very concerned about the reception that we would be given for not having an onward air ticket, the greeting was as always when I'm involved, total indifference. Even the drug sniffer dog ignored me. Well it cocked its leg against my naked leg but I tapped it firmly on the nose and it danced away and moved on, enthusiastically sniffing at passengers bags, legs and in one memorable case (well memorable to me), groin!
The immigration officer asked me in all seriousness if I intended to look for work in Australia!!!
"No! And I can assure you if I see any I will certainly ignore it!"
The first impression of Australia was good, wide-open roads, warm sunshine and cold beer! What more could anyone want, but jet lag was hitting, that strange almost euphoric feeling that you get when you miss sleep, my body clock and my mind were in different time zones to each other and to everyone else, the latter of course not being too unfamiliar to me.

We were met and accommodated by Alison and Roman, another of the ever growing "You must come and stay with us" innocents

On Sunday they had an air race in Perth, in my innocence I expected to see some aircraft flying round a track, not unlike any other race. In the event all you saw was one aircraft zipping around a course which being in the sky didn't have any marking, then suddenly diving down and skimming the surface around some large inflated road cones! Then flying off.. Only to be immediately replaced by another plane indistinguishable from the previous one doing the exactly same thing!

Definitely not a spectator sport! Especially as it rapidly became apparent that they weren't going to crash.. Boring!! It's at moments like this that I get an overwhelming urge for a beer, if only to alleviate the boredom, and so when Roman suggested that we try the local brew (again and again) I declined with such a transparent insincerity that was obvious to all, they thankfully ignored me and we went to Freemantle, the port of Western Australia which was buzzing.

A covered market selling ethnic crafts and food; a vegetable market with every storeowner shouting and negotiating creating a cacophony of sound. Everyone dressed without needing to worry about the temperature, a gentle sunny Sunday afternoon. Buskers, firstly a large lady singing opera (I now know the source of the expression about fat lady and singing!), and the John Butler Trio who apparently are famous and award winners and only the previous week appeared on national television, sitting in the street busking and seemingly happily collecting money in a hat.

Everyone happy cheerful and chatting, the beer cold (yes I finally agreed to have one! Well I finally agreed to have more than one in truth) and the food good, well except for the broken plastic that I found in mine when I neared the end of the food, and which they insisted on refunding me the full price of the meal so apologetically that I almost regretted breaking the plastic into the meal.. almost!!!

The overwhelming feeling though was of security, which we wore like a fluffy blanket after five months in Africa when lack of security became a way of life, it was good not to be looking over your shoulder all the time, and no begging! Whilst waiting for the Land Cruiser we hired a small camper van to look at the west coast of Australia, and suddenly realised just how big the bloody place is, and paradoxically the excellent roads make it seem bigger as you just sit there and see the road disappearing into the distance in a ruler straight line.

And some of the road trains!, gigantic lorries towing three large trailers, thundering along and coming right up behind you trying to bully you out of their way .. And do I let them? .. Too bloody right I do.
And where, you may wonder, because I certainly was, was my Land Cruiser all this time!! On a round the world bloody sea-cruise that's where! It was no doubt enjoying a rest after five month hard travelling; relaxing in the bars and restaurants and even going to the disco's all at my expense.
Bloody cheek!

Whilst we were waiting for the car we flew to Alice Springs and Ayres Rock.. Blimey it's hot there. Looking out of the plane windows you're reminded again, as if you could forget, that Australia is a bloody big place...

Ayres rock, from now on we'll call it Uluru which is its original Aboriginal name, Ayres being a politician after whom it was named, is coloured brilliant red or dull rust, dependent on the time of day you see it, and that of course why its red! It contains a high proportion of iron and it's the iron going rusty that causes it!

Although it was originally taken over by the Australian Government, the aboriginals claimed ownership and after much negotiation they (the Australians that is) gave it back to the Aboriginals who immediately leased it back to the government (keep up at the back!) so visitors could look at it, but, it being a traditional sacred place to the Aboriginals, they ask you not to climb it although under the terms of the lease climbing is allowed (Did you follow all that?).
We walked slowly around the base, 9.4 kilometres in 40 degrees of heat and the guide insisted we drink a litre of water every half an hour!! Well some of that water certainly replaced what I sweated off, but the rest went, as liquid always does, inexorably
straight to the bladder.

So if climbing Uluru is disrespectful then pissing up against it certainly is!! And I now await the retribution of Aboriginal elders who will no doubt throw boomerangs or didgeridoos at me (or whatever it is they throw), that is if they can be bothered to sober up and get off their arses.

(If anyone now says "what's Uluru" you haven't been concentrating and you should go back to the beginning and start again and this time concentrate!!)..

CHRISTMAS 2006
Having finally cleared the Land Cruiser we eventually, and reluctantly, left Alison and Roman's wonderfully comfortable house in a select suburb of Perth. Well, it was select until we arrived and put the tent up, but that, as they say, is another story.
I love the Aussie sense of humour and some people wouldn't have realised that Roman was joking when he greeted us each morning with,
"Oh are you two still here I was hoping you'd have buggered off by now!"
"Oh no Roman it's so comfy here we were thinking of staying longer!" he laughed until he cried at that one!

Well he cried!

Christmas day was spent on the beach! Decadent or what? Surrounded by half dressed (or half naked) bodies and drinking champagne, then home (as an aside I said that to Roman " let's go home!" and he said "Jesus he really does think it's his home!") to a turkey dinner, (or being Australia it could have been Emu!)
Christmas Day Perth 2006
But like all good things it had to come to an end and it was the day after Boxing day that we drove away with Alison shouting "Come and again anytime!" and Roman shouting, "But not too soon!".

We drove away shouting and sounding the horn, then realized we were heading in the wrong direction and drove past the

426

house again...just as the locksmiths van arrived to change the locks!

Heading south before turning east, the high spot, or so the guidebook says, are the trees!! Big bloody Karri trees, but at the end of the day, just trees. The Karri tree only grows in a small part of the world and is denser than any other tree.. (Fitting as it's Australian!) And with the best will in the world it's difficult to find anything exciting to say about them except that they're big, very big and old.. Some apparently four hundred years old!

Oh yes! They used to pick the tallest, and we're talking seventy metres here! to climb up and look for forest fires. There is one called the Gloucester tree named (keep up it's going to get interesting!.. honest) after the Duke of Gloucester who, when he was Governor General of Australia, (a position he got because of his intelligence , industry intellect, and .. er.. oh yes and the fact that he was related to the King!), visited the area so they named the tree after him.. Seventy metres high! one can easily imagine some Australian muttering
"Try looking down your nose at that one mate!"

To get to the top they have hammered bloody great steel rods into the trunk and you can climb up and look out over the forest which is what I did.. and the most memorable thing about it wasn't the view, which as you would expect was panoramic.. But in truth just a carpet of the tops of trees.. No! The most memorable thing was the pain in your legs that climbing vertically for seventy metres, then climbing down again, inevitably brings,
"Weren't you scared Jeff!
"Nahhhhh! No problem! Remember my brother used to be a fireman, so it's in the family"

"Oh I see! Just a point though didn't he fall off a ladder, injure himself, and have to retire!"
"Bloody hell yes he did.. I'd forgotten that.. Why didn't you tell me before I climbed the sodding tree?"

We saw in the New year in Pemberton.. just! .. Sitting with two German couples we drummed our fingers until two minutes past midnight giving me just enough time to break my New Years resolution (again) before going to bed! Yet another New Year on the road, remembering friends and family and feeling homesick!

ESPERANCE
A tropical cyclone called Isobel (I seem to remember reading somewhere that tropical storms in the southern hemisphere are called cyclones and are named in alphabetical order using female names and northern hemisphere ones are called typhoons and named after males). Isobel entered the north east of Australia and immediately began to diminish but when it reached the south coast what was waiting for it?
"I said what was waiting for it?"
"Oh sorry I was somewhere else then, I don't know! What was waiting for it?"
"Another low depression that's what! Which helped to resurrect its strength and create the biggest storm in Southern Australia for decades and guess what?"
"What?"
"I'm stuck under it! and have been for two days!"

We were driving along happily and we heard the weather forecast threatening dangerous and heavy storms so we raced into Esperance and took some self catering accommodation (the last in town) to use until the storm passed over.. But it didn't!, pass over that is, it liked it so much that, like us, it

428

stayed here and for the last two days it has rained.. Really rained.. and we can look smugly over the camp site opposite and play "watch the tent fly away!" which is infinitely and definitely more interesting than Australian Television.

I wrote earlier that we found the last room, what really happened was that at Jeans insistence we joined the long queue at the Tourist Office all looking for the last of the limited accommodation. We finally got to the front,
"What do you want?" said the nice, but harassed lady.
"Anything!" said Jean,
"Anything cheap" I said quickly,
She looked doubtful, and was about to speak, when the 'phone rang, she listened then covering the mouthpiece she said,
"Do you want a self catering flat? It's just become available"
"Yes!" said Jean,
"How much?" said Jeff,
"YES!" shouted Jean,

We'd got the last room in the town, so the chances of negotiating were low.
Some places had half their annual rainfall in one night, but more importantly for me the beer ran out. For a while there I was quite concerned .. No! Panic ridden is closer to the truth .. but the TV has just given out an emergency telephone number to ring in case of .. well emergencies! Which I think I will call now for some beers.. and perhaps a couple of packets of crisps.
Oh yes the good news is that the power has just gone off!!
Why good news you might ask??
 "I SAID WHY GOOD NEWS YOU MIGHT ASK!!!"
"Oops sorry! Might I ask why that is good news?"
Because it means we don't have to watch Aussie Television!!
Right that does it where's that bloody phone?

LATEST

In the Australian National News it says that 200 mm of rain has fallen today in Esperance, and that it's going to get worse by nine o'clock tonight.. (it's now seven o'clock!) ..I am not sure whether I should be worried or not as I have absolutely no idea how much 200mm is!

NEXT MORNING

Flooding, trees fallen down and roofs off and here's me wondering if I had enough sun cream to last.. Oh well it will make interesting reading on the web site,
"What will?"
"Reading about the storm"
"I've got news for you Jeff .. It didn't!!"

CROSSING THE NULLABOR

The Eyre Highway (named after Edward Eyre the British explorer) runs across the bottom of Australia and it's a bloody long way! .. and where do you think the word Nullabor comes from?
"The original Aborigine?"
"No I think it's more likely that its from the Latin "Null" meaning no and "Arbour" meaning trees"
"Oh ok, so are there any trees?"
"Well no! I've just told you!"
After the 200mm downpour in Esperance we left and headed across pausing at Norseman ..
"Hey how do you think that town got its name?"
"Well obviously from the original settlers who were men from Norway.. That's easy!"
"Well you're wrong its the name of some blokes horse who founded the place!"
"Bloody good job his horse wasn't called Nellie then wasn't it!"

On the way over to Norseman I realised that 200mm is in fact 8" which is a bloody lot of water and most of it finished up in our tent so we spent the day drying it out.

There's one stretch that's 90 miles long without a single bend,

Hang on you skipped past the pictures of the GPS.. This screen shows the track you are on so that if you get lost you can simply turn round and go back.. it's called at breadcrumb trail (of course you can't use actual breadcrumbs because the birds follow you along and eat them! So that would just be silly).. and if you look at the writing in the bottom left hand corner you will see it's set at 100 miles.. so the straight line is 90 miles long

"That's really interesting Jeff!"

It took three days of hard driving but eventually we hit Adelaide .. Oh yes before that we stayed at a great camp site miles from anywhere and the couple who we working there were working their way around Australia ..

"Oh get to the point Watts"

"..the point is she had tattoos on her tummy you want to see?"

"You took pictures of a strange woman's belly, or even a woman's strange belly?"

"Yes I told her I was a reporter for Tattoo world!"

"And she believed you?"

Her name was Janice, smashing girl, gullible but smashing!!

INTO ADELAIDE!!
You remember the Aussies we met in Ghana?? No?? Well
look back at the Ghana write up and you will remember that
John and Sharyn said,
"Anytime you're near Adelaide etc. etc!" FOOLS!
We found them even though they moved house!!!(People do
that a lot! But I'm sure it's coincidence). The first night we
met them in Adelaide and were watching them doing African
drumming and they got a phone call and Sharyn said,
"We've gotta go, there's a fire!"

Following Sharyn to her house high in the hills we rounded a
bend and there on the horizon was the fire, lots of it. (The
question did enter my head as to why we were driving
TOWARDS the fire?). When we eventually got to her
(wooden) house high in the hills at the end of a dirt track road,
she immediately logged onto the fire service web site which
updated every half an hour with the current situation, and the
current situation wasn't good.. The only saving grace was that
the wind which was, at least not blowing towards us.
We stood outside watching the fire lighting up the sky,

"Bloody hell Sharyn how far away is that?"
"About ten km!"
"Er so we're safe enough here then, we'd have lots of time to get out!"
"Well forest fires have been measured at sixty mph!" (By whom?)
"Right so that would take .. bloody hell six minutes to get here!"
John arrived and tested his fire defense system, which consisted of sprinklers on his roof attached to a bloody great tank of water, which simply, but hopefully effectively, covered the house with water. His own personalised tropical cyclone! The curtains in the house were all "quick release" and could be pulled off the runners instantly!

At one stage Jean said,
"Excuse me I need the wee!"
"I should hang onto it, if that wind turns we're going to need all the water we can get!"

It was a long night watching the fires, getting the updates and of course testing the wind direction. It was only later that John said,
"The problem is of course there is only one way out!"
"So John, if there's only one way out what do we do if it's blocked!"
He looked at me as if it was a stupid question, which I suppose under the circumstances, it was!
So in the last two weeks we've been under the biggest storm in Western Australia for a couple of generations and then we drive 1500 miles across country into the biggest forest fire in the Adelaide hills for years..who said I'm bad news!!
"HEY!!!! Guess what?"
"What?"

"You remember Sharyn skinny dipped when she was in
Ghana and there was a picture?.. Well you know we've been
staying with Sharyn and John"
"Where the forest fire was?"
"Exactly anyway she said that I could copy the pictures of the
hotel where we were all staying and guess what?"
"You found the picture of her skinny dipping!"
"How did you know?"
"Just a hunch! And how's this for another hunch you pinched
a copy didn't you?"
"It was an accident!"
"So you thought you'd send a copy of it to Simon Billson who
e mailed you and promised you money if you could get him
a copy!"
"Yes but it's only for him to see no-one else, because I asked
Sharyn if I could have a copy for the web site and guess what
she said?"
"Yes?,"
"NO no!!"
"No No?"
"What?"
"She said no no"
"No just the one no!"
"OH! No, or do I mean Oh no!"
"I've no idea what you mean!"

So in deference to her wishes I want everyone to promise that they will not look at the photo.

God! I wish the water was as shallow as I am

Right that's it.. Onto Sydney across the Hay Plain! bloody hell Australia is big and hot (trying to make Hay whilst the sun shines! Bill Bryson said that first!)

SYDNEY

Well I've said it before and I'll say it again (and again) Australia is a bloody big place and I wish there were lots of interesting things to write about but there isn't!! The Hay plain, like the Nullabor, is long and boring, not unlike this web site, so let's skip quickly to Sydney where we stayed with Mark and Charlotte, who let us in, showed us our room and how the TV and internet worked and went to work, exactly what we love in hosts.

We did all the touristy things in Sydney, looked at the Sydney Harbour Bridge, the Opera house, took a ferry to Manly beach (crowded and full of young people who, in my day would still have been at nursery school), Bondi beach (ditto above), had my waist line checked by a young girl who said,

"You're too fat, you are in danger of being a diabetic" cheeky sod,
"And you are in danger of a slap!" (I didn't say that because she was bigger and fitter than me.. in fact most of the females in Australia seem to be bigger and fitter than me!)

I tried body surfing, and resisted the temptation to try on one of Mark's rubber suits for two reasons, the first being sexual (don't ask!) and the second because there are so many Japanese tourists around they would probably have mistaken me for a whale and caught me for sushi (memo to self .. Diet!)

We reluctantly left Sydney (that was a split infinitive in case you hadn't noticed) because we had failed in our record and not outstayed our welcome, but the great outback beckoned and Australia is a bloody big country...(did I tell you that?)

Theres something I wanted to tell you! I was standing on a train and this rather attractive female sitting in front of me smiled! I looked over my shoulder to see who she was smiling at, but it was at me! Blimey! Result! I breathed in to show her my six-pack, unfortunately all this did was make my shorts drop down a bit. (It was only the fat that was keeping them up) I smiled back and was seriously considering moving to Australia if the females fancy geriatric overweight pommies. She leant forward, so did I, she smiled again and whispered, "Would you like my seat?"
I breathed out!!!
The east coast is very different to the west, the motorways busier and faster, the campsites crowded and noisy and frankly the trip ceased to be fun!! The visa expiry date of sixteenth of February meant that if we were going to see the Great Barrier Reef we would have to drive some 1800 miles north and of course the same distance back so a couple of

days hard driving saw us making not the slightest impression on the map!

Oh yes! Have you ever heard of the song "A Pub with no beer!" if you admit you have we all know your age.. It was written and sung by an Australian country singer called Slim Dusty and we went to see it...it was twenty miles off the road ..

"Hang on you drove twenty miles to visit a pub with no beer.. why?"
"Because it's famous and guess what?"
"I know! When you got there it had no beer!"
"No! it had plenty of beer!"
"So you had a beer from the pub with no beer"
"No I had a cup of coffee!"

What is noticeable is that no matter how small the community there is a war memorial which is inscribed with the names of the Australian dead from the first and second world wars, Borneo, Korea, Vietnam and Afghanistan in fact all the conflicts of the last 100 years..

Opposite the "Pub with no Beer!" there was the memorial for that one small town including three brothers.. Wherever we go in the world there are memorials!!

HEADING NORTH

Many years ago I worked in Africa with Barry Lee, not true, I played cricket with him and he wrote and said "if ever ..etc. etc..." So we did and it was good because it forced us off the main roads onto the quieter back roads and we saw another facet of Australia...green rolling country side interspersed with small towns to all intents like the ones you see in any American movie.. except there is no one around.. each has a general store a hotel and a garage, perhaps if you are lucky an IGA (a supermarket) and a cafe!

I was reminded of the joke about an English comedian who was doing the rounds of Outback pubs and he stood in front of a group of big hairy Australians (men not women! Oh! I don't know though) with a boomerang in his hand and he said,
"If I throw this out there will it come back?"
A voice from the back said,
"If it f......g hits me it will!!"

THE TOWN OF 1770

The story goes that Captain Cook "discovered" Australia in April 1770. As in most things the truth is somewhat different!

The idea of "Terra Australis" a "Southern Land", was originally introduced by Aristotle and his ideas were expanded on by Ptolemy in the 1st century AD, who believed that the Indian Ocean was enclosed on the south by land, and that the lands of the Northern Hemisphere must be balanced by lands in the south. Ptolemy's maps, which became well-known in Europe during the Renaissance between the 14th and 17th centuries, did not actually depict such a continent, but they did show incorrectly that Africa had no southern oceanic boundary and therefore might extend all the way to the South Pole, and it also raised the possibility that the Indian Ocean was entirely enclosed by land.

So history credits Cook with discovering Australia and New Zealand, but what is forgotten (or as with many European discoveries is ignored) was that it had all been done many times before.

After the "discovery" by Cook, Captain Dalrymple, head of the Map Department at the British Admiralty. . . wrote a furious,

"Cook could hardly have discovered Australia since he had in hand Admirality maps already depicting that continent!" The Chinese regularly journeyed to the "Australia" as early as the ninth century to mine copper, and fifteenth-century Chinese voyages of exploration led directly to the maps Cook used.

About another writer Gavin Menzies, concluded; "Cook was a great man, and the greatest navigator of all time, but he discovered neither New Zealand nor Australia. More than two centuries before he embarked on his voyages maps from the Dieppe School showed Australia with remarkable clarity. The Jean Rotz map was in possession of the British Admiralty when Cook set sail, and Joseph Banks, who sailed with Cook, had acquired another of the finest, the Harleian (Dauphin) map, showing Australia with the same precision as the Rotz map.

The Endeavour Reef, on which Cook ran aground, is clearly shown on these earlier maps, together with what became known as Cooktown Harbour. When Cook had extricated himself for the reef, he sailed directly for Cooktown, the only harbour in a thousand miles of coastline. "This harbour will do excellently for our purposes, although it is not as large as I have been told." Earlier maps do show it larger, for sea levels were lower when Admiral Zhou Man originally charted the coast in 1422-23".

So when Cook sailed from England in 1768 he had in his possession accurate maps of the region but that notwithstanding he mapped the complete New Zealand coastline, making only some minor errors. He then sailed west, reaching the south-eastern coast of the Australian continent on 19 April 1770, and in

*doing so his expedition became the first recorded
Europeans to have encountered its eastern coastline.*

*On 29 April Cook and crew made their first landfall
on the mainland Australia at a place now known as
the Kurnell Peninsula, which he named Botany Bay
after the unique specimens retrieved by the botanists
Joseph Banks and Daniel Solander. It is here that
James Cook made first contact with an Aboriginal
tribe known as the Gweagal. He returned to England
via the Cape of Good Hope and Saint Helena,
arriving on 12 July 1771*

*The name "Australia" is derived from the Latin
Australis, meaning "of the South", and the name
"Australia" was popularised by the 1814 work "A
Voyage to Terra Australis" by the navigator Matthew
Flinders, who was the first recorded person to
circumnavigate Australia. Despite its title, which
reflected the view of the British Admiralty, Flinders
used the word "Australia" in the book, which was
widely read and gave the term general currency.*

*In 1824, the Admiralty agreed that the continent
should be known officially as Australia.*

There's a story about when Cook landed and was trying to
talk to the local aborigines when a kangaroo bounded by and
Cook said,
"What's that animal called?"
The aborigine replied,
"Kangaroo!"
Cook said,
"Make a note of that chaps that jumpy thing with a big tail is
called a kangaroo!"

In fact Kangaroo in the Gweagal language translates as, "I don't know!"

"Oi Watts is that true, can I repeat that's story?"
"Best not!"

On the list of "must do must see" is the Great Barrier Reef, and we'd resigned ourselves to a 1500 mile drive north to Cairns, which in truth we were not looking forward to at all, and it was Barry who pointed out that the reefs southern tip was off the towns of Agnes Water and 1770. That's right there's a town called 1770..and ......"Why?" I hear you asking "is it called 1770?"
"I still can't hear you asking!!"
"Oh sorry! Why is it called 1770?"
"Thank you! well it was discovered by Captain Cook!
"Oh really and what year was that then?"
"Well 1770 obviously! look you're really not concentrating are you?"

We took a day trip out to Lady Musgrave island (named after the wife of a Governor of Queensland) and did a bit of a walk round and saw the white headed terns nesting and shitting, and we also saw the tracks where the turtles had come ashore to lay their eggs, and I learnt something!,
"I said .. oh never mind I'll tell you anyway"

The female guide was telling us that the female tortoises mate with lots of males and she can store the sperm (yes she said sperm!!.. sheesh modern women again!) from up to eight different males and then release the sperm individually and fertilise it (yes she said fertilise without even blushing!) so the clutches of eggs are from her but from eight different males.. I said it sounds a bit like a 18-30 holiday in Benidorm, an old

441

joke and she ignored me, everyone does but that has never stopped me yet!

The trees there have sticky pods which attach themselves to the baby birds that fall from the nests, and the weight of them prevent the birds escaping and they die a slow death of starvation and their bodies decompose or are eaten by the centipedes and eventually the nutrients return to the earth. It was so hard not to release them but we were warned against it! Natures balance again!

SNORKELING IN THE REEF
I snorkelled in the reef and it's difficult to describe the wonderment and serenity that I felt. Drifting over sheer cliffs of coral, different shapes, sizes swirls and colours. Some like granite, others like petrified leaves. Living amongst the coral, fish of every conceivable shape and size, reds and yellows, zebra fish. Large groupers, silver gar fish, clams slowly opening and closing in the current and I felt honoured to be part of their lives for a few too brief minutes, alone with them and the coral, no sounds intruding just shafts of turquoise sunlight intensifying the colours. Yellow fish with patterns like an electrical circuit board. Mysterious caves and canyons in the coral invite you in, large black seaweed waving the in the water and all the time the coral reef, older than time, reminding you of the transience of your life. Unfortunately the reef itself is in grave danger!

The Great Barrier Reef is located in the Coral Sea off the coast of Queensland in northeast Australia stretching for over 1,600 miles with an area of approximately 133,000 square miles and is composed of over 2,900 individual reefs, 900 islands and is the world's biggest single structure made by living organisms, and is the only living object that can be seen from space.

The reef is made up of of billions of tiny organisms of coral which live in colonies made up of identical individuals and exist as small sea anemone–like polyps, some of which secrete calcium carbonate to form a hard skeleton. The present reef is about 20,000 years old but is growing on an earlier plate some 600,000 years old.

The reef reproduces sexually each year during a mass spawning. The majority of inner reefs spawn around November with the outer reefs spawning later in December. Spawning always takes place at night, at any time up to six days after the full moon. Eggs and sperm are released into the water where they eventually combine to form a free swimming plankton.

The reef is home to 1500 species of fish, 400 species of coral, over 4000 species of molluscs, 500 species of seaweed, 215 species of bird, 16 species of sea snake and 6 species of sea turtle, 30 species of whales, dolphins, and porpoises including the dwarf minke whale, Indo-Pacific humpback dolphin, and the humpback whale.

Salt water crocodiles live in mangrove and saltmarshes on the coast near the reef along with 125 species of shark, stingray, skates or chimera

It is also home to large populations of dugongs or sea cows.

A large part of the reef is protected by the Great Barrier Reef Marine Park, which helps to limit the impact of human use, such as overfishing and tourism. But the Reef is under attack from many fronts; the water quality from run off of chemicals used in farming finding its way into the rivers and then into the sea; climate change accompanied by mass coral bleaching and cyclic outbreaks of the crown-of-thorns starfish.

The Crown-of-Thorns is a carnivorous predator that preys on reef coral. They climb onto reef structures, and then extrude their stomach onto the coral. This releases digestive enzymes that allow the starfish to absorb nutrients from the liquefied coral tissue. They are voracious predators. An individual starfish can consume up to 6 square metres (65 sq ft) of living coral reef per year

Perhaps this is the highlight of the trip, the Great Barrier Reef, the sight and experience marking the end of the time in Australia.

AND HOME!!!!
Well that's another trip over, in truth although we came home without the car via Singapore. Kula Lumpa and Bangkok, don't ask about the brothel in Singapore (do you want the room by the hour or all night!) and Pussy Ping Pong in Bangkok (no it's not cats playing table tennis and it's unlikely to be an Olympic sport and if it was I dread to think where they'd hang the medal), the trip finished mentally in the Great Barrier Reef

Perhaps now it's time to reflect on the trip as a whole, which had many different facets.

Australia was intimidating in its sheer size.

Africa down to Namibia challenging in the day-to-day immediacy of the problems faced.

Asia we haven't given a fair chance, we were tired of travel by the time we got there and were well into the "yeah yeah" mindset.

As I look back some events are outstanding

Nearly losing the car in the Atlantic was the scariest, when we suddenly realised danger was for real and that that we could lose everything.

Robbed in Gabon, inevitable.

The night in village in the Congo which reminded us that in a modern world of instant communication some people lives haven't changed.

Cyclones and Bush fires in Australia, nature can still show its teeth.

The impact of religion in West Africa driving through Ghana on a Sunday, listening to the hymns from the churches of every denomination, but to this agnostic and atheist, at least the religion sounded fun, which is about all that can be said for it. How did the Nigerian women manage to look tall clean and elegant in the filth, rubbish and motor fumes?

The traffic everywhere where the driving is so bad that it almost makes it safer, you EXPECT bad driving therefore you never relax.

In Angola and Mozambique the shells of empty buildings stripped of everything, roofs, plumbing, doors but no attempt made to occupy the building as a whole. Why? I never found out although there were various explanations the main one being superstition of ghosts of the former residents.

Long days lost in Angola acutely aware that there are millions of uncleared land mines, and the route had precipitous climbs and falls, thinking we were alone in Angola cowering behind rocks when three vehicles came by after midnight

Begging. Begging by people who had nothing, begging by people for whom it was a way of life. Begging is endemic in Africa from the smallest child on the street corner to the Government Minister being paid off by the west, to salve I suppose, the tribal guilt we all feel about slavery.

My over riding memory as I sit her remembering the people we met on the road is that we are so fortunate that we have freedom of choice in our lives, so many of them do not.
I am not of course being so arrogant as to think that they want my life! I do know there are very few whose life I would want.

So few of them, from the prostitutes in Nigeria, through the man sorting out traffic chaos in Gabon, to the mine clearing man in Angola, whose profession or the environment in which they work will kill or disable them, have the option to chose NOT to do it.
Africa was a challenge but it's changing. I have to be careful here not to judge whether the changes are an improvement because
firstly you have to define improvement. Certainly the new roads that are being built make movement easier, so children can travel to schools, hospitals become closer, perhaps emergency food and water can be distributed. But these same roads make hunting easier, make the villagers envious of what they see, increase urban migration, enable the forests to be stripped of their hardwoods, diseases to spread more easily, so I don't know.

In parts of Africa now you can use a mobile phone but can't drink the water, you can get designer sunglasses but not medicines you can trust.

We travelled through two countries (Zambia and Congo) where they were "electing" a President. Western democracy does not work in Africa; it hasn't worked since we imposed it as a price for Independence. It has not improved African society; all it has done is created a breeding ground for corruption and inefficiency under a façade of democracy.

The elections in Congo and Zambia were corrupt, everyone knows that but the electoral monitors didn't see anything untoward, or chose not to see knowing that if they did see anything, it wouldn't make any difference.
Not many were killed during the elections so they are getting better.

But at the end of the day does it matter. Africa's problems can only be, and will ultimately be, solved by Africans, not by the west giving charity or imposing an inappropriate political system. It will take a long time but it took the west a long time and I'm still not convinced that we have the best system.
So that's it another trip over! Full of incident, surprises, challenges and disappointments but that's why we travel.

SOUTH AMERICA HERE WE COME 2008

Right that's it I've been sensible, I've decorated the house, dug up all the flower beds and covered them with wood chips, cut the trees down and generally been terminal with the bushes, and we're ready to hit the road again. So when the map fell open at South America I thought,
"Why not" and the planning started.

In the past we've always shipped the vehicle in a container but this time we're trying Ro Ro, which for the uninitiated means that the car is driven onto a boat and driven off the other end, (well that's not strictly true! what happens is you deliver the car to one port and it's driven onto the boat, then when the boat arrives at the other end you drive it off, well in truth you don't drive it off, it is driven off ..).

"Get on with it Watts! You're waffling.. and you still haven't told us what Ro Ro means…!

Ro Ro is short for "Roll on Roll off and is cheaper than a closed and locked container but of course not as secure, but who would want to steal used personal stuff from the back of the locked van?...well! Who except the crew of the ship and the teeming masses of West Africans who were at Tilbury when I took my Land Cruiser to Grimaldi Ferries receiving area?

If you've ever wondered what happens to all the knackered cars, I can now tell you, they are filled with used tyres, second hand fridges and the general remnants of house clearances and shipped to West Africa.

I could have been forgiven (but wasn't) for missing the queue for Grimaldi's ferry, it looked like a scrap yard, but as I said it was in fact the vehicles being shipped to West Africa.

I got talking to one of the Nigerians there,

"No! I don't want to sell my Land Cruiser; no I don't want to sell the spare tyre!", and it works like this. They trawl round the streets looking for MOT failures and give the owner a few pounds to take it off their hands, they then fill the car with crap (sometimes with an S which makes it scrap) and ship it to Lagos, where after making a contribution to the "Customs Officers Benevolent Society" the vehicle and the contents disappear into the West African economy...don't laugh he reckons to clear £3000 each trip!!!

The one thing I couldn't help but notice was that all the doors were welded up and that the external lights had been removed, stupid me asked why,
"Well everything gets stolen by the crew whilst it's on board!" and he looked at me pityingly, whether it was because I'd asked a(nother) stupid question or that I'd simply relied on my car on industrial strength chains and padlocks.
It's at this point I should point out that Grimaldi had agreed to take the vehicle on the condition that they wouldn't be responsible for any losses. So of course I went to the office and said politely,
"OI! How do I know that nothing will be pinched off my vehicle?"
"Oh it's perfectly safe! Only the crew have access to the car deck!"
"Oh that's ok then! Erm.....?"
So you tell me what's going to happen, but if any of you are offered the lights, wheels, engine, body, chassis etc of an 80 series Land Cruiser buy them! I'll pay you back! (eventually, possibly)

So we waved off the car as it was driven away hopefully to Buenos Aries, getting a warm feeling that we'd at least got the paperwork sorted (the warm feeling could have been because we were sh*tt*ng ourselves!

BUENOS ARIES AND QUAINT ARGENTINEAN CUSTOMS

It took five minutes short of thirteen hours to cover the 11,200 kilometres between Paris Charles De Gaulle and Buenos Aries Airports. The first hour or so being spent eating airline food and drinking wine. I skipped the desert, opting instead for a sleeping pill and woke up, mouth open, dribbling, somewhere over the Atlantic, helped my self to a free ice cream and went back to sleep.

Being a well behaved and law abiding English people we had followed the rules on hand luggage size, not carrying on board liquids, nail files, firearms, thermo nuclear devices, ground to air missiles etc and endured being body searched at Birmingham airport (endured!!! It's the nearest thing I get to a sex life). Everyone else of course ignored it and crammed mountains of hand luggage into every available corner, in the overhead luggage lockers, under the seats and in the aisles.

I know the Security Services have to do their job, but do I really look like an El Quaida operative trained in the mountains of Afghanistan and capable of highjacking a fully laden Boeing 777 with a plastic fish knife! but what do I know?

The fact that they provided steel dinner knives tended to make the whole security search pointless (except for improving my sex life), the breakfast knife was plastic and broke when I tried to spread the butter, which must I suppose say something about the strength of French plastic or perhaps the strength of French butter.

I thought I might have a problem entering Argentina as we didn't have a return air ticket and fully expected the immigration officer to refuse us entry on the grounds that they already had sufficient geriatric idiots in the country without allowing in yet another. She didn't even look at us when she stamped the passport, believing I suppose that no one would forge a picture that looks like me.

So there we were at Buenos Aries airport on a Sunday morning with nowhere to go, what to do?? Easy! Go to Tourist Information!
"Necessito una hotel por favor!".. See all those hours of learning Spanish has enabled me to be totally fluent, and to speak Spanish like a native (but obviously not a native of Spain!)
"And where would you like to stay?" her English was better than mine!
"Where do you recommend?"
"We cannot recommend but we can give you a list!" which she did! And the list was three closely typed pages of hotels, "Which one do you want?"
"I don't know which do you suggest!"
"I cannot recommend"
"Give me a clue!"
"I cannot!"
I waited, an old trick designed to make someone feel guilty and do something they don't want to do.
She waited!! She had obviously read the same book as me or more probably was bored and was thinking of something else entirely!

In the end I remembered that I'd previously emailed Ed (more about him later!) and he'd recommended the Grand Orly hotel and when I mentioned it to her she shrugged and dragged herself reluctantly back from whatever was making her smile to herself, some bloody dark hard swarthy bloke I suppose, and 'phoned them.

They had a room!! Sorted!

Next stage is getting there! You are always at your most vulnerable of being ripped off after a long flight when you don't know what you are doing, what the rate of exchange is and when you don't know the rate for a job, in this case the taxi from the airport to the hotel.
I immediately started busily rehearsing my,
"How much? Are you bloody mad??? Do I look as if I've just come off a long flight, do you really think I don't know the rate of exchange and how much the fare should cost?"
When the lady said,
"Don't try taking a taxi, just go over there and they'll get you an official taxi and you wont have any problems!!
And that's what happened, you pay your 98 pesos (about £22) get in a taxi and they drop you at the hotel! No arguments, no hassle, but not half as much fun!!!!

The Grand Orly is on a glide path (a steep glide path!) to seedy and the first floor room they gave us was full of atmosphere, the atmosphere being dust, road fumes and music from a bar!! Where's that bloody 'phone.
The next room was on the ninth floor!

The bed looked comfortable so I lay on it just to test it, and woke up three hours later ready to take in the exotic sights of Buenos Aries!! It was Sunday afternoon and the exotic sights of Buenos Aries consisted of an expensive shopping mall and a tacky street full of cheap tat.
Isn't international travel great!

We had a pizza and coffee and paid the bill leaving what I considered to be a generous tip! (Any tip I leave no matter how small it may appear to others I consider generous). As we were leaving the waiter chased after us and reminded me

(Nay! demanded of me!) that it was usual to tip more than that and he considered my tip derisory.

After a bit of a chat (and me taking the money back from his outstretched hand) I believe that on that Sunday afternoon he learnt something much more valuable than mere money, namely that demanding money from Grey Haired Old English men is a pointless occupation, and we parted, not so much good friends, but at least I was happy and had started the holiday exactly as I meant
to go on being a miserable tight bastard whose idea of fun is upsetting local waiters

In the Square St Martin is the Argentinean monument to the dead of the Malivinas, yes I do mean the Falklands, but in the presence of the monument to the 4200 odd dead it seems appropriate to at least to refer to it as The Malivinas. I wonder if the two leaders who led the countries into what to me (and many others) was a pointless war, in an attempt to perpetuate their days in power, ever reflected and felt guilty at the loss and stupidity of it all.. Somehow I doubt it!

I'd had this great idea before arriving that we'd use the we bought in South Africa and just put in a local SIM card so we could make the phone calls we needed, good idea? Yes?

No! Bad idea! What the hell are bands anyway? apparently we only had three of them instead of four, and presumable the one that we didn't have was the one we needed

Once again proving again that nearly all of my good ideas have a basic flaw... namely that they are in fact bad ideas.

As I said earlier I'd been in contact with Ed George by email, having found him through HUBB overland, a travellers

website, and, after a couple of phone calls (not from the mobile which doesn't work) we finally met Ed in the coffee shop in the Grande Orly (a little hint here for you.. any hotel with "Grande" in the title usually isn't!) He'd not been idle and had found us an apartment, an apartment that came with free Internet access and a cell , and an owner named Ozvaldo who speaks English, having lived in London for many years! Sorted!!
Back in the room we packed! Do we need their towels? No!

The Parque Patricios area of Buenos Aires (they are called Barrio's) isn't a tourist area, well let's be honest it's pretty run down and certainly more run down than pretty, but it was attractive to me in that it was cheap.
Ozvaldos house was traditional with large rooms, high ceilings with a fan turning lazily, (it was an Argentinean fan after all!), tall pine doors and courtyard where we could sit and drink cold beer, whilst we waited for the Grimaldi ship to stop buggering about on the ocean and deliver our car to the docks.

We experienced our first Asado! Now an Asado is what the Argentineans call a BBQ, and this was my first, but not my last, experience of the traditional Argentinean way of cooking and eating meat...and I soon learnt that attempting to eat all the meat on offer is a big big mistake.. But my reputation as an Englishman was at steak (there's a pun there somewhere but I can't think of it!). I persevered and perspired and failed! If you want to stay in Buenos Aires away from the city and close to local shops and restaurants and with a great bus connection into the centre you should try it!

Ozvaldo is a DJ in a Tango club (I just remembered he also suffered from severe back pain caused by a slipped disc and I have been desperately trying to think of the joke that connects a DJ with a slipped disc but I can't..You'll have to do it yourself!) And he invited us along to watch him perform, I sounded a great idea until he told us that he started at midnight and finished at 5 a.m! Silly sod!

Anyway back to Ed, he's ex Peace Core and is now setting up a business providing safe temporary storage for motorbikes and cars for travellers, and who appears to know everyone in Buenos Aries.

Whilst in a cafe I got talking to another expatriate American, a long term resident named Chas! (Also Ex Peace Core and I couldn't help speculating why a country that spent so much money on the Peace Core appears to be permanently at war). Chas asked us about our itinerary and when I mentioned that we were going to the Pampas he stiffened, looked around as if nervous of being overheard and leant forward. Instinctively I did the same.

In a hushed almost conspiratorial voice he whispered,

"If you're going onto the Pampas be very very careful!" and looked around again

I too looked around and whispered,

"I certainly will Chas .. Erm! careful of what?"

Jean shuffled closer,

"Aliens!"

"Aliens?"

"Aliens!"

"There are Aliens on the Pampas??" I leant back,

He nodded,

"Yes and they take the cows!"

"Just cows not humans?" he looked at me as if it was a silly question,

"No! cows, and sometimes sheep!"

"So Aliens like Asados then?

By now both Jean and I had moved back and were checking the exits,

"No!" again the tone intimated a silly question,

"So what do they do with them"

"Who?"

"The cows"

"When?"

"After they've got them in the spaceship?"

"They disembowel them!"

"And!"

"And?"

"After they've disembowelled them!"

"Obviously they throw the carcass out of the spaceship and sometimes you can see the dent in the pampas where the cow landed"

"Ahh!" (It wasn't obvious to me!) I looked at Jean and she ignored me, concentrating on looking interested, she's much nicer than I am in that way "Right Chas I'll remember that! So Jean!" (she was still avoiding looking at me!) "When we're crossing the Pampas we must remember to keep the sunroof closed!"

I got the "Stop taking the piss Jeff" look but Chas nodded in agreement, and said,

"If you don't believe me look on the internet!" I didn't so I did, and sure enough it's there so it must be true.. Err mustn't it?

TANGO!!

There are things in the world that you've to do! Eating Sacha Tort in the Sacha Tort hotel in Vienna; drinking Champagne in the vineyard where it was produced; eating fish and chips on the sea front at Whitby; moules and fries in Belgium and watching Tango in the place where it was created.. Buenos Aries! And more importantly at the Gran Café Tortoni on Avenue de Mayo.

The decor in the actual cafe was wonderful, original paintings large ornate candelabras ancient furniture....

"Yes I was just looking...she's a big girl!"

"Who? "

"The one in the yellow jumper in the picture!"

"You mean the one with the black bra under her jumper? I never noticed!

"Yeah right!"

"Anyway about the Tango!"

"You sure you haven't any more of her?"

"Hang on I'll have a look"

…………………..

"No sorry!"

"Pity for once I was vaguely interested, Oh well get on with it!"

The Tango has been danced in the café Tortoni for 150 years, coincidentally this also being the average age of some of the waiters, and when you are finally ushered into "theatre" it is amazingly small, no more than thirty yards by ten yards, and with more tables than you'd get in a cheap Indian restaurant, you share a meal and a drink at a small table with strangers, eating so closely that when someone sprinkles salt on their meal, everyone gets salt!

The show was, not surprisingly in Spanish. Now Spanish singing I can just about take, Spanish dancing is ok, but the Spanish jokes weren't funny, well I didn't think so but then as I don't speak Spanish that's not really surprising.

The Tango originated I am informed (but remember I'm the one who believed the bit about Aliens abducting cows!, Cows! for God sake!) in the brothels of Buenos Aries mainly to keep the male customers entertained whilst they were queuing for …well you don't need me to tell you what they were queuing for, although my immediate reaction is that if you have a crowd of drunken randy men standing impatiently (to coin a phrase!), getting someone to dance for them wouldn't have been my first thought.

I'll be the first to admit that all dance and me are strangers. I stopped jiving and twisting many many years ago and only do it now to embarrass the family, but even I understand after seeing the Tango that it's a whole theatre of dance!.

Each dance is a playlette, and in one I remember particularly well the male made his approaches to the female but is rejected and turns away dramatically, only for the female to slink up behind him drape herself over him, and when he turns they cavort around finally striking a very "Rodin" like pose in a spotlight before the lights go out..

Cue rapturous applause from the audience and a haughty stare from the Maradonna look alike (before the drink and drugs got him!).
"I like her!"
"Who?"
"Madonna"

I've missed out the fancy footwork and hips swivels, various lifts and tragic expressions but I think you've got my drift now.
I can't help feeling that if a British man had met with such rejection after the initial approach, rather than holding the back of his hand to his forehead and jumping in the air twisting and wriggling his hips, he'd have said,
"Oh ok then I'm off to the pub!"

Tango is an obsession in Buenos Aries and I can, in truth see why, it's not an erotic dance but it's an intensely passionate one, and I don't know if what we saw was a mediocre, good or great example of the Tango, but I'd like to see more.

We didn't exactly have the best seat in the house but the place was so small that when the dancer kicked her legs out you had to duck. One last point though, the male dancer was young, athletic, tall, a superb dancer and handsome..

I console myself by thinking he's probably gay!!!!

CLEARING THE VEHICLE AT THE PORT
Unless you're planning to be stupid enough to ship your own
vehicle by Grimaldi Lines from UK to Argentina you can skip
the next bit. Even if you are you will gain very little from it as
I completely lost track of what and why I was doing anything
and simply went where pointed and waited whilst each
successive official looked through the ever growing pile of
paperwork, added a bit more and pointed me to the next desk,
occasionally looking through the pile, looking at me
quizzically, looking through again signing and without adding
to the pile pointing me to the next desk.
If you're still with me here goes,
INSURANCE
I bought insurance from Parama Seguros It cost 620 pesos for
six months and of course is only third party but does include
free transport to the nearest garage if you break down.

CLEARING THROUGH CUSTOMS
If you're going to use RO RO you will be given the local
agents in Buenos Aries who are Mrs. Inez Charpentier. at J.E.
TURNER
But don't bother to e-mail as all emails are directed straight
into the "junk" which we soon found was how Turners and
Grimaldi think of customers. Inez explained how to clear
customs and it transpired explained it clearly, concisely and
totally incorrectly.

What I should do now is to list the procedure for clearing
customs and getting your car from the docks in Buenos Aries
but in truth I can't! For after spending eight hours in an
around the docks and offices I still have no idea what
happened!
Turners told us to go to an office on the docks and pay your
dock fees!!! Which we duly tried to do at eight o'clock and at

eight thirty when we finally got to the teller he looked at the papers looked again and said,

"Where are the customs papers"

"What customs papers"

"The customs papers you need before you can pay, you need to go to EMBA (which I think is the Customs) and clear customs!! There's a bus outside!"

It was only 8.45 so I smiled and caught the bus to the customs office, which was hiding behind a plain unmarked door, in a cavernous empty building, but the give away was that there were other Europeans standing there!

It said on the door that they opened at 9.30!!! but they didn't!! At 9.45 they let the first one in, we were fourth so it shouldn't take long, it shouldn't but it did. We were finally given the papers at 11.30 and still had to wait for the "chief" to sign them!!! How long could it take for Gods sake to sign one piece of paper??? Twenty bloody minutes that's how long!!!!

Back on the bus to the office where we started from to pay the fees, another wait and finally we faced the cashier again,

"You want to pay in $US or pesos?" Not a smile just the question,

"$US!"

"We only accept pesos!"

My little inner voice which up to this time had been behaving suddenly woke up (it was still early!) and said,

"She's taking the piss Jeff, she needs a slap!"

I paid the 630 pesos and so at 12.15 we'd finished, not bad four and quarter hours!!

WRONG!!!

All we had to do know was jump back on the bus to the terminal where the car was allegedly parked.

With papers clutched in hand I passed through a Security check and we (by this time there was an Austrian, a Belgian and us) were directed to a Portcabin office who directed us back to the security who pointed us back to the Portcabin, and this went on for four times before I finally flipped and obeyed my inner voice, shouted very loudly and the voice was for once proved to be right!

After listening politely (or more likely disinterestedly) to my opinion of the system, the port, the weather and (for good measure) the state of Argentinean Soccer and Madonna the manager, we were directed to the customs office..
Aaahhhh I can see you thinking that can't be right because he did customs three hours ago.. and I can understand that because that was what I thought.. this apparently was another department (Don't ask!) who completed another set of forms and made me sign something!! And that was it!
Finished!
WRONG!!!
Off we went to another office and waited and waited, which at least gave us the opportunity to ask the others what the FFF... lipping hell we were doing now,
"This is to get permission to leave port !"
Right!
He was a nice man very helpful but I guessed there was something wrong when he looked through the papers twice and then looked at me and then looked at the papers a third time.
"You must go and pay your fees!"
"I have paid my fees look there's the paper!"
"No that is the bill what I need is the receipt!"
"But we paid!....."

The combination of the all of our assertions (and my fingers around his throat!) persuaded him to phone the girl who took our money (if you're asking which girl you've not been paying attention this is the "dollars or pesos?" girl from hours ago!).

He finally got her to understand what we could see, that he was highly fed up by her incompetence and that he should not have to face the wrath of elderly Europeans because of her incompetence or indifference (perhaps both). At this point I released his throat leaving him free to disappear for half an hour and to reappear clutching our receipts.

A few entries on his computer and his printer rattled out a gate clearance!

At last we could go!

WRONG!

Back to the customs and another queue, to a very friendly, but inefficient and ineffectual, man, who suspiciously examined each document, looked at us before examining each one again, and reluctantly signed them off!!

Eight and a half hours!!!!

SORTED!!!

Our trip could start at last!!!!!

WRONG!!!!

The battery was flat, but apart from that the car appeared at first sight to be in good condition; perhaps for once in my life I'd made the right decision and saved money by not putting it in a container!!

We were surprised that nothing had been stolen, as we learnt from the other passengers the reason why on the Bill of Lading Grimaldi deny all responsibility, they let "dock workers" on board and they rob the cars! When you ask why they allow it there's a Gallic (or Argentinean) shrug of the shoulders and a

"What can we do?"

"GET BLOODY SECURITY SORTED! THAT'S WHAT!"

The first thing I noticed after getting the car started was that all of the switches for the differential locks were activated!! Why? I've driven through deserts and only used them occasionally. All the bloody idiots had to do was drive on and park, I drove off and the centre diff light stayed on!! Not good.. it means that all four wheels are locked and rotate at the same speed, not good when you are going round corners and certainly not good for the car!

I drove back to our accommodation and contacted Toyota! Not happy but at least I can get them to sort it and I can be on the road!!

WRONG!!!!
Toyota was in the middle of a strike and has a two-week backlog before they can even look at it.
Am I happy???? What do you think?
SOME DAYS ARE DIAMONDS SOME DAYS ARE STONES
And the last few days have been bloody big boulders!!!!
It started with a visit to San Telmo (a famous street market) and got pick pocketed!!! You realise that they are so good that you're never really going to stop them all you can do is make sure that you're not carrying too much money and fortunately that's what we had done. I had about £30 and no cards but it still pissed me off.

I know you will have been concerned about me after my suicidal thoughts of the previous posting, particularly those foolish people to whom I owe money, but you can relax, because after intervention by Ed a very nice man at Toyota sorted the car and it turned out to be corrosion on the switch, caused by it being left on (not that it should have been on in the first place!), anyway £40 not bad!! He refused my offer of a kiss in gratitude in fact he backed away so quickly that he fell into a pit!!!

I mentioned earlier how helpful Ed George had been, not only with the accommodation with Ozvaldo but also getting in via the back door to Toyota through a friend of a friend, and becoming a strike breaker!!.

I'd phoned him up on the Sunday prior to our traumatic Monday, to say thanks and he invited us over to a café where he was sitting with another British traveller, a round the world motorcyclist, not a wimp like me who does it in a Toyota!

So we met Warren, now this isn't his real name for reasons that will become clear, his real name is Walter, whoops now you will all have to be killed!! In fact I'm much too busy, you'll all just have to kill yourselves
Warren has led a fascinating and full life, having, now let's get this right, visited 82 countries; been a mercenary in Africa; served with the Rhodesian Light Infantry; has got three degrees from different universities, one being from Wisconsin (?) in Electrical Engineering, another from Oxford in English and another in something else from somewhere else; he's discovered a way of washing silicon chips that no one else has (I exhibited my ignorance by asking what was wrong with soap and water, the look he gave me showed he'd already decided I was an idiot, and that question simply confirmed it!)

He was also well respected in China having done some groundbreaking work installing water systems, but it might have been Malaysia (I was tempted to say it's difficult to install a water system without breaking the ground but, as I say, I was already being considered an idiot so why confirm it?)

He was flying to back to England to go to the Palace!!
My little voice asked me "Crystal?"
"Crystal?" I asked
"Buckingham, I think Phillip has another job for me!"
"Oh right!"
Little voice inside said "What job?" I ignored it,
A pause, and he said,
"I was in Brecon!"
"Brecon?"
"Yes doing some training of the lads from Hereford"
"Hereford?"
"Yes you know the Regiment! "
"Oh the S.A.S"
He looked round quickly in case we'd been overheard, in
which case he'd probably have to kill me!.(I mean really and
not just by boring me to death) He changed the subject to
when he was elected a Fellow of the Royal Society
"Of Arts? Oh you're a painter then!"
"No!" That look again! "The Royal Geographical Society!"
"Oh sorry!"

At this point Ed showed me a little instrument that he was
holding, a small box with a dial on it,
"What do you think of this Walter, sorry Warren, and I have
designed it!"
"Wow that looks great very impressive! What does it do!" (I
suspected I would regret asking!)
"It's a bullshit meter whenever anyone speaks bullshit near it,
it bleeps" (I regretted asking!)
I knew it couldn't have been switched on because whenever I
said anything there was a deathly silence and we all know
what a bullshitter I am.
I always admire people like Warren who can pack so much
into their lives, people,

Like Marco Polo who conquered vast areas of land between China and Europe and still invented a mint sweet; Mozart in between composing developing chocolate: Epstein managing the Beatles and developing then theory of relativity!

It makes me realise how little I have achieved! So much to do and so little time and more to the point so little ability to do it with!
Walter was quiet, I asked him,
"What's the Mitty?" Jean kicked me under the table.

South of Buenos Aries
Where was I, I'm rambling again... Right the car was mended at Toyota so it was a quick return to the accommodation and a drive out of Buenos Aries (well it was a slow drive, this being Buenos Aries) until suddenly we were clear of the town on open empty roads.

Heading South on Route 3 with Jean once again proving what a wonderfully natural navigator she is by finding her way through and around towns, armed only with a very large-scale map and an amazing sense of direction.

We're heading south to see the whales mating in Peninsular Valdez! I've never seen whales mating, and unless they actually leave the water to mate on the beach I'm not sure how this is going to work, because as sure as God made little apples I'm not getting into the water for a better look!

I'd just closed the computer down when I rembered he'd also been trained as a chef in Rheims and taught English as a foreign language in Spain!! Sorry!!!
"Who?"
"Walter!"
"Busy man!"

Puerto Madryn Peninsular Valdez 19-11-08

Route 3 which heads south on the east of Argentina is long and boring!!! And that's the good news. In Buenos Aries there is a car within inches of you at all times, on Route 3 you get quite excited if you even see one!!!. Which explains why we've done over a 1000 miles in four days or so! I spy become a little tedious when the clue is "P" and you say "yeah yeah Pampas!" which in truth is all there is! There's not even cows any more, just flat featureless scrub grass. After the story of Aliens lifting the cows I was even looking hopefully upwards, anything for some interest.

In 1865 a group of Welsh people arrived in Argentina having left Wales because they were fed up of the English and didn't want to be near them anymore, they were not alone, a group of South African Boers did the same a few years later! Both, of course, could have saved themselves the trouble and waited a while, then moved to London, where now there's not an Englishman to be found!

The Welsh families landed and dug caves in the rocks and lived in the caves for a couple of years!! Now when I'm talking caves I'm not talking a Rhondda valley mine entrance with a room for everyone. I'm talking about a scraping in the rock perhaps four feet deep and they lived like that for two years! Now allow some time to start a rugby team and a male voice choir, but even so two years!!!!…Eventually they moved south to where they live now, a little principality, serving welsh scones and singing, "saucepan Bach" at the drop of a hat!!!

A FEW DAYS LATER

Well the last few days have certainly been diamonds and Stones. The diamonds being the Cullinan and the Koh-I-Nhor

468

rolled into one and the stones being the biggest bloody chunk of rock you can imagine.

Firstly the diamond, which is Peninsular Valdez where we saw whales, We've never seen whales before, and the first sighting is surreal. You cannot imagine any living creature being so large and graceful.

Firstly a bit of background. The Southern Right Whale commutes between Antarctica and Peninsular Valdez, where it meets up with all its friends between June and November where they chat, dive, play and generally flirt whilst looking to mate! For those of you who are interested what happens is that the female swims on her back (so I'm informed) whilst the males vie to erm, what's the word I'm looking for? F…..
"NO!! "Mate" is a perfectly good word"

The female lays there on her back doing nothing except waiting to be mated, (you will notice I've refrained from commenting), and as each one mates she stores the sperm then, later, and when she's looking back over the days activities (as it were!) she selects which one's sperm she wants to use and expels the rest!, (you will see now why I resisted the temptation to swim in the bay!). She then swims off to Antarctica and returns a year later to give birth, in the same bay, where she feeds the baby and builds its strength up until the baby is strong enough to make the journey back to Antarctica and to avoid the killer Whales.

To be close to these massive creatures is daunting and spiritual; they float in the water then with a sudden turn and a flick of the tale they disappear, but although massively large they are not carnivores, but feed on Krill plankton.

The problem with a digital camera is it's very difficult taking photos of the whales as they appear briefly then just as quickly disappear. If you look carefully at the picture you will see a seagull and they are a bloody nuisance to the whales as they land on them and peck them, breaking the skin leaving an open wound which is prone to infection. It's tempting to suggest that the answer is to eradicate the seagulls but that of course presupposes that seagulls are less worthy than whales.. mankind has a history of interfering with nature with catastrophic effect.

Everyone takes pictures of Whales Tails and it's satisfying when you eventually get it right, but believe me its not easy! Digital cameras have a lag on them, which can be very frustrating.

There are now an estimated 12000 southern right whales living in the southern hemisphere. Right whales were called the "right" whales to catch by early hunters because they are large, swim slowly, have long baleen plates, contain lots of oil, and float when killed. The blubber thickness being about 23-24 cm (9-10 inches) for a 15 metre whale! The current population still being far short of the number that existed a couple of hundred years ago.

When, in 1937, it became clear that stocks were nearly depleted (down to around 400), a worldwide total ban on Right whaling was agreed. Although the ban was largely successful, some whaling continued in violation of the ban for several decades. The slow recovery in numbers between then and now is due to a number of factors not the least of which is continued hunting.

It's wet work watching whales

Madeira, for example, took its last two right whales only in 1968. Illegal whaling continued off the coast of Brazil for many years. The Soviet Union is now known to have illegally taken over 3,300 Southern Right Whales during the 1950s and '60s, although it only reported taking 4.

Another factor is that the Southern Right Whale also has a relatively low birth rate of perhaps one calf every three to four years; and then there are collisions with ships. Predation of mature whales doesn't exist but as calves they are attacked by killer whales, which is why they don't leave the safety of the birthing areas untill the calves are big enough to make the journey to the summer feeding grounds in the antarctic.

And they are big and grow to a maximum length of 17.5 m and weight 80 –100 tons, with mature females often slightly larger than males. The calves at birth are about 5.5 m long and weigh between 1000—1500 kg, and are solitary during migration, unless accompanied by a dependent calf or occasionally a yearling offspring.

They form large groups in breeding areas, where unaccompanied whales are frequently engaged in mating and socialising behaviours. Female-calf pairs generally avoid socialising, despite spending extended periods on the calving grounds with other whales. They have a life expectancy of around 50 years and Southern Right Whales tend to return to the same breeding location each year.

Although Baleen whales include the largest animals on the planet, they feed mainly on tiny organisms such as zooplankton (crustaceans, such as krill, and copepods) and small fish (capelin, herring, sand lance, etc.). The baleen plates act like sieves to filter water and retain prey.
Each baleen plate is composed of a number of rigid hairs sandwiched between two plates made of a hard flexible material, and the baleen plates are positioned in the mouth like vertical blinds suspended all along the upper jaw. Baleen whales will have between 150 and 400 baleen plates suspended from each side of the upper jaw, depending on the species. Like our fingernails and hair, baleen plates grow, and wear, continuously. The plate edges that rub against the tongue wear faster than the hairs they contain. This results in the hairs extending beyond the baleen plate "sandwich". The resultant fringe of hair formed becomes matted and serves as a filter that, whilst allowing water to flow through easily enough, efficiently retains prey.

Baleen whales use three different general feeding strategies.

Some species are "engulfers", and feed by engulfing large quantities of water and prey with each enormous mouthful. The water is then expelled while the prey is retained and then swallowed. Whales that engulf their prey possess ventral grooves, or folds of skin, that enable the throat to expand like an accordion allowing them to scoop up impressive volumes of water. These are commonly known as "rorqual" whales, from a Norwegian term meaning "pleated whales".

Some are "skimmers", and these include the right whales. They do not possess ventral grooves. Instead of engulfing large volumes of water at a time, they simply swim along with their mouths wide open, filtering water as they go and capturing tiny crustaceans known as copepods.

Finally there are the "excavators". They use their short baleen plates to filter sediment on the ocean floor and capture small organisms that live buried in the sediment. Their technique consists of diving to the bottom, turning sideways and using suction on the sea floor to draw in small organisms.

It's estimated that during the four to six months feeding season they eat 4% of their body weight, that's 4% of 100 tons each.

The peninsular Valdez is also home to colonies of Elephant seals, the male of which is alleged to mate fifteen times a day, which believe me takes it out of you!

"I wouldn't know"

"Trust me"

In the time I spent watching them all they did was lay on the beach, sleep and sunbathe, then periodically chase a female and mate! Why has the image of a British male on two weeks holiday in Benidorm yet again sprung back to mind?

In Trelaw we visited the palaeontology exhibition and came out to find one of the local Neanderthals had broken into the car! This wasn't your subtle pickpocket, this was screwdriver into the locks and when that didn't work it was a brick through the window and stole couple of sat navs, an Ipod, a Leatherman, a new pair of binoculars, all of our toiletries and worst of all Jeans Filo fax.

BASTARDS!

About one hundred yards up the road was a police station and it was there I attempted to report the problem, attempted being the operative word. The lady on the desk listened with rapt attention to my problem before turning to her colleague and saying something, which I hoped would be,
"Right block all the roads, cancel all overtime, we'll get these thieving buggers who rob our tourists!" but which was, I suspect,
"Have you any idea what this silly old sod is rambling on about?"

She called her boss and they reluctantly opened a book to record the robbery and I was describing what had happened and how they
had broken my window after attempting to hammer a screwdriver in the locks. To emphasis the point I hit my hands together hard, forgetting that I was holding the car keys and stabbed myself in the back of the hand! Now that did interest them and they watched fascinated as I bled onto their book.

475

The worst part of the robbery is that they have damaged all
the locks on the car and as it happened on Saturday lunchtime
I'm stuck in Gaiwan until Toyota opens on Monday, where I
hope they will just happen to have in stock a window and a set
of locks for an 80 series Land Cruiser!

So in a three weeks on Argentina I've been pick pocketed and
had the car broken into!! The stones in "diamonds and stones"
are coming thick and fast! It's so easy to become disillusioned
and just say "bugger it" let's just go home!

But it's not an option, we are going to see Tierra Del Fuego
and the Andes and nothing is going to stop us, even if this
does turn out to be a whistle stop tour of all the Toyota
garages in Argentina.
To all those who ask if it's all worth it, believe me at the
moment the only thing that makes it worth it are the whales,
and I wouldn't have swapped that for anything. Well! Except
for a sat nav, a gps, a Leatherman etc etc

RADA TILLY 26-11-08
We are on the road again with mended locks and windows!
Having spent the weekend in Gaiman, the centre of Welsh
Patagonia where with nothing better to do, we learnt about the
movement from Wales to the Gaiman valley of various Welsh
families who were fed up with living near the English, and
how they were allocated 100 hectare plots (which although I
nodded knowingly made me realise that I have no idea how
much an hectare is) and how after a year they said "Bugger
this boyo!" and moved back to the cave on the coast but then
decided that it wasn't too bad in Gaiman and moved back!!
There was a lot more but that was the gist of it!.
The towns of Trelaw, Triawky and Chubit have tearooms
selling Welsh teas in streets called "MD Jones, JC Evans and
D Roberts alongside Belgrano and Yrigoyen".

Fabio, the guide at Gaiman Museum spoke fluent Welsh although he was Argentinean of Italian descent! He was well into a description of the passing of the local law that allocated water rights to different families on an equitable basis (fascinating!!!) when in walked an attractive young female and his interest in water rights (and me) noticeably diminished, and disappeared completely when she spoke to him in Welsh!
She was Welsh and was visiting from Pembroke shire!
Not wanting to ruin the start of a beautiful friendship (or in truth to hear any more about the Water Allocation Act of 1878, fascinating though it was) we left!

Monday morning saw us awake bright and early still with a broken window and door locks and another visit to the police station needed to complete the list of items stolen on Saturday by the thief who, if there is a God who answers prayers, is in mortal agony as his testacles fester and drop off.
The police station, was full of nice policemen, which was disappointing as I was fully convinced that by now they would have cordoned off the town and be performing house-to-house searches. The police forms were needed because the insurance company probably wont believe that we have been robbed again, and, having been duly completed (by me!), I followed one of the nice policemen to the car locksmith, not keeping up as he was speeding and I didn't want to give him the opportunity to give me a ticket for speeding as well! Paranoid!! Who's paranoid?

The locksmith was the spitting image of Keith Floyd the television cook (apropos of nothing!), and when he looked at the locks which had been attacked with a screwdriver, he sucked his teeth looked
at the policeman and shook his head! then he looked at me blew back out through his teeth and shook his head again!!

God that made me feel good!!

But give him his due he went and got his tools and in no time he'd taken the door handle off and disappeared. The Policeman smiled at me and he too disappeared. I'd like to think to join all of his colleagues looking for my stolen property but somehow I doubt it.

I stood for a while feeling decidedly spare then decided to disappear as well and go and tackle Toyota, who were fortunately just a few hundred yards away.

The Spanish language that I studied before the trip enabled me to say,

"Two beers please" or " I think I have missed my period!" (Don't ask!)

 But not,

"Some bastard knackered my door locks and broke my window!" so after three attempts at telling them my problem, when all I got was two beers and packet of Tampax, they sent for Laurent who spoke perfect English, Spanish and French, and who understood immediately the problem and came up with the solution!

"We will ask Buenos Aries!" easy! All we had to do was to wait whilst Buenos Aries checked their stock records, which they would do immediately! Well immediately after they came back from lunch in three hours time!!

Cue inner voice!

"He's taking the piss Jeff! Slap him!"

I didn't! Instead I smiled and Laurent suggested that the window glass could be replaced with plastic which they could start that immediately cutting and shaping!

"Great!! You mean immediately?"

"Oh yes!"

Well immediately after they too came back from lunch in three hours time!!

So we sat in an empty Toyota showroom and I studied my Spanish tape, desperately looking for Spanish for, "Three hours! You're having a laugh!"

A very Argentinean nice man (or a very nice Argentinean man) came and spoke to me in incredibly fast Spanish and indicated (I think!) that the parts were available in, "Shabon!"
"Excellent! Shabon?
"Si Shabon!"
"Right!
So that was it we could get the locks from their branch in Shabon and all would be sorted!

Three hours later (well three and a quarter in truth but who was checking?..well me as a matter of fact), back came Laurent from his long lunch and he repeated that the locks were available in Shabon and could be ordered and express couriered to their branch in Esquel. I was impressed! And also that the man would start work on the plastic window immediately, well immediately he came back from lunch!
"Great news Laurent! Erm ! So tell me Laurent where exactly is Shabon?"
He looked at me as if I was stupid (that look again!)
"You don't know where Shabon is? Shabon! Oh sorry, you call it Japan!"
Little voice inside says "JAPAN? BLOODY JAPAN! Do it Jeff, do it now!"
He only wanted to send for the parts from Japan special delivery for me! The day looked black again!
Just then he had a message, the locksmith had mended the lock!
The day had colours!

So whilst the nice fat mechanic (it's not suprising he's fat with all the bloody time he spent at lunch) was cutting the new window glass, it's back to Keith Floyd the locksmith, who's assistant was triumphantly turning the key in the lock, which he had stripped down and rebuilt, and it worked.

As you know homosexuality is not something I've tried or ever wished to (well in fact there was that …no! too much information!) but at that point I was close to giving him my body to do with what he wanted. I think he spotted this, backed away and quickly got to work refitting the lock!

A thought! If he could mend one why couldn't he mend the other? I asked Keith, who sucked in through his teeth and looked doubtful and spoke to his assistant, who obviously was new to the game and instead of looking doubtful and sucking his teeth, just smiled and nodded enthusiastically.

He stripped out the handle and went to the back of the workshop. Now this I had to see! I followed him and it was interesting to see him at work, the speed that he stripped the barrel down was impressive, and the confident way he looked at bits that he pulled out, some of which he shook his head at and threw over his shoulder onto a surprisingly large pile of bits and pieces of other locks, was in a way both comforting and worrying.

Now call me a cynic if you want but if they weren't needed why did those very nice designers at Toyota put them there in the first place? So without being too obvious I recovered them, and put them in my pocket.

He saw, smiled sadly and continued stripping, looking, keeping, discarding, filing and in some cases hitting with a hammer!

I left him too it…back to Toyota to get the window fitted! The mechanic smiled at his handiwork and with a final clean of the new window (probably to brush off the remains of his lunch) I now had a complete set of windows!

Back to the locksmith and sure enough there he was clicking the lock back and forth, successful again!

I wondered what the bits he'd left out did, but not wanting to finish up with more beer and Tampax I didn't bother to ask! I did however feel in my pocket for the excess bits and vowed to keep them safe just in case.

I didn't! I lost them!

Nice people all round, with the cost of the hotel and meals the whole break in, not including the things stolen, cost £220, so I'm thinking of leaving the car open in future. It's difficult to know what else we could have done to prevent it. The items stolen were not on display, the car was locked and in a public place, and near to a police station!!!
Oh well insurance company here we come

We have decided that we are not going to change what we do, just not throw any more money at the trip, when our kitty has gone we will stop, whenever and where ever that is!! We have had more expenses than we budgeted for but then again that always happens.

PHONING THE INSURANCE
A quick note about 'phoning the insurance! There's a three hour difference between where we are and England so when we finally arrived at last nights camping and could get network coverage on the mobile it was six o'clock Argentina time (and probably about 1952 in the village where we were) and nine o'clock British time but as they say the claims section is open 24/7! So I felt confident in phoning!
Firstly I got the answer and the music! (I could feel the money clicking away) then a message about the company being regulated by the FSA (GET ON WITH IT I DON'T GIVE A

481

TOSS!) then a nice lady answered and went into a long pre-set speech before I interrupted and told her I was calling on a mobile from Argentina and would she mind shutting the f**k up and listening!! (I might have exaggerated that a little!). Apparently she couldn't give me a claim number because the computer doesn't work at night.

I resisted the temptation to ask what happened to the "24/7" and arranged for her to take my e-mail address!! It was at this point I regretted using Iamabigboy@hotmail.com, which I had to repeat four times! this call was getting expensive!

Her final question of "Is there anything else I can help you with?" was left unanswered!

PUNTO TOMBO

There are 250,000 Magellanic penguins around the coast of South America! (Or is it 25,000 or even 2,500,000 I'm not sure, and frankly don't care) because in truth unless you're a penguinologist or another Magellanic penguin, it's not important.

I have to say once you've seen one you've seen them all. We went to see the breeding colony at Punto Tombo where as we speak scientists are studying them; although what they find to study I'm not sure.

Let's be honest penguins are pretty boring, and they quickly stop being "cute", especially when you get down wind from them, and after watching them stand, do their silly walk for a few yards stop as if they've remembered something, and then a silly walk back, you've seen it all!

I was walking along the path when, right in front of me stood a Male Magellanic (in case you're asking why Magellanic, come on!! Magellan?? As in straights of Magellan, Ferdinand Magellan ???..Sheesh!) Where was I? Oh yes! So there stood

482

this penguin that looked at me, and there stood me looking at the penguin, each I suspect as bored as the other, but it seemed churlish to show it, I didn't want to hurt its feelings! "And you know what?"

"No what?"

"He walked away first!!! I had managed to bore a penguin! Now a penguin can't have much excitement in its life!! All they bloody do is walk back and forwards, catch a few fish, shit and then walk back and forwards again!!! And I couldn't even hold its interest!!!… Who says I'm paranoid!"

The Route 3 down the east side of Argentina links Buenos Aries and Ushuaia and it's boring, flat and boring, long, flat and boring. The boredom being relieved only by the music from my Ipod, oh sorry I've just remembered I haven't got one now! .

Occasionally every hundred miles or so there's a petrol station and perhaps if you're lucky a half a dozen cars an hour! The clue in the games of Eye Spy is now F.A.! But we are still about 900 miles short of Ushuaia on the Route 3 having already travelled for 1600 miles on it and seen F.A!..

Blimey even alien cows would be a bonus!

I'll leave you to guess what he's just asked her!

PETRIFIED FOREST
There's a Petrified Forest forty km off Route 3. Well it's not quite a forest it is in fact a few trees that have turned to stone, but it's taken then 130 million years to do it.

I'm not sure if you will be able to tell from these pictures but the trees are stone, well they are now, they were originally trees and when the volcanoes covered them with ash they slowly turned to stone. I wish I could think of something more interesting to say but in truth I can't

During the Jurassic period (between 145 and 200 million years ago) the climate in this area of Argentina was wet and covered with forests of giant trees. At the beginning of the Cretaceous (between 60 and 145 million years ago) massive volcanic activity connected to the uplifting of the Andes, buried vast areas of Patagonia in ash.

The forest remained buried under the ashes until millions of years later, water and wind eroded the area and uncovered the, by now, petrified trees. All this happened some 1,400,000 years ago and the great logs of jasper and agate were now lying on the ground surrounded by the varied colours of endless fragments and small chips, which have remained unmoved since. Some of the trees were already 1,000 years old before dying under the ashes.

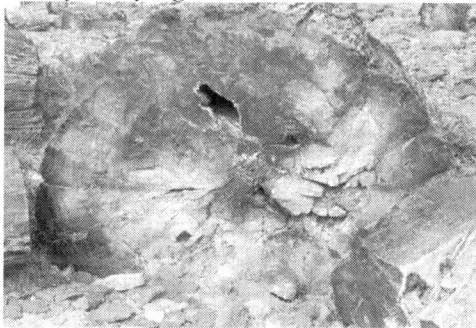

The process of petrification needs three ingredients: wood, water and mud. The mud that covered the logs contained volcanic ash, a key ingredient in the petrification process. When the volcanic ash began to decompose it released chemicals into the water and mud. As the water seeped into the wood the chemicals from the volcanic ash reacted to the wood and formed into quartz crystals.

When the crystals grew over time, the wood became encased in the crystals, which over millions of years, turned the wood into stone.

Elements such as manganese, iron and copper in the water and mud during the petrification process give petrified wood a variety of color ranges. Pure quartz crystals are colorless, but when the mud is contaminated with other elements colours are added to the process the crystals take on a yellow, red, or other tints.

CAMPING AT THE PETRIFIED FOREST

The sanitary arrangements in campsites in Argentina can be difficult to get used to and this campsite was no exception, there are very few exceptions come to think of it. I can forgive (almost) the business of putting loo paper into a waste bin and not down the toilet, I can never quite understand why this is necessary and if you know please DO NOT email me I get enough emails talking s**t already..

But why can't they build showers with heads that aren't in imminent danger of falling off the walls, and why does the water come out, not just from the showerhead but also from everywhere else. Blimey how difficult can it be to tighten the connections so the water does not spray indiscriminately onto you and which has an uncanny knack of wetting your clothes that have been carefully slung over the shower door because of course there are no hangers. And then they have the bloody cheek to put up notices asking you to save water!

In some places they have a great idea! The shower and the toilet are combined so you can do two jobs at once...

The campsite at Petrified Forest was, in a land of doubtful toilets, the most doubtful. We should have known what to expect the campsite being forty km from the main road along a gravel road.

The pampas wind so strong that we had to ease forward in low gear, the scenery becoming more and more desolate with each kilometre.

When we finally arrived, the whole campsite was in need of care and attention, and failing that demolition, old cars and lorries abandoned at the end of their final journey, the wind blowing sand into the building through ancient cracks or into ancient buildings through cracks!! Take your pick and use it on the building!

I was in the toilet compartment (no seat of course!) having, well having completed the task in hand, and remembering to put the loo paper in the bucket and not, as once memorably happened into my pocket (don't ask)...so I reached up to pull the chain and the cistern fell off the wall covering me, and everything else, with water.

After wiping my eyes I checked and saw that the whole unit was simply balanced on top of the pipe and not fixed in any way.. So I did what the person before had obviously done, simply balanced it back onto the pipe and backed away soggily careful not to slam the door. I warned the others! I

nearly didn't as they had laughed at me for being wet...so
there it is, a loo with a shower...and if you were the next one
in after me ..Sorry!!!!!

USHUAIA
Pronounced Ushwaya or Ushwya, it claims to
be the southernmost city in the world, in truth it's not! There's
a couple of small cities called Puerto Williams and Puerto
Toko that are in fact more southerly but as they don't have tea
rooms and souvenir shops selling badges that say
"Southernmost City in the World" they don't count.

We arrived at Tierra del Fuego from Patagonia crossing the
Straights of Magellan by ferry accompanied by black and
white dolphins, or maybe porpoises, I'm not sure I know
which. Crossing from Argentinean Patagonia into Chilean
Patagonia then into Argentinean Tierra del Fuego! (Since
found out that they are porpoises!) (Later found out that they
could have been dolphins that look like porpoises!)
I'm not sure how it can take so little time to pass through
customs from Chile into Argentina when it took eight and a
half sodding hours to clear them at Buenos Aries, and what's

more all of the paperwork that they gave us in Buenos Aries has been met with blank uncomprehending looks from the customs officers at the other borders who smile and stamp odd bits of paper and wave us away!

Ushuaia is a tourist and travellers town (and the stop off for Antarctica) the two mixing, but each easily distinguishable! The tourist usually just off from a luxury cruise ship, dressed in pristine "expedition" clothes browsing in expensive shops, the travellers in well washed (in some cases let's be honest not so well washed) "T" shirts and trousers walking quickly past the expensive shops to the supermarket to buy the food! We looked at the possibility of going to Antarctic but at £4000 each for a ten day cruise we couldn't really justify it, we spoke to a very nice girl (but not very nice enough to reduce the price!) who said,

"You will see many penguins!" that decided us. More penguins!!! No thanks!!! But in truth we both wanted to see the Antarctic and wonder if in time we will regret the decision not to go.

The Antarctica starts at the Beagle Channel

The Beagle Channel was named, as I am sure you know after the ship captained by Fitzroy, who found the passage! On

board was Charles Darwin who wrote his famous book " A treatise the ascent of man" (On thinking about it, it wasn't him that was Dr Bronowysky. Darwin wrote "On the origin of the species!") which contrary to the views of the Church at the time showed that we were not all created by God in his own image! But were in fact evolved through millions of years into what we are today, and that evolution is still taking place. So for example an English football hooligan will, over the next million years evolve into a human being, or a chicken or something!

If I have offended anyone with that last paragraph, such as the Pope or a English football hooligan, I'm sorry!!

Or I'm not sorry whatever!

So we've now completed Route 3, 3000 plus kilometres down the eastern side of Argentina and Ushuaia is the lowest point, lowest point geographically not emotionally, and now we start heading northwards, mainly on route 40 but with side trips into the various national parks to see glaciers and the Andes, and hopefully no more bloody penguins!

The campsite in Ushuaia before the Christmas invasion of German and Argentinean camper vans is occupied by hitchhiking back packers and long term travellers all of whom can easily "outstory" anything we have done.
It's all very Monty Pythonesque..as each one tops the others tales.
"You drove down? I motorcycled!"
"You motorcycled? I cycled!"
"You cycled? I walked!"
"I walked barefoot
"I hopped!"
"I hopped barefoot"

Not quite true but you get the idea!

I was talking yesterday to a Swedish man about Wadi Halfa and the problems of driving through the desert, and how difficult it is to dig a car out of deep sand in the Sudan.. he commented that he never had that problem when he cycled through the same desert! Another French man was talking about the problems he had travelling alone through the middle east and the Old Russian states on a bloody tandem!!! Alone on a tandem? I know I should have asked but I never! All right!

The days travelling down have been filled with nothing but flat, and in many areas barren country; but this has now suddenly changed to snow covered peaks with very cold nights and warm days, or in some cases very cold nights and very cold days!
Ushuaia is a strange mix of buildings; a few grand old houses now turned into Museums and wooden, badly maintained shacks, inhabited by the Indian looking local people.

In the Museum it showed early pictures of the local Yaghan tribes, as they were when "civilization" arrived, naked and adorned with only body paint! Now I know that some societies evolve faster than others but in this climate it wouldn't, I'd have thought, take much for them to think "Bugger me it's cold I wonder if I should cover myself with some clothes!" but then having seen how little some of the females wear on a Friday and Saturday night in mid winter in England! Perhaps "civilisation" and "evolution" are over used words!!!
Written later!!!
I've learnt something!!! Apparently it was wearing "western" clothes that finally finished them off!! The missionaries persuaded them to wear clothes but they never quite got the

hang of washing them (not unlike many of the travellers that we meet) and because they then were hot, sweaty, flea and lice ridden they succumbed to disease…just goes to show what I know! NOTHING!

Coming down through Patagonia and into and out of Chile there are Department of Agriculture road blocks to prevent the movement of vegetables and meat and thus to prevent the spread of disease! Now I'm all in favour of that but what I'm not in favour of is that no bugger tells you beforehand and when you turn up at the road block they demand you eat it, destroy it or they confiscate it!
This is even more frustrating when you've just been to the supermarket to stock up!! So I'll leave you to guess what choices I made.
Right!
So there I was mouth full of cheese and cold meat, cheeks puffed out like a bloody hamster, having already just eaten five bananas, three apples, a carrot, two raw potatoes, and a garlic clove, when he looks at what was left of the cold meat and cheese and indicated that they were allowed and handed them back
If my mouth weren't so full I'd have told him what I thought!!! The same thing happened in Australia and I still suspect that they decide what is and isn't allowed by what they fancy for dinner.

Entering Chile was the same, they hand you a form which asks if you have any prohibited goods..(Fruit? cheese? meats?) We answered, "yes" partly because we are law-abiding citizens but mainly because there were notices that indicated that you would be heavily fined if you were found out.
When we got outside he started to search the car and we saved him the trouble by pointing out where the "contraband" was.

"Did you declare this!"

"Yes!"

"Really?"

"Yes!"

He muttered something in Spanish that could have meant, "That's a first!" or "Silly old Sods!" and took the fruit! He didn't go inside to look at the form so the old "he looks old and trustworthy" routine worked again! We were talking to a couple later that didn't declare and they were fined £20 for each orange!!

Chatting to a German couple Manfred and Lottie about the problems on the road with theft and he said,

"Everyone knows that you don't park near the museum in Trelaw because of the robberies!"

I bloody didn't!!!

Oh yes! You know I told you it was windy welll!!!!

The Beagle channel, situated between the islands of Tierra Del Fuego on the southern tip of South America, was named after HMS Beagle which made two trips performing hydrographic surveys off the coasts of the southern part of South America between 1826 to 1833.

*During the first expedition the Beagle's captain,
Pringle Stokes committed suicide and was replaced
by Captain Robert Fitzroy, who also went on to
captain the second trip, a trip made famous because
he selected as his companion and on board naturalist
Charles Darwin which gave him the opportunity to
make the scientific observations that led to the
ultimate publication 29 years later of his "On the
Origin of Species by Means of Natural Selection, or
the Preservation of Favoured Races in the Struggle
for Life" usually shortened to "On the origin of the
species".*

*Darwin is generally credited with the theory of
evolution by natural selection, which is the theory
that the strongest survive and propagate and
therefore increase the strength of the species.*

*As an aside Robert Fitzroy almost refused to let
Darwin sail because his "nose did not appear to be
that of a man with character" (on such whims were
decisions made), and Darwin was only accepted after
he got testimonials that he was "suitable for dining at
the Captain's dinner table" presumably in spite of his
nose!*

*Captain Fitzroy, a fundamentalist Christian, didn't
always see eye to eye with Darwin, who was once
banned from the dinner table for several days after an
argument, which has led to speculation that this
further hardened Darwin against traditional religion.
Fitzroy was a staunch believer in a literal
interpretation of Scripture, and he wanted Darwin to
confirm the biblical account of creation and appealed
to Darwin give up his "evolution and adaptation"*

theory, and felt guilty that his expedition was being used to undermine Scripture.

During the the first survey, some of Fitzroy's men were camping onshore when a group of Fuegian natives stole their boat. They gave chase but when they failed to catch them, the culprit's families were brought on board as hostages. Fitzroy decided to take them back to England to "civilise the savages, teaching them English ... the plainer truths of Christianity ... and the use of common tools".

The three Fuegians spent a year in England, and were taken back to Tierra del Fuego as missionaries. Darwin found them friendly and civilised, yet their relatives seemed "miserable, degraded savages as different as wild from domesticated animals". To Darwin the difference showed cultural advances, not racial inferiority and unlike his scientist friends, he now thought there was no unbridgeable gap between humans and animals, except for football hooligans!

Although the geological surveys were the primary objective it was Darwins observations, particularly in the remote Galapogos islands, for which the voyages became the most famous. One of the questions that fascinated him was how so many different plants and animals arrived on the Galapagos and what happened to them once they were there. Some, such as sea lions, fur seals, and penguins, could swim with the help of the currents, as could the giant tortoises.

It is possible to imagine (just) a single specimen arriving at Galapagos from the mainland sometime since the creation of the island, around five million years ago, but imagine the odds of a male and a female arriving at the same time and of finding each other in the sixteen thousand square miles of the islands.

During the rainy season rafts of vegetation break off from the mainland and float out to sea and the reptiles and the only terrestrial mammals (the rice rats), and insects must have arrived like this.

The light spores of many smaller plants probably arrived in the islands by wind. Spiders, small insects, and tiny land snails are frequently transported by the wind, and birds and bats, weak fliers, would have to have been blown to the islands, although the seabirds would easily have flown there, carrying seeds with them either in their digestive system, or attached to the feet and feathers, the birds would aid plants by ingesting seeds before takeoff and then expelling them at their destination. Other seeds, with tiny hooks, would have attached to feathers and feet and been given a free ride. Still other seeds were caked in mud and clung to a bird's feet.

Once on the islands, the various species established themselves and determined territories. Evolution then set in and many unique species, such as Darwin's finches, resulted. As an example of how evolution and adaption works, the finches probably descended from a common ancestor and then, due to isolation and through chance, different climates and natural forces such as food availability and type, they evolved into thirteen different unique types.

After the trips on the Beagle, Fitzroy was appointed Governor of New Zealand and later in 1854 he was appointed Chief of a new department to deal with the collection of weather data at sea which was the forerunner of the modern Meteorological Office. He arranged for captains of ships to provide information, and for the collection and publication of the data collected. One of the instruments that Fitzroy had previously developed while on the Beagle was a storm glass which is a type of weather forecasting device, composed of a sealed glass container, filled a mixture of distilled water, ethanol, potassium nitrate, ammonium chloride , that changes appearance dependent upon the forthcoming weather.

A massive storm in 1859 inspired Fitzroy to develop charts to allow predictions to be made, which he called "forecasting the weather", thus coining the term weather forecast, and fifteen land stations were established to use the new telegraph to transmit to him daily reports of weather at set times.

The first daily weather forecasts were first published in The Times in 1860, and in the following year a system was introduced of hoisting storm warning cones at the principal ports when a gale was expected. They also distributed storm glasses to many small fishing communities around the British Isles.

Unfortunately, many fishing fleet owners objected to gale warnings that prevented fleets leaving the ports and FitzRoy's system was abandoned for a short time after his death but inevitably and eventually fishing fleet owners succumbed to the pressure from normal seamen and the system was reintroduced.

Fitzroy retired in 1863 but suffered from depression and in 1865 he committed suicide and in his memory the British Isles weather forecasting sea area Finisterre was renamed Fitzroy in 2002.

Darwin returned home and continued his work towards the publication "On the origin of the species" which was published some 29 years after his return, and 12 years after that he published his other most famous work on sexual selection "The Descent of Man, and Selection in Relation to Sex".

Darwin defined sexual selection as the effects of the "struggle between the individuals of one sex, generally the males, for the possession of the other sex". We distinguish between "male to male combat" because it is usually males who fight each other, "mate choice" (females usually choose mates, in both the human and animal worlds!). Traits selected for male combat are called secondary sexual characteristics sometimes referred to as "weapons" (horns, antlers.etc); and traits selected by female choice called "ornaments", the mane on a male lion, or the feathers on a peacock.
Darwin died on 19 April 1882 and is buried in Westminster Abbey.

CHILE UPDATE

HEADING NORTH
So we got to the southern most (ish) tip of the American continent, Cape Horn, and started to head north, leaving Ushuaia behind and retracing our steps up to and over the Magellan straights and Tierra del Fuego and into Chile and the ever present wind of Patagonia!

The Patagonian wind manages to blow in all directions at the same time and we are talking WIND here!! The sort of wind that would create "severe weather warnings" anywhere else, the sort of wind that makes umbrellas pointless, and as for reading the newspaper in the street.. Forget it!!!!
Even the hardy long distance cyclists give it up and catch the bus! When you walk it's at a crazy angle so that if there were wonderful scenery (which there isn't) you'd miss it!

I'm trying to remember now (and I could look it up but can't be bothered!) whether I've told you about the sheep .. hang on I will look it up…don't go away I'll be back…
Ok I've checked and I didn't tell you
"So I suppose that means you're going to now.. it must be really interesting if its taken this long to remember.. Not of course that you did!"
"Did what?"
"Remember!"
"Remember what?"
"Just get it over I've got something more interesting to do than listen to you!"
"What?"
"Any bloody thing! Just get on with it!"
"I've forgotten now!"
"Sheep?"
"What about them? Oh yes! Do stop interrupting and listen.. It appears that in Argentina if you are hungry you can catch a sheep and eat it but you must leave the skin so they know it's not been rustled but that you were simply hungry! You sure I haven't told you this before?"
"Believe me I'd have remembered!. Go on!!"
"That's it!, and that's why you sometimes see sheepskins hanging on the fences."
"That was fascinating!! And is it true? Have you tried it?"

"No! But extending the principle I did go into a bar the other night and helped myself to a bottle of beer, drunk it but left the empty and walked out!"

"What happened?"

" A bloody great Argentinean chased me and made me pay!"

"So you wont be trying the sheep trick then!"

"Probably not!"

"As a matter of interest, and not that I really care, how much of that was true.. the sheep story?"

"It was true that I was told it!"

"The beer story?"

"Absolutely not complete pack of lies I just made that up!"

They have a flightless birds called Rheas on the Pampas, that look like ostrich's and have this game called "let's scare the motorist" which involves walking with its family slowly along the side of the road then when a car comes along rushing across the road and making them brake hard on the gravel causing them to skid and roll off the road, the car not the Rhea, which works for most drivers except Old English men who are bored!

I have to report that the Rhea's have a wonderful turn of speed, which nearly always gets them out of trouble, when I say "nearly always", I also have to report that they taste dreadful on a BBQ.

PUERTO NATALIS

Puerto Natalis is the stopping off pint (that should really be "point" but on reflection pint is better!) for treckers to the Torres del Paine national park!.. And it's full of "Treckers" hostels and "Treckers" outfitting shops, hardy people walking around the streets in "trecking" gear even if they are only going to the supermarket.

We went to a talk on "trekking" (American spelling!) given by a hippy American called Rustyn, and if I tell you his name suits him perfectly you can guess what he's like! Rustyn owns a trekking (American spelling!) hostel and outfitting shop (trekking outfits of course!) and is a guide in the Torres del Paine national park. And his set up is called "Erratic Rock". By now you should be able to get the complete picture of Rustyn!
And yes he has got dreadlocks!!!

We were all sitting round in a small room for his talk on trekking (American spelling!) in the park and he greeted us saying how pleased he was to see real "trekkers!" who were going to walk "The W" (5 days!) "The circuit" (9 days!) or for the real MEN!! (Some of who were women) "The Q"(12 days!!)

I settled myself lower into my seat trying desperately not to look like a tourist who was just popping into the park for a drive round in my four wheel drive before having a meal at a restaurant with a nice bottle of Chilean red!.
Which of course I was!.

Spotting me he looked doubtful but I exuded a knowing smile and a waft of body odour to show that doing the "Q" was the least he could expect from me!! I might even throw in a "Z" and a "P" whilst I was at it!!!

Right back to the story! When I said twelve days to do the "Q" that's walking! Sleeping in a tent carrying all your own food in and rubbish out AND!!!! Now listen to this! AND! If you're a female carrying out the used Tampax!!!

It was at this point that I gave myself away as being the wimpy tourist that I truly am, by sticking my fingers in my ears and singing "la de la de la!!" until he'd changed the subject!
There are some things I just don't want to know!!!!!!!

Sorry Rustyn!! Counting out sheets of toilet paper for twelve days, and mixing up just enough porridge oats, powdered milk and jam to make a nourishing breakfast leaves me cold! (A lot like the Patagonian wind)

I've told you before that the wind blows permanently and horizontally in Patagonia and as I look at the peaks I can imagine the real trekkers high in amongst them doing the "W" the "circuit" and the "Q" their packs stuffed with just the right amount of toilet paper (new and used), Tampax (new and used) and porridge oats and I envy them not at all!! Because at the moment I'm a tourist!! Drinking a cup of English breakfast tea with a complete toilet roll ready and waiting!!!

The park is a indescribably wonderful scenery harsh mountainous peak and turquoise lakes and I could prattle on more but as I've just told you it's indescribable I won't bother!

In the Torres del Paine (the Paine is pronounced PINEY not Penis as I once heard someone (me!) pronounce it) we went to see the glacier at Lago Grey (which for some reason I keep calling Lady Grey!) and it's impressive. The icebergs in the lake, surprising shades of blue, the wind carving them into surreal shapes! the water icy turquoise.

Torres del Paine at sunset

Glacier Lago Grey

Memorable but not as memorable as the notice on the edge of the lake,
"NO SWIMMING!"

No bloody swimming!! Imagine if you will water cold enough not to melt icebergs and they're worried that people will contaminate the lake by swimming in it?? I can tell you this! I was near the lake for an hour and at no time did I see anyone turn up dressed in just a swimming costume, rolled up towel under their arm, turning away disappointed on seeing the notice, and thinking!

"Well bugger me! I really fancied a swim out to that iceberg and now they say it's not allowed!"

As a stupid notice it ranks alongside the one in the game park in Africa, which said

"WILD ANIMALS ARE DANGEROUS DO NOT APPROACH"

This is a guananco, (stop saying Aaaaah!) a relative of the camel and llama, but it can be a pain when it stands on the side of the road then suddenly jumps out. It happens so often that it can't be a coincidence. It's the staple diet of the puma,(and of Land Cruisers) a picture of which I haven't got, a puma that is not a Land Cruiser!

Now this is a Condor the famous raptor of the Andes, which we came across feeding on the carcass of a Guanaco. (Don't worry there are thousands of the bloody things) It would have made a great picture but by the time I had stopped and found the camera, switched it on then realised I still had the lens cap on, took the lens cap off and pressed the little button to reset the camera, the condor had got bored with waiting and flown away Sorry!

We are happily jumping back and forth between Chile and Argentina with the immigration and customs formalities being better described as informalities. Now of course we make sure that our fridge is devoid of anything that could conceivably tempt a Chilean Agricultural Officer, all of whom incidentally, but not coincidentally, are as fat as roasting pigs, but not I'm sure because of all the food they confiscate off poor innocent, and after they've had their way, hungry British tourists.
Who's bitter??? ME?? Never!!!

At the moment we are dealing with three currencies simultaneously, the Argentina Peso (3.4 to the US dollar and five to a pound) the US dollar (1.6 to the pound) and the Chilean Peso (150 to the Argentinean Peso, 630 to the US dollar). Now the clever amongst you will be able to do the maths and say,

"Hang on that can't be right, Jeff's being ripped off there!"
are absolutely right, but when all you want is cup of coffee
you really can't be bothered to argue, although I must confess
to being quite assertive AFTER he'd filled my tank with
Diesel and I enjoyed watching his face as he tried to interpret,
"That's all you're getting sunshine if you don't like it try
taking the bugger out!

ESQUEL
Route 40 which forms the southern leg of the Pan American
highway is long. I know I've said that before about other
roads in Argentina, such as route 3, which runs down the
eastern side, but the difference with route 40 is that for
hundreds of miles the road planners seem to have forgotten it.

The scenery is lunar, I know that is an over used description
but its exactly the right one, and when the guide books
describes it as "infrequently travelled" and "Argentina's
loneliest road" I have to agree, but when it goes on to say it
inspires introspection, I don't agree, "moments of terror
mixed with sheer bloody boredom" is more apt!

I've already told you about Route 40 being mind- blowingly
flat and boring, and how the wind blows horizontally at ninety
kph but I haven't yet told you about the "RIPIO" the local
name for the loose harsh gravel road surface, with the
adhesion quality of ball bearings. That, and a horizontal wind
conspire to take you where you would really prefer not to go;
off the road and into the ditches, but it's difficult to fight it! It
shakes you and the vehicle, and has the same road holding
properties as ice! Of course when you do meet the occasional
vehicle you're scared for your windscreen, and the local idea
is that if you touch it with your fingers you will prevent any
cracks... but then you wonder if people are just waving and

being friendly..I wonder if it depends on how many fingers you use!

So that's Route 40 remote and challenging, lateral winds corrugations and a slippy surface..GREAT FUN!

But enough of that! We went to see a glacier!! The Perito Moreno Glacier near El Calafate, blimey it's impressive. A sixty-metre high wall of ice being pushed forward until it breaks away and falls into a turquoise lake.

We'd parked about ten miles away and I thought I had heard thunder, it was only when I got close that I realised that it was the movement of ice within the glacier, sometimes groaning like an arthritic old man other times roaring like an enraged elephant!

I waited for a couple of hours to get the obligatory picture of ice falling off into the lake to make icebergs (apparently it's called calving!) but it was only when I turned to leave and had packed the camera away that it happened!! So you'll have to imagine it.

You may remember that in Buenos Aries I had a problem with the diff lock, well it happened again. As I went to drive out of Lago Roca campsite the warning light was on again, glowing like a bloody fairy on a Christmas tree, I tried everything to get it to work (or not to work) but of course it didn't (or did)!

Oh yes! it was also Saturday so we were stranded as all the lazy bloody mechanics who had obviously made enough money for one week weren't interested in doing anything until Monday, so there we were! .... STUCK!
A stroke of inspiration, why not have a look and see if I could do anything myself?

"But you know nothing about cars!"

"True but what harm is there in having a look..?"

"You said that about the dishwasher as I remember and what happened?"

"Well we were going to buy a new one anyway"

So, remembering what the nice Toyota mechanic said in Buenos Aries about the "corrosion" I stripped off the dash board panels and opened up the diff lock switch which still had sand from the Sahara in 2004 on it..so that wasn't the right switch!

A quick crawl under the car and I located the transfer box (Paul and Julian had said you can't miss it!! At least that was true, I bumped my head on it!) and there was the diff lock activating unit which pulled apart surprisingly easily...and inside the switch was corroded!!

There's nothing to this mechanicing business! I'll just clean it up with Jeans' nail scissors and we'll be away.. well we would have been had the whole damn thing not disintegrated as soon as I touched it!!!

Now I won't bore you with the details

"Oh Do Do!"

But for the next six hours I lay on my back under the car and I rebuilt the switch from others that didn't seem to be serving any useful purpose (I hope) and from the camp site owners tool box and, though I say it myself I did a good job!

"I'm impressed! So it worked?"

"No! I switched on and the bloody light was still on!"

I had a few beers and sulked,

Roll forward to Sunday.

Wandering round the site I met up with a Dutch man and his baby son who I'd been chatting to the previous day and he introduced me to Alberto and Ricardo who listened to my tale of woe, and offered to have a look (Alberto was driving a Toyota and Ricardo a Land Rover.. sheesh the embarrassment) .

Who said electro mechanics was difficult?
Ricardo wriggled under the car, suppressed a giggle at my handiwork, and did mechanicy things!
Suddenly Alberto said
"What's this switch for"
"I never use it ….erm..ermmmm bugger!"
(Thinks to myself "that's the diff lock switch!")

I then remembered the night before I was sitting with the little Dutch boy in the car and he'd played with the switches and he must have…er…er
"Switched your central diff lock switch on?"
"Yep!"
"So you'd stripped the unit down and spent six hours on your back when all you should have done is checked that it wasn't just switched on!"
"You make it sound obvious!"
"Isn't it?..so no one thought to check?"
"Well Jean did in fact say "are you sure that nothing has been left switched on?""
"And you said?"
"Don't be stupid woman!"
"Not wise!"

So all I had to do was cancel the flat bed lorry that had been ordered and try and not look like an incompetent idiot in front of everyone.

"Did you succeed?"

"What do you think?"

We went to visit Alberto the next day and he took us to meet his wife Angie and his son Alex (all in all an all round alliterative family!) both of whom really wanted to see again the stupid English man who has travelled round Africa and Australia and still doesn't know what switches do what.

So there I was doing my daily tyre check, which I do without fail at least once a month, and another effect of the Ripio was apparent.. it rips great chunks of tread from your tyres. I was showing canvas where there should have been rubber, in fact I was showing so much canvas I could have taken up oil painting... and talking of oil, that needed changing too, so back to Toyota for another stage in my "tour of Toyota garages in Argentina!"....

I explained in my best Spanish what the problem was to a very nice man but who was obviously a foreigner as he looked at me blankly.. Now I've come across this a lot since I've been here peoples just don't understand Spanish...I speak to them in perfect Spanish and they just look at me...I wonder what language they speak? They lost interest and wandered off.

So the upshot is still a knackered tyre and I'm still using the same oil!!!

ST MARTIN DE LOS ANDES

Christmas

Well we tried looking at Barilochi "the chocolate capital of Argentina" it was bloody horrible! But then I've never been a chocolate lover; there were some very strange people there, some obviously totally off their heads and others extremely effeminate.

So we left, very quickly, who needs to stay in a chocolate town full of fruits and nuts?

"That wasn't clever! We all saw that coming!!!"

"Sorry!"

"You're not!"

"True!"

We drove into St Martin in the middle of a rainstorm and, now listen to this, I was informed by Jean, that's it informed! that we wouldn't be sleeping in a wet tent over Christmas but that, WE WOULD GET A HOTEL FOR CHRISTMAS WEEK!!!! I explained that as explorers we should laugh in the face of rainstorms, that we should scoff in the face of high winds, that we should.....

"YOU CARRY ON LAUGHING AND SCOFFING!!! I'M GETTING A ROOM!"

Now you know as an independent thinker and a MAN! I am not willing to be dictated to do! No one tells me what to do I decide where we stay and....

"So what's the hotel like?"

"It's good, thank you for asking!"

The robbery has had a greater effect on us than we imagined. We now dislike towns and are very very nervous about letting the car out of our sight when we visit places, which of course makes sight seeing very limiting. But against that the lakes and the Andes are all that we expected and hoped for

A week in San Martin de los Andes was good, wandering around the streets having "café con leche" and ice creams, sitting outside cafes in the early evening and drinking ice-cold beers, or chilling out watching interminable films on cable TV, selecting not by the quality of the film but by the language. Hugh Grant in English is bad enough but Hugh Grant is Spanish is even worse.

It was after we'd sat through two episodes of Kojak that we realised it was definitely time to hit the road again, that and the fact that the "tourist high season" arrived with a bang, overnight prices went up by 50%, and the shopkeepers started smiling again, and happily ignored my,

" HOW much? You must be bloody joking!"

In a country of, let's be honest, mainly unattractive towns San Martin was an exception, probably because it's a custom built tourist town that has a winter tourist season as well as summer trade.

The streets are lined with tearooms, bars and souvenir shops everything that we normally dislike, but after some of the depressing towns we have travelled through so far it was, like the beer, refreshing!

The Internet is widely available in Argentina and many garages have free WiFi and it was at one of these when we picked up our e-mails, that we learnt that a good friend had died unexpectedly. We felt so badly for his wife and family, and to be honest this made us question the trip even more.

In every trip there are highs and lows, you spend long days driving on poor roads with uninteresting scenery, staying in poorly built noisy campsites with unsanitary showers and toilets waiting for the next high spot ever aware that at the end of the day you will need to find somewhere to stay.

Towns marked on the map, which look to be large, turn out to be just ribbon developments of dirty grey low square buildings, the only colour being the political graffiti on the walls. Small sad shops with dark interiors stocking a depressing range of cheap Taiwanese plastic rubbish.

I hate us being so conspicuous, driving past rows of men sitting backs against the buildings and you can imagine them valuing the vehicle and its contents (and for all I know the occupants) so you resist the temptation to ask the way, knowing that when you do all you'll get is blank stares as they try to understand my Spanish whilst looking into the car assessing, always assessing.

You start looking early for somewhere to stay, searching hopefully for a campsite and all too often when you eventually find it, it takes one minute to decide you don't want it.

Aaahhhh! You may say, there is always the option of a hotel, yes of course there is! and sometimes it can take as long as thirty seconds to decide that the hotel is not quite what you're looking for unless of course you're looking for a dirty unkempt brothel!
It's at times like this that you wonder what the hell you're doing here, after all what's wrong with a perfectly good house in middle England with central heating TV and shops but then you drive round a bend and you gasp at the magnificence of a landscape.

Or you are awed by the presence of a whale; or have a night drinking beer around a campfire with other travellers; or experience the magnificent spontaneous hospitality of people or you live again what it must have been like to sail for the first time through the straights of Magellan and you know what you're doing there…you're living!!!

Where was I?? Oh yes! We decided to leave San Martin and head northwards with the Andes on our left, snow covered shadowy peaks rising in the distance looking for somewhere to spend New Year.

"Now as you know I'm not really an anti social bastard!"
"You are!"
"But I really fancied a quiet New Year"
"In Argentina the noisiest country in the world?"
"Well a man can hope!"

A day driving round the vineyards "interesting and informative" the guidebooks say, well yes I am sure they are and would have been had they been open, but they'd all closed up for Christmas so we looked at rows of vines, waiting in vain for interest and information, and then gave up and searched for a campsite.

I braked suddenly after spotting a small faded lopsided and almost unreadable notice and apologizing to the driver behind (the only other bloody driver on the road that day) and we bumped down a track for a couple of miles, convinced we'd missed it but suddenly there were signs of civilization, well that's an exaggeration, it was in fact two men standing by a bridge holding fishing rods (the men that is not the bridge)
"Buenos dias! Como esta? Hay camping agua?
Now what's difficult about that? Perfectly good Spanish spoken with a superb accent, even if I do say so myself. Mystified looks firstly at me and then at each other!
"Campeeeeeeeeeeng agua?"
"Si camping!"
"Oh! you're English!

What's wrong with these people don't they understand their own language; blimey it's not that difficult! Well it is in fact "derecha" meaning right and "derecho" meaning straight on which alone explains our somewhat circuitous trip around Argentina..
"I've forgotten where I was again?"
"Campsite!"

"Oh yes!"
So he pointed vaguely down the road "derecho derecho! I tried to turn right but he was in the way and his frantic pointing sent me off straight on.

Whilst driving I went through again in my mind what I'd asked him and suddenly realised that I'd used the word "agua" meaning "water" instead of "aqui" meaning "here" perfectly understandable (the mistake as opposed to the language) especially if you're dyslexic in Spanish.
After following a small track for a couple more kilometres we found a quiet campsite just us and two others tents…
PERFECT!! A couple of beers perhaps a steak and in bed by five past midnight leaving just enough time to break my News Years Resolution!! (again)
And so it remained until ten o'clock when thirty two cars with tents and music centres arrived, the fires were lit, the tents were erected and everyone shouting at each other as only Argentineans can! So much for a quiet night!

It was at this point a cow wandered through the gate from an adjoining farm. Now having seen how much beef your average Argentinean man, woman or baby (I'll come onto the business of breast feeding later) can consume at a single sitting, if I were a cow there is no way I'd come anywhere near fifty-odd campers with sharp knives and fires at the ready, but sure enough in it wandered and grazed, happily unaware of the lustful looks his bovine bum and legs were attracting.
Jean commented that this must be the Argentinean equivalent of a pizza home delivery.
Surprisingly I slept well that night unaware of any noise, it's amazing what three bottles of strong red wine, a sleeping pill and a thunderstorm can do.

"In 2009 I will be teetotal!" my annual and perennial New Years resolution lasted seventeen minutes, seven minutes longer than my previous best!

Silence is a precious commodity, so is gold, but in Argentina silence is harder to find. No matter how remote, no matter how empty the campsite, sooner or later there will be noise. Bloody music, Asados, dogs, cars, motorbikes anything designed solely to piss me off, so it was with surprise and gratitude that we found a camp site in Tupungata that was totally silent, not a dog, not a disco, a motorbike nothing! A great nights sleep with the lower rolling hills of the Andes in the background absolute blissful silence.

Well silence until the bloody plumber arrived at seven in the morning, turned his radio on full and proceeded to bang seven types of shit out of copper pipes!!

And! AND!! He had the bloody cheek to ask if we had slept well

Bastard!

The Asado, or bbq, is fundamental to the Argentinean way of life, but it's nothing like any BBQ you have had in your life. Not for them a pork sausage and a square of steak, perhaps a chicken leg and breast! Oh No! Great slabs of beef, yards of spicy chorizo sausage sand complete chickens are dropped onto the glowing embers and then you wait.

This is one mans Asado portion

You wait because whereas in England we have a red hot fire with the steak and sausages given a quick blast turning the outside black and leaving the inside a nice salmonella pink, the Argentineans cook their meat sloooowly, having the main fire to one side then moving embers under the meat; not worrying about the time it takes and letting the fat drip onto embers which keeps the fire nicely warm!

And they think nothing of cooking half a pig (ok it's a small pig but come on!) stretching it out as if it's crucified alongside a few sticks of wood, and you know what? It works... but the life expectancy, or more properly the social life expectancy of a vegetarian in Argentina is limited.

The cuts of meat are different too, and there's so much of it, the actual Asado cut is a vertical cut down the length of the rib cage about four inches wide and about eighteen inches long and if you are not careful you get one of them to yourself...and that's the just the starter, then there's chorizo, a spicy sausage each one big enough for four people to eat or to beat each other to death with, and then there's choripan, which is a chorizo sausage in half a baguette, and then just as you think,

"Well that's me finished eating for a few months" there's more meat. Do you give up?? Do you let them think that and Englishman can be beaten by a few kilos of beef, sausages and chicken? You bet your bloody life you give up, if you didn't you'd explode and become part of everyone else's Asado!

BUENOS ARIES AGAIN

I've seen a job I fancy, dog walking!!! Not your British one
man
his dog but one man and eight dogs!!! I got my camera ready
and waited..Bugger where are all the stray cats when you need
them?

The problem is of course that "cleaning up!" after your dog
hasn't arrived in Buenos Aires so a walk in the park becomes
a tap dance and inevitably a shuffle in the grass to clean up!

LA CAROLINA
We met Arrica and Ricardo in a car park near San Luis. We'd
parked in petrol station and Arrica came over and started
talking to us Arrica said,
"I like all English people!"
Jean said,
"You haven't met Jeff yet!"
Jeff said,
"Oi! I am still here!" but they ignored me.
We chatted for a while and she told us about the beauty of a
wonderful area they were going to, picturesque, quiet and best

of all a cheap Hosteria (I suppose the nearest English equivalent would be a guest house) in La Carolina! That'll do for me! Not the Hosteria, just the region where we could wild camp! WE don't need bedrooms with en suite! WE don't need three course meals! WE don't ….
"Ok! Ok! You've made your point you don't like spending money!"

We had one great night wild camping in the hills, under a cloudless sky and in total silence well except for a rooster that I'm sorry to report died the next day but its death wasn't in vane it was in wine with a few onions and garlic!!!! (for that joke to work you need to say it with a poor German accent!)

But Jean got a bug and was ill! she was so ill she even stopped criticising my driving, now that's ill!! So we looked for a Hosteria, having forgotten of course the name of the one Arrica
had told us about, but everywhere was full with bloody Buenos Aireans (or hairy Buenosians) on the first weekend of their annual holidays, each Hosteria giving us a sorrowful shake of the head, and a look as if we were mad even asking! One last try along a small track and guess what?
"What?"
Coming the other way was Arrica and Ricardo! I explained the problem and after doing a U turn on a track narrower than their car (Argentinean drivers can do this!). They returned with us to the Hosteria to try to try get us a room. Arrica asked only to be met with the same sad shake of the head from the lady in charge, which had absolutely no effect on Arrica at all, she wheedled, she bullied, she charmed and suddenly there was a room.

Arrica and Ricardo took us under their wings, appropriate as Arrica is an airhostess, and our time with them confirmed that the Argentinean people are, with the exception of the thieves, sociable, friendly and generous, but dreadful vegetarians

HEADING HOME
Suddenly we'd had enough, it was time to go home!!
Crowded noisy expensive campsites, busy roads and David's death were enough. In truth the trip had never quite been the same since the robbery, and we were surprised at the profound affect it had on us. Instead of wandering and looking at the scenery we wouldn't let the car out of our sight, we became suspicious of strangers and finally we were running out of money.

You have to set a budget on these trips and the additional expenses had eaten into it, eaten??? It had wolfed it down and was searching hungrily for more
So how to get home?
There are a number of options.

Put the car in a container and fly back. We've done this before when we left Capetown and Australia. It's safe but with all the paperwork it's also expensive because you need to employ an agent and every time the container is handled there are additional costs.

RoRo for car and fly back. In case you've forgotten RoRo means the car is actually driven onto the ship just like a cross channel ferry. Again there is still paperwork but the handling charges are less, but you rely on the drivers not to mess about with switches they don't understand, and of course there is the security problems in the African ports

Finally, RoRo but travel with the car on the boat. The car becomes just another piece of accompanied luggage but the cost of the boat is higher than by air, and who wants to sit on

a cargo vessel for thirty odd days whilst it meanders from South America to Europe?
Well to tell the truth I wouldn't mind!

We contacted Turners in Buenos Aires to be told there was a cabin and space on the Grande Buenos Aires sailing on the 14th or the 10th or the 16th January (it was a freighter after all!). I made that sound easy! It wasn't in fact, as they don't answer emails unless you follow them up with a phone call, and you can only phone from "telefonika" cabins the Argentinean public phone boxes or by using your UK mobile, which works out about the same price as the first class air fare; and it's great waiting, drumming your fingers and watching the extortionately expensive minutes ticking away as they go and try and find Inez, pausing along the way, no doubt, to talk about bloody Asados or tangos or whatever else they can think of, so it takes ten sodding minutes to walk across the office..
"But you're not bitter!"
"Bloody people!"

When get into their office n the middle of downtown Buenos Aries we finally get it sorted leaving only the small (well not so small) matter of payment, and do they accept credit cards?...noooooooo!!
"I ask you, who doesn't accept credit cards in the 21st century?"
"Turners?"
"Right! How did you know that!"
"You just told us!"
To get round the problem we had to arrange for our son Ian to transfer the money to New York to pay the bill in Genoa and get the ticket in Argentina.. Three different currencies in three different time zones..
"Did it go smoothly?"

"What do you think?"
"No?"
"Yes!"
"Yes? It went smoothly?"
"No it didn't go smoothly!"
"But you just said yes!"
"No! the "yes" was to your "no" try and keep up!
"Sorry!"

The final hope was that Ian our son would pay for the passage
and forget to take the money from my bank account…
needless to say it was a forlorn hope! Don't you just hate
genetics!

The departure formalities were as complex as the arrival ones
but as we had a man from Turners helping us all went
smoothly, well smoothly until we were stopped by the anti-
drugs (or it may have been anti-chemical or anti-explosives)
squad at Buenos Aires. We were waiting to clear customs, our
vehicles parked in a row, us, also in row, looking bewildered,
when a large white vehicle drove by, stopped reversed, drove
by again and stopped.
Two men got out and from a safe distance looked suspiciously
at my vehicle, and shouted,
"Open lid (the bonnet)"
I opened it and they edged nervously closer and peered in!

I joined them looking in, John, another overland traveller,
joined them and we all looked at my engine. They looked at
me and I looked at them then they looked at John pointed to
his vehicle (which is the same model as mine) and said,
"Open lid"
We all looked at Johns engine, it was the same as mine,
cleaner but the same,

"Problem?" I asked, well in fact I spoke to them in fluent Spanish "Problemo?"

"Come!"

In their vehicle was a TV screen, apparently it was an anti-explosive drug smuggling X ray thingy and sure enough in the X-ray of my vehicle was a suspicious shadow. We all went back and looked again at my car, working on the principle that if you look hard enough something will spring to mind.

It didn't!

They made some phone calls, and we all looked again. I took the air filter apart and we all looked in there!

It was an air filter!

The only other thing it could be was the fuel injector unit all firmly bolted down, still with the sand of Australia on it (memo to self! must clean car!).. We were perplexed, or as we bilingualists would say, perplexedo,

"Did I tell you I was bilingual?"

"Dirty Sod!"

Jean appeared

"What's wrong?"

"It's man stuff dear!"

"WHAT'S WRONG?" sheesh that look again

"The fuel injector is showing up a shadow on the x-ray machine and that apparently could be explosives or drugs or chemicals or a couple of Kurdish refugees"

"Could it be the additive you put in!"

"Sheeeeeeesh silly tart! of course not! that wouldn't....

" Ahh Additeeeeeeeve?...ADDITEEEEVE" the men smiled nodded climbed into their vehicle and departed.

Jean managed to look triumphal and scathing at the same time!

So apparently the additive to clean the injectors is radioactive or explosive or something but then I knew that!, memo to self buy some more and try sniffing it!

THE TRIP HOME
After spending eight and a half hours getting the car into Argentina it only took us half an hour to get it out, almost as if they were pleased to see us go.

There were eight other passengers, John and Denise who had just driven from Panama to Alaska and back down in a Land Cruiser; Marie and Brian, French-Canadian motorcyclists who had ridden from Canada and were now travelling to Europe and then through to Asia. Arno a lone German motorcyclist travelling home; Suzanne a Dutch lady travelling alone who had sailed down from Europe on the boat and was now travelling back and Jean Marie a lone male French doctor doing the same.
Our mortality was brought home to us yet again when Jean Marie collapsed and died in Rio, a quiet man who only spoke French, so couldn't communicate with us apart from "good mornings" and "good afternoons".
We all had regrets, could we have tried to communicate more, could we have included him? could we have taken more pictures that included him so that his family would have had a final record?.
But we didn't
RIP Jean Marie

A NIGHT IN RIO DE JANEIRO

The bar on Copacabana beach was full of ladies (ladies?) who to my shock, horror and yes I'll say it, disgust, were in various (and in some cases almost complete) states of undress, not surprising on a beach bar you may think, but this was nine o'clock at night and raining.

"I'll be honest with you I didn't know where to look!"
"You mean you didn't know where to look first!"

Their outfits, as my mother used to say, (through pursed lips, arms firmly crossed under her bosom)
"Only covered where they touched!" and they didn't touch in many places! And I tell you something else! There were some big girls there, some of them with so much meat on them that if they'd have been in Argentina they wouldn't have known whether to cook 'em or F……..
"JEFF NO!!!!"
"What?"
"You know what!"
"Well! they were big girls"
"How big"
"This big!"
"Is that both or just one?
"Just one!"
"Blimey that's big! I don't suppose you got any pictures?"
"No sorry!"
"Pity!"
The females with us were of the opinion that the amount that the girls smoked must be bad for their chests! I commented, quite reasonably I thought, that it didn't seemed to have done their chests much harm so far and received a very severe and painful slap on the back of the head!

We had our first cold beer for days and the waiter, obviously impressed with the speed that the beers disappeared, immediately brought us another and another.
Rio de Janeiro is an intimidating city where you get dire warnings even from the locals of the dangers! (I suspect that

even the muggers will warn you of the dangers immediately prior to robbing you!). The Corcovada, the famous statue of Christ, overlooks it and I think he spends much of the time with his eyes firmly closed, as the commandments "Thou shalt not commit adultery" and "Thou shalt not steal!" are enthusiastically ignored.

It's interesting that the taxi driver who took us to town took great pains to ensure that we were dropped off in a "safe area", which was nice! He warned us to be careful which was also nice! But he ripped us off! Which wasn't nice!

The crew of the Grande Buenos Aires, the gargantuan car freighter on which we travelled, was comprised of Italians, Indians and a smattering of other Eastern Europeans communicating in a strange mix of Italian and Anglo/Indian. The chef was Italian and whilst cooking sang opera enthusiastically at the top of his considerable voice enthusiastically and tunelessly; simultaneously drumming with a wooden spoon on the metal tins.

The only thing that's flatter than his voice is his soufflés. Being Italian he bases all his meals around pasta and after thirty days it's not funny any more!

"Pasta joke?"
"I was going to say that!"
"Believe me I know you were!"
I have in the past before running marathons "carbo loaded" that is eaten pasta so that you build up your carbohydrate reserves. I've eaten enough pasta in the last three weeks to have the energy to swim back to England and his bloody singing makes swimming very very tempting.

Let's put it this way before much longer one of us will be swimming! Probably him but at least his cries for help will be heard for bloody miles.

The boat kept stopping, which can be a bit disconcerting. Firstly because a fuel pipe broke in the middle of the Atlantic and come to think of it secondly because the same fuel pipe broke. It is soooo comforting drifting in the middle of the Atlantic whilst the Indian Engineers finish their bloody curry before reaching for the "Marine Engineering for Beginners" manual.

The third time was in the lee of Fuertaventura, one of the Canary Islands, hiding from a storm which they assured us is to make our lives easier when crossing the Bay of Biscay but more likely because the Italian first mate was worried about his hairdo.

The "mess-boy" a young large Italian who's normal conversation is conducted at 105 decibels, his function ito serve the food and clean the cupboard err cabin. Now when I say serve I use it in the tennis sense. He distributed the food over the tablecloth, your lap and occasionally when he's lucky onto the plate. He resented the paying customers (us!) and expects a tip!

A combination of the cooks' singing and the mess boys' shouting reverberates through the boat, and neither of them speak English, so they now think "For Christ's sake shut the f..k up!" is our way saying "good morning!"

It's interesting that in a world of Electronics that ships still use flags. On the bridge are banks of flickering electronic screens and equipment, no large spoked wheel though, and ready to hand are

old-fashioned coloured flags. Each flag represents a letter of the Alphabet but they also give messages to other ships.
The red and white flag means that the pilot is on board; the yellow one indicates that there is no disease on board (apparently my athletes foot doesn't count.. I was itching to complain about that!) The red one a dangerous cargo (the chef perhaps!), the red green and yellow is the Senegal flag, (they always fly the country flag of the port they are visiting); the blue one is the Grimaldi line flag; and the middle one is the Italian flag.
Was that interesting! Not really but time is passing slowly!

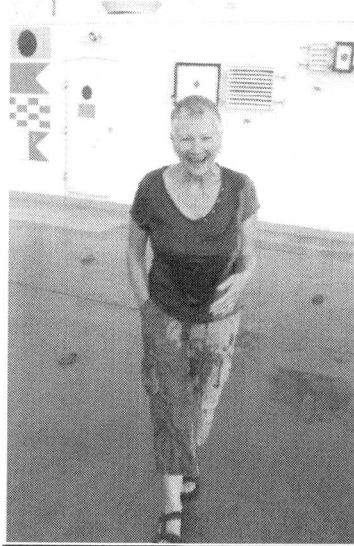

Jean "GOT" crossing the line

ROUTE

Grimaldi is a freighting company first and foremost so the route and timing depends entirely on the freight and the mood of the captain but our trip was,

Buenos Aires
Paranagua
Santo
Rio de Janeiro
Dakar
Hamburg
Tilbury

A total of thirty days filled with, erm, reading looking at the sea, watching for flying fish, eating pasta (always pasta!) using the exercise bike in the gym (it hurts your bum!) and sleeping! I'd love to say drinking but we had a teetotal captain! It was a long 30 days!

We had a couple of days Hamburg and was informed that one in every three hundred inhabitants is a millionaire, I was going to find him and beg some Euros but I really didn't know where to start counting!

"And there was an Edgar Degas (so so near to being an anagram) exhibition, which we walked to!"

"You like Degas?"

"Oh yes love him!"

"So how was the exhibition?"

"Closed!"

"Why?"

"It was Monday!"

"Ahh that always seems to happen to you! Remember a few years ago when you arrived in Rio the day after the Carnival finished?

"Do I ever!"

"And of course the best month for viewing whales in Peninsular Valdez is..?"

"October!"

"And you arrived in?"

"November!"

"Going to see Boca Juniors soccer team play in Buenos Aires?"

"They were playing away that week!"

"The flowers in fish river canyon Namibia at their best in July?"

"You arrived in?"

"August!"

So the trip is over now, it had highs and lows but I leave with indifferent memories of South America but great memories of the Argentinean people. I suspect that this will be the last trip, perhaps it was one trip too many.

We've sold the Land cruiser time for new challenges.

We were fortunate to see Africa before new roads and communications will change it forever. It will evolve and change the poor will remain poor the rich will become very rich, diseases that we have virtually eradicated in the west will continue to kill, political systems will evolve that will work for Africa, but most have all we have seen felt and for a short while been part of a magnificent continent.

And this is what you wake up to!!!! You know now why we do it!

Printed in Great Britain
by Amazon.co.uk, Ltd.,
Marston Gate.